Orpheus at Eighty

Nonfiction by Vincent Sheean

Orpheus at Eighty
First and Last Love
Lead, Kindly Light
This House Against This House
Between the Thunder and the Sun
Not Peace but a Sword
Personal History

. . . You have that in your countenance
which I would fain call master.

King Lear, Act I, Scene iv

Orpheus at Eighty

Vincent Sheean

 Random House, New York

First Printing

© Copyright, 1958, by Vincent Sheean
All rights reserved under International and
Pan-American Copyright Conventions
Published in New York by Random House, Inc.,
and simultaneously in Toronto, Canada, by
Random House of Canada, Limited
Library of Congress Catalog Card Number: 57–10054
Manufactured in the United States of America
by George McKibbin & Son

To Arturo Toscanini
Et lux perpetua luceat ei.

1
Verdi's Milan

1   The third night of *Falstaff* at the Scala in Milan was in the truest sense Verdi's farewell to the theatre. He went through the motions once more in Rome, and last of all in Paris, but on those occasions there was not much more than the weary repetition of duty done, all passion spent. We have his own word for it. It was after the third night of *Falstaff* that he said to himself: *Tutto è finito*. It is all over.

The tradition of the theatre, from which Verdi seldom deviated, was for the composer to be present at the first three performances of a new work and then to efface himself. In the earlier days of the Scala it was actually the custom to put the poor composer into a corner of the orchestra pit, on the theory that he might be useful in an emergency; he thus had no means of avoiding the tumultuous demonstrations which anything new was likely to evoke. By 1893 all that had changed, and the position of Verdi himself in the world at large was such that any demand he felt to be just and reasonable was instantly granted. He had full power over every detail of the production, and if he had not had it, or if anything had been done contrary to his wishes, he was at all times ready to withdraw his work both from the theatre and from the publishers. He was rich; he was old; he was immensely famous. He had suffered throughout the greater part of his working life from the exactions of managers, publishers, censors and public officials; he had struggled, often in vain, with stage interpreters; he had found himself helpless against scene designers, chorus masters, conductors and all the other potentates of the opera house. Now it was his turn, and the fullness of his authority over every particular in a highly complex whole was never questioned. For this once, the Scala belonged to him—it was his festival theatre now, his Bayreuth, his to command as much as Bayreuth had been Richard Wagner's. Aside from the *Falstaff* production—the greatest effort the Scala ever made for a composer—there had been a revival of *La Traviata* with the admirable, the exquisite Adelina Patti singing in it. "Dear little Adelina," or sometimes "naughty little devil," as Verdi had often called her, was now nearing fifty, but she was still without an equal on the lyric stage, and no doubt it was hard for him to remember that she—who had first enchanted him long ago in London, when she was eighteen—was also accumulating years.

The years, of course, were important to everybody, and none had complained of them more assiduously than Verdi during the past two decades, but this winter of 1893 found him in a state of health and spirits which seemed to defy time. He had started the *Falstaff* rehearsals on January 4 in the theatre—at first in the Ridotto at the back of the house— and had worked every day from then until the opening night on February 7. Some days he rehearsed six hours, some seven, and some eight. Some days the task was finished by dinner time, but if there were a night rehearsal Verdi never missed it. Neither did he miss his good meals, his good wine or his good cigar after dinner. The phenomenon had so startled Milan and all the international visitors who had come for the *Falstaff* production that learned physicians gave learned opinions about it. The esteemed Cesare Lombroso, who had already conclusively proved (to his own satisfaction) that the "man of genius" was a result of degeneration from a norm, and thus related to the criminal or to the insane, had little support for his pet theories from the example of Verdi; and when the *Gazzetta Musicale* asked him for an article on the subject, he supplied one which concluded that the case defied explanation.

Explanations there were, of course, and we can all think of them. Nobody could have written *Falstaff* without realizing that it was a masterpiece. To have done it when one was, so to speak, canonized and put on a shelf—when the whole nation had insisted on a "jubilee" celebration, four years before, as if for the immortal dead—was a very special source of glee. The work itself, much of it written against the deadening influences of illness or of grief for the friends who kept on dying without respite, is filled with lyric joy. Who could have felt this more deeply or known it more securely than Verdi himself? Reason enough, we think now, to give an incomparable vigor and elasticity of mind and body to an old man whose whole life had been directed toward this end. At the time it seemed to defy reason, especially medical and physiological reason; the critics, musicians and other special correspondents from Paris, London, New York and Berlin were generous with the word "miracle." The miracle was in the composition itself, the work of three years: given the ability to write such work at all, to "invent the truth" alone in his own study down in the country, it was not at all surprising that he displayed such youthful energy and uncommon good humor that winter in Milan. *Falstaff* rejuvenated him, as it has many another since. And there is no use asking any doctor or physiologist how it occurred in the first place; the only answer there may be lies in the long, gradual but absolutely inevitable progression of Verdi's own work from first to last.

He felt the rich rarity of this event. His abundant common sense, his native irony, his keen perceptions, must have placed all the circumstances in perspective, molded the entire parade into something both funny and sad. (We know from his letters that this was so.) Fame no longer meant anything at all to him except a nuisance and a deception. The behavior of mankind, however, called forth his unceasing comment, and although he was too busy to write letters during the production of *Falstaff*, his wife Peppina wrote a few, and so did many others; we have quite a shrewd idea of how he bit his lip, controlled his smiles, did his work and kept a straight face at the moments of solemn ceremony and adulation. He had taken the measure of the world long, long ago. For a great many years he had struggled against any form of public honor, celebration or monument. He would *not* have music schools or conservatories named after him; he would *not* permit any theatre to plaster his name across its front or put his statue in the public square; he would *not* attend sessions of the Senate at Rome, although it was impossible to decline the King's appointment; and he would *not* give any countenance to the nationwide "jubilee" for the fiftieth anniversary of his first opera. All this seemed to him unnecessary and foolish, an intrusion on the privacy of a man who only wanted to do his own work in his own way and otherwise—in fact mostly—to cultivate his garden down at Sant' Agata. What is more, he felt that there was something a little indecent, or anyhow profoundly wrong, about great commemorative honors being given to living persons. It may have crossed his mind (I should be astonished if it had not) that such things were all right for Richard Wagner, who was a monster of vanity anyhow, although a composer of genius; but for one convinced, as Verdi was, that only time and the will of the great public can determine the value of work done, the headlong rush of so many men in so many countries (especially Italy) to make him into a public monument while he was still alive was downright repugnant.

And yet, in spite of everything, in the year of *Falstaff* he accepted his apotheosis with grace and good humor, perhaps because he knew that this was the end of it all and perhaps also, even more, because his common sense told him it was not to be avoided. He had sworn a mighty oath that this, his last work—his "lyric comedy" of which he had dreamed almost forever—would be done right or not at all. He had repeatedly told everybody concerned in every country (through Ricordi, his lifelong publisher and agent) that he would happily withdraw the work altogether and destroy the score rather than see it subjected to the horrendous maltreatment of the ordinary theatre production. Now, if he were to see it done right, must he not do it himself? And if he did it himself, how could he avoid the public demonstrations and the speeches, the homage and the frills? My reading of the evidence is that when he finished the orchestration and sent it off to Ricordi, in the preceding October, he had already made up his mind to do what he did. If he could not have it performed for himself and a few friends down at Sant' Agata with a smallish orchestra—another dream—the only alternative was the great commercial opera houses, in Milan, Paris, Berlin and the like, beaten down, for once, into complete submission to the will of the composer.

So, in return for their surrender to his work, he surrendered himself to the requirements of what he called "personal exhibition." If he had to take bows, he would take bows. If the public insisted on standing up and cheering at the mere sight of him, he would even pretend to like it. These were the conditions of the trade. He would be grateful to the King and Queen and to the Prime Minister for their fulsome telegrams; he would let the Mayor of Milan make speeches to him; he would show himself on the balcony of his hotel to the cheering mob in the street. This was part of the business, a necessary part, too—once and once only: now that it was all over at last, now that he was eighty.

One thing only threw him into a serious state of fright, just a few days later: the newspapers reported that the government of Italy was about to create him "Marquis of Busseto." This seemed so ridiculous, so incongruous for the old peasant that he felt himself to be, so utterly out of line with his life and work, that he sent an imploring telegram to his friend the Minister of Public Instruction to have the act prevented. (Once it had become a royal decree he could have done nothing.) The Minister reassured him and the calamity did not occur.

All his friends, and even his best friend, his wife Peppina, who almost knew him, were surprised at his equal temper, his benevolent mood, his spry and amiable converse during the *Falstaff* winter. January and February in Milan are never pleasant months; raw, wet, cold, they bear heavily upon the throats of singers, the temper of conductors and the feet of the populace. The old Maestro was almost constantly in good mood, working harder than anybody else and showing less strain under it. His overwhelming melancholy, the curse of his life, does not seem to have shown its dark power during those weeks at all. Peppina took extremely good care of him, of course, and for a great many years past he had been such an honored guest at the Grand Hotel of Milan that if Peppina had ever forgotten anything, the Cavaliere Spatz, manager of the hotel, would have remedied the deficiency. However, the Verdi ménage depended little upon the transitory blessings of hotel food or service. They had their own cook, their own personal servants, with ample room for all concerned, just as they did wherever they went. The Maestro had been accustomed to these comforts for so long that he hardly even noticed them any more (except in their absence). Peppina took all the trouble. We have her letters in which she tells exactly what is required: the kitchen of their own, the bedrooms and baths, the rooms for their three personal servants, the sitting rooms all on the same floor. The Grand Hotel of Milan was, and is, only about a block away from the Scala, and Verdi could easily have walked to and fro as he had so often done in the past, but for this a carriage was provided—to guard against the curious crowds as much as against the cold, wet streets.

He was even physically handsome this winter, within the limits of the possible: his hair was amply curled around his ears, his beaky nose twitched not too much, and his beard was neatly trimmed. We can depend upon it that Peppina saw to his clothing and linen, which were as good as it was possible to obtain. Between Peppina and his valet there was not much he was permitted to forget in those categories. What no valet and even no wife could have provided was the keen and steady gaze of his gray eyes which saw everything and conveyed the information to a brain cool enough and high enough to understand. The slightly dandified portraits by Boldini—an artist overestimated at one time and underestimated at present—give some suggestion of this public Verdi, the combed and curled and faintly scented old man who was equally accoutered for the adulation of the Queen or the acclamation of the people. In fact, the Boldini portrait of 1886, seven years before the *Falstaff* winter, seems to me to convey not only a slight dandification, but also, in the eyes of the subject himself, a certain delicate amusement at this strange presentation. For, after all, Verdi was a peasant born and bred, a peasant through and through, with every peasant characteristic, and it must have afforded him some ironic inner laughter to be thus turned out for public consumption. When he put on his rubber boots and tramped down his long *allée* of Lombardy poplars at Sant' Agata (all planted by himself) to look at the fields and estimate the yield of the potatoes or the beet root, slouching along in the rain in an old hat and whacking at the weeds with a stick cut from his own trees, he must frequently have laughed aloud at the fate which had made him, the most private and the most unpretending of men, into a national and an international idol. What was it the Czar had said—Alexander II, autocrat of All the Russias? "Ah, Verdi, you are more powerful than I!" *Ah! Ah! Ah! Ah! Ah!* (That is how Verdi writes it out in his letters—his indication

of loud laughter to himself.) And all of them, all of them, the Khedive
of Egypt with his wretched little Suez Canal, the Emperor Napoleon
III, the presidents and princes and prime ministers, with all their flowers
and their telegrams and their letters and their handsome payments, were
alike in that they did not know how to grow a decent patch of radishes or
when to cut the hay. Could they tell by the sun and the wind whether it
was better to grow the peaches in an orchard or against a wall? If any
of them had had to build a house and a garden in a plain, and sow the
surrounding fields with suitable crops, and bring up chickens and geese
and care for a few common country horses, what would have been the
result?

Verdi knew. We have all those letters, too—from Paris, from Turin,
from wherever he happened to be, to that Paolo Marenghi (poor fellow!)
who was the farmer at Sant' Agata for years, and to others in his train.
Why have you used the irrigation motor when I told you not to touch it
until I got back? Why don't you tame that captious filly? You don't
make Milord (another horse) work enough! I don't want my horses to
get fat and heavy. Tell that coachman that the horses must be exercised
every two days, so long as they stay out of Busseto. What are the stone-
masons doing now? Where is Carlo? Where is Ettorino? I have to go to
Paris tomorrow, but how can you have expenses amounting to 518 lire
and incoming payments of 276 lire? How can you have spent so much, and
where did you get the 276 lire? Write to me at once, *Poste Restante*, Paris.

Most of the time he was at Sant' Agata himself, working and watching
and building. The house itself, the garden, the trees, the lake (which he
called a "mud puddle"), the surrounding fields, the crops, the livestock,
the walks and little bridges and the beloved *allée*—all of it, every single bit,
was his own work. He would have been perfectly happy to stay at Sant'
Agata all the year round and tramp about in his rubber boots and talk to
the other peasants and quarrel about the accounts. After all, he had given
up the theatre long, long ago—just twenty-two years before this *Falstaff*
winter—when the lavish Egyptian Khedive paid so much money for Aïda,
to open his Suez Canal with, and except for the really interesting suggestions afforded by an Egyptian subject, Verdi never had for one moment
thought it sensible to open a canal with an opera. It was only that young
poet Boito, so full of talent and so highly educated, who had finally
brought him back to the theatre; Aïda had been supposed to be the last.
Thanks to Boito there had been *Otello*, a genuine satisfaction, reluctantly
engaged upon, triumphantly finished, after sixteen whole years away from
the wretched grease paint and fustian, sixteen years without an attempt

to write anything new—sixteen years of rubber boots and radishes. Suiting himself, Verdi would have stayed in Sant' Agata and attended to what he considered his own business, but Peppina could not endure the long, cold, dull winters with nobody but him to enliven her; as she herself testifies, he was not lively, and spent most of his hours either alone with his music or alone in his fields. She was bored to the point of misery; and that is why they took a big apartment in the Palazzo Doria in Genoa for the winters, where she could have friends in to tea, and even the Maestro would consent to receive company in the evenings.

The old peasant must have felt a little "dressed up," a little *endi manché*, in the regalia with which we see him represented during the *Falstaff* winter and spring. He was used to it, but less and less as time passed, and more and more with a twinge of irony. The statues and busts of Verdi which are strewn all over the world, but particularly in Italy—and there is scarcely a town of any size in Italy which does not possess one—are all more or less of this period. Very few of them were studied from life: the two Boldini portraits were, as was the bronze bust by Vincenzo Gemito, now at Sant' Agata. (The original is in the house and there is a plaster cast in the garden, so it is clear that the old man liked it. There is another in the Scala museum.) In these representations we are given some notion of how he seemed to all the musicians and singers, stagehands, designers, artists and fellow workers in the *Falstaff* production, as well as to the crowds in the streets and to the (relatively) few who could get into the Scala during those nights. In most versions he seems both venerable and energetic, which indeed he was; and in the statue which stands in front of the Home for Aged Musicians ("my best opera," as he called it), the effect is positively cocky. The old man has his head slightly on one side and his hands folded behind his back, holding up his frock coat in an attitude not at all monumental but at any rate decidedly brisk. It is impossible for me to escape the conclusion, or at any rate the strong belief, that during these weeks—the weeks of his last creation in the theatre—Verdi felt serene, confident, powerful, assured, as he had almost certainly never felt before in all his long life. The "Big-Belly" (*Pancione*) had done this for him, the immortal clownish knight of Shakespeare, now welded all in one in a music beyond compare. We shall never know, as indeed he never knew, how it happened: often "Big-Belly" would refuse to move for days upon end, and then suddenly he would take possession of the composer and of everything else in the house. All the rest of life stood still on those days when "Big-Belly" was rampant. Verdi's letters to Boito describe how this possessive or obsessive phenomenon took place, how irresistible it was and yet how undependable; how the pen could hardly keep up with the flow of the musical and dramatic idea. There have been a good many writers and composers whose work is done in this or some comparable way—that is, by fits and starts, with intervals of gloom and discouragement; but such had not been Verdi's way. Considering that he composed all at once (that is, from the top line right on down to the bottom of the score, although he could not get it all on paper), it is remarkable how swiftly and confidently he had always been able to work up to now. Aïda, for instance, written some twenty-two years before, was entirely composed and orchestrated in four months, one month to each act. It is a mature work for many voices and a full modern orchestra, all of which he bore in mind at each step even though he had to go back afterward and write it down in detail. Four months for Aïda—three years for Falstaff. Arrigo Boito, as the author, naturally was delighted at all this (the obsession, or the possession, and its irrational nature). It suited his own temperament and, we may suspect, his ideas of how genius ought to work. In effect, he urges Verdi to yield completely to the caprices of "Big-Belly": "Let him do as he likes, let him go; if he breaks all the glass and all the furniture in your room, you can buy more: if he smashes your pianoforte, you'll buy another. Let everything be turned upside down, but let the great scene be finished! Evviva!" It sounds as if Boito had been at some particularly violent spiritistic séance with "Big-Belly" as the medium's control.

The Maestro's plenitude in every way, his achievement and its acceptance, his own inner sense of the goal attained, his ability (at last!) to get out of a theatre what he had put into it—this, we think, accounted for his remarkable health and serenity during those weeks. He had been ill before and was to be ill again; but in the Falstaff time we do not hear a word of any complaint—not even of his legs, which, as all know, are likely to suffer in a Milan winter. The massage, and the "waters," and the various medical men of high repute—all these, which are so often mentioned in the correspondence of the late years—seem to fade to oblivion before the omnipotence of the Pancione. The whole enterprise was blessed, really, as we can see from the beginning—and blessed, most of all, by the devotion of that extraordinary man and poet, Boito, who knew how to coax the old Maestro into working again by providing him with the best of all texts written for opera. The secret was, in this case, double: the Maestro's tremendous love for Shakespeare and his lifelong desire to write a "lyric comedy." Boito, so wise and (I think) so good, very nearly giving his life for the Maestro, understood both of these private passions and their strength. He wrote his *Falstaff* before Verdi had even consented to write the music, and gave it as an offering before an altar. The old Maestro was so shaken and so moved that while he was still able to breathe he would have worked on this text, which he regarded as being (independently of the music) a great Italian poetic comedy. It is the sober truth that this *Falstaff*, this *Pancione*, as the two of them called it, was the only work of all Verdi's immense life in which he did not ask for the alteration of a single word. For a man who had suffered agonies during more than half a century from the inability of any theatre poet to provide the kind of text he wanted, this—even more than Boito's *Otello* six years before—was in itself bliss.

And, finally, as we separate and label the strands of his contentment, we must perceive that he had obtained on this occasion the best stage interpretation it was possible to get at the time, and the best he had ever obtained. Nothing else, not even *Otello*, satisfied his own ideas as much as this *Falstaff*. A man works alone in his study for four months or six months or two years, creating a work for the stage, with absolutely definite characters in mind—each movement, every sound, every detail of appearance and gesture—and then finds himself obliged in practical life to submit to whatever is "available," whatever can be put upon the stage under given circumstances of time and place. Verdi had yielded constantly, as every composer must—as Wagner did, too, for all his haughtiness—because otherwise no work can be performed. If you have dreamed of a willowy red-haired Irish princess and have to submit to a beer-barrel (as Bernard Shaw calls the Wagner sopranos), you learn in all bitterness what the practical stage is like. Verdi went through it for decades before he even had the chance to choose his own interpreters: when he could finally do so he was (like everybody else) limited to what there was at hand. In this ultimate work he had very nearly the choice of all the singers, conductors and musicians in the world. He chose with great care and without the slightest regard for the judgment of any other than himself. He would have Edoardo Mascheroni as conductor, and Mascheroni only—and this not only for Milan but for all the capitals of Europe except Paris. (He knew the provinciality of Paris better than the French did: he refused to send Mascheroni and the Scala cast there, but insisted on a French production in French.) For "old Big-Belly" himself he chose Victor Maurel, the French baritone whose fame had by this time penetrated more or less everywhere, but who was still capable (on the stage, at least) of surmounting it. From the evidence I doubt if Verdi ever liked Victor Maurel in the least, as a human being. Maurel was vain, handsome, boastful—a Provençal—with a fixed conviction that his own career was the most important element in the life of the time. He had "created" Verdi's Iago (how the Maestro hated that word!) and never allowed anybody to forget it. He was now to "create" the *Pancione*, and did so with the most resounding success. Verdi chose him out of sheer common sense. Whatever Maurel's defects, he had obviously a most remarkable gift for acting and singing without permitting his audience to take the two apart. Madame Maurel, as Verdi pointed out more than once, was "very intelligent." Then there was a robust young Italian baritone, Pini-Corsi, to play Ford; and the light tenor part, Fenton, went to Edoardo Garbin.

The girls were probably even more exactly suited to the Maestro's intentions. The *comarelle*—little gossips, merry little wives—as he was wont to call them, are composed together in a way quite unlike the usual treatment of solo sopranos and contraltos; in fact they are hardly "soloists" at all except in single phrases. (Nannetta has a song, it is true, but she is the only one.) Musically a great deal depends upon Alice, that is, Mistress Ford, who must have voice, style, presence, skill, charm and everything else, but nevertheless has to content herself with scenes which, brilliant though they are, involve a constant participation with others in intricate musical patterns—no "arias." For any leading soprano in those days (or even now), a part without an "aria," without one single "aria," was not a choice plum. Verdi chose Emma Zilli, who seems to have adored him and did everything he told her to do with superb results. "La Zilli"—thus she is invariably called in the letters and other works on the subject—had the merit also of engaging the Maestro's own liking. He was fond of pretty young ladies and in this *Falstaff* cast there were at least two, La Zilli and La Pasqua, who were his particular favorites. Giuseppina Pasqua was a contralto who managed to keep her looks, figure and feminine status in spite of having a big, deep voice. Verdi had already picked her out to play the Princess of Eboli when he made his final revision of *Don Carlos*, nine years before, and she was now Dame Quickly. For La Zilli and La Pasqua he had a particular place in his heart because they had understood his meaning and carried it out, but also—for in this he never changed—because he liked them anyhow.

Peppina, whose wisdom in such matters had grown deep and wide, accepted the Maestro's liking for the company of young women just as she had accepted everything else in his powerfully defined character. Indeed, it is more than likely that this aspect of his being was more comprehensible to her, and therefore easier to condone, than the other two peculiarities which had caused her to suffer: his passion for the fields and the crops in all weathers, and the terrible necessity which locked him up alone in his own room for many hours every day. The two sovereign elements, peasant and genius, were deeply painful because she was essentially shut out from both; but the ladies she knew quite well (having been one) and long experience had taught her how to deal with the situation. After all, she had been living with Verdi for forty-six years by this time, and had been actually married to him for thirty-four years, so there were few surprises. She may have compressed her lips and averted her eyes now and then, but if there was ever anything at all serious involved—such as with the Countess Maffei and, later on, with Madame Teresa Stolz— Peppina knew what to do: she firmly, resolutely, irresistibly adopted the "other woman" as her best friend, with such vows of sisterhood as never could be broken, and thus put a stop to whatever two-sided relationship there might have been before. Now "my Verdi," at eighty, could not be expected to wander far, and if he became a trifle skittish or sentimental, Peppina, whether she liked it or not, could ignore it. She was an imposing old woman, in spite of her arthritis, and like all old ladies of the period she bore some slight resemblance in general style to Queen Victoria. Nobody, looking at her, would have dreamed that she had once figured in the imagination of a master as "the one who had gone astray"—as the "deviated one," we might say now—as the *Traviata*. Peppina was not in the very least astray or deviated at the present moment. She was in firm control. So far from being *Traviata*, she was about as thoroughly *Viata* as any woman of the nineteenth century.

And then, of course, she did love the old man. There was that. Who is to say what kind of love it had become by this time? We read her letters in their whole range from the earliest passion and tenderness to the final adoration. (Why are such things kept? And yet we know it was Peppina herself who kept everything, every scrap of paper.) We know her tremendous sense of his greatness: it comes out from beginning to end in her words and deeds. She could not follow him into those recesses where composition occurs, and as the years passed she gave up trying, but when the result could be perceived she perceived it. It is very touching indeed what she said to Giulio Ricordi down at Sant' Agata one evening, after the Maestro had played and explained to him some passages from the work then in progress, *Otello*. (This after sixteen years when nothing new had been written.) Peppina turned to Ricordi and said in Milanese dialect: *"L'è ancamò bravo, el me Verdi!"* *Bravo* is a difficult word, ranging between good and excellent and fine and true, but we may trans-

late anyhow: "He's still good, my Verdi!" Peppina loved the Maestro with
a single-mindedness which changed its hue but never its essence all
down the years. Long before they began to live together, to "set up
housekeeping," as we say in the Middle West, she had befriended him;
his earliest steps in the theatre were accomplished with her help; she was
the mistress of his impresario, Bartolomeo Merelli, and whether or not
Verdi was her bel ami at that time we shall never know, but at the very
least she recognized him for what he was. It may truthfully be said of
them, as of few others on record, that his entire life as an artist was
warmed by her love. She presided over his last work just as she had over
his first, and there is every likelihood that in this case the artist and the
man were one to the heart of the woman. Such cases are rare.

2   We do not know precisely what took place on the third night of
      Falstaff in Milan, except that it was the Maestro's eternal fare-
well. Everybody was profoundly stirred, but, as he says in a letter to La
Zilli afterward, it was La Zilli herself and La Pasqua, the two favorites,
who betrayed their feelings. The Maestro himself was the most deeply
moved of all, or so he thought. The two singers must have had tears in
their eyes or he would not have mentioned it to La Zilli in such terms.
And yet—and yet—what grizzled veteran of all the wars could have re-
strained the feelings of pity and terror aroused at such a moment? The
master of the theatre was here and now, in the hour of triumph, saluting
his human instruments and the stage itself: morituri te salutamus. For
us as fellow artists (I am paraphrasing his own words) this is the end. We
may meet, yes, here and there, but this theatre is no longer mine; the
theatre of this world is no longer mine; I go toward another stage now.
    "Imagine what my salute was," he says to La Zilli in the letter of the
following December. "It meant: as artists we shall not meet again." And
to himself: Tutto è finito.
    The young ladies may have wept and I am sure they did. But can we
be equally sure that even that hulking monster Maurel, the idol of three
continents, and his "very intelligent" wife, not to speak of the conductor

Mascheroni and a good many others, kept their eyes dry? We see them clustered on the stage of the Scala—actually in what was only a few minutes ago Windsor Great Park, with Herne's Oak on the left—in the disillusioning brightness of a stage setting which has submitted to ordinary illumination. Here was where that last bewildering manifestation of the old man's genius, the fantasy in the park, the strange twittering and glittering of unearthly sprites, had turned into a human resolution of all problems in a great, roaring fugal laugh: the eight-part fugue on the words: "Everything in this world is a joke." Here, under these painted branches in the cold working lights for stagehands, where canvas is only canvas and papier-mâché shows its quality, the lyrical soul of Italy (for what else was he?) said good-bye.

Verdi's farewell could not properly have taken place under other circumstances. The magical presentation as seen from the audience was one thing he could do better himself, in his head: he had better magic down at Sant' Agata, in his own study, than anything they could do at the Scala or anywhere else. But here, in the thick paint and strong smells of the working men and women of his theatre, he could feel to the full what it was to which he had given so long a life. For this—alas!—and for this only had he lived. Bitter resentment of its conditions and an engulfing melancholy over its results had been his lot for fifty-four years. Nothing had ever really been right up to just now, just when it was all over. This very theatre, the Scala, which pretended to be "the first theatre of the world" (and how that phrase irked the Maestro, too!), had caused him more heartaches than any other except, perhaps, the Opéra in Paris. It had always seemed impossible to get anything done right in the theatre —any theatre, anywhere. It was an impossible situation to begin with, since one's dreams were turned into lyrical drama and this itself—lyrical drama—could never even approximate one's dreams. Negation, nothingness, was the only result, and if it had not been for the imperative need to live and work one's own way out of the labyrinth in the apparently foreappointed manner, what was the use of having written thirty-two operas? Thirty-two cornfields would probably have been better.

Thus we follow Verdi's essential thought about his own life in the theatre, as shown in an enormous number of letters over many years, and we know how it all must have welled up in him during that February of 1893 when he was taking his leave. But it was directly contradicted by another flood of feeling which had equal validity, even to him, and much greater decisive power, which was that he could not help loving the theatre even when he hated it. It was blood of his blood and bone of his bone. When he uses the word *arte* it is with love; when he uses the word *teatro* it is generally in profound bitterness. Yet his *arte* was the *teatro* and he knew it; they could not be separated; these Siamese twins of love and despair were the tyrants of his being. Aside from his Requiem Mass, which is an opera for the church, he never gave the fullness of his genius to any work which was not directly for the theatre—that is, a work to be rehearsed and produced with living men and women, fantastically disguised to represent that which they could seldom even understand, and subject to every conceivable or inconceivable accident of daily circumstance. What a thing it is to spin a web and have it turned into an icicle or a lump of mud! This is the fate of all who write for the theatre. And yet if there should be any person indissolubly linked to this kind of writing, as Verdi was, it will be forever as it was with him, an inescapable obligation, a torture and, at times, a joy.

That night on the Scala stage the paradox of *Hassliebe* seems to have reached its last climax for the old Master, and profoundly as the theatre had caused him to suffer, he was filled with a great sadness on leaving it. How could it be otherwise? Every resentment of the years, all the bitterness and gloom that had come to him from this cup of illusion, this cardboard universe, this trap of dreams—all vanished now as he walked, with firm step and misty eyes, Peppina on one side and Boito on the other, toward his waiting carriage. The hushed actors and stagehands, the awed and stricken musicians, must have wanted to go on their knees as he left the stage of the Scala forever, but none would have dared to do so: his departure was in silence and tears.

The carriage was as close as it was possible to get to the side door in the Via dei Filodrammatici, and the coachman had his own way of driving through the back streets to the Grand Hotel of Milan without entering the crowded square in front of the theatre or the Via Manzoni leading out of it. The system had worked on the first night, with all its excitement, as well as on the second; it worked again tonight. Verdi, with Peppina and Boito, passed from the carriage into the side entrance of the hotel without difficulty, was recognized and applauded by the street crowd and was saluted with deference by the hotel visitors downstairs. They reached the big apartment on the third floor at last. We are at liberty to suppose—since there is no record of the exact proceedings—that Verdi bowed from the balcony once or twice, as on the other evenings, and then went to bed.

One ceremonial of the Scala tradition, at least in the case of successful productions, was omitted at Verdi's fervent prayer. This was the se-

renata performed in the street by the whole orchestra, or a large part of it, under the composer's windows on the third night. Such a demonstration would, in this case, have turned into a kind of public concert, with a mob for audience and considerable unnecessary fatigue for the old man. By this time it must have been getting on toward one o'clock in the morning, and what with rehearsals and performances all together, it had been a grueling five weeks; five weeks of hard work, exemplary companionship in effort, supreme fulfillment.

To this he had come, and in the very theatre of his beginnings, after an ardous pilgrimage. Back again where he had started, yes; but with what a difference! His first opera, a work of little or no merit in his own eyes afterward, was produced at the Scala on November 17, 1839—fifty-four years earlier—through the benevolent intervention of that very Peppina who was now and long had been his wife. Since that far-off night he had had many a quarrel with the various managers, performers and conductors of the great theatre; and for twenty-five years he had never given it first choice in producing a new opera. He had produced them elsewhere: Venice, Rome, Naples, Florence, Trieste, or else in Paris, London, St. Petersburg, Cairo, anywhere but at the Scala. The Milanese assumption that this was "the first theatre of the world"—in dialect, *el prim teater del mund*—never failed to arouse Verdi's scorn. "So many firsts and no second!" he remarked, speaking of the claims of all these houses, particularly Paris, Milan and Vienna, to primacy; and none in his view deserved the title, although he once said that he might give it to Vienna. The chorus, orchestra and stage management at the Scala drew scathing words from him many times through all these years, and even the soloists—who were much the same everywhere—took advantage of lax management and bad conductors in this house; it was provincial, self-satisfied, unmusical, careless; so he scolded away. He was just as severe about the Opéra in Paris, of course, but for other reasons. The emphasis on stage machinery, settings, trickery with lights and all the other non-musical elements annoyed him there, along with the vagaries of the management and the vocal shortcomings. Perhaps if he could have combined the Paris stage, the Milan vocalism and the Vienna discipline (with the Vienna chorus and orchestra), he might have been satisfied; but in the nature of things it was not possible for Verdi to be satisfied with any work of his own in a human theatre. The nearest he had ever come to it was now, with this *Falstaff*, and even here, as the letters of the next few years show, there were annoyances which had been firmly concealed at the time. The pretensions of Maurel, for example, were hard to digest, and even in his own work (such as the ending of the second act) he found occasion to reconsider and rewrite. The score of *Falstaff* as we have it today—the only score, since he ordered the earlier one destroyed—contains two revisions of considerable importance made after the Scala production was over.

He had been forced in his later years to concede that the Scala was getting better, particularly in all those respects (stage, chorus, orchestra) in which it had displeased him before. In various letters discussing the Italian theatres he makes it plain that the best of them is the Scala. As he almost never went to hear any but his own work any more, we must assume that the rehabilitation of the Scala in his own mind was based upon its productions of his last three operas, *Aïda*, *Otello* and *Falstaff*, all under his own keen eye and absolute authority. They were far apart, of course: *Aïda*, 1871; *Otello*, 1887; *Falstaff*, 1893; and the very progress of all stage work, the world over, must have made the Scala in 1893 better than it was in 1871. What a revolution, for example, was the introduction of electricity! *Aïda* was lighted by gas, *Falstaff* by electricity. But aside from the stage itself and its new conveniences or resources, the musical values had all risen; a race of new conductors (Mariani, Faccio and Mascheroni) had given authority and discipline where once there had been almost musical anarchy; moreover, Italy, the new Italian kingdom, was prosperous, and whenever Italy is prosperous Milan is gorged with ready money. As the financial, commercial and industrial capital (the speculative capital also, with its great Bourse) Milan disposes of far more surplus funds than any other city in the country even today, and sixty or seventy years ago (while Rome was still relatively small) this condition was more marked. There was bound to be a lifting of standards in the opera house, which is the city's pride.

One element in the improvement, however, Verdi was most unlikely to recognize explicitly, although in his heart he must have known that it was true. That is, the vogue of Richard Wagner had introduced into Italian orchestral playing a sonority and discipline hitherto unknown. It is impossible to play Wagner as carelessly as the Italian orchestras had once played the earlier Verdi. Moreover, all this Wagner and Beethoven—this invasion from across the Alps—had forced upon the Italian orchestras just that kind of authority they most needed, as exemplified in the conductors Mariani, Faccio and Mascheroni, culminating, a decade later, in Toscanini. Verdi himself, bitterly though he resented the dominion which he felt Wagner was beginning to have over the musical youth of Italy, and angrily though he might preach against false gods and foreign values, was one of the very first to benefit by the changed conditions thus brought about. As he grew older his own orchestration grew more complex, until, in *Otello* and *Falstaff*, it reached symphonic dimensions. How could the Scala orchestra have played such music forty—even thirty —years before? *Aïda* would have been more or less impossible for the orchestras, choruses and stages of Verdi's youth. The intrusion of German art into the Italian theatre, although it may have led a good many Italian youths astray and produced a considerable number of absurdities —kittens dressed as tigers, musically speaking—was responsible for the enlargement and enrichment of the orchestras, the correction of public taste and the elevation of the conductor to a position of genuine authority, all of which were essential if Italy was to get beyond *Rigoletto*.

When he was a boy of twenty-four, lean and anxious, shabby and unwashed (no valet then!), the Scala was a very different establishment in every respect, run as a court theatre for the Milanese aristocracy and the Viennese viceroy. The impresario of those days, Bartolomeo Merelli, had to manage two seasons, one in Milan and one in Vienna, and there was in 1839 no considerable repertoire of old work to draw upon; many productions had to be new. Lombardy and Venetia were an appanage of the Austrian crown and Verdi, who came from the state of Parma (governed by the Archduchess Marie Louise, Napoleon's widow), was therefore a "foreigner." Most of all, the difference was in his own condition: then the poor young man thought of admission to the Scala as a prize to be won, performance of his work upon those boards as a daring ambition. Now it was all his to command, a greater organism than the wildest fancy of 1839 could have imagined, with an orchestra almost three times the size of that for which even Beethoven had composed. If we were to ask the classic question in such cases—that is, whether the old man in his glory would not have given it all to be that youth again—my own answer would be the opposite of what is expected by sentiment. I do not think he would have "given it all," or anything else much, to be that youth again, to suffer so much poverty, sorrow, hard work, disappointment and downright despair.

For Milan and the Scala meant many things to Verdi, by no means summed up in the splendor of this golden hour. Once the city had meant nothing but cruelty and the theatre nothing but the unattainable to an ignorant peasant boy harassed by genius. These were wounds that never went away, and although he was quite capable of getting the sheer facts of his own life a little muddled in his final years, he never lost the sharpness of those abiding impressions. He could get his own birthday wrong (and did for years); he could telescope the tragedy of his own young family into a fourth or fifth of the time it actually took; but he could not shake off, nor could he fail to convey, the memory of the youthful work and the pain.

3 Verdi arrived in Milan for the first time when he was eighteen, to apply for admission to the Conservatory as a student of pianoforte and composition. His native town of Busseto was responsible: his very early aptitudes in music had aroused enough interest to assure at least some opportunities there, on a most meager scale, and he had the immense good fortune to find one teacher, Ferdinando Provesi, and one patron, Antonio Barezzi, who firmly believed in his gifts. Barezzi, a prosperous wine merchant, was regarded by Verdi to the end of his days as his one great benefactor, even though the financial amount of the benefaction was small and was repaid. Provesi, director of the Philharmonic Society of the little town, and church organist as well, thought so highly of Verdi's abilities that he wanted the boy to go to Milan and study, with a view to taking over those positions in Busseto eventually; and since the scholarship fund available in the Monte di Pietà could not be touched in time, Antonio Barezzi advanced the necessary sum.

That is the briefest summary of how Verdi got to Milan in the first place. Volumes could be written (and have been) about the small-town drama behind these simple facts—the jealousies and savage feuds, the politics and the civil wars, of a provincial town in the duchy of Parma. The boy himself, although his hours of work could have given him little time for political discussion, was more or less anticlerical because his teacher, Provesi—playing the organ in church and training the choir—was anticlerical. Of this much was to be heard thereafter.

In Milan he was lodged with a fellow townsman, of the same family as his grammar-school teacher, and presented letters to the learned Professor Rolla of the Milan Conservatory. Provesi had known Rolla, as he had known may others of his own profession, before ill health and the provincial appointment had sealed him up in Busseto. Rolla was able to make the arrangements for a "kind of examination," as Verdi called it in retrospect, which consisted of two trials, one at playing the piano and one in composition.

Another small literature has accumulated on the subject of those trials. Was Verdi stupidly and ignorantly rejected by a committee of pedants who were afraid he might outdo their own pupils? Was he refused (as the Belgian critic Fétis seemed to think) because the head of the committee did not like his looks? These and many other hypotheses, all most unflattering to the judges, have been printed repeatedly; Verdi never troubled to correct anything written about him and was parsimonious of his answers to questions, so a considerable misunderstanding had already accumulated during his own lifetime. Besides, his remark about the Milan Conservatory, made at the time when that institution wished to call itself by his name, was repeated and printed everywhere: "They wouldn't have me young and they can't have me old."

The truth, as established by much research on the part of Professor Carlo Gatti and others, is that the boy from Busseto was already over the age of admission to the Conservatory and could only have entered, even as a paying student, by a special exception made "for extraordinary merit." In fact, the age of admission to the Conservatory was fixed between a minimum of eight and a maximum of fourteen years. Such were the provisions of the original decree creating the institution in 1807, and signed by Napoleon's viceroy, Eugène de Beauharnais. Most of the boys were leaving the school at just the age when Verdi tried to enter it. They were chiefly scholarship winners, paying nothing, living in the school and sleeping in a dormitory which was by this time overcrowded. (Almost every conservatory in Italy began as a sort of charity school.) Exceptions were made when necessary. For example, in the year of Verdi's failure a boy of his own age did get in, but as a student of singing—he was a *basso cantante*, and such a voice could hardly have been formed at the earlier age stipulated in the rules.

Verdi took his "kind of examination," therefore, as an aspirant to exceptional treatment on the ground of "extraordinary merit," which puts a different light on the whole affair. He played a show piece by a certain Heinrich Herz, who was in vogue at the time. The judges were his friend (or Provesi's friend) Rolla, a composer; two piano teachers; and the head of the committee, the Censor of the Conservatory.

His failure was decided by the piano teachers, in particular by one Angeleri, the head of that department, who considered that the boy held his hands wrong and employed an incorrect technique. It was Angeleri's opinion that such a method could not be corrected after the age of eighteen, when the hands were already formed, and the application was accordingly rejected.

There is no doubt that Verdi played the pianoforte extremely well as a child, and continued to do so until a very late age; but he played it in his own way. His first teacher had been a bumpkin, and his second, Provesi, was more a theorist, composer and contrapuntalist than an executant either on the piano or the organ. There is good evidence that Verdi played both instruments much better than his teacher. However, he may have done so with a faulty position of the hands and wrists and a good deal of wrong fingering. Those would be grievous shortcomings in a pianist, of course, but since he had no pianistic ambition and had come to the Conservatory to learn how to compose, the objection seems in our later days a little pedantic. It was, however, in accord with the rules of the institution. Nobody could study composition without being able to play the piano correctly, and even though the compositions Verdi submitted were judged passable, his sins at the pianoforte determined his fate. After all the papers had gone through all the offices, all the way up to the Austrian governor and back again, the application was rejected (July 9, 1832). In the formal rejection no reason was given; Verdi may never have known precisely all those details which now, after much ferreting in the archives of the Conservatory and the government, have been made public. As a matter of fact, those documents show that there were a number of reasons for rejecting the young man, although if he had been more acceptable at the pianoforte they might not have counted. One official said the dormitory was overcrowded anyhow, and another official noted that there were too many pianoforte students for the available instruments and time. Still another gentleman noted on his bit of paper that Verdi was a "foreigner" (estero), coming from the state of Parma. All of them (including the Austrian governor) took care to mention that he had reached the advanced age of eighteen.

There have been worse tragedies, of course, and perhaps in the long run it may have been better for Verdi not to get into the Conservatory. But the blow to all his pride and hope was terrible: he had been the prodigy of Busseto ever since his tenth year, and now he was to disappoint those who had put their faith in him—Barezzi and Provesi and his own parents and his beloved sister. The savage energy with which he worked from then on—twelve, fourteen, sixteen hours a day almost every day for years—a cruel grind even to contemplate—was undoubtedly generated, in part anyhow, by this early failure, so icy and unexpected, so hard for the boy and those who believed in him to understand.

On the advice of his mentors and, above all, of his benefactor, Barezzi, the young Verdi then gave himself up to the direction of a private teacher, Vincenzo Lavigna, who had composed operas and ballets in his youth and enjoyed high repute as a contrapuntalist. The boy studied far harder than can have been normal in those or any other days; by his own account he composed "canons and fugues, fugues and canons, in all the sauces" for the next two years and more. We also know, although he did not himself mention it, that he studied the work of Corelli, Bach, Mozart and Beethoven at the same time, so the regime Lavigna imposed was not quite so dry and military as Verdi's letters forty and fifty years later might indicate. In addition to studying scores and composing all these "canons and fugues," he was encouraged to go to the Scala whenever he could do so, with particular attention to instrumentation and "the presentation of dramatic music." His progress was rapid enough to justify two testimonials from his teacher, both of which were sent back to Busseto to fortify the enthusiasm of the old folks at home. Among these old folks there was one young one who already counted for a great deal with the student Verdi: this was Barezzi's daughter Margherita, whose sad and brief idyl with him had already begun.

Provesi's death (July, 1833) brought another stinging disappoinment along with its great grief. The ecclesiastical and civic authorities of Busseto, falling again into a state of civil dispute, went through a period of unimaginable intrigue over the succession to that worthy pedagogue. Verdi's friends had always assumed he would get the place, and it was for this that he was being trained in Milan; but after a whole year's delay the church authorities took their revenge on Provesi's anticlericalism by appointing a stranger, one Ferrari, to the post of organist and choirmaster. This was only half, and less than half, of Provesi's job: the greater part was that of music teacher to the town and director of the local Philharmonic Society. Barezzi and his friends of the Philharmonic held out against this "treachery," as they called it: if the church would not appoint Verdi, they held that the post should at least be open to a free public competition, in which they were certain that Verdi would win. In this situation Verdi, who had returned just in time to receive the blow (June, 1834), was put into the directorship of the Philharmonic and remained in Busseto for six months, giving concerts and otherwise proving himself to the satisfaction of the "Verdian" party. The amount of correspondence and the number of incidents to which this civil war in music gave rise could hardly be believed by one who sees the little town of Busseto merely in passing. It became a battleground between clericals and anti-clericals, the "pigtails" (codini, those who wore their hair in a queue) and the "cockades" (coccardini, those sporting the white cockade of the French Revolution). It was characteristic of Busseto that these insignia, now a good forty years and more out of date, should have been adopted by the respective partisans. Underneath all the extravagances of the dispute, which continued through the summer of 1834 and actually led to blows on more than one occasion, ran a sober economic fact: there was not enough money in Busseto to support more than one music master, and all the jobs had therefore to be combined. Verdi's rival, the the unfortunate Ferrari, had a brood of children and could not survive on the meager stipend of church organist and choirmaster: neither could Verdi as director of the Philharmonic Society. The civil war ended with an agreement between the church authorities and the Philharmonic: the appointment would in due course be thrown open to competition, and in the meantime Verdi could return to his studies in Milan. This, of course, he did as soon as Barezzi gave the word (December, 1834), and remained with Lavigna until the following summer.

All the early struggles and disappointments may seem of little or no consequence compared to the immensity of Verdi's later career, but they left scars which never disappeared so long as he lived. Those years from eighteen to twenty-one were spent in grueling work, and the immediate reward was one drenching shower of ice water after another. When a boy of this temper—of indefatigable energy, spurred by genius in all its impatience—faces the difficulties of the workaday world, no matter if all other conditions are favorable, the result must be pain. In Verdi's case the other conditions were far from favorable. He had no real education, nothing but his own reading to provide those clues to poetry and history which were his lifelong delight; he was a peasant of the poorest, and his birthplace, the village of Le Roncole, an appendage of Busseto, exhibits even today the signs of its original poverty. He could have had no money at all for clothing, must have known little about the customs of educated society, and probably did not even know how to eat properly when he first went into the house of his benefactor, Barezzi. These are really decisive circumstances in the life of such as he, and to the end of his days we find their echoes. We shall find him going to almost any length to avoid the town of Busseto or any of its activities or inhabitants. And, as we have mentioned, for twenty-five years he absented himself, professionally speaking, from Milan and the Scala. These facts or deeds are accompanied by many sharp words. He was not a vengeful man, indeed, and was capable of great generosity toward those who had injured him, but pain and disappointment, if they were accompanied by any suggestion of injustice, left deep marks upon him.

Slowly, all too slowly, the difficulties about Busseto and its music mastership were straightened out, with all the creaky and cumbersome deliberation of a provincial bureaucracy. The position of *maestro di cappella*, which included that of organist, was declared open to competition (December, 1834); the official authorization for this arrived from Parma at the end of June, 1835; the proclamation of an open contest was made January 23, 1836. Verdi went to Parma in the following month, sustained two examinations (February 27 and 28), returned to Busseto victorious, received his appointment in April and was, at last, in a position to marry his Margherita (May 4, 1836), about six months before his twenty-third birthday.

Of his feeling for Margherita there can be nothing but certainty: it was love's young dream. They had known each other since childhood and we have the virtual proofs, from Lavigna's certificates and the record of his student days, that Verdi had never really looked at another girl. The gentle Margherita lived her brief life so completely in his shadow that we can hardly discern her separate existence across the density of subsequent events. She loved him, lived with him, bore him two children, lost them, and then herself was lost to him, all within four years, leaving a ring and a lock of hair which he treasured ever after. They may be seen today at Sant' Agata, but he kept them so securely for himself that we are not at all sure that Peppina, his second wife and companion for so many years, ever knew of their existence.

All this took up the years of Verdi's first youth and gave it that somber tint which seems to suffuse every reference he ever made to it in later time. He was only twenty-seven when his Margherita ("Ghita," he called her) died; their son Romano, a year and a half old, had died the preceding October, their daughter Virginia the year before. He was eighteen when he failed to obtain entrance to the Conservatory, twenty-one when he failed to obtain the Busseto appointment: these were, it seems, the principal events of those all-important years, outweighing the success he eventually secured for himself in the contest of 1836 (when he was twenty-three) in the competition for that appointment.

For, as might have been expected, the Busseto appointment did not, when it finally came, give him any genuine satisfaction. It enabled him to marry Margherita, which was the one great joy of his youth, but so far as music was concerned it did not fulfill his own expanding or aspiring nature. He was conscientious in all of it, both in the rehearsing and conducting of the Philharmonic Society and in the direction of the church choir; he taught the young to the best of his ability; in whatever time all this work allowed him, he also composed, but it was time taken from sleep, for he had no other. And the fact was that by now (when he was twenty-three) he was a composer through and through, blood and bone, and nothing else. He did not want to give lessons on the piano or play the organ in the church. He did not even want to prepare and conduct works for chorus and orchestra (the Philharmonic Society), although this, of course, was far better, far less like drudgery. He wanted to compose operas and had already made some attempts, even before he left Milan and his old teacher for good (1835). Moreover, there was one thing Verdi always resented with a towering passion all his life long, and that was the attempt on the part of anybody or anything to hold him in servitude. He had not been long in Busseto, in that appointment for which he had been trained and which had given him the long and anxious wait, before he discovered that the whole town regarded him as its servant, its bond slave, in all matters musical. The financial obligation incurred for his training in music had never been great and was quickly discharged, but the sense that Busseto owned him—that he was under an eternal obligation to Busseto and to every citizen of Busseto—was in the air and remained in the air for long, long years after he had left it. This was intolerable to Verdi and poisoned his existence. We find him complaining to his friend Massini in Milan that here in Busseto he was "passing the best years of his youth" in a void.

We can easily imagine how bewildering it must have been to Verdi's own family—as to many another in the neighborhood—to find that this wonderful appointment for which he had been so carefully groomed was not what he wanted. It was an appointment for three to nine years and with the merest modicum of industry and politeness he could have held it for life. It gave him 627 gold lire a year to begin with, which, if multiplied by about ten (as would be necessary to obtain real values) would today make something like $1,250 a year, and this, to his parents, must have represented a lordly revenue.

Antonio Barezzi, now his father-in-law and always his most loyal adherent, was perhaps the one and only Bussetano who truly (although perhaps sadly) understood the necessity which made Verdi leave Busseto for good in early 1839 (February 6). It was not possible to produce an opera in a little town in the midst of the Parma plain, and Verdi had written an opera. It was more important to get this opera put upon a stage than it was to do anything that fell within his range during those laborious days in Busseto; he had not even filled out the entire three years of his appointment, its minimum; he was twenty-six and the world called; his departure was as inevitable as the change of the seasons. Barezzi let him go, no matter how many difficulties this defection might bring upon himself. By all the evidence, Barezzi was a remarkable man and fully deserved not only Verdi's unfailing gratitude but also that eloquent marble plaque which today ornaments his house in the principal square (the Piazza Giuseppe Verdi) at Busseto.

On the third night of *Falstaff*, as we glance back at the composer's hard-driven youth, we cannot but see how differently the momentous departure must have been regarded by those who beheld it. To Verdi it was an imperative necessity and no other course could have been either logical or possible, given the laws of his being. He was an opera composer and he knew it. The chief purpose of an opera, practically speaking, is to get itself heard in a theatre, whatever may happen afterward. To go to Milan was the only way. And yet to Busseto, by and large, and to many inhabitants of Busseto for decades afterward, this departure was a form of treason. What? Had they not dragged up this insolent peasant youth from the very gutter, and put shoes on his feet and sent him to a good teacher, so that he would in turn give Busseto the benefit of his services as universal music master, for all purposes, for the rest of his life? Most of the good citizens forgot that the actual money spent upon Verdi's training came out of the benevolent funds of the Monte di Pietà, and the rest of it from the pocket of his father-in-law Barezzi, and never a penny from the pockets of those who complained so loudly. The feeling and its expression were there, just the same, and there was not much hesitation about letting the composer know. This, too, rankled forever after, and although he returned to that immediate neighborhood for the indispensable earth which his nature demanded—a familiar earth for the plow and the manure, and no other would do because any other would have seemed agronomically alien—he never actually made his peace with the town. Now, as you go from the Via Giuseppe Verdi into the Piazza Giuseppe Verdi, passing streets named after his various teachers and friends (including even the Abbé Seletti, who taught him grammar), and read the plaque put up on Barezzi's house, and look at the statue of Verdi in front of the Teatro Verdi, the whole irony of the situation becomes downright comic. To him it was never, even half a century later, a situation to which a proud spirit could become reconciled: it contained that which he most hated, which was injustice.

So he and Margherita went to Milan, for good and all, and his first opera was actually produced in the autumn season of 1839. It was called *Oberto, Conte di Bonifacio*, had a moderate success (fourteen performances) and retired to oblivion soon afterward. The departure for Milan was precipitated by the promise that the work could be put on as a benefit (once) in the carnival season of 1839, but a tenor fell ill and it could not be done; the autumn performances, however, were a still better opportunity, and Verdi was given a contract for three more operas at 4000 gold lire each. For a young man of twenty-six—indeed for any composer of the period—these were wonderful terms, and he owed them to the interest and the active intervention of the soprano Giuseppina Strepponi (Peppina). She was young and, we gather, beautiful; she was the mistress of the manager, Bartolomeo Merelli, by whom she had a son; it is not possible to know, from the very sparse evidence, whether her interest in the young composer was based only upon her perception of his genius. She sang in his first opera and in his third (*Nabucco*), but in no others, and it seems possible that their relationship did not begin until they met again in Paris, eight years after that first encounter, and discovered that they were (as they may have been, one or the other or both, obscurely or uncertainly, from the beginning) in love. In the days of the composer's first experiences with the Scala neither of them was free, in fact or in fancy, and there is nothing to suggest that they behaved otherwise—nothing, that is, except the general possibility involved in human weaknesses.

Verdi was devoted to his young wife Margherita, his first love, who had been so sadly stricken by the loss of their two children; and her own sudden death (from meningitis) in June, 1840, was the cruelest blow of all those which fell upon his youth. He took refuge in his brother-in-law's house at Busseto and locked himself up with his grief, but the impresario Merelli had a contract and demanded his opera. It was, as luck would have it, a comic work, only partly finished when Margherita died, and in the depths of his melancholy he had to complete it, just the same, for the autumn season. It had its first and only performance at the Scala on September 5, 1840; the composer was compelled, by the custom of the time, to spend that evening in the orchestra pit, listening to the whistles and catcalls with which it was stormed off the stage. It was called *Un Giorno di Regno* and was the most unvarnished failure of all his life, a genuine disaster which he could never forget. In his despair he resolved never to write another opera. He sent his and Margherita's furniture off to Busseto and took a furnished room where he spent weeks and months in gloomy inaction and aimless melancholy. He was twenty-seven years old that October, and all his hope in life and art seemed already dead: wife, children, work, everything gone.

These were the memories of his early years in Milan. It was to this first decade—something less than a decade but something much more in retrospect than any span of years—that his mind must have turned back as he said his farewell. Verdi's recollection of all the slings and arrows was tenacious. In common with many of us, he remembered the suffering more keenly than he did the joy; he never forgot the bitter taste of tears. There is something of this in all his later attitude toward fame and fortune; he was glad to get any money he could reasonably get, and stood by his rights in such matters with a peasant's fortitude and (too often) suspicion; but the trappings of fame—"glory," as they always called it, —were never congenial to him. Beneath the laurel wreaths he always seemed to feel the thrust of thorns, and every triumph came too late to be savored to the full. No compensation of that sort could restore the brightness of his morning or bring his dead to life again.

4 Milan was kind and more than kind thereafter. In the year after Margherita's death he was able to resume work, at first with reluctance and no confidence, later on with gathering force. The impresario Merelli was again responsible, by thrusting upon him the libretto of a work called *Nabucodonosor*, by Temistocle Solera. Bartolomeo Merelli would appear to have been a good-natured man, and he was no doubt moved to humane sympathy by the spectacle of Verdi's helpless and hopeless grief, even without prompting by his friend Giuseppina Strepponi. In addition, he had a contract with Verdi, and the clamorous failure of the young man's second opera had not destroyed either that contract or Merelli's faith in its possibilities. Still further, as we have observed, the repertoire was not so large in those days as to permit a whole season of old work. Every impresario had to find a few new things to produce before he could open the doors of the theatre, and the public would

have been vociferous in disapproval if he had failed them. Merelli had returned the contract to Verdi at the moment of the young man's deepest depression and at Verdi's own request (it was during the period when he had resolved never to write another opera). However, in the meantime the script of Nabucodonosor, which Merelli had already bought and paid for, and therefore regarded highly, was going begging for lack of a composer. It had been submitted to the German Nicolai (composer of Die Lustige Weiber von Windsor), who did not feel inclined to attempt it. The good-natured Merelli had said to Verdi, on returning his contract: "I can't make you write music by force. But if you ever do write another opera, give me two months' notice before the beginning of any season and I will produce it."

One evening in the winter of 1841, as the melancholy young composer was walking home through the snow from the cheap restaurant where he had all his meals, he encountered the impresario with this manuscript in hand. Merelli admonished him, pleaded with him: "A stupendous, magnificent, extraordinary libretto! Effective dramatic situations, grandiose; beautiful verses," and so on, but, unfortunately, that obstinate German maestro had refused to set it to music and the poor manager was at his wits' end to find another composer. All this, of course, led up to the proposal, made as they walked along toward the Scala, where Merelli was bound, that Verdi should go back to work again and write the opera, the text of which was then and there thrust upon him. Verdi refused, but Merelli insisted and would not take the script back. The young man then returned with it to his furnished room, where, for months on end, he had done nothing but lament his fate. In the savage mood of those days, resentful of the world and his own presence in it, he was in no mood to read a libretto. He threw the manuscript on the table in his bare room and it fell open at the words: "Va, pensiero, sull'ali dorate!" (Go, Thought, on wings of gold!) which struck him by their closeness to a Bible text he had only recently read. He picked up the script and tried a verse here and a verse there; before long he was reading the whole thing from beginning to end. He had already felt very strange on his way home with these papers in his hand—there was some disturbance of his whole being, as if Merelli had made an appeal to instinctive powers or desires that were not dead, but sleeping. Over and over again, all night long, he read and reread the libretto of the Biblical tale. Afterward, long afterward, in telling the story to Ricordi in a famous autobiographical letter, he declared that he had almost memorized the libretto before that night was over. Nevertheless, he did not weaken in his resolve:

he was never going to write another opera, life was over, art was finished, he must eke out his living by teaching idiot children how to play the piano, or in some other modest way. He would not keep this libretto. During the day he went to the Scala to see Merelli and gave the manuscript into his hands. The impresario said: "Beautiful?" and Verdi agreed that it was very beautiful. "Then set it to music!" Merelli said excitedly. "Set it to music, set it to music!" Verdi's protests went unheard. The manager put him out through the door and thrust the manuscript into his hands, all in a flurry of words, shoves and pushes, and then locked the door behind him. Verdi, sorely puzzled and ill at ease, made his way home again, libretto in hand, and from then on he could not get it out of his mind. The music for this verse or for that verse would come into his head and eventually he started writing down what came in this way, unbidden and more or less against his own will. Thus, in a haphazard way at first, without plan or intention, and with some obscure sense of guilt at being engaged again in composition after such a vow against it, he found himself working full tilt. Before the end of that summer (1841) he was writing with excitement and confidence, and by his twenty-eighth birthday, that October, the opera was completed. *Nabucodonosor*, re-christened *Nabucco*, was his first great success with the general public of Italy, the foundation of his whole career as an artist.

Verdi's confidence in his own work began with *Nabucco*. After all his sorrow and despair, this effort, started in such an accidental manner, gradually aroused his moral and physical being to a higher pitch than ever before, and we may be amused, but scarcely surprised, to find him clamoring for its immediate production. The young man who, six months before, had struggled to avoid another trial of strength, was now so sure of himself that he wanted Merelli to put on *Nabucco* before any of the other new works of the season. Merelli, of course, had other contracts, other obligations—he was a man of large interests, the principal impresario of the time throughout Europe—and held his impatient protégé in leash as best he could. He had three other expensive new works by famous composers (one of them Donizetti, the king of the opera houses at that time) and could not afford to put on *Nabucco* in the carnival season. He asked Verdi to wait until the spring—a sort of post-season at the Scala, after Easter. In the meantime, he might see if Giuseppina Strepponi wished to sing it.

La Strepponi had made progress as a *prima donna assoluta* throughout Italy in the past two years. Her talent, not for technical display but for musical and dramatic expression, beauty of tone and action, was admired by the best judges and by a rapidly growing public. She certainly had more musical training from childhood, more natural perception and general musical intelligence, than was common among singers then or even now. Her father, Feliciano Strepponi, director of music at the Monza Cathedral—an appointment for which Verdi was suggested in later years—had composed a number of comic operas as well as church music and had seen his work performed in several Italian cities before his death, at the age of thirty-five, left his family penniless. Giuseppina was then at the Milan Conservatory, where she had been admitted at fifteen for "exceptional aptitudes for music." She had been a paying student for two years when her father died, and rather than see her studies interrupted for lack of money, the Conservatory itself applied to the Austrian government for a scholarship grant. She thus completed her training as a pensioned student and emerged from the Conservatory on September 25, 1834, a prize winner, adjudged "very distinguished" in every test. Within a few months she had made her debut at Trieste (carnival season of 1834–35) and was in demand throughout northern Italy by the time the all-powerful Merelli met her and took her, first to Vienna and then to the Scala, on the road to fortune.

We have already seen how La Strepponi had championed Verdi's first opera with the management and was responsible for its production (November 17, 1839). She had herself made a formidable success at the Scala in the preceding spring, and after a year's absence was now about to return for the latter part of the carnival season of 1841–42. In her first five years after leaving the Conservatory she had sung in no less than twenty-seven theatres, including all the principal ones of Italy and Austria. Aside from her personal influence upon Merelli, she exercised the natural power of a brilliant young soprano with special gifts, for whom the public had shown a marked predilection: Verdi could have had no better friend at court. Consequently, when Merelli advised him to consult La Strepponi, he lost no time: with his friend, the lawyer Francesco Pasetti, who possessed a carriage, he called upon the singer and received an appointment for the reading of the opera the next day. (This was October 21, 1841, and Pasetti's carriage was probably welcome in the Milan weather.) La Strepponi declared herself highly pleased with the music as soon as they had read it through at the piano, and the three of them took the score then and there and drove to the house of the baritone Roncoli, whom Verdi hoped to obtain for the title part in the opera. The same scene was repeated: Roncoli also was pleased, and the composer could then hold the management to its promise.

There were other hitches, of course. Merelli, in spite of great gains and successes, did not have a limitless purse, and four new productions in one season meant a great deal of expenditure. The announcements for the carnival season (that is, from St. Stephen's Night, otherwise December 26, through Lent) came out with no *Nabucco* and no Verdi on the list. The composer lost his temper altogether and wrote Merelli a rancorous letter, which, he says, he regretted as soon as it was sent; but that wonderfully even-tempered man merely laughed and said: "Is that the way to write to a friend?" If Verdi would accept a production without new scenery and costumes—that is, one pieced together out of the theatre's storehouse—his opera could go on at the end of the carnival season as a special bonbon for the subscribers. Verdi professed himself to be glad of anything, any kind of production, so long as the work could be produced. Assured, as he was by that time, of his favorite singers for the two principal parts, he felt strong enough to risk the rest.

The rehearsals for *Nabucco* began toward the end of February, 1842, and before they had gone far they caused a ripple of excitement to run through Milan. Everybody concerned in the matter had a tale to tell. It was said that the music was so fresh, new and exciting that the main difficulty was that of getting any work done: all the workmen, stagehands, musicians, choral singers—everybody—fell to listening at once, with the effect of paralyzing the rehearsals over and over again. Whether this was strict truth or somewhat mixed with legend, it is of record that the first performance, on the night of March 9, 1842, was one of the most triumphant in the history of the Italian theatre, as well as one of the most decisive in its results. In a single night Verdi became famous; his characteristic musical utterance, already defined although not developed, was accepted with rapture by a public which had never heard anything quite like it; his work from then on might succeed or fail, but there was never again the smallest difficulty in finding theatres and managements anxious to produce it.

Along with the actual triumph in the theatre, which was rare enough, there went a curious series of overtones and suggestions which made the most powerful appeal to Italians of that period, whether Verdi deliberately set out to create it or not. *Nabucco* deals with the suffering of the Israelites under the alien tyranny of the Babylonian Nebuchadnezzar, half mad with dreams of greatness, and with the promise of their redemption. In some ways it is as much a hymn to freedom as was Beethoven's *Fidelio*, even though not on the same level of musical maturity, and I find it worth noticing that both these works (*Nabucco* in Italy and

Fidelio in Germany) had a highly unusual number of performances during the decade which followed the second world war. Even today their significance in that respect—politically, let us say—seems undimmed in the countries for which they were written. In 1842 *Nabucco* was immediately taken as an allegory of the anguish of Italy, divided into small states and much of it under foreign misgovernment. It was a period in which some of the finest spirits in northern Italy had wasted their years in the Austrian prison at Spielberg, in Moravia, and the atmosphere of Milan, conspiratorial, glowing under the ashes, was like that in George Meredith's Italian novels.

Verdi, of course, was liberal and republican in feeling—even his ill-fated children bore names which were like proclamations of the Roman Republic, the one Virginia and the other Romano—and although he had no time or temper for politics, there never was a doubt about where his heart was. When he first moved to Milan, the Emperor of Austria (Ferdinand) had just descended upon Milan to be crowned in the Cathedral there as King of Lombardy-Venetia, and Verdi's comment in a letter to Busseto is contained in one word: "The Emperor has gone and the brothel is over." Whenever or wherever his views show through, they are of the same stamp, fiercely Italian and patriotic.

Naturally, inevitably, the *Nabucco* subject aroused this fever of the blood, but we may be sure he knew exactly what he was doing. He was far too intelligent to be unaware that when he wrote so fervently of the Israelites he really meant the Italians, and when he promised a liberty to come he was thinking of his own country and people. However, he need not have known, and I think did not know, that his own fierce ardor would be instantly understood and taken up by the whole of Italy. He can hardly have expected that result, since nothing like it had happened before. It was as if his music, joined to Solera's text, meant two things at once, on two successive planes: one the ostensible story, which could offer nothing offensive to an Austrian censor, and the other which immediately communicated its passionate message to every Italian soul. When I suggest that he may not have done this deliberately, I mean that he did not set out to arouse his fellow countrymen, so far as I can tell: he set out merely to write an opera, in the course of which his own patriotism caught fire and illumined the whole work. Nobody could have known, until it happened, that what he wrote out of his own intensities would prove to be an expression of the nation's soul at a given moment in its history.

The chorus "*Va, pensiero, sull'ali dorate*" ran through Italy with something like the velocity of light, and Verdi found himself at the outset of his career aureoled in a national patriotism, the aureole of the Risorgimento, which clung to him for decades and in fact never altogether faded in Italian eyes. Such consecrated and recognized patriotism had both good and bad results for the artist: in an era like that of the Risorgimento it kept his pulse beating in time with that of his audience and assured him of a special emotional loyalty, but it was also a great temptation to easy effects, which the Verdi of that decade could not always resist. We may be sure of one thing, the sincerity of the original feeling. "Va, pensiero" is a page of authentic musico-dramatic inspiration, perfectly fitted both to its place in the theatre piece for which it was written and to the larger world outside which so quickly adopted it. It is impossible to know how much such music contributed to the rekindling of the Italian spirit which we call the Risorgimento. Poetry and music defy measurement, not only in themselves but in their results as well. Men who lived through those stirring times did not hesitate to say that Verdi's work, even by sheer accident and even when least patriotic in significance, did much to awaken Italy. Who can tell? Something sent the volunteers out on their desperate enterprises—something in the air, perhaps, more complex and inclusive than any music but less specific than Garibaldi's red shirt or Mazzini's pamphlets. One song may do more than any number of pamphlets and red shirts, or it may be only another manifestation of the same vibrant and unseen reality. Who is to say?

In Verdi's own life, certainly, Nabucco was a turning point of dramatic sharpness. It seems to divide his journey into two parts, like a pass in the high mountains, so that where all had been poverty, suffering and struggle up to then, everything afterwards was lighted by the sun of fortune. He was to have failures from time to time, notably La Traviata, but they had no more power to throw him into despair. He also had resounding and memorable successes, but they did not upset his equilibrium. It would be hard to find in the annals of the theatre any more crashing failure than his second opera, Un Giorno di Regno, with its one disastrous performance, or any more total triumph than Nabucco. He had thus touched the two extremes of a theatre life early, very early, and before he was twenty-nine—with nearly sixty years yet to go—he already knew that lesson of Falstaff: "Cammina, cammina," keep on going. Whatever happens, keep on going, on your own way.

And his way was not, in spite of fortune's sun, by any means smooth. The very conditions of the Italian theatre in his time were fundamentally inimical to the free, spontaneous and independent development of an original talent. Composers worked under contract for a specific theatre. Such an opera, on a subject agreed upon in advance, would be ready for performance at such-and-such a date, would be rehearsed under the composer's eye with such singers as the theatre happened to have on hand. Often the subject would be suggested by the management, or changed by the management; more than once a musical scene written in a certain manner would have to be rewritten to suit the vocal abilities (or disabilities) of the singers. Every word and note was subject to the censorial review of the police in the Austrian territories, the Papal States and the kingdom of Naples, which between them controlled all the larger cities and theatres. Only the grand duchy of Tuscany and the duchy of Parma were relatively lax toward "liberals" and "liberalism," more out of laziness than benevolence, but Milan, Venice, Rome and Naples were in the full grip of that monarchist-clerical reaction to which the Congress of Vienna had assigned them. From *Nabucco* onward Verdi was always suspected of subversive ideas and possibilities; indeed, it was remarkable how many meanings of this kind the public could hear in his work, even when he had least intended them; and the police had a tendency to examine each new opera of his with a magnifying glass in search of political unorthodoxy. It was not easy for even the most skillful, industrious and professional of all theatre musicians to meet these practical difficulties head-on, time after time, and surmount them; great popularity, which Verdi so quickly attained after *Nabucco* and never lost, was in some respects a disadvantage in the preparation and production of any new work. It did assure an ultimate revenge, in most cases, but it made the initial stages more arduous because more was feared from him, just as more was expected. Every opera he wrote from *Nabucco* onward, until Italy was free and united, encountered the same difficulties. It is a curious circumstance that his own full maturity and the great work that came out of it—*Aïda*, the Requiem Mass, *Otello* and *Falstaff*—occurred only after the free and united Italy had come into being. Everything that went before was composed and produced against a sea of troubles.

But he took arms—oh, yes, he took arms. Chief of his arms was an absolute inveterate professionalism which made him (however fiercely he might growl) curb and clip and prune his own rugged talent to suit the conditions of the time. He bewailed his fate but he accommodated himself to it with the military efficiency of a commander beset by bad weather. There was nothing he could do in practice to change the conditions of the Italian theatre, or of Italian politics, society and economics. Like famine or cholera, the rule of the foreigner and the secret police held Italy prostrate. Verdi's course was to fight with every weapon he could command—and his great popularity made him no mean opponent—but to yield, when it became necessary, rather than have a work totally suppressed. And such was his ingenuity, aided at all times by that aura of invincible and incorruptible patriotism which clung to him, that no matter how many times the police might change the subject or the words or the treatment of a theme, it always did come out, just the same, in a way which the Italian people understood. As I have suggested, the people sometimes understood a little too much—more than he put into the work; but it is more than likely that the instinct of the people was right. Verdi's unconscious was pervasive. He did not always realize how his melancholy and passionate lyricism, at its most sincere, affected the very circulation of the blood in his countrymen.

The discipline of a professional conscience was that which kept him going through something between two and three decades of virtual impossibility. No matter how complex his musical utterance finally became, it was always subject to this professional criterion of the theatre man thinking of theatre production. When he timed the first act of *Falstaff* for himself, down at Sant' Agata in the valedictory years, it came out to forty-two minutes. "Two minutes too long!" said Verdi.

His melancholia, the curse of his life and the source of much unhappiness to himself and others, arose in great part from that poverty-stricken and disappointed youth, ending, as it did, in a clean sweep of his every hope at the age of twenty-six; but his subsequent life in the theatre, even as a so-called "successful" composer, made heavy contributions to the disease. He felt the iniquity of the theatre system, the subjugation of Italy, the tyranny of the police, the helplessness of the composer, the impossibility of getting anything produced, sung or played in accordance with an intention. In one very deep and true sense opera itself is an impossibility, and although every composer is irresistibly drawn toward it (perhaps for that reason), it cannot but defeat an intention. How many times in Verdi's letters do we find expressions like "*Triste, triste, triste!*" They refer to the passage of time, to old age, sickness and death, to the general human predicament, just as often as they do to any specific event such as the loss of an old friend or the misfortunes of Italy. Melancholia, once it has taken possession, needs no more than the falling of a single leaf in the September woods to set its clouds afloat over the consciousness of a man like Verdi.

Yet Milan—Milan after *Nabucco*—was more than kind, and the old man going to bed on the third night of *Falstaff* must have had many softer recollections to dim the bitterness of his far-off youth. He could not have forgotten his beloved Clarina, the Contessa Maffei, for whom he felt an indissoluble friendship for so many years; he must have remembered La Frezzolini, the vivid and devoted little soprano who said to him on the first night of *I Lombardi*, "If I have to die on the stage, your opera will conquer!" He could not have forgotten the hospitable and amiable, if somewhat inconstant, Giuseppina Appiani (born Contessa Strigelli), who transferred her affections from Donizetti to him—or Donna Emilia Morosini or the Contessa della Somaglia or any of the other lovely ladies who welcomed him to their houses after *Nabucco*. All were gone now: all dead. Both in the city and in the theatre he had much of the kind to remember, not to mention his own Peppina. Milan had opened all its doors after *Nabucco*; all, that is, except those of the Austrian and clerical officialdom which held him suspect.

Indeed, after *Nabucco* Verdi was himself a changed personality in some notable externals. He was never again in sharp need of money—the days when his little Margherita had to take her trinkets out and sell them to pay the rent were gone forever. He learned about clothing, manners, carriages, hairdressers, conversation, the customs and usages of the upper classes—all those things which had never come his way before. The "bear" was tamed and the "peasant" groomed. In his later days he had no use for society, in Milan or elsewhere, and never accepted an invitation unless it was from an old friend, but in the *Nabucco* time it was all new, strange and interesting; he would have been lacking in ordinary human curiosity, one lively section of the intelligence, if he had not availed himself of the opportunities offered. Moreover, it is clear that for some years he liked all this, and the manners he learned at that period lasted him to the end. He was punctilious as a countryman who had learned the rules rather late, but once and for all, and expected others to conform. The fine ladies of Milan, who taught him all this, delighted in the task and showered their invitations upon him. Most of them were Italian patriots by instinct because of the prevailing winds, even though their own fathers or husbands might have been knights of the Holy Roman Empire; there was a curious combination of Austrian and Italian in the Milanese aristocracy, within many families, one member at the Emperor's court and another in the Emperor's jail. Intermarriages with Austrians had taken place, and an education in Vienna—a polyglot capital anyhow—was not unusual for an Italian aristocrat. All these muddled loyalties, for they were not even divided just yet, were swirling about in whatever intellect there might be to contain them. One simple reason for the confusion of loyalties in an aristocratic society was that the families of Hapsburg and Savoy, which were only gradually moving into their historic positions on opposite sides, were still closely related. The Empress of Austria at this period was a princess of Savoy (Maria Anna Carolina). Victor Emmanuel II (then still duke of Savoy, King of Sardinia a few years later, and King of Italy from 1860) was about to marry the Archduchess Adelaide of Austria. In fact, *Nabucco* itself, an undeniable document of Italian patriotism, was dedicated to this young lady when it came out in printed form: such were the contradictions of the period. Indeed, aristocratic society, always monarchist by nature however many exceptions it may contain, did not veer toward the house of Savoy until the next decade—the great decade of Cavour (1851–1861), who made Victor Emmanuel II the symbol of every Italian aspiration. At the time when Verdi first frequented the salons of the Milanese countesses there were few clear-headed monarchistic patriots, and the very word "patriot" was obscurely associated in most minds with the more subversive word "republican." Verdi was both a patriot and a republican—in those days a determined and uncompromising republican—so that he had not only the vogue of the successful composer and the halo of partisanship, but carried a suggestion of danger and daring as well. It was very "advanced" to have Verdi as a guest in one's house, and the Milanese ladies, although not themselves republicans and not at all sure of what they really thought, were anxious to be "advanced."

We can be quite certain that the patriotic instinct was well developed in them, just the same, no matter how little they may have attempted to think it through to a conclusion. Contessa Maffei, Verdi's lifelong friend, was a woman of intelligence and sensibility, and in her case the political principles went deep. We know, for instance, that her final separation from Andrea Maffei was brought about not only by his hopeless passion for gambling, his general looseness of behavior and his incurable propensity for debt-making, but also by the fact that he was very lukewarm toward the freedom of Italy. The Maffei pair, Andrea and Chiara (whom Verdi almost always called "Clarina"), were ornaments of the cultivated society of their time: he wrote poetry, made translations from the German, graced many salons besides that of his wife, and seems to have been debonair and companionable at all times. He was Verdi's friend before, during and after the legal separation (to which Verdi was a witness). Clarina was sixteen years younger than Andrea, and her celebrated salon began its existence only two years after their marriage (in 1834). She was from Bergamo, a countess of the

Spinelli family (Spinelli-Carrara). This title from her father's house—although, of course, strictly honorary or "by courtesy," like those of the peers' daughters in England—stuck to Clarina throughout her life; she was always called "Contessa Maffei" and the marble plaque which is now in the wall of the house where she died, in the Via Bigli, calls her by this name. Andrea had no title; he was a member of the high bourgeoisie, originating in the very mixed Austro-Italian region of Trent, and was educated in Munich by a priestly uncle. He came to Milan as a counselor at the Court of Appeals, and by the time Verdi knew him he was a man of forty—Clarina, therefore, twenty-four. If one were to apply a knowledge of life in general to the affairs of the Maffei couple, it might seem that their respective advantages, which were distinctive, set up something like a competition rather than a collaboration between them. Clarina's title and her Spinelli ancestry, her wit and grace, her good sense, her private fortune, her ability to attract men of remarkable intellect to her house, all contrived to set her at odds with the elegant, careless, and more or less good-for-nothing Maffei. Andrea, whose father had been a knight of the Holy Roman Empire, became in due course himself a knight of the Austro-Hungarian Empire, and this alone contributed to the dissonance with Clarina. Gradually, under the influences of Manzoni and others, including Verdi, the Countess became more and more politically mature and less inclined to temporize with the foreign oppressor. It was a period when every Italian of the politically conscious classes had at least some friend or friends in Austrian jails. Some had been tortured; some had been condemned to death. The Maffei marriage ended in a legal separation for all of these reasons—thus saving Clarina's personal fortune from the bottomless pit of his debts—but also because she had transferred her affections to a devoted young man, Carlo Tenca, editor of the literary periodical *Rivista Europea*, who gave her what Andrea had failed to give. Tenca was "of humble origin," as the phrase goes, but Clarina's affection would not deign to conceal the relationship, which was perfectly open from the very beginning. And Tenca, too, was Verdi's friend.

In all this Maffei story it is difficult to discern any romantic or sexual element for Verdi. He seems to have known Andrea and Clarina separately, both in the early days. It is likely that he met Andrea first, as he had met other male members of the upper classes, through musical doings of one sort or another. However, it was not until the extraordinary success of *Nabucco*, a few years later, that the ladies of these same classes began to invite him to their houses, and Clarina Maffei became important in his life. Putting together all the dates and circumstances, there is no probability that this friendship had a directly sexual origin. If, indeed, we should start with the assumption that no man and woman can have a lifelong friendship without such an origin, then something of the kind might be understood, but there is not a shadow of evidence to prove it. On the contrary, Verdi's friendship for all three of the persons in the Maffei story (Clarina, Andrea and Carlo Tenca) seems to have been deep and sincere.

Verdi never paraded his intimacies. He was not of the same breed as those nineteenth-century exhibitionists who were his contemporaries—Wagner, Liszt, Balzac, Victor Hugo—all of whom made their bedrooms into a notable part of their collected works. We have only to think of Victor Hugo's statement that he "possessed" his wife (Adèle) seven times on their wedding night. Could Verdi ever have said anything of that kind, to anybody, or in any form? We have not one scrap of writing from his hand, or from the hand of any friend of his, which gives this kind of information. There was a period when, according to the gossip of Milan, the young composer had a plurality of sexual triumphs all at the same time—"every prima donna in the theatre," they said, and an assortment of the countesses as well. If this were ever true it cannot be proved. We do not even know when Peppina became his mistress—whether it was in the year of *Nabucco*, when she was La Strepponi and was gradually releasing herself from Merelli, or whether it was even a little earlier or (more likely) later. All we do know is that in Paris in 1847 they began to live together openly. Verdi was not the man to label locks of hair, like Byron, with the dates of their conquest, or to keep notes on his own assignations, like Victor Hugo: he did not kiss and tell.

However, between them, the prima donnas and the countesses did unquestionably bring him out into a sunnier world than he had known before, and his letters to a number of these ladies revealed a new—and sometimes rather awkward—effort toward the arts of courtship, flattery and badinage. Madame Appiani, who was also a countess by birth but did not use the title, evoked some of the most skittish of these epistles; Donizetti had graced her salon and probably her intimacy, but on his removal to Vienna for the music directorship at the imperial court she passed fluently on to his successor in popularity. It is notable how constantly Donizetti and Verdi are mentioned in the correspondence of both men with Madame Appiani; whether from jealousy or mere professional awareness, the older composer and the younger one could not forget each other in writing to the beautiful lady. She kept all or most of their letters, and although her own do not survive, there is a strange sense as of a three-cornered relation in the papers as published. Donizetti's letters are urbane, elegant, sometimes a little sad (for he was the loser in the case), and he does not trouble to disguise the fact that he and the lady were on the best of terms; indeed, he calls her Peppina (her name, too, was Giuseppina— there were a surprising number of them in Verdi's life). Verdi, by contrast, is a little clumsy even when he most wishes to be light and airy; he pays court, he bows and scrapes too much; he could not hope to compete with Donizetti as a man of the world. There emerges from this correspondence a perfectly clear apprehension of the fact that both Donizetti and Verdi knew, somehow or other, just how things stood with them in the world of art as well as in the esteem or affection of Madame Appiani. That is, Donizetti refers to the younger composer in terms which suggest a rather unwilling admiration, a recognition—sad, in the circumstances— of undeniable genius, whereas Verdi not only suggests, but in one passage quite bluntly states, that he cannot admire the work of the older man. (He asks after Donizetti's health and says that he is interested in the man although not in his art.) Donizetti's triumphs were by this time in the past, and he had not long to live; Verdi's were still to come, even though Nabucco, I Lombardi and Ernani had all rocked the opera houses of the period. It is a great tribute to Donizetti's taste and judgment that he realized, even then (in the mid-1840's), that there was a great deal more to be expected from this young man. He was somewhat in the position of the priest of Diana on the lake of Nemi: he was aware that here was the young man who must kill him to take his place.

Those were extraordinarily busy years, just after Nabucco—that is, from 1842 to 1847. Verdi in his early thirties was not only savoring worldly life for the first time but also working with a pertinacity and speed which make us wonder how many hours he could find in a single day. I Lombardi was produced at the Scala on February 11, 1843, and Ernani at the Fenice in Venice on March 9, 1844. In the autumn of that same year I Due Foscari went on the stage of the Teatro Argentina in Rome (November 3, 1844), and Giovanna d'Arco was ready soon afterward (La Scala, February 15, 1845). It may be difficult for us to realize it today, since all four of these works have disappeared from general circulation, but they were tremendous successes in their time and even Giovanna d'Arco, the poorest of the lot, made a highly lucrative tour of all the opera houses for a few years. Alzira (Naples, August 12, 1845), Attila (Venice, March 17, 1846) and Macbeth (Florence, March 14, 1847) testify to the regularity with which Verdi was grinding out the product even though his musical inspiration was very nearly standing still. He himself calls these "the years of the galley slave," and nothing he wrote during that time would survive of itself, that is, if it were not the early work of a great master. Not even *Ernani* or *Macbeth*, each of which contains some element of his characteristic genius, could stand on its own feet today; when they are revived, as they occasionally are, it is because they have pages of great beauty and occasional foreshadowings of the work that was yet to come. Constant toil with the pen and constant practical experience in the theatre were storing up in his own mind the resources which were to bear fruit later. But the operas themselves, if they could be divorced from the whole body of his achievement and considered singly, would not be long remembered. He was not only composing vocally—he always did that, from first to last—but was making little or no progress in instrumentation, harmony or genuine invention. His own idiom, already expressed in *Nabucco*, had a tendency to repetition rather than to expansion during these years, and its facility— that is, its lower half if one may so express it—had too much freedom, was too often allowed to aim straight at the organ grinder rather than at the musical or dramatic intelligence. We have eyewitness accounts of the way he made his orchestrations in those days—"as fast as the pen could write"—so that a great part of the orchestral score consisted of simple guitarlike accompaniment. For a composer of his skill and erudition, thoroughly acquainted with the resources of the instruments, it seems a waste of time. Even in these simple touches, of course, he was generally ahead of his predecessors (Rossini, Bellini, Donizetti), but his originality consisted principally in his insistence upon fitting the music to the words and the characters, that is, in the vocal line. This he made truly dramatic, responsive, emotionally and musically true, however sketchily it might be sustained in the orchestra. In so doing he got rid of a great deal of the excess ornamentation (most of it rubbish) which had overgrown Italian opera, and by the persistent effort toward *true* expression he was, naturally, preparing himself for the vocal splendors of the two succeeding periods.

I have used the words "vocal" and "vocally" so emphatically because they govern the progression and, in every practical sense, obliterate other considerations at this time in Verdi's life. Furthermore, I should like to state my conviction, which could not be shaken by all the medical faculties put together, that Verdi's recurrent sore throat, which came upon him toward the end of the composition of every opera for so many years, was of psychogenic origin: that he suffered from it because he was composing purely vocally, or, let us say, that his work was purely vocal music. He *sang* in his throat, not literally of course, but psychologically, every note and every word of every opera. The intensity with which he did this produced not only the extraordinary voice-writing which revolutionized the singing of modern times, but also directly exhausted his own throat. The phenomenon is very well-known among music listeners and even among musicians—there is a celebrated passage of Nietzsche in which he complains that Wagner's music gives him a sore throat—and I have myself experienced it often. By consulting other listeners, singers, musicians and persons concerned in various ways with music I find that in greater or in lesser degree the occurrence is common, although until recent years the medical doctors would have dismissed it as nonsense. Verdi's voice-writing was dramatic throughout, and even the occasional passages of more old-fashioned ornamentation have a dramatic content; he had a passion for color and contrast; he required a very long melodic line from his sopranos, dark deep notes from his contraltos, difficult high declamation from his tenors; he pushed the baritones up and the basses down; it was the most effective voice-writing the theatre had ever known, but for about thirty-five years it gave him a sore throat every time he wrote an opera. It was not until he had begun to compose all the way from top to bottom of the score—that is, with a much more evolved musical structure straight through the orchestra—that this malady dwindled and departed. The nervous stomach disorder which usually came along with the sore throat, displaying itself chiefly in nausea, was part of the same psychogenic affliction involved in finishing an opera.

But, somehow or other, he always finished them, and although his first eager acceptance of worldly success led him into making too many commitments, too many contracts in too many directions, he did keep his word in every case known to us. There were delays, of course. No man could take upon himself the amount of work Verdi promised in those days and deliver it with mechanical precision. Even in these delays we suspect the dominion of the subconscious, for they came chiefly in work for the opera houses of Paris and London, both of which he was fundamentally reluctant to approach. So far as Milan and the Scala were concerned he kept all his agreements impeccably on time—that is, to the end.

And *Giovanna d'Arco* was the end. When he finished that season at the Scala (carnival, 1845), he had no more use for that theatre and did not work there again for twenty-five years. It was very nearly a Verdi festival that year, for the season opened with *I Lombardi*, conducted by the composer. This work (*I Lombardi alla Prima Crociata*, to a libretto in four acts by Solera) had been a resounding success with the public only two years before, but in the meantime the Scala itself had deteriorated rapidly, and with it some of the principal singers. Merelli was falling back upon an ancient device of successful theatre managers: he paid an exorbitant fraction of his available funds to a few popular singers (sopranos and tenors mostly) and then economized severely on chorus, orchestra and stage settings. La Frezzolini (Erminia Frezzolini) had been stricken by some malady incident to maids, and as a result her voice, at the age of twenty-three, was already much impaired. Verdi went through the rehearsals of *I Lombardi* like a smoldering, and at times an erupting, volcano. We are told that he stamped his feet "as if he were playing the pipe organ," that he poured sweat down upon the score in front of him, and that he yelled at times like a man beside himself. He had not only this initial production to see through the mill, but also his new work— *Giovanna d'Arco*—and at the end of the season a revived *Ernani*, then only a year old. Toward the end of that carnival Merelli was presenting *Giovanna d'Arco* four times a week along with *Ernani*. It may not have been too much Verdi for the Scala; at all events it was too much Scala for Verdi.

We may wonder a little about all this. Is it possible for a great opera company, with machinists, resident orchestra and chorus, stagehands and all the rest of its permanent equipment, to deteriorate so drastically in only two years? No doubt Merelli had had so much success that he was getting careless, and we have Verdi's word for it that the orchestra was not only insufficient but was indeed badly placed. Could the resident chorus have gone to seed so thoroughly in only two seasons? We are pushed into the suspicion that Verdi had some reason other than purely artistic dissatisfaction for his attitude. He was bitter toward Merelli and quarreled with him when occasion offered. He refused to consider any offer from the Scala for new or old work. He would not go into that theatre again; he would not set foot upon its stage. And, as usual, he kept his word. The world had to change before he relented.

The truth is probably a mixture of the ostensible and the arcane reasons which have been put forward. The Scala had deteriorated to some extent, but it is also beyond question that Verdi was becoming more difficult to satisfy. Either his standards were going up or he was acquiring the courage to insist upon them. Successes in Vienna, Venice and Rome had taught him that the whole world did not revolve about the Piazza della Scala. And, in a realm where all the evidence is hazy, we are at liberty to assume that by this time his relationship with Giuseppina Strepponi had become very serious indeed. We know that it was already becoming dominant from the time of Nabucco onward, and by now, three years later, if Verdi were jealous of Merelli for either the past or the present, the violence of his temper may be understood even without blaming the artistic standards of the Scala company. Of this personal imbroglio we are so ill informed that we do not know exactly how things stood with Merelli, La Strepponi and Verdi at any given date between 1842 and 1847. The quarrels between Merelli and Verdi were all of a professional nature, and the personal undertones may have exacerbated them but were not put into words that have survived. The informed guess is probably that of Professor Gatti: that by this time Peppina longed to escape from Merelli and the Scala and was skillfully urging Verdi on to break his ties with Milan for good. Even if she ceased to be Merelli's mistress (which is likely) and even if she had not yet become Verdi's (which is less likely), her wishes in the matter were strong. For one thing, she was about to bring her stage career to an end, owing to one of those quick vocal declines which seem characteristic of the period, and it would be only natural for a woman of her vigorous temperament to strike out for fresh fields—and, if possible, to bring Verdi with her.

Some such amalgamation of the motives, private and public, must have taken place before a man of Verdi's sensible and kindly nature could have lost his temper quite so often as he did that winter. He had, of course, been through a period of overwork and was in for another: his signed contracts called for new work in Naples, Venice, Florence, London, and Paris. He was at his wits' end for subjects, for librettos, for librettists, for anything which he could consider "musicabile," fit to put into music. Under these various stresses we may also guess, from his own words used later on, that he was dissatisfied with his work itself, which in these "galley-slave years" did not often express his own intention to the full. And with this, a galling thing to any artist, was the growing discontent with theatre conditions and possibilities—a discontent so fundamental that he could actually say that he "hated" the theatre and longed to escape from it. "The theatre," in a sense, was the Scala. At any rate, the Scala was the theatre of his youth and of his dreams. In his bitter adieu to this house he may have been doing what men so often do, that is, avenge themselves upon the particular and the near at hand for a hurt too big and general to be cured. It is like the child who pummels his mother because the sun does not shine or the water is too cold.

5 When he took up his wanderings Verdi was not alone. He had the company—and the abject devotion—of his one and only pupil, Emanuele Muzio, who had been living under his care since 1844 (the year of *Ernani*). Muzio was a boy from the Busseto neighborhood, who, like Verdi, came of a poor family and wanted to study music; his father was a cobbler; he, too, encountered the benevolence of Antonio Barezzi and the Philharmonic Society of Busseto and was sent to Milan to study. Again like Verdi, he was too old for the Conservatory, and the similarity of all these conditions may have influenced Verdi in taking him as pupil, companion and, as it turned out, worshipper to the end. Muzio was only eight years younger than Verdi, but the older man seems to have treated him more or less as a son from the very beginning; even in their old age the filial tone is heard; Verdi is forever admonishing, Muzio is forever reverently learning. And, although his original talent may have been limited, Muzio obviously did come to understand Verdi's work in its later phases, although he was given to indiscriminate adoration in all the earlier years. It was Muzio whom Verdi recommended to conduct the first *Aïda* in Cairo, and by virtue of kindred recommendations the "pupil"—the eternal pupil, as he seems to us—had quite a satisfactory career in his profession. He was director of the Théâtre des Italiens in Paris for six years and ended as a highly respected teacher (or, as we say nowadays, coach) for singers. To his death in 1890 he remained the simplest, truest and plainest of all Verdi's idolaters. He composed four operas himself, and although no opportunity occurs nowadays to hear them, it is a fairly safe guess that they follow—at a great distance—the Verdian line.

Muzio was in many respects an enchanting character. Industrious and determined though he was, it would be hard to find much self-confidence in his attitude toward his own work. Perhaps if he had not been taken into Verdi's house, had not had such a powerful example before his eyes during the formative period, his own gifts—whatever they were—would have come out more freely. An immeasurable good fortune, as he considered it, descended upon him, and the "Signor Maestro" actually began to teach him counterpoint; thus he came under the spell which lasted all his life. "*Il mio Signor Maestro*," which we might translate crudely as "my Mister Master," was obviously so much the greatest musician, composer, contrapuntalist and man in the whole world that Muzio himself never dreamed of self-assertion. During the three years he spent with Verdi in Milan, and afterward on their journeys together to London and Paris, he considered it his duty to keep their mutual benefactor, Antonio Barezzi, fully informed of every detail in their lives. It is thus that so much information has filtered down to us, for Barezzi, of course—like many others associated with Verdi—never threw away a piece of paper which related to the life or work of the wonder child of Busseto. Muzio's letters are gossipy, racy with comment and supposition, filled with small circumstance and busy fact. His style of writing gives them a flavor quite unlike those of most others in the same category: he has learned no airs, no graces, and what he has to say is as plain and pungent as a farmyard in summer. Anything that happened to Verdi was in his eyes worthy of detailed report, and through these reports there shines an unfeigned reverence and love, mixed with Muzio's own sense of astonished gratitude at the privilege of being pupil to such a master. Verdi, who refused to take pupils at any price—and many students, says Muzio, "would pay even two or three thalers for each lesson if the Signor Maestro Verdi would give them" —very nearly adopted young Muzio, giving him not two lessons a week but one every morning, and luncheon afterward. Later on, this extended to the other meals and to the single hour from noon to one o'clock when they played billiards in a café.

Two years and more later, Muzio is more under the spell than ever, and more constantly in his master's company. "If the Signor Maestro had not existed what could I have been?" And the answer: "A poor devil without knowing anything." When it is suggested that he should enter the competition for organist at Busseto (the same post which Verdi had once held) Muzio refuses. He cannot abandon "my Master who has given me a second life." He is deeply sensible of the honor done him by the writing arrangements in the house—one big table, with the Maestro on one side and Muzio on the other, both composing, the difference being that Muzio's work is submitted to the Maestro's eye and comment from time to time. Moreover, the Maestro takes him everywhere in Milan, introduces him to the Gentlemen and always tries to make him appear well in Society. Muzio will never give this up. "Let them say what they like; I don't care; it is enough for me to be with my Master."

We go from this pure devotion to an account of the Master's intestinal troubles and his bowel movements; we hear a good deal about the weather; if anything untoward occurs—a fire in the streets, for instance— it is fully noted. The letter writing continued for as long as Muzio remained with Verdi, and although they were both very busy in London and Paris, Muzio by this time as an assistant not only in copying scores and parts but in rehearsal and in a dozen other ways, Barezzi in Busseto was always fully informed.

This simple, honest and shrewd young man was obviously worth his weight in diamonds to Verdi during those busy, crowded, overworked and lonely years. After his own family had been swept away and the world had descended upon him, Verdi needed help more than he could fully realize at the time, and his severe regime with the one and only pupil ("Remember, I am *inexorable!*" he said) was an anchor. Muzio thought that he had been "born most fortunate" to be part of this relationship. It seems to us at our greater distance that the more fortunate of the two was, in truth, Verdi, and his unfailing regard for Muzio throughout almost half a century afterward is a suggestion that he came to know it in due course.

And, when all is said, Verdi's desperate unhappiness in youth may have overshadowed his later memory, but the Milan years were full of such compensatory blessings toward the end. Up to 1841 all is black, but love and friendship (not to mention popular success) did grace the next few years. Andrea Maffei, whatever his shortcomings as a husband, was an excellent friend, and there are few more eloquent testimonials to that effect than his letters to Verdi. His actual contribution to Verdi's work was of some importance because, little as he knew of the theatre, he had an enthusiasm for Schiller. It was Maffei who first suggested that *Die Jungfrau von Orléans* should be metamorphosed into *Giovanna d'Arco,* although Solera wrote it; and Maffei himself made *Die Räuber* into *I Masnadieri.* The results were not felicitous, but the third Schiller subject, *Luisa Miller* (*Kabale und Liebe*), played a great part in Verdi's transition to his middle and most popular phase of composition. It was Maffei, again, who came to the rescue in the unconscionable confusion of the *Macbeth* libretto, writing the two most important scenes at a moment when Verdi was in despair (the chorus of witches and the sleepwalking scene). All this work was for friendship and Maffei did not want payment or presents—in spite of the fact, which we know as well as Verdi did, that he was generally hard pressed. There must have been an element of consolation, to say the least, in the presence of such as Maffei and Muzio, no matter how out of joint all the rest of the world might seem to be.

But if Verdi was cruelly overworked in the "galley-slave years," whose fault was it? Why did he take upon himself such a burden of contracts all over Europe? He never ceased to complain, either then or afterward, of his sad fate, his appalling profession and the wretched conditions of the theatres. To us it might appear that all he had to do was to say no (not every time, but now and then), and the work itself, not to speak of his own health and nerves, would have shown a benefit. In the five years from 1842 to 1847 he produced no less than nine operas, ten if we count the French revision of *I Lombardi* (produced at the Opéra as *Jérusalem*). Except *Nabucco* itself, the first of these works, which can never disappear for long from the Italian stage, all have faded into musical history. Once in a while a theatre in Germany or America may revive *Ernani*; a few years ago there was a vogue for *Macbeth*, chiefly in Germany and England. All the others are names on paper today, and from what we are able to see and hear of them (chiefly through recordings) they have deserved oblivion. A few set pieces from these early operas, chiefly the choruses and trios, have survived to show what passionate vigor and eloquence there was in them for the time in which they appeared. Otherwise their principal historical function was that they made Verdi rich and famous— rich enough to work more slowly, famous enough to impose his own wishes in growing strength upon the recalcitrant theatres. It has even been said that the motive power of the work done was precisely this and nothing more: that is, to make Verdi rich and famous. He was certainly ambitious in the simplest worldly sense. He wanted money and wanted to be "established" in the opera theatres of the world, because only thus could he have any feeling of security for either his life or his art. He wanted money also for a characteristically peasant reason; he wanted to buy land and build a house. Every peasant must have land, a house, a mule and, eventually if not simultaneously, a wife. This was the cast of Verdi's mind and he did buy the land and farm at Sant' Agata in 1848, when he was thirty-five. A great part of the rest of his life went into that farm, not only in the constant building and improvement of the house itself and its spacious park, its garden, its lake and streams, but also into the crops and the livestock; they absorbed time and attention as well as a great deal of money, although he was (like all such affluent farmers) anxious to show himself that he could also make money out of it.

Of course he wanted to be rich and famous; most composers, writers, painters and other artists would like the same thing if they could get it. The essence of the accusation against Verdi is not that he wanted such things, but that he was capable of writing inferior work to get them. "Inferior work" must be defined here, as in everything concerned with art, not by comparison with something else, but as judged by the laws of its own being and the powers of its creator. It would be useless to contend that Verdi did his best with every work he wrote in the 1840's—he too obviously did not, knew he did not and allowed it to be known afterwards. His haste, a regrettable side-product of the divine impatience, made it impossible.

But to say that Verdi wrote all this early work only for money and the most vulgar forms of success would be to misunderstand his nature profoundly. The peasant and the artist were at variance in him, and the civil war they conducted ran through the work itself for all these and a good many subsequent years. That is, he certainly did want land, a house and a mule, and was willing to be a galley slave to get them, but at the same time he tried agonizingly to make the work itself come out as well as the circumstances, the environment and the speed of labor permitted. If he had been an ordinary hack in an ordinary Grub Street, he would have manufactured operas without a qualm, since the market demanded them so gluttonously. Qualms, however, beset him like gadflies during this whole period; he was never satisfied; his melancholia would immobilize him for days on end, and then he would set to work with even more frantic industry, spending fourteen and sixteen hours a day at his desk scribbling down those obstinate notes of music. His ordinary day at this period began at eight in the morning and ended at midnight, with time off only for meals and for the one hour of billiards with Muzio. The sore throat and the nervous nausea were so inevitable that he grew to expect them toward the latter part of every composition thus elucubrated. A common hack, making hay while the sun shines, does not work in such a way or undergo such suffering. The turmoil within Verdi's own mind was created, not by the peasant's necessities or the demands of the market, but by the imperious assertion of the artist's nature every day and every hour in conflict with them. Hacks of genius— Balzac, for instance—wrote with frenzied speed to meet the demands of an anxious market, but did so quite naturally, without even reading over the sheets that cluttered the floor; nor does it appear that this state of things ever mitigated Balzac's self-satisfaction. Verdi was the victim of a dichotomy which did not resolve itself until the sovereign years of his old age.

There were, in the brighter aspects of his Milan life—what I have earlier called his compensatory blessings—elements which would have encouraged him to self-deception and, for a time, probably did. The loyal Muzio, the greatest of these blessings, was one such. To Muzio every note the Master wrote was sublime, or if not quite sublime, at least undefeatable in the theatre. Muzio admired everything of Verdi's with the utmost sincerity, finding a different reason for each according to its nature. If there was a tune of that easy banality which suited the taste of the 1840's, Muzio would say: "If you hear it twice you'll be singing it." Of one such tune in *Giovanna d'Arco*, one of the weakest operas of the galley-slave years, Muzio remarks that it "makes its way" straight to the grind organs and the military bands! This, to him, indicated the infallible success of the work. He could, of course, find purely musical reasons for admiring many other pieces by his Master (the *Lombardi* trio, the chorus of Hebrew slaves in *Nabucco*, the terzetto of *Ernani*), but if the higher reasons did not exist he was proud and happy to adduce lower ones.

Thus to be living with Muzio, although it was compensatory and consolatory, could not precisely have sharpened Verdi's critical sense with regard to his own work. We know Muzio's views because we have them in his letters home to Busseto. We do not have Peppina's views because none of her letters of the period survives; but is it possible to doubt that she, too, found all the Master's work superb? She had not the naïveté of Muzio but she had, or was rapidly acquiring, every bit of his concentration upon Verdi intellectually, along with that love which by now must certainly have been declared between them although not to the world. Peppina, however, saw Verdi less often; she was absent from Milan a good deal; Merelli was for some years in the way; her flame was, had to be, qualified. What we see through Muzio's letters is principally a masculine world of musicians and *dilettanti*, of which the connecting tissue was a vast admiration for Verdi. This admiration, determined by musical form and expressed in musical terms, was in part (we must always remember) patriotic in essence and therefore impossible to reduce to rational limits. The days when Verdi's name itself was the synonym for Italian freedom and as such was painted on the walls throughout Italy had not yet arrived, but from *Nabucco* on through the 1840's he contributed, sometimes accidentally and sometimes deliberately, to the rising tide. Political or patriotic demonstrations at performances of his operas had shown how difficult it was for anybody (even the composer) to foretell just how his music was going to strike upon sources of the people's passion: sometimes weird transpositions took place, as in Rome a little later (1849) when the entire audience at the first night of *Ernani* changed Charles V of Spain into Pope Pius IX and joined with the singers on the stage, turning the finale of the opera into a political demonstration. "*O sommo Carlo!*" became "*O sommo Pio!*" because the new and relatively young Pope was at that time the hope of liberalism and of Italian freedom. Of course, when *Ernani* was written, Pius IX, as such, was not yet in existence and no such implication could have been foreseen by the composer, yet incidents of a similar character occurred so often that his music obviously had some electrical communication with the spirit of the time.

In June, 1844, when Muzio had been with Verdi for less than two months, *Ernani* was produced in Vienna with resplendent success. The opera was itself only three months old, and from its triumph at the Fenice in Venice it had already traveled far. Muzio in a letter to Barezzi gives an account of how the news from Vienna reached Verdi's house in Milan. Leaving his language as near as possible to the original, with no effort to improve upon his grammar or punctuation, I translate as follows:

"*You, sir, should have been in the house of Mr. Master Verdi on the day when the news arrived of the most happy results, to see how for a whole hour, first one would come with a letter from Donizetti, then another who had received the news from some Count, I don't remember his name, and then another who had a letter from Merelli, and so many others that they never seemed to come to an end, and to hear the wonderful things they wrote about Mr. Master and his Ernani you would have surely wept, sir, because you are very sensitive, and then to see them all sitting there, now one reading his letter and then another reading his, and with their papers in their hands they were like so many boys in school reciting their lessons; and Mr. Master there in the middle of them at his table seemed a preceptor, and I big-eyed in my corner seemed the dunce of the school. It was a thing which gave pleasure and delighted.*"

All the admirers sitting in a circle with their letters from Vienna must have gratified Verdi in that part of his nature which required, at least sometimes, to be appreciated, but we can scarcely imagine one of them coming forth with a critical observation, or even concurring in one if Verdi had chanced to make it upon his own work. It was, therefore, entirely up to him to determine whether or not he had carried out his intention in any given composition to the best of his ability at the time—the one true test. There would be no earthly use asking the Verdi of 1844 to have the mind of the Verdi of 1893: *Ernani* is a planetary distance from *Falstaff*. But he might have struggled through the "galley-slave years" with greater satisfaction to himself if he had been not only less overworked, but also less admired. The combination of unremitting labor and extravagant success was one in which his critical faculty had small chance, and everything, even his compensations (even Muzio), conspired against his progress as an artist. Of the ten operas which, in defiance of credibility and common sense, he put upon various stages in those years, the best that can be said is that they gave him practical experience as well as worldly confidence. There is no real musical or dramatic progression to be discerned after the first three (*Nabucco, Lombardi, Ernani*), and the final pair—*I Masnadieri* for London and *Jérusalem* for Paris—were the weakest of the lot. Indeed *Jérusalem*, a reworking of *I Lombardi* on a French text, has the distinction of being the only Verdi revision which was notably less good than its original. Aside from musicologists and historians of music there are few today who even care.

The old man going to bed after the third night of *Falstaff* in Milan knew this just as well as we do. He insisted upon one thing, which was that all his work from beginning to end was his own, written in his own idiomatic style, all vocal, all personal; and he pointed out how many adumbrations there were in even his earliest and most forgotten operas of passages much admired in his latest ones. He did not insist upon any other value for the work of his apprentice years, and for some of it he had a scarcely disguised contempt (*Alzira*, for instance). Once when a well-meaning enthusiast dug up a "*Tantum Ergo*" from the Master's student days and wanted to publish it, Verdi rebuked him angrily and ordered the piece destroyed: it had, he said, "no merit of any kind." He never went so far in disowning anything he had written for the theatre, and there seem to have been isolated passages in almost every opera, even the least effective, which were to him steps on the ascent to Olympus.

When he shook the dust of Milan from his feet in 1845 he was leaving his youth behind—he was thirty-two years old. Now, at eighty, he could see that it had not all been bad. Love, friendship, the cheers of the crowd—they had been worth something. It was his custom in referring to all those years of Busseto and Milan to say, dryly and without exaggeration, the plainest truth that remained in his mind, as he did to the French critic, Camille Bellaigue, in extreme old age. "My youth was hard."

6   It was always difficult for Verdi to rescind a decision well taken and firmly intended. He could not chop and change; he was as stubborn as any of his hard-fisted forebears behind the plow. When he said nothing new of his would be given to the Scala again, he meant it. In his new contract with the publisher Ricordi—who had alternated and at times associated with Lucca, but was henceforth to be Verdi's only publisher and agent—he stipulated that Ricordi's right to make arrangements was from now on limited in one very important respect: Verdi, and only Verdi, would choose the theatres which could present his operas. Verdi's main purpose in introducing such a clause was to exclude any possibility of an arrangement with the Scala. He blamed Ricordi (no doubt unjustly) for permitting the Scala to make a sloppy and careless production of *Ernani* at the very end of the carnival that year, without proper rehearsal—thrown in, so to speak, to catch whatever extra money might be made out of Verdi's popularity. To all four generations of the Ricordi family who had to deal with him, Giovanni, Tito, Giulio and the second Tito, Verdi showed similar signs of suspicion and distrust where money affairs or contracts were concerned. They were his friends otherwise, but when it came to a contract—or, more specifically, the composer's rights in any given instance—he was up in arms against them. They were so close to the Scala, *per forza*, that he could not trust them to maintain his own interdiction of that house for his work. It applied, of course, only to the all-important first production, by which in those days the fortune of an opera was usually made. The Scala could, like any other theatre, by payment of the normal fee, produce Verdi's operas, and did so for the next twenty-five years, but without the composer's assistance or his presence and without the prestige of the "first."

Rome, Naples, Venice, Trieste, Paris, London, St. Petersburg and even, toward the end, Cairo, were all preferred by Verdi to his own natural capital and the theatre of his youth. He went to Madrid, to Vienna, to Cologne and Frankfurt, he wandered and he wandered and he wandered, he fought with everybody in every opera house, kissed the hands of the queens and empresses, bowed before the sovereigns, struggled against the tyranny of Meyerbeer and the pretensions of Wagner, made his own way against what he invariably considered to be tremendous odds. Such a revulsion against the native heath (the mother, the father, the nest) is probably quite natural; at least it occurs often. Mozart was overjoyed to escape from Salzburg, Beethoven from Bonn; Wagner had no choice when he was driven from Dresden as a dangerous revolutionist, but there is not a shadow of doubt that he welcomed the release; Shakespeare himself seems only to have gone home to die. Verdi's unhappy and often gruesome youth ruined his whole view of Milan, or so he thought for years, but at least he did return—and what a return!

For twenty whole years he did not even see the city of his young ardor and aspiration. "Youth's dynamite and dear remembrances"—a phrase of Stevenson's about Fontainebleau—meant nothing to Verdi in his first maturity. He was dry and unsentimental to the point of being antisentimental; he was a practical man doing practical work. When the Italian government wanted to build monuments to Rossini, he thought, characteristically, that they might better put the money into some decent performances of that composer's operas. All his passion and power were for music (his own). When it came to remembrances he tended to think—and in the case of Rossini openly said—that they were hypocrisy.

We can see through all that now. He loved Milan and the Scala, and they were the same thing. That was why he stayed away for twenty whole years. It took a considerable amount of ingenuity, stubbornness and sheer ungovernable will power to do so. To get from Paris to his own villa at Sant' Agata he had either to go through Milan without getting out of the train or to take the longer route through Genoa. He generally chose the latter, particularly since a comfortable apartment in a palace in Genoa suited Peppina and was therefore a convenient stopping place. Milan is such a central point in the Italian railroad system (as it was in the system of stage coaches earlier) that only a very clever and obstinate man can avoid it now, or could have avoided it then. Verdi avoided it for twenty years, and avoided its theatre, the Scala, for twenty-five years. He was drawn back—and we can trace it all out so clearly that it looks like a map—by his own youth, by himself as a young man, by youth's dynamite and dear remembrances. He went back to Milan in search of his youth, to find it again and to redeem it. Unlike so many others who have done the same thing, he succeeded.

Clarina Maffei, that woman of so rare a quality that all who beheld her perceived it, was the wonder worker in this case. Verdi had not seen her, either, for twenty years. They had written letters, yes, and we have many of them now, but twenty years are twenty years: she must have looked very different and so must he. In the meantime the Countess had also become famous in her own way, although perhaps not quite so splendidly. Hardly any distinguished foreigner ever came to Milan any more without asking to be presented to her. The houses where she had her evening conversations, her salon—first in the Via Monte di Pietà, near the present American Express Company, afterward in Piazza Belgioioso, and finally in the Via Bigli, only a few steps from the Grand Hotel—were known to Europe in general, Italy in particular. The unity and freedom of Italy owed something to her because many of the men who made it were able to meet and talk in her house. Writers, composers and painters from other countries were welcome too; Liszt and Balzac were there; but the presiding genius was Manzoni. The old lion of Lombardy had a paternal affection for Clarina and during the twenty years of Verdi's absence from Milan this had grown into a positive association, so that Manzoni was almost as much a part of the Countess' life as Chateaubriand in that of Madame Récamier, although without the same sexual history. For most of the time they lived in such proximity that he was able to visit her, if he chose to do so, in five minutes' walk. When the Countess finally came to Sant' Agata (May, 1868, for one week), she not only brought Verdi her own grace, wit and charm, her sense of what was valuable and her exquisite company, but also an invitation for him to meet Manzoni in her house in Milan.

Clarina was subtle and daring. Like all the great *salonières* of history, she knew at what time to make the stroke that would count, as a military commander knows when to attack and when to feint or evade. She could estimate just when and where, as if with a micrometer caliper. Verdi by this time had endured so much and received so much that the wounds of old counted less, and he was returning in his own heart to the familiar, or what he called the "natural," sources of his being. Most of the old friends and enemies in Milan had died or gone elsewhere; the map of Europe had changed; the kingdom of Italy had come into being, although it still lacked its inevitable capital, Rome. The tempests of time had transformed or disfigured everything. Pope Pius IX, once the hope of Italian liberalism, had become its only remaining obstacle; the Austrians did not matter (after 1866) but the French still did, and Napoleon III, whom Verdi had originally liked and trusted, had become a Sphinx without a secret; Victor Emmanuel II was King of Italy. The golden decade of Cavour, the radiant period of Italian nationalism, had come and gone: Cavour died in 1861—too soon, very much too soon. Through all this Verdi had lived, loved and suffered. He had been Cavour's friend, to his own astonishment, and for Cavour had undergone the penance of being a deputy in the Italian parliament at Turin. He had done his best for Italy, most of all in his music but also in his frequentations and occasions: for Queen Victoria he had done one thing, for the Czar Alexander another, for the Queen of Spain another. The unification of Italy had been the work of many men and of a tremendous collective national passion, but very much of Verdi, too. In the Cavour decade—the Risorgimento at its height—Verdi's name, which, spelled out, signified Vittorio Emanuele, Rè d'Italia, V.E.R.D.I., had become the national symbol and was painted, scrawled or scratched on walls from the Alps to the tip of Calabria. The police had never been able to do anything against him; what can you do against music? They might cut and chip and change and quibble, but whatever they did, all his music served mightily to unite the ravaged and divided country.

Now he was old and tired, especially of the theatre. He was fifty-five, an infant alongside of what he was yet to be, but in his own eyes tired and old. In all his wanderings he had really never found anything better than the Scala. That, in itself, was a sobering thought. What was the use of giving up one's birthright if nothing else was any better? When he first went to the Opéra in Paris he thought he had never heard worse singing, a more deplorable chorus or an orchestra which so fully deserved the word mediocre. The Opéra, or the Académie Impériale de Musique, or whatever else it chose to call itself through the years, was nothing more nor less than the Big Shop, the whorehouse. The singing was far better at Her Majesty's in London, and at Covent Garden; both London and St. Petersburg were more satisfactory than Paris in every respect, except, of course, climate. You could do whatever you liked in London or St. Petersburg but you never could get warm. Madrid was all right, and in some respects Vienna—the abode of the tyrants of old—was best of all. But no theatre had really exhibited any greater response, even under ideally favorable conditions, than the old Scala in the old Milan. This we may be sure was at the very root of Verdi's feeling in 1868.

The Countess knew, estimated and struck. And of all weapons she might have used, the idea of a meeting between Manzoni and Verdi was the one most certain to reach the heart.

Manzoni was at this time eighty-three years old. His masterpiece, *I Promessi Sposi*, had long since become the most widely read of all Italian books, and Verdi had known it from childhood. It is to this day the most widely read of Italian books, and rightly, because no other contains so much of the essential Italy. At one of its frontiers this novel touches Walter Scott, whose impetus helped to instigate it, and at the other frontier it touches Tolstoy. The book is continental or planetary; it is said to be as good in Chinese and in Icelandic as it is in Italian; but what gives it immortality is its full expression of the relation between Italian people and the land fertilized by the bones of their ancestors, that from which they come and to which they return. This is what Verdi really felt. He was no literary critic. He merely *knew*. Manzoni had also written poetry which was more appreciated in the early nineteenth century than it is today; his ideas were noble, akin to those of the great spirits of the Risorgimento, and that whole wonderful rebirth of Italy owed much to his hymns and odes; there was not one of the makers of modern Italy who did not acknowledge the debt. But Verdi above all, who had spent his life looking for a poet and never finding one, felt an immeasurable reverence for this great writer. Next to Dante and Michelangelo, we know of no Italian in history who exacted from him anything like the same awe and worship.

Clarina understood all this—wise woman!—and brought Verdi back to Milan on June 30, 1868, to meet Manzoni in her house.

At the end of this narrative there will be an opportunity to speak of the results of that momentous meeting. Just now, as we think of the Maestro going to bed after his *Falstaff*, it is Milan itself that must come first. He had left Milan in 1845 with the bitter taste of tears. He returned in 1868 to meet the old man who was to him the greatest of Italians. But he could not help seeing Milan also, coming and going. And it shook him; it really shook him.

"It is completely transformed," he said in a letter to Léon Escudier, his French publisher and agent. Much of the city had been renewed or rebuilt; the Galleria Vittorio Emanuele, which connects the Cathedral with the Scala (church and theatre, church and theatre), was particularly suited to Verdi's frame of mind. He thought it was "*artistica, monumentale.*" Then, with little apparent relevance, he declared that in Italy there still can be the feeling of the great united to the beautiful. He had heard no music in Milan and had not entered the Scala for twenty-three years at this moment, but he wrote to Escudier: "That the French composers are the only men of genius, as they say, could be; and let it be. That the French singers are the first in the world . . . let it be. Even so they ought to learn how to place their voices. But that music is well performed at the Opéra . . . no, no, no, no, no!"

Why the outburst? He had suffered considerably at the Paris "grand" Opéra, which is the undertone of his statement that in Italy the great (or grand—same word in Italian) and the beautiful can still be felt united in one. He is in effect saying that the Opéra in Paris, that perfect reflection of the Second Empire, was so busy with the "grand" that it had forgotten the beautiful: it was his usual complaint about the Big Shop. But the outburst occurs in this precise connection not only because he was keenly excited over having met Manzoni, the greatest of his countrymen, but also because, after all this time, he had actually seen the city of his youth. Above all he must have seen the Scala and the Piazza della Scala, so inextricably concerned with every important memory of his life and art, several times in that one day, and although he had vowed not to work there again, he had taken no vow not to *look* at it. He was deeply stirred; his letters from Sant' Agata for sometime afterwards betray an agitation not usual with him. The words *grande* and *bello* recur over and over; writing in French he uses *beau* and *bien* and *grand* and even *parfait*, referring to Manzoni but also in some inexplicable way to everything connected with his visit to Milan. One need not have been a prophet in the summer of 1868 to predict that somehow or other Verdi would forgive the Scala all its sins and return to it as the sailor comes home from the sea.

The occasion arose very soon. We may suppose that Clarina Maffei and Giulio Ricordi talked it over; certainly all concerned with the management of the Scala must have discussed it with longing. It had, of course, been most painful to the Scala and to Milan to have Verdi roaming through foreign theatres and never setting foot in *their* opera house: for the Scala, like the Opéra, and like the imperial houses of Vienna, Berlin and St. Petersburg, firmly believed itself to be the best in the world. ("So many firsts without a second!" said Verdi.) The Scala had mounted everything of Verdi's at second hand, sometimes most extravagantly, but had never been able to persuade him even to attend a performance, much less to work there. And it was not only galling, but in some respects positively disgraceful, that a quarter of a century should pass without the Scala's being able to get the greatest of Italian composers to cross its threshold. (Verdi himself, who had a keen sense of fitness, must also have reflected that he had punished them enough by now.)

Ricordi made the proposal which did the trick. Verdi had been dissatisfied with *La Forza del Destino*—not with the production in St. Petersburg, November 10, 1862, which had been superb, "imperial" indeed, but dissatisfied with his own work. He had had, as usual, nothing but pain and trouble with its libretto, and the composition had suffered. There were a number of scenes and passages he wanted to cut, change or rewrite, and above all he was unhappy over the ending—the *maledetto scioglimento*, he called it. (In English we should probably say "accursed denouement," as usual borrowing a French word when none of our own will fit.) Verdi's feelings on the subject were so strong that he would not allow this opera to be performed anywhere in Italy, after a few trials in Rome, and denied it also to the managements in Paris and elsewhere.

Ricordi's proposal was that Verdi should make the changes he had in mind, get rid of the "accursed denouement" in favor of something else, do, in fact, anything he chose to do with it, and then produce it at the Scala as a new work. In the meantime the Scala had produced *Don Carlos* that same spring in a translation of the French version as done in Paris the preceding year (not with changes—those came sixteen years later). Two new operas by Verdi in one year, along with the first production of Boito's ambitious *Mefistofele* and five other new works (including Gounod's *Roméo et Juliette* and Meyerbeer's *Dinorah*): this was the kind of thing the Scala could do then and still can do, with a lavishness practically unknown elsewhere. (Eight new works in one year would bankrupt any house in America, England or France.)

Verdi hesitated and made conditions, of course, but from the time he first saw Milan again his final course was assured. He would not be present at a performance but he consented, at last, to go back to the Scala and rehearse the *Forza del Destino*. The Scala was in difficulties; it had had too many failures lately, and Ricordi in appealing to Verdi for help was not exaggerating the seriousness of the situation. He also brought in the Mayor of Milan, Count Belinzaghi, to support his appeal. *Mefistofele*, in March of 1868, had been one of the most calamitous failures in the whole history of the theatre, with hostile demonstrations becoming more violent at each of its three performances. Verdi must come back—and did.

He kept his name off the posters outside the theatre and, furthermore, he left Milan for Sant' Agata before the first night, but he did see *La Forza del Destino* through its crucial rehearsals and was, at the time, highly pleased, especially with the soprano and tenor. That soprano was the Bohemian Teresa Stolz, trained in the Prague Conservatory and afterward, for Italian style, in Trieste; she was now thirty-four, a woman of beauty and personality, with a dramatic voice of great power, range and flexibility. She seems to have been a true Verdian soprano by nature, and the species was more unusual then than it is today because it was still in the process of creation. La Stolz sang in the first Italian *Don Carlos* (at Bologna, conducted by Angelo Mariani, praised to the skies by some of the same critics who had been lukewarm to the Paris production) and went on to do the same thing at the Scala. From his rehearsals with her in *La Forza del Destino* Verdi derived not only a sense of fulfillment, which was rare for him with any interpreter of his work, but also a fascinated absorption in her charm. No doubt it was an inextricable mixture of the woman and the artist, for in the conditions of intimate daily work it is not easy for anybody to say which is which, but there cannot be much doubt that La Stolz dominated his imagination for a very important period—the period which saw the composition and production of *Aïda*.

And this it was—*Aïda*—which really brought Verdi back into the Scala. It would be rash to state, without documentary proof, that he wrote *Aïda* for La Stolz. He never did write any part (much less an opera) for any one singer. But it is difficult to avoid the reflection that a composer getting on toward sixty, having found a soprano perfectly adapted to the kind of music he wanted to write, and having, what is more, found in that soprano an enchanting personality, a rejuvenating force, must have borne her in mind, willy-nilly, while he was writing the immense opera which centers about just such a one. Is it not common sense? How could Verdi, who was at this moment virtually bewitched by La Stolz, get her out of his head while he was writing music ideally suited to her gifts? Even though there exists not one scrap of evidence admissible in a court of law, I think the circumstances themselves powerfully suggest that she was Aïda in his mind before she became Aïda on the stage of the Scala.

Aïda stands all by itself in the creations of Verdi's genius. You can group the others and relate them, easily enough: there is the "early Verdi," from *Nabucco* to *Luisa Miller*, in which a powerful talent struggles through inherited or traditional forms toward increasing freedom. There is the "middle period," which erupts all at once into the most popular works of this master, *Il Trovatore*, *Rigoletto*, *La Traviata*, filled with human truth in musical form, containing everything it is possible for vocal music to contain—literally everything, from vulgarity itself to exquisite lyricism as pure as Shakespeare or Mozart. It was such a profuse talent that it could not stop to explain. The "middle period" simply occurred, like Niagara Falls or the San Francisco earthquake, and you can take it or leave it, but there it is forever. And then there is the "final period," as it is called—a time of harvest—when two supreme works, one a tragedy and one a comedy, reconciled and blended, enhanced all the elements of an incomparable gift into true masterpieces: *Otello* and *Falstaff*.

Outside of these three categories, belonging to none of them except by a form of cousinage, of blood relationship, is the extraordinary creation called Aïda. It is a work which, like *Carmen*, could all alone have justified the lifework of its composer. And—again like *Carmen*—it has that rare combination of instantaneous popularity and prolonged interest: you like it immediately, that is, but after the tenth hearing you find that you have never *really* heard it before, and so on and so on until one fine day, after almost innumerable hearings and discoveries, you wake up and realize that this, too, in its way, is a masterpiece.

Its way is peculiar, not because of the occasional "oriental" turns of melody or harmony—these are easy enough—and not even because of the new subtleties and richness of orchestration. The "oriental" themes are mere decoration: they are a compliment to the Suez Canal. Even the instrumentation, although we are grateful for it, is not enough to give this work its peculiar, its downright unique, quality. Verdi always had known the instruments superbly well and had always been able to compose for them; if he was content with guitar music too often, it was due to haste and to a concentration on composition for the voice. No: what gives Aïda its immediate effect and lasting interest is that it qualifies under all the Paris definitions as "grand" opera but at the same time is passionately human and supremely Italian. Nothing of the kind can be found before it and nothing anywhere nearly so good after it. A "grand" opera, as defined in Paris and performed only at the "grand" Opéra, had to have heroic characters, large-scale action, very ample and grandiose scenic effects and a whopping, bang-up tragic denouement in which the largest number of persons possible would meet their deaths. It could not be tolerated without a ballet somewhere along about forty-five minutes or an hour after the rise of the curtain, because that was the time at which the members of the Jockey Club entered their box (and the ladies of the aristocracy entered theirs). It had to provide the maximum effects for climactic scenes, rather like the old-fashioned three-ringed circus, and it had, if possible, no relation of any kind to ordinary life in recognizable forms.

In other words, "grand" opera is Meyerbeer, essentially. The proto-types are *Guillaume Tell*, Rossini's great effort in that direction; *La Juive*, Halévy's one contribution; later *Samson et Dalila*, in which Saint-Saëns did his best to fulfill the formula. But the real "grand" operas of the whole period are *Le Prophète* and *L'Africaine* and the rest of Meyerbeer, the juiciest of course being *Les Huguenots*. Wagner, for example, never wrote a "grand" opera under the Paris definitions, the nearest thing being *Tannhäuser* as revised for Paris, but even there he put his ballet so early in the work that the Jockey Club could not see it and there were riots.

Neither Wagner nor Verdi could write "grand" operas by nature because each was ruled by an inexorable genius: Wagner's was for significant or symbolic myth, epic abstractions symphonically composed; Verdi's was for human beings as the prey of tragic circumstance, pouring out their emotions in song. He was a composer for the human voice and could only give the voice its expressivity in the situations of emotional stress well known to mankind. *La Traviata*, for example, at which more tears have been shed than at any other opera ever written, is not a "grand" opera: in Paris, until recently, it was always performed at the Opéra-Comique.

Well, in a word, "grand" opera as defined in Paris (and it is only in Paris that either the word or its definition can be found) is first of all a big show. Everything else is secondary. In Italy and Germany, where music is important, the concept is unknown: there is opera, yes, but no "grand" opera, in either of the countries where opera is most native and has been most extensively written and performed. *Fidelio*, *Carmen*, *La Traviata*, all the works of Wagner, all the works of Mozart and almost all the works of Verdi are outside the "grand" category. *Pelléas et Mélisande*, *Wozzeck*, *The Rake's Progress*—none of these is "grand" opera.

Verdi had tried his hand, even though he detested the formula; he was so professional that he found it difficult to suppose that there was a kind of opera he could not master if he tried. His *Vêpres Siciliennes*, the first thing composed directly for the "grand" Opéra (1855), had unsatisfactory results; and *Don Carlos*, the last effort (1867), left positive wounds. *Don Carlos* is a real "grand" opera, of course, and until *Aïda* it came the nearest to filling every requirement of the idiotic French definition, but it was one of the most painful of Verdi's mature experiences because he could not obtain the result he wanted. (The rehearsals were a nightmare—under the system at the Opéra everybody had an opinion and expressed it; the composer had no real authority; there was no unity and no feeling of need for it; hardly anybody in the opera house knew how to read a score, and consequently the first actual hearing of any passage, even the smallest chord, was a revelation.) And what happened to *Don Carlos*? After that frosty experience in Paris, where all sorts of absurd things happened—the Empress turning her back on the stage during the scene with the Grand Inquisitor, for instance!—it was translated into Italian and had just been performed, wonderfully and ecstatically performed, by La Stolz and Tiburini and other first-class singers under a real conductor, Mariani, to the delight of enormous audiences.

Verdi, I think, had learned his lesson by the summer of 1868, what with the *Don Carlos* experience and his first view of Milan again and his conversation with Manzoni and, finally, his return to the Scala to rehearse *La Forza del Destino*. The lesson was that he was an Italian through and through and belonged in Italy; that his music would be best understood and therefore best performed in Italy, where it would find its best and most natural audience; and that the Paris "grand" Opéra would have to struggle along without him henceforth. He never says all this quite so bluntly, but it is clear enough: his letters to Escudier and to Camille du Locle (his French translator, who had just become director of the Opéra-Comique) are full of outbursts about the differences between French and Italian orchestras, French and Italian choruses, rehearsal systems, styles of singing, etc., etc., all very much to the detriment of Paris.

And at the very same time he knew that he could write a big show. He had done it in *Don Carlos*, and it was the fault of the French that they did not know how to sing or to play instruments or to make a unified production of any stage work. This was proved by the fact that in Italian (as also soon in German) *Don Carlos* could be properly done with enormous effect. So we find, at the very outset of his work on *Aïda*, that all these things had come together, and that he fully intended this time to write a big show *in Italian*, not for the Opéra but for the man in the moon, and prove that it could be done. (Besides which, the occasion demanded a big show if any occasion ever did.)

The reconciliation of the spectacular style of "grand" opera to the natural genius of Italian lyric drama is what makes *Aïda* unique, technically speaking, and gives it both spaciousness and intimacy at the same time. Of course, it happens to have been written at the full tide of Verdi's mastery, in his own vein of passionate dramatic expression, and, furthermore, at a time when he had given a great deal more thought to the orchestra than ever before. He had just been presiding over a commission named by the Ministry of Public Instruction to recommend reforms in the study and performance of music, and he never accepted a task of that sort perfunctorily. His commission reported the exact constitution of a "normal orchestra," as it ought to be: fourteen first violins, fourteen second violins, twelve violas, and so on, all through the winds, brasses and percussion instruments. With the exception of some extra demands made in the drums, the orchestra for *Aïda* is precisely the same—and a great deal more than Verdi would have thought "normal" only a few years before. With some shift in the balance, more strings and less woodwind, it is about the same as Wagner's orchestra for *Die Meistersinger von Nürnberg*, produced for the first time in Munich the preceding year.

The way in which *Aïda* was presented to Verdi and caught his imagination; the way in which, also, it encountered extremes of both good and bad luck on its way to the stage, might be taken as eminently characteristic of his whole theatre experience. The personal and the professional were deeply intermingled in his life as an artist: witness the very first of his decisive efforts in the opera house, *Nabucco*. The imbroglio of Verdi, La Strepponi and Merelli at that time was about to be repeated almost thirty years later with Verdi, La Stolz and Mariani, all transposed and differently colored by age and circumstance, but bearing a strong family likeness. (It almost looks like what Nietzsche called "the typical experience.") Similarly, many of his operas in the past had been hopelessly entangled in external events, wars or revolutions, popular movements or tyrannical suppressions, and had been held up, changed, suffocated or at times enhanced by these seemingly irrelevant events—which, too, often had an effect upon the composer's own mind and spirits while he was doing the work. *Aïda* was very nearly the syndromic case in all these respects.

It came to him anonymously, to begin with—that in itself shows how difficult he had become to persuade, how reluctant he was to accept new work. After *Don Carlos* he was more than ever disillusioned with the theatre, especially in Paris, and although he consented to read every new play or story that was sent to him, he found fault with everything. There exudes from his letters at the end of the 1860's a feeling that unless his imagination was touched, really touched into activity like the spring from the rock, he was now capable of leaving the theatre for good. He did not even want his own more recent work performed unless he felt sure of how it could be done. He refused *Boccanegra* and *La Forza del Destino* for Paris—the former was "too gloomy" and the latter too "muddled"—and although in principle he would not refuse to compose a new opera if he found the right subject, he was sufficiently dissatisfied with all the librettos he had ever had to make this an extremely difficult provision.

Camille du Locle, who had worked with Verdi enough to acquire unusual understanding of that stubborn and ingrown nature, kept on trying. Du Locle was new as director of the Opéra-Comique and would have

liked to get Verdi into that house for the first time. Perrin at the Opéra
and Bagier at the Théâtre Lyrique, who had put on Verdi's previous
work, were also importunate but with less success. Du Locle had made
a journey to Egypt in the preceding winter, had gone up the Nile with
Mariette Bey, the archaeological director, and perhaps even at that time
had acquired the germ of his idea. At all events, however it got started,
the Khedive himself, Ismail, eventually got the idea (and always thought
it was his own) that the opening of the Suez Canal should be signalized
by a new and very brilliant production at the Cairo Opera House (which
was also new). Khedive Ismail had traveled in Europe a good deal, had
read books and listened to music; it is by no means impossible that the
original notion came from him. Mariette Bey had written a story about
ancient Egypt, and in the course of the discussions it occurred to him
that this might form the basis for musical and dramatic treatment. He
proposed to the Khedive that Du Locle should write the scenario and
the verses: the composer might be Gounod, Wagner or Verdi, the
recognized masters in their three countries. Du Locle quite naturally
preferred Verdi, with whom he had a good working relationship, and the
Khedive agreed—all of this, it seems, before Verdi had any idea of what
was going on. On a brief visit to Paris that winter Du Locle did sound
him out, most cautiously, on a composition for "a very distant country,"
but Verdi seems to have paid little attention. Finally, after Verdi and
Peppina had gone back to Sant' Agata, Du Locle sent him a scenario
on the original story by Mariette. The Egyptian story (they called it
"un programme égyptien") took up four short printed pages, but was in
the form of a sketch for a stage production, with its action presented as
dramatic rather than narrative. Along with the Egyptian story, the
crafty Du Locle sent a Spanish comedy by Lopez de Ayala, one of the
many he had been submitting for the past year or so. The four-paged
Egyptian sketch was anonymous.

Verdi instantly liked it. He could see its musical *tinta*—its color, its
tint—which was for him the most important thing with any subject. If
he got the *tinta* right off, instinctively, then everything else could follow
in due course. He was eager to know who had written it; whoever it was,
he said, knew the theatre and theatrical situations.

Du Locle then confessed that it was his own, on a story by somebody
else. (Verdi somehow got the notion, in the earlier stages, that the
Khedive himself had written the original.) After a considerable correspondence, Du Locle set to work and made a full stage scenario, without versifying or otherwise attempting to fill it in; and at this, finally,

Verdi's imagination took fire. If he could compose to an Italian text by a poet of his own choosing, who would work with him and for him, and if he could be given ample time for the necessary development both of text and music, he would accept the commission. By this time he knew that it was for the Khedive and for the Suez Canal, although no terms had been settled.

It may have been a disappointment to Du Locle not to be able to write the text of the work, in French, but an element of relief was probably not absent; Verdi was captious and at this moment, as we have seen, was most at odds with everything French; he wanted to compose to his own language in his own way. Whatever he wished would be done (so the answer came from Cairo) if the Khedive could be sure to have the full score, ready for production, by January, 1871, to celebrate the opening of the Canal. That was his only condition. Verdi was to retain all musical and dramatic rights to the work in every country except Egypt; he was to be paid 150,000 francs, gold, at the Rothschild Bank in Paris, for those Egyptian rights and the right to the first performance; he would himself suggest the proper conductor and the appropriate chief singers; he would supervise and pay for the libretto himself, so that it would be his own property.

Rarely has there been such a magnificent stroke of business, and Verdi did it himself: he did not tell his publisher-agent, Ricordi, until it was all settled. The Egyptian rights and the Cairo première for 150,000 gold francs! Such rights were of value to the Khedive for one occasion only, the ceremonial festivities to which kings, princes and notables from many countries had been invited. The world rights to Aïda, which Verdi retained, were the real fortune. The sums of money involved under the gold standard were worth a good deal more than the figures indicate— 150,000 gold francs, roughly $30,000 or 6,000 pounds sterling, would be worth about five times as much in "real" value, translated into contemporary terms. And this, so to speak, was a present, a princely gift: for the Egyptian rights could really be worth nothing like so much. Verdi no doubt took keen pleasure in carrying out the negotiation himself, but, although he was shrewd enough, it really did not require any great business skill to bring about the result: the Khedive and Mariette Bey were already determined on their course before Verdi was even approached, and the money did not matter to them.

Ricordi was beside himself with delight. He did not feel in the least injured at not being consulted: Verdi had saved for himself, which meant the House of Ricordi, everything that really mattered, the world rights. Furthermore, Giulio Ricordi knew how to value to the very fullest that part of the enterprise which Verdi at first did not understand and afterward cordially detested—that is, the fantastic publicity of such a first performance. There probably has been none other, before or since, which compelled such interest throughout the world, not even *Parsifal* at Bayreuth. It was, of course, not a musical interest exclusively or even primarily: it was merged into the general fanfare of the Suez Canal inauguration, of which it was supposed to be the crowning event. Ricordi did not mind how unmusical the fanfare might be: he saw at once that the House of Ricordi, which had greatly gained by Verdi's work for over thirty years, was now going to reap an even greater harvest.

All summer and autumn the villa at Sant' Agata was turned into an incubator for Aïda (that was its name from July first onward). Verdi had chosen Antonio Ghislanzoni to write the scenes and verses, but hardly a situation, hardly a line or a word, came into being without his own collaboration, far beyond the ordinary limits assigned to that expression. He had always fussed and fretted over the texts of his operas, not one of which had been satisfactory to him throughout, and to be sure, he had been cursed by some of the worst ever written; but this time he had learned so much, was so sure of what he wanted, and perceived the entire text in such a clear musicality—the *tinta*—that his librettist was in effect a specialized kind of secretary, able to take dictation in verse. Ghislanzoni, a man of skill but no great ambition, did not mind—in fact he was delighted; he made no terms even about money, but would take whatever the Maestro wanted to give him; he probably knew quite well that if he were to be remembered it would be for this work. Du Locle had provided the broad lines, the situations, the very bold, simple, highly effective drama; Ghislanzoni had to supply that *musicabile* which Verdi always sought, the text that could be put best into music. Sometimes the Maestro asked for verses of such a length in such a meter, evidently because a certain kind of music was already taking form in his head; at other times he wanted broken cadences, or verses in this color or that. Often he simply wrote the verses himself and told Ghislanzoni to improve on them or polish them—which, we learn, the poet did not do. A great many touches in the text of *Aïda* remain, word for word, as Verdi wrote them, because the poet said he could not better them.

In the midst of this absorbing work, the most absorbing and the most rewarding to himself of any for years past, Verdi was greatly shaken by the outbreak of the Franco-Prussian War and its rapid evolution. All at once the tone of his letters to and about France is changed: he follows the course of the war with anxiety and deep foreboding. If he had been Garibaldi he would have done as the red-shirted hero did, and volunteered to fight for France. He was not only anxious and concerned for France, to which every friendly emotion he had ever felt was now revived, but for all of Europe, for Italy and for the world: he dreaded the hegemony of the German, the iron heel, the Gothic fist. The composition of Aïda was accompanied by these larger concerns and was to some extent influenced by them: the speech of the conquering Prussian King, in which he appropriates God as a Prussian commander, is exactly the tone Verdi wished Ghislanzoni to give the Egyptian priests (in the triumphal scene). The work went on relentlessly, in spite of these enormously depressing events on a large scale, and by November was finished: as we have said before, the actual composition occupied four months, one month to each act. It is an astounding example of Verdi's fertility, the boundless energy with which he could compose on a subject which he had fully absorbed; and, furthermore, a demonstration of how he managed the simultaneity of text, vocal line, color and instrumentation. Granted, the orchestration was accomplished only by brief notes and sketchy indications while he was racing through, but it was *real* orchestration (not piano music): he had only to go back afterwards and fill it in, because at the time when he composed a scene he felt the orchestra in his mind while he was writing the top line down to fit the text. Similarly, he was able to set a portion of an act, in this way, while the text of the end of the act was not yet written, because he had the text, too (and its writer), completely under control. This uncanny speed was in material or physical terms the result of a willingness, or rather a determination, to work any necessary number of hours in a day or days in a week; it was also due to the rude physical vigor which at this time, in his late fifties, had never been more marked. But most of all, it came out of the full mastery of all means, all elements, which he had now attained: he could if necessary have written the poetry himself, the scenes, the whole drama, and in an inner sense this is pretty much what he did do. He had the orchestra within him by now, and the vocal flow—that endless melody of which the Wagnerians spoke but which was native to Verdi without theoretical assistance—had never been lacking: it was as abundant as ever, perhaps more so, but held in check by the taste and judgment of maturity, the growing sense of dramatic significance, the conviction of the *oneness* of a work. "This is no place to stop and sing," he said to Ghislanzoni about one passage, and out it went. Yet everything sang, on the stage and in the orchestra, in quite a new way, continuously, so that although the separate pieces are marked down in the score in the conventional manner, they no longer seem separate—they merge into the whole.

So the work was completed on time, a work of white-hot enthusiasm, inspiration and distinctive *tinta*—the things Verdi always valued most— and he wrote to Mariette Bey in Cairo to tell him so. He did not know that Mariette Bey was locked up in Paris, then undergoing its long siege by the Prussians, and that all the scenery, costumes and stage properties, which had been made under Mariette's supervision for the Cairo production of *Aïda*, were also locked up by the siege. Verdi had harassed Mariette with many questions during the summer, about ancient Egyptian customs, traditions, ideas, dress, even ancient instruments of music, but lately he had been so engrossed in composition that he had lost track of his mentor. Draneth Bey, director of the theatre for the Khedive, replied: it would be impossible to produce *Aïda* in January, 1871, because the stage materials were unobtainable.

This was a blow to Verdi because he had already set his mind on the Scala production, to follow that in Cairo by about a month. He had signed papers and picked singers and conductor. He was in the midst of that tenebrous affair with La Stolz and Mariani, the exact sequence of which will never be fully established, but by this time La Stolz had certainly left Mariani's bed and board forever. There exists a letter from her to the conductor (October, 1870) in which she tells him that between them there can no longer exist anything but the "simple friendship of artists."

The letter "of rupture," as the French call it, was written after she had spent three weeks at Sant' Agata in Verdi's house, with his wife present, learning the meaning of *Aïda* and some of its music. Mariani, working desperately at Bologna on his production of *Lohengrin*, the first work of Wagner's ever performed in Italy, and already corroded by cancer, struggled to retain the remains of the love (it was to have been a marriage) which, as he felt, Verdi was taking from him. La Stolz was living in Florence, alone, and Mariani went there to try to persuade her not to enter Verdi's house. They traveled together as far as Bologna, where he returned to his work in the theatre and she, imperturbably, went on to Parma and to Verdi. She was to have stayed a week at Sant' Agata and she stayed three. On her return from Parma to Florence she had to change trains at Bologna, where she saw Mariani for a few moments only; he could not deflect her from her course; she got into the other train and they never met again.

La Stolz had already decided not to go to Cairo for the first *Aïda*, since

Verdi's obvious wish was to keep her in Italy so as to mold her performance of the work exactly as he intended it to be. Mariani had refused
for both himself and La Stolz, but Verdi now seems to insist. He had
wanted Muzio, as we know, but the good and faithful Muzio had obtained the lucrative and permanent post of conductor at the Théâtre des
Italiens in Paris and the Maestro did not want to rob him of it "for all the
gold in the world." Poor Mariani, whose letters on this subject to various
friends, particularly if they had Verdi's confidence, are heart-rending, thus
found himself in the position of being urged to go off to Egypt—very ill
as he knew himself to be, and dreading the sea voyage—leaving his
beloved Stolz to the mercies of Verdi under the conditions of forced
intimacy provided by long hours of rehearsal in a new work. He would
not or perhaps could not do it.

There should be some words of mitigation, lest Verdi appear too
cruelly egotistical in the matter. In the first place it is doubtful if the
Maestro knew of Mariani's illness at all, or at any rate of its gravity. In
the second place, La Stolz was herself an imperious lady and had been
growing cold to Mariani for a good two years by now. She had much
to do with all this; it was not altogether or even primarily Verdi's doing,
no matter how much the singer fascinated him. And, so far as Verdi's insistence on Mariani for Cairo was concerned (and La Stolz for Milan
where Mariani was unable to conduct because of intrigues), the artistic
reasons were sufficient: Mariani was still the best of Italian conductors
and Aïda would have been safe in his hands in Cairo, whereas young
Faccio, known to Verdi from La Forza del Destino, could take charge in
Milan, under the Maestro's own eye. We see all this, and we can also see
how La Stolz had wearied of Mariani—whose infidelities, she complained,
had never even been concealed—and no longer wished to marry him. Nor
is it at all mysterious that a soprano should be dazzled by the role of Aïda,
ideally suited to her talents and, as I think, consciously or unconsciously
written for them; what flattery could equal this? The composer had
formidable advantages in fame, fortune, prestige and power over the world
of opera, and in his own person had never failed with the ladies to the
best of our knowledge. La Stolz herself, Teresina, was prodigiously willful
and, according to the best contemporary evidence, had a blazing talent of
the rarest dramatic quality; would not such a woman be difficult to
manage, would she not do what she wanted and what seemed best for her
temperament and her career? That Mariani was, in fact, a dying man
might not even have occurred to her; she was so bored and impatient with

his complaints that she may even have thought he was inventing his own illness.

The one most curiously silent partner in the affair is, of course, Peppina, who had already gone through a good deal of turmoil during her quarter of a century of life with Verdi. She was jealous by temperament, very, but she had a commanding brain and knew her Verdi about as well as anybody could. We see her smoldering beneath all that self-control, biting her lips a good deal and perhaps occasionally the nail of a finger, but re-solved to keep the Verdi-Stolz relationship as levelly as possible on the plane of a composer's necessary traffic with his leading interpreter, and if it ever fell off that plane, to ignore it. Peppina had one technique which had worked before and would work again as soon as all this passionate agitation over *Aïda* had come to an end: she could join the enemy.

In the meantime the Wagner-Verdi feud, which never was a feud between the principals but between their fanatical followers, cut into the whole *Aïda* tangle.

Verdi never wished to bar the Italian theatres to Wagner, or at any rate never tried to do so; he only disliked the Wagnerian theory and dreaded its effect on young Italians, just as he bitterly resented the way in which most of the young people were unable to praise Wagner without at the same time denigrating Verdi and all the rest of their own heritage. He suffered from the enormous literature created in the wake of Wagner; it afflicted him in many ways, all unjust, since he really had no theories and was not *opposing* Wagner so far as he knew, unless it were by his mere existence. He had found out in the unpleasant experience of *Don Carlos* in Paris that his own maturing use of harmony and instrumentation was likely to be called—*by Wagner's enemies*—"Wagnerian," so that as be-tween the irrational Wagnerian fanatics and their equally fanatical op-ponents he had little chance of going his own way unmolested. A resent-ment of Wagner, not yet accompanied by any great knowledge of that master's work, was inevitable, and for Mariani, an old friend, the best conductor of the latest and most developed Verdi work (*Don Carlos*) as of so many others, to turn to Wagner—well, it was too much. We can see that in his indignation as an artist Verdi quite easily forgot that he was not himself without fault toward Mariani. He must have known that the world of music and the theatre buzzed with stories at this time, and not in Italy alone: it was said that Mariani had turned to Wagner as a means of revenge on Verdi for stealing his ladylove. The whole affair was worked up into a great historico-musical event; and at one time Hans von Bülow, the most extreme Wagnerian in existence, who had publicly

recorded his scorn for Verdi two years before, was considered by the
Bologna management as conductor for Lohengrin. Mariani, principal
conductor and artistic director of the Bologna season, could hardly put
up with this, but he did accept Von Bülow as Wagnerian adviser at his
elbow throughout the preparation of the work. Wagner himself was only
just dissuaded from invading Italy for this performance; if he had done so
there would have been riots; there very nearly were anyhow. If detach-
ment or irony had been possible to anybody concerned in this affair, it
might have seemed at least a tiny bit odd that Von Bülow, whose wife
had at first lived with both men and then with Wagner alone, in a union
sanctified by divorce and remarriage only the year before, should now be
acting as mentor to an Italian in more or less the same position; but
under the banner of "the music of the future" neither irony nor a sense of
humor was permissible.

Lohengrin had its first performance November 1, 1870, with a triumph
which echoed through the public prints for a long time thereafter. Wagner wrote a letter to that impertinent young man, Boito, who was anti-
Verdian in those days, and Boito printed it all at length in La Perseveranza about a year later. (In Wagner's works it is called Brief an einem
Italienischen Freund.) There were crows of triumph from the "futurists."

Such was the state of affairs, with La Stolz sulking in Florence and
Mariani dying on the podium in Bologna, when Verdi decided to go and
listen to Lohengrin. He thought he would be able to get to Bologna and
back without notice—a delusion. Two men came from the House of
Ricordi to guard over him and were instantly spotted by Mariani himself and other members of the Bologna company, as well as by some of
the Milan visitors. Mariani went to the railroad station to meet somebody
(a friend in the suite of the Grand Duke Michael of Russia) and ran into
Verdi in the crowd, carrying a small satchel. Mariani offered to carry it for
him and was curtly refused. The Maestro, as he says in his woeful letter,
scarcely spoke to him, except to order him sharply to keep silent about
his presence in Bologna. Mariani says he went home to rest, in bed, then
had his meal and went to the theatre without having said one word to
anybody about the Maestro's presence. He had hardly been in the theatre
a quarter of an hour before he was aware of some unusual excitement, and
after the performance began he knew it was serious. Many slips and
laxities and inexactitudes occurred both on the stage and in the orchestra;
a kind of orgasmo, as he calls it, was going on. When he went backstage
at the end of Act I, he found out that everybody in the whole company
knew Maestro Verdi was in the audience. It was nearly the last chance to

hear *Lohengrin*, and Verdi was yielding to a natural curiosity, but the effect on the singers and orchestra was apparently disastrous. They must have slipped from their first night's keenness anyhow, as is usual in the theatre, but Verdi's presence in any audience was as rare as his power in opera was great, and Mariani could not pull the company together again. Verdi followed the performance attentively with a voice-and-piano reduction of the score open in his lap, marking it as he went along. The score and the marks are preserved, and an industrious student has tabulated them: 114 remarks, 78 adverse in greater or less degree, 25 cautious praise, the rest between the two. The general judgment was not good for Wagner's work but was much worse for Mariani's performance.

Madame Stolz arrived in Genoa for the Aïda rehearsals—or, more accurately, lessons—with Madame Maria Waldmann, originally from Vienna, who was to sing Amneris, and with the masculine trio of Capponi, Pandolfini and Maini. The end of 1871 was spent on this work in Verdi's apartment in the Palazzo Sauli. It consisted of explanation at the piano, much work on character, tempo and style, but not much of what might be called straight rehearsal. At the beginning of 1872 the whole troupe moved to Milan, Verdi and Peppina in those ample rooms in the Grand Hotel which they were to occupy afterward whenever they returned. Somehow or other we detect a change which had either already taken place or was now taking place in the relationships of the persons involved, for by this time "Teresina"—Madame Stolz—had become a dear, dear friend of Peppina. That, as had been shown before, was the end of any romance with Verdi.

Aïda had been produced in Cairo on Christmas Eve, 1871, with stupendous success. The Khedive had not only invited his own chosen guests from all over the world, but also some chosen critics from Europe: a circumstance which, savoring of "réclame," aroused Verdi to sharp anger. The performance was evidently good, with settings and costumes created according to Mariette's ideas and some of the stage management also supervised by the expert. The long accounts which appeared in Europe were profuse in their compliments to the composer and his work, but to us nowadays they sound extremely puzzled and uncertain. What were they to make of this huge leap forward on the part of a composer whom they had known so well for three decades? Ernest Reyer, the French Wagnerian (composer of *Sigurd*), was one of those invited by the Khedive to the opening in Cairo; he had never had much to say in Verdi's favor before. This time, he informed his newspaper, the *Journal des Débats* in

Paris, Verdi was using all the artifices of fugue and counterpoint, blending timbres with rare ingenuity, breaking the old forms of melody, reaching out toward new harmonies, "*les plus étranges quelquefois*," with the most unexpected modulations, giving the accompaniment more interest and sometimes more value than the melody itself, so that, says poor Reyer in his bewilderment, it is like what Grétry said of Mozart: he sometimes puts the statue in the orchestra and the pedestal on the stage.

Verdi cared little about this. He was back at the Scala at last. It is my feeling that he never did care much about the Cairo première of Aïda after he was well into the composition of the music: the Scala was his aim. With this work, so rich, big and new, with such tremendous opportunities for everybody concerned, he could make his real return to his native heath. From the time the Aïda rehearsals began in Milan he was absorbed in them all day every day, and sometimes at night as well. Peppina spent her days with the Countess Maffei; Verdi in the theatre. La Stolz, under his tuition, was becoming what the contemporaries heard and beheld in wonder, a perfect Aïda, a soprano and actress ideally conterminous with the part she had to play. The young conductor, Franco Faccio, after some anti-Verdian years (he was another of the wayward young, a friend of Boito, an admirer of Wagner), was now learning all he could from the Maestro and giving everything he could in return. The singers and the orchestra and the chorus, all of whom understood the challenge, were working as never before. Ricordi might have told them that Verdi was back at the Scala, but that it was up to them to keep him there. The demands he was making were musically great for that time, or indeed for any time, and the manipulation of the masses on stage and of the orchestral novelties in the pit made it a task for which none of the participants (not even Faccio) had been prepared by previous experience.

The first night was February 8, 1872, and would appear to have been a rare amalgam of resurrection, apotheosis and coronation all at once, with such storms of approval as even Milan, in all its extremes, has seldom recorded. Verdi was forced onto the stage for thirty-two calls in all: this time he went through the entire gamut of a return to the theatre, with the first three nights and their required bows, the demonstrations in the streets, everything all together.

The composer went on back to Sant' Agata after a while and devoted himself to his garden. It was sixteen whole years before the Scala saw a new work of his, but in the meantime all the old wounds had been completely healed by Aïda; he went back to Milan and to the theatre whenever he felt so inclined, and on two occasions, in producing revised versions of *Simon Boccanegra* (1881) and *Don Carlos* (1884), he returned to work again as before. His next return was with *Otello* (1887), which he owed, like this miraculous *Falstaff* now, to the evolution of the once impudent young man, Arrigo Boito. Half-asleep and half-awake, remembering in those almost instantaneous glimpses to which time makes no difference, it must have seemed to the old Maestro that the most unexpected of all his fortunes had been the coming of this young man at the end to crown the day. *Va, vecchio John*—he could say the words of his Falstaff, as he did so often in his letters—be on your way, old man; it was work well done and there is little more to do; a farewell to the theatre there must be sometime, and this, at last, is it; be on your way.

2

Rome and the
Risorgimento

1   The climate of Milan in winter was no better in 1893 than it is today, but Peppina and "her Verdi" stayed on at the Grand Hotel a few more weeks. He said it was too late in the year to open up the big apartment in Genoa, and of course it was too early to go into the snowy plains and darkened rooms of Sant' Agata. We suspect that both he and Peppina were actually enjoying the glow of the world's esteem at a moment when it was unalloyed and when the composer could feel that it was deserved. There had always been something wrong before, something lacking, some carping footnote to be resented fiercely; Aïda and the Requiem Mass, even, in fact, Otello, had brought forth a few criticisms of the obtuse and wrong-headed kind which hurt most. The terrible and enduring wound of Aïda, which seemed almost to count more than its triumph, was that numerous critics saw in it some influence from the theories or practice of Richard Wagner. Even Otello was occasionally subjected to the same kind of abuse. "Forty years in this career," Verdi said to the Countess, "and I must end as an imitator!" Now, however, years later, nobody in all Europe made any such suggestion. Falstaff was received as being what it was, the ultimate evolution of Verdi's own style, mood and gift—complicated, yes, and composed in polyphony with great erudition, but as much his own as Ernani. This was akin to his own inner realization that he had obtained a good result from his own work and also in the theatre. He was content; he was in good humor; he was willing to be agreeable to large numbers of Milanese friends and visitors from overseas. He did not go back to the theatre and, in fact, he did not go out much at all, even in a carriage, but his very large and comfortable rooms at the hotel were enough to accommodate an agreeable amount of movement and company. Peppina, whose rheumatism (or arthritis) surpassed his by a good deal in discomfort, was content to stay in one place for a while, and to enjoy, as she really did to the marrow, every evidence of the world's esteem for her old man.

Under contemporary conditions the Verdi troupe—for it was hardly less than that—might have gone easily enough to the Palazzo Doria in Genoa. Travel was not quite so painless then; nor was it quite so simple to open up a big house at a moment's notice. Verdi's two fixed establishments, that in the Palazzo Doria and the country house at Sant' Agata, were by now of a size which implicated many persons and much work;

to open or to close either house would have been, for a housekeeper of Peppina's standards, a major operation in the month of February; but aside from these valid practical arguments I find it most probable that both of them relished the general atmosphere of the *Falstaff* triumph. For one thing, there was a great deal of business connected with it. Theatres throughout the world were demanding the right to produce the opera, and Verdi would not yield a single point of his demands for integral execution, note by note, exactly as he wished it to be performed. This meant tremendous long contracts and an immense amount of correspondence, although the House of Ricordi could attend to most of the details. Berlin, Vienna, Lisbon, New York, London, Paris—all of these had to be considered very carefully as well as the great houses of Italy, which had already made their arrangements. So far as possible, Verdi would have liked all the world's theatres to produce the work exactly as he had prepared it for the Scala. This, naturally, would be best accomplished by using the same instruments (conductor and principal singers at least; chorus and orchestra when possible) with which he had worked. The old man had vowed a mighty vow that this last work, above all others, must not be done anywhere on earth in less than the full measure of his intention so far as it was possible for a theatre to do it. The parade of the agents, managers and other persons coveting a share of "Big-Belly" passed through the Verdi rooms at the Grand Hotel all through February and a good part of March. Without much trouble he succeeded in imposing the conductor, Mascheroni, and most of the principal singers—especially Maurel—upon most of the opera houses, but then arose, of course, the question of when these successive premières could take place. Nobody could be in more than one theatre at a time, and theatres have the unfortunate habit of running their seasons simultaneously. It was an intricate but eminently successful series of negotiations: it would be hard to find another case in which a composer's wishes were more widely obeyed, in spite of the difficulties.

Aside from the business of getting the *Pancione* on his way, there was another close to Verdi's heart: the Home for Aged Musicians, it is generally called in English. The Milanese called it simply Casa Verdi and still do. His name for it was the *Casa di Riposo per Musicisti* (House of Rest for Musicians). He had come to this title after much discussion, because the names suggested—especially anything of the nature of "refuge" or "asylum"—seemed to him lacking in respect toward the elderly or aged artists who would live there. Nobody knew better than Verdi how the careless word might hurt, and he wanted his fellow musicians in their old age to be spared unnecessary humiliation. "There but for the grace of God go I"—it is in this spirit that he set up and worked on the Casa di Riposo, one of the main interests of his last years: he called it, toward the end, "my best opera." It involved a great deal of legal work and much planning, to which Verdi gave close attention and all the time that seemed necessary. It is impossible to look at it even today without a slight catch in the throat: there are many princes and potentates in history who built their own monuments, from Cheops on down to Richard Wagner at Bayreuth, but I know of none better than the Casa Verdi, in the Piazza Michelangelo at Milan.

Verdi had tried institutional philanthropy on two previous occasions and had discovered how extremely difficult it is. The first, a hospital, suffered from his own inexperience in such matters; there were troubles about the director, the doctors, administrative intrigues, etc., etc., which were new to him and disturbed him greatly. His second hospital, at Villafranca in his own native region, was a model institution to which both he and Peppina gave every effort as well as money. His determined effort to fight malaria and other periodic fevers in his own region—which was combined with the struggle for irrigation—must also classify as an experience in institutional philanthropy, because it, too, involved a great amount of legal foresightedness and social accommodations or combinations. He had been generous in a personal or private way on innumerable occasions, had contributed for decades to every public fund or purpose of intrinsic concern to him, and clearly possessed from the early years of his accumulating wealth a sense of responsibility toward those less gifted or less fortunate. When the first payment for Aïda came to Paris from Egypt, he instructed Escudier to take 3,000 francs out of the 30,000 and use them for the wounded in the hospitals of the besieged city. Just as he was intractable with Ricordi or anybody else when he thought his material interests were at stake, so he was stubborn and practical, painstaking and patient, in matters referring to the money he wanted to use for others. There was not one minor circumstance of architecture or engineering, lighting or comfort, to which he did not attend closely, both in his Villafranca hospital and in the House of Rest for Musicians. The latter—the Casa Verdi—became, after *Falstaff* was launched, a leading preoccupation of his life.

So the Verdi ménage, busy as always, remained at the Grand Hotel of Milan until it was time to go on to Rome. There they had promised to be present at the first presentations of *Falstaff*—promised the Teatro Costanzi, which by implication meant also the King and the government as well as the people. Verdi knew to a nicety what he was in for; he had had a considerable number of Roman triumphs, although only four of his operas had received their first productions there. *I Due Foscari* (1844) and *La Battaglia di Legnano* (1849) were the earliest of these, both works which made a tremendous impression in their own time upon political as well as musical feeling. It would have been difficult for him to separate the political idea of Rome from any other: it was the foreordained capital of Italy, the heart-town of the heart-land, even though he had never himself lived there. "We must be careful," he once admonished his librettist Cammarano, "because, remember, it is for Rome!" He seems to have been a little shy of it, a little in awe, even in those far-off days when it was really only a small provincial capital without properly paved streets or sanitation. The parade of the years, whenever he glanced back at it, presented to him now, at eighty, a progression almost unimaginable in its slow, inevitable course. As a child he had dreamed of Rome—of the Roman Republic, the severe, the grand, the virtuous Republic—and never had ceased to think of it as the natural destination of every Italian effort. His friend Cavour, who was, next to George Washington, the political hero of his mind, had been equally steadfast, and even in days when it would have been so easy and so popular to say that Turin was the Italian capital, Cavour had never wavered: if there was to be an Italy, its capital must be Rome. He was no longer a republican. Cavour and history and circumstance had convinced him that the constitutional monarchy was the best practical system for Italy. He was not even an anticlerical any more (he referred to the Pope as the *pover papin*, in dialect, and had been quite moved at the death of Pio Nono). To go to Rome now was to reconcile many beliefs, hopes and dreams in one, and see them unified, for the last time, as they best can be in an imperfect life. *Tutto nel mondo è burla*—as he so often wrote in his letters just now: everything in the world is a joke. It was perhaps to savor this joke at its best that he consented to go once more to Rome.

Rome was the capital of a free Italy, strong and united, prosperous as never before in history, abounding in vitality and producing so many children that the land could no longer feed them or keep them busy. They were streaming across the oceans in a tumultuous migration which was within a few years to introduce a strong Italian element into the populations of North and South America. The capital itself was growing and building, the monarchy was firmly established, Crispi was Prime Minister and the great powers of the world (which was still an exclusively European concept meaning the six nations which exchanged ambassadors—it did not yet include the United States of America or the Japanese Empire) accepted Italy as one of them. This, at eighty, Verdi saw with his own scarce-believing eyes, remembering the powerless poverty and division, the hopeless prostration and despair, of Italy in his youth. His country was like his theatre, an idea which had grown up to meet his own demands. It was not quite everything he had so ferociously intended in his first youth, when he, too, had been starved and anxious and impatient, but it was as near as life can ever fill out the scope of dreams. After all, he had entered the theatre when it was lighted with candles, and lived through the time when it was lighted with oil and then (1851) had seen it blaze into the new brilliance of gas; now, this very year of 1893, after a partial adaptation occupying ten years, the cautious conversion of one part after another, the Scala was completely electrical in every section. Such were the revolutions, such the changes, through which his consciousness had gone on rendering into music, like the *élan vital* of the plants and the animals, an essence less mortal than any of their forms.

The King and the Prime Minister were at least historically and politically percipient. That is, they knew Verdi to be more integrally Italian, more part of the root and branch, than they were themselves. He was the friend of their elders and betters; he had spoken for the people, or at least had sung for the people, half a century and more; his was the incontrovertible voice. By his age alone he brought to mind such as Michelangelo, the half-eternal, and by his associations he recalled Cavour and Victor Emmanuel II, Garibaldi and Mazzini. True, his late work was not instantly comprehensible by everybody, but the King and the Prime Minister could scarcely have boggled at such a trifle, if, indeed, they knew of it. What they faced was the invasion of Rome by a national idol of difficult character and indeterminate limits, the "Italian song" indeed, as was so often said—*il canto italiano*—but something so much more than simply the song that they did not really know what to do about the singer.

Humbert I was not at all a clever man but he had been blessed by the tutelary genius of the house of Savoy (i.e., Cavour) with a wife who made up for many of his deficiencies. Margherita di Savoia, his first cousin— daughter of Victor Emmanuel's brother Ferdinand, duke of Genoa—had been crown princess for eighteen years, in a country where the queen was dead, and now had been queen for fifteen years. She thus had already, during thirty-three years, been first among Italian women. To this experience of social rank and public duty she brought beauty, charm and intelligence, a proper education and a lively sense of music, art and literature. Mar-

gherita had won many victories for the house of Savoy, particularly among
the hard-crusted old republicans, some of whom came to have a positive
adoration for her in spite of their antiroyal principles. The whole country
remembered her instinctive behavior in the early days of Humbert's reign
(1878) when, during their parade through the flower-strewn streets of
Naples, an anarchist assassin leaped to the step of their carriage and thrust
a futile dagger toward the King's chest. "Cairoli, look to the King!" Margherita called out to the old republican stalwart who was their Prime
Minister, and simultaneously thrust her whole armful of flowers into the
face of the assassin and blinded him. Cairoli grappled with the idiot until
the guards took over, and he was thereby wounded. Such stories of Margherita reveal a woman whose mind did not desert her. She was able to be-
witch the poet Carducci, one of the most inflexible republicans of the lot,
into writing a poem in her honor. This royal lady, who had grown up on
Beethoven and Bach—her culture was German and French as well as
Italian—knew as much about Verdi as he did himself, or probably more,
and there is every likelihood that she was responsible for the skill and tact
with which they all conspired to make his final triumph in Rome. For
myself, I have no doubt of it. Francesco Crispi, with all his gifts, was no
Cavour, and I cannot in my own mind credit him with such sensitivity;
whereas King Humbert could not possibly have known, unless he had
been carefully instructed, just how difficult the problem was.

In substance it was this: how to give Verdi the public, national honor
which was his due, and which it would have been dangerous for the
monarchy and the government to refuse. Verdi wanted no honors; he had
already refused everything. If he had been told, before he left Milan, that
he was to be made into a public effigy and, so to speak, deified in the
Roman Forum, he would never have gone to Rome at all. And yet, as I
have said, he knew what he was in for. Both these statements are true. If
they had submitted an official program he would have refused to go—and
yet he knew, as a man of supreme intelligence, that he could not at this
late date enter Rome for the purpose of producing a new opera without
causing an outburst of acclamation. In his nature, as I understand it, he
was now perfectly prepared to accept the acclamation, if it were natural
and came from the people and could not be avoided. What he never
would have accepted was an official or national program of public glorifica-
tion.

The Queen, by my reading, understood all this through and through;
her particular talent for dealing with difficult men had been proved
and was to be proved many times over. We know her habits—

how she studied; how she worked. The voice-and-piano reduction of *Falstaff* had been published by Ricordi in Milan on the day of the first performance there (February 9, 1893). I have no doubt in my own mind that the Queen, who was a pupil of Sgambati, played it over to herself more than once between then and April, and that if it did not go right she got somebody else to play it to her. These things are within the evidence of her character and her life—we do not need documentary proof if we know the woman. *Falstaff* is not musically very easy even today, and it was far more difficult to understand in 1893, but among my more confident guesses is one that Queen Margherita had a tolerable conversance with its intricacies before Verdi came to Rome.

Mascheroni and all the principal singers from the production at the Scala came to Rome and rehearsed again at the Costanzi under Verdi's eye. The composer and Peppina, with their domestics and adherents, moved into the Quirinal Hotel on April 12. We do not know if the dogs and cats were also there, but even without them there must have been a large section of the hotel set aside. The crowds began to gather from the moment they arrived in Rome. This, which he defined as an interest in his person rather than in his work, was the only complaint Verdi put into words during the *Falstaff* period either in Milan or Rome, or even afterward in Paris. He would have preferred the curiosity and enthusiasm which surrounded him to be transferred to the theatre where his *Pancione* could justify it. He did not like having to acknowledge cheers as he made his way out of his habitation to go to work: he thought it useless, foolish, misdirected. All the same, he was in Rome just as he had been in Milan, willing for this last time (and, so far as I can see, the only time) to put up with whatever came along, understanding all and forgiving all, just so that the work could be put upon the stage with every chance of conveying what he had written into it. He was commanded to the Quirinal immediately and had his audience with King Humbert (no Queen Margherita, no Peppina). They can have had little to say to each other, but there was evidently some sort of recognition scene, as from king to king, because they both betrayed it afterward. Humbert's homage to Verdi became more explicit after that, and when Humbert was assassinated (1900) Verdi briefly thought, in his very last days, of writing some music to his memory. Humbert was a kind of *vert galant*, really, and the whole world could have been contained within two skirts and a bottle of champagne so far as he was concerned, but he does appear to have experienced reverence for this old man. It was Italy personified whom he received in the throne room of the Quirinal that day.

The first night of *Falstaff* in Rome was on April 15, 1893. The royal box, which at the Costanzi, as at the Scala and at the San Carlo in Naples, is large, central, and during the monarchy was used only for official appearances, was not occupied. Queen Margherita sat in a box on the far left, second tier, with her ladies and gentlemen in waiting. Just beneath her, in the first tier, Madame Ricordi and Madame Stolz sat in the front of the box with Peppina concealed behind them. After the house was dark the King came in and slipped into his place in the royal box, with his gentlemen and officers behind him. This was, of course, all carefully arranged, so that Verdi's work would not be disturbed or interrupted by applause or the playing of the national anthem. (No foreigner, neither Queen Victoria nor the Czar of Russia nor the French Emperor and Empress, had ever been so tactful.) At the end of the second act the King sent for the composer and advanced to the front of the royal box with Verdi's hand in his, and "presented" him to the public. The acclamation which followed—the cheering audience, its back to the stage, looking up at the sprightly King and the aged composer—is described in sober texts as "interminable."

After the interminable had terminated the King took Verdi around behind the other boxes to the extreme left and presented him to the Queen. Margherita was enraptured with his work and exquisitely kind to the composer, as we know; but if she had only said—or if she had only been able to say—"I wish you would let me know your wife . . ." It was not said. Peppina, directly underneath, remained concealed behind La Stolz and Madame Ricordi while this was going on. The nineteenth century, even at its last gasp, was faithful to a set of standards which no longer had any connection with reality. Italy was strewn with the King's mistresses and even—well—no more of that; but Peppina was *La Traviata* in the eyes of the 1890's even though she had been Verdi's legal wife since 1859. Queen Victoria, who dominated all the courts of Europe at the period, would have been shocked and indignant if Queen Margherita had received Verdi's wife.

Poor Boito, and why we so often say poor Boito I shall never knew (since he found his god), but anyhow, as we often do say, "poor Boito" was worried. He was afraid Verdi might stop composing again and that he, Boito, would be blamed for the disaster, conceivably with justice. Now that he had extracted so much blood from a turnip, so much water from a stone, so much flower from a dead branch . . .

Verdi himself, as we know, said his farewell in Milan on the third night of *Falstaff*. Nobody else seems to have known that this was the truth.

Boito was sketching away busily, scenes here and verses there, on a possible *King Lear*, which he knew to be a subject the Maestro would find difficult to resist. Now, in all these Roman triumphs, sanctified by "the grace of God and the will of the Italian people" (as the King's commission reads), the Maestro suddenly turned on the poor fellow one evening, as they were on their way back to their rooms in the Hotel Quirinal, and said: "You'd better find me another libretto right away." He was only joking and the chances are that Boito knew it, but some answer had to be made. Boito said: "*Antony and Cleopatra.*" He had translated the play into Italian for Eleonora Duse and now almost immediately began to recast it as a libretto. Verdi had never liked the subject, which was presented to him by other poets in other years, and in any case the idea of composing another opera was dim and distant, really, was hardly more than a quip late at night. Boito worked on both subjects, and Italy resounded with stories to the effect that Verdi was about to embark upon one or the other of them. Verdi himself kept in mind what he called (in a letter to Calvalho in Paris) "*un tout petit, petit détail, mes quatre-vingts ans sonnés.*" There was an almost superstitious belief in Verdi's inexhaustible fertility, and, indeed, after *Falstaff* one can scarcely wonder. The tone of that triumphal week in Rome—for it was just that: eight days to be precise—was more suitable to the high middle of a career than to its end, for there was a steady expectation of more miracles to come.

Verdi made his offhand remark to Boito on the way home from an exceptional demonstration which took place on the night following that first *Falstaff* at the Costanzi. There was no performance at the opera that night and the orchestra seized the opportunity to give a serenade in Verdi's honor. This he had avoided in Milan with considerable effort, but in Rome, where the proceedings had taken such a regal and national aspect, he could not successfully decline it. The orchestra placed itself on the terrace above the grand entrance to the Costanzi and performed its unrehearsed concert to an immense audience which filled the whole square and the streets out of it. So vast a crowd had seldom gathered in the city, and the observers are at a loss to guess how many persons it contained. "Thousands upon thousands," is the phrase we find used; the space might accommodate ten thousand if it were as crowded as is said, but nobody could guess how many were packed into the side streets. The serenade was long, the demonstrations tumultuous, the cheers for Verdi every time he bowed to the mob became more frantic. We may rightly suppose the occasion to have been irresistible to most Romans: a national glory of the most distinctly Italian character, Verdi himself, archpriest of the opera, combined with a free public concert by the best available orchestra. We are not surprised at the size of the mob or at its unfettered enthusiasm; what does surprise us a little is that Verdi not only stayed up so late and displayed such good humor, but actually seems to have enjoyed, for once, the "personal exhibition" which he had long detested and often avoided with stubborn skill. His remark to Boito about a "new libretto right away" was jocular, of course, but at that hour of the morning (half-past one or thereabouts), and from Verdi of all men, it betrays a soaring vigor and contentment which were not his characteristic response to such ordeals.

Why? Well—it was for Rome. He did not go there often or stay there long, but he had a regard for the capital which was in a different dominion and climate from his feeling toward other cities or parts of Italy. It was originally planted in him by that early attachment to the heroic virtues of the Roman Republic and grew, with the painful rebirth of Italy, into a passionate desire for Rome as capital and as living symbol of the new nation. By his own fireside or at his own writing desk he lived through the struggles of Mazzini and Garibaldi, and we know how they dominated his mind.

All this formed his view of Rome, and although in other countries it might have seemed an irrelevant concern, it was much of Verdi's life and pervaded the rest. In no other country would there have been such an intimate, indissoluble and yet undefinable interpenetration of politics and music, or precisely, of politics and opera. Opera was the primary art of Italy in the nineteenth century for all classes and regions; it was in itself (even aside from Verdi's work) a force of union because it transcended the foolish frontiers of the petty states and became truly national. It was no longer, as it once had been, the toy of princes; no art presenting anything like its technical difficulties has ever been more truly popular, of and for the people. What Verdi wrote for the theatre dramas of the 1840's and 1850's made its way into the streets at once. That he was a national force—a force of the national revolution, that is, of the Risorgimento—no thoughtful Italian ever denied, and the vast demonstrations of that night in Rome put the seal upon a recognition which was already deep and permanent. Verdi himself could recall—and perhaps he was almost alone now in such memory of the past—how so many of the Roman first nights—Nabucco, I Lombardi, Ernani, coming there from Milan and Venice, or I Due Foscari and La Battaglia di Legnano, which were unveiled in Rome—had caused outbursts of popular excitement directly political or revolutionary. And his constant, pettifogging but maddening difficulties with the Papal censors: those, too, must have come back to him as quaint mementos of a Rome that had vanished. There were two categories of humanity in which any surprise might be experienced, and in Verdi's life many had been: one was the censorship as set up in such anxious little principalities as the Papal States and the kingdom of Naples, and the other was the opera audience on a night of agitation (such as a première) when there was a tingle of hysteria in the atmosphere. To the mind of a censor almost anything might be censorable, and to the emotions of such an audience even the simplest or most innocent musical composition might be a call to arms. Rome—like Venice —had always taken a Verdi first night as an excuse for trouble, and the old man could not refuse them now, at the very end, that modicum of tumult which was the people's joy.

There was one of his Roman first nights, and only one, in which neither censor nor public could find much political argument. That was *Il Trovatore*, which made its memorable appearance for the first time at the Apollo Theatre on January 19, 1853. The Papal officials had been squeamish about one thing only, the use of prayer or of sacred symbols on the stage, and although they looked with anxious care all through the monstrous libretto for a sign of revolutionary meaning, they could find none; nor could the Roman audience which cheered it on that night.

Il Trovatore probably gave Verdi his first taste of a purely musical give-and-take with the Roman public, and he seems not to have been greatly satisfied. The opera was immediately successful and has remained one of the most successful in existence, but he did not much like the stage interpreters in Rome or, as might be expected, the audience's choice of favorite sections. Those parts of the work which meant most to him, and mean most to us today, are the accents of human passion in the parts, particularly, of Azucena and Leonora, but what the first audiences, not only in Rome but throughout the world, relished above all were such pieces as the Anvil Chorus, a lapse from the stage of evolution to which Verdi had now come, and the tenor arias in which high C's (not written by Verdi) could be interpolated to arouse the galleries. The libretto of this opera is one of the very worst ever written, with a plot which contains so much complication of past events and mistaken identities that it has to be narrated, not acted on the stage. The verses are deplorable, abounding in an absurd Italian archaism, with inversions and elisions which all together go by the name of "librettoese," a language never spoken on this earth. Verdi had struggled with it—first with Cammarano, who died, and then with the eager and complaisant Piave—but to no avail. What attracted him to the original play, a Spanish effusion, was the breadth and simplicity of its motivations (filial love, mother love, along with romantic love and jealousy as always). These became so tangled up in the bad verses and bad scene-writing that even he despaired; and then the librettist, showing excellent judgment, died in the middle. The finished product is something which cannot be regarded as a whole, an integer; it has passages of utter vulgarity and banality, along with many pages of fluent beauty and dramatic expression; it is one of the mysteries of Verdi's entire creative contribution in that it touches such wide extremes. In this case he was not in a hurry; he actually took twenty months over this score, which is longer than he spent on any preceding opera—longer than he spent on the exquisite *Traviata*, which was its immediate successor. He was accused throughout Italy of "destroying *bel canto*" by the style of vocal writing adopted in *Il Trovatore*, in which cries of distress or pain sometimes interrupt the flow of singing; but his insistence upon the dramatic meaning of each character, each scene, had grown stronger with every year, until now he did not much care whether *bel canto* survived in its earlier form. The two women in *Il Trovatore* are wonderfully composed, and their moods are expressed in music which does, in fact, introduce a new kind of singing to Italian opera. Most of us nowadays, observing the monotonous *cantilena* which was the rule under all situations in earlier decades (particularly with Bellini and Donizetti), may think that it was high time.

The middle operas of Verdi, of which *Il Trovatore* is the middle one, have kept him alive in theatres which could never attempt the musical and dramatic difficulties of his later work. *Rigoletto* (Venice, 1851), the first of the trio, depends upon three good principal singers; the chorus and orchestra are modest, to say the least; the instrumentation, although at times wonderfully effective, makes no demands which a provincial opera house cannot easily meet. Its power is that of all Verdi's work, in the characterizations and in the theatrical situations; a blaze of talent expended upon human passions which every member of the audience can recognize (no abstractions, no symbols, no legends—suffering human beings in very plain, broad situations, visible and comprehensible in every part of the house). It is aesthetically superior to Victor Hugo's pretentious drama *Le Roi s'Amuse*, upon which it was based, but at the same time it benefits by a certain coherence or theatrical explicitness which it gets from Hugo's play. Its libretto, anyhow, as compared to that of *Il Trovatore*, seems almost a masterpiece, and a whole century has not dimmed its appeal to the oncoming generations. Hardly anything in it is as bad as the Anvil Chorus in *Il Trovatore*, although some of the writing for the Duke (particularly the first air) is meretricious; some of its dramatic intensities—as in the clown's outburst against the "*Cortigiani, vil razza dannata!*"—never can fail in a theatre.

Then, after *Il Trovatore*—very soon after—there comes *La Traviata*, in which most of the dross has suddenly been washed away and we have a work of art which approaches perfection within its own aesthetic limits —that is, within the frame of what it sets out to do and the instruments it uses for that purpose. There are lapses: in the second act, most of which surpasses criticism, the tenor has an air at the beginning and the baritone one at the end which we are forced to think Verdi merely put in for the sake of convention, because each of these voices had to be given an air, however feeble or vulgar it might be. The writing for the soprano has a true pathos which even Verdi never touched again, and others who have tried it—such as Massenet in his *Manon*—have shown in their attempts how difficult and rare it is, how substantially unattainable. In the middle trio of Verdi's operas every Verdian has a favorite— this is, in my experience, an unbroken rule—and to most of us nowadays —certainly to me—the favorite is *La Traviata*. Its intimacy, its departure from every canon of "grand" opera, its simplicity of treatment and unshrinking sentiment, make it, however slight its orchestral basis, a singularly modern work in feeling.

Rome had no chance to riot at the celebrated trio of middle works, even though *Rigoletto*'s meaning was so antimonarchical, but there was enough trouble over *Un Ballo in Maschera* to retrieve the omissions. It was the last time Verdi ever produced an opera in Rome (1859), and he had enough to contend with on that occasion to last him for a while. Starting with the court of Gustav III in Sweden (sixteenth-century costumes and settings), he ended up in a locale of colonial Boston, with a large number of changes in names, period, verses and meaning imposed by police censorship. His struggles left a bitterness from which he did not easily recover, and the passage of a hundred years has not made the mutilation any less pitiable, for *Un Ballo in Maschera* could have been (still is, in a great many pages) a beautiful work of music for the theatre. It was cursed from the start by a libretto which never could have been more than a farrago of nonsense, but in its stage scenes Verdi thought he had found something *musicabile*, something of which he could get the *tinta*. He saw it in Paris originally. That is, he saw an opera by Auber on this subject (entitled *Gustave III*) and thought he might put it to music. He reminds us of Beethoven on the first night of an opera by poor Ferdinando Paër; the composer of the work saw Beethoven and asked him how he liked it; Beethoven replied, "I like it very much and I think I'll set it to music." He did; it was *Fidelio*.

Ah, well, we can imagine Verdi thinking: if twenty men write twenty operas on the same subject, what survives, if anything does, will be the best. That was his frame of mind throughout. Such were the ways of the opera house (and even of the theatre itself) in the nineteenth century. There had been a certain amount of trouble with Victor Hugo—"a mercenary fellow at best, like all the French"—but by and large, if you were a composer, you took your subject where you found it, and the only author you had to pay was the "poet," so-called, who actually made the scenes and wrote the verses for the characters. The Maestro had a few fixed beliefs in such matters: "Time will judge," repeated in a dozen forms, was one of them, and "the box office is the only barometer" was another. He could tell one thing with absolute certainty, I believe (the certainty of a very old artist at his culminating point) : there never would be another *Falstaff*.

2   The passions of other days had dwindled away and may have been hard for Verdi to remember any more. Everything that was bound up with the idea of Rome had affected his life from childhood, but he had passed through so many modulations and transpositions by now that youth's dynamite must have seemed like a very small, far-off firecracker. What happened to Verdi was what happened to the greater number of the passionate Italian patriots (not only politicians, agitators and publicists, but also poets and engineers, professors and businessmen) who had struggled for freedom and unity. They got what they wanted: after 1871 Italy took its place among the nations. There followed what Croce has called "the anticlimax of success," a peculiarly bitter form of disillusionment. In this, too, Verdi was supremely characteristic of his generation and those just before and after it. He was disgusted with parliamentary procedures and political bargains, electoral subterfuges, the hypocrisy of public men, the dead-rot of bureaucracy, the general well-fed professionalism of government. He would not go near Rome and tried not to hear too much about it during those last decades. There was, obviously, a sharp decline in the intellectual or moral standards in public life after all the dreams came true, but at our safe distance in time we can reflect that the same thing has happened before and since. The struggle for freedom inspires great words and deeds; the achievement itself often belies them. In the United States, for instance, a galaxy of truly extraordinary men presided over the birth of the Republic—Washington, Jefferson, Hamilton, the two Adamses, Madison and Monroe were all alive at the same time, if not precisely of the same generation—although the population which produced them was very small. It seems the peculiar property of a struggle for freedom to throw up remarkable men, and in the cases where such struggles have succeeded the men appear to have, in retrospect, an uncanny adaptation to their historic function. How could the American Republic have found a more excellent personification of its special character and genius than in its very first government, its main (and permanent) tendencies stated by Hamilton and Jefferson, with Washington as their mediator? This was what the historic situation demanded, but in such cases it is a never ending source of wonder to see that the demand was satisfied.

Italy in the nineteenth century, a patchwork of petty tyrannies, some alien and some native, had little chance of making its way into the modern world as a nation without a powerful interaction of circumstances, among which leadership for the people was primary. After all, the word "Italy" was forbidden after the Congress of Vienna: Metternich had decreed that the word was only "a geographical expression," corresponding to no political or social reality. If you used the words "Italy" or "Italian" in a national sense, as if the congeries of little absolutisms constituted a unit, you were, ipso facto, a revolutionary. The Italians themselves had grown so used to this state of affairs that even when movements of insurrection did take place (as in 1821 and 1831) they were never national in scope: Naples might revolt against the Bourbons, or Rome against the Pope, but neither one cared about the other or about what might be happening in Venice or Turin.

To overcome this parochialism and give the Italian nation a *feeling* of unity—the indispensable platonic idea to precede and create the act—there were required indigenous forces called forth and directed by indigenous leaders. There had to be some kind of theory or principle which could arouse this national feeling: came Mazzini. There had to be a sword, a plume, an appeal to the imagination: Garibaldi. There had to be a practical wisdom, a genius for combination and government: Cavour.

Between the three of them, Mazzini, Garibaldi and Cavour created the Italian nation, and it is difficult to see how it could have been done without any one of the three. It is true, and always has been true since the Roman Empire, that the fate of Italy largely depends upon the maneuvers and rivalries of other European powers; in particular, France and Austria (or Germany). A national movement, such as Mazzini conceived in its abstract purity, could not have come to fruition, even with the aid of Garibaldi's sword, unless it had been directed by Cavour in such a way as to take every advantage of the political state of Europe in each successive phase, month by month and almost day by day. When we consider the whole process for, say, forty years, from 1831 to 1871, we are struck not only by its inevitability: inevitability is the truism history makes in retrospect. Once the grass has grown, says the German proverb, everybody knows he heard it growing. What strikes us most is not the resistless surge of these events but their direction under men so unlike. Mazzini and Cavour never understood each other in the least and were incapable of reconciliation; Garibaldi, who began with the one and worked with the other, was essentially different from both. Yet, divergent and even inimical as they were, they all directed the forces under their control into a momentum converging upon one single end, the creation of the united, independent Italian nation.

The awakening, the rebirth, the flowing forth again of springs long desiccated, the reflowering: these ideas are put into the single word Risorgimento (resurgence), which applies to the era during which Italy was created anew. The Risorgimento was, like the Renaissance, a social, political, literary and aesthetic awakening, a dawn of the Italian soul after a long night. In this remarkable confluence of life forces there were so many elements that it is difficult for the most expert historiographer to sort them all out; to weigh and measure is even more difficult; Italian scholarship will dwell upon the subject for ages to come. The directly political events, which are of chief interest to history as recorded, may not be—almost certainly are not—the decisive or determinant elements. They are more like results than causes, more like that which is borne on the stream than like the stream itself. Verdi was part of the stream itself.

The task of deciding how much he gave to the power of that stream was one he never would have undertaken: so far as I can tell, he never thought of it. He would have put it the other way around. He had done little or nothing for Italy, he would have said, and Italy had done everything for him. He had known Mazzini, Garibaldi and Cavour; he made music for Mazzini, bought rifles for Garibaldi, accepted the friendship of

Cavour and (for Cavour) the ordeal of public office. At every step of the way he had been with the Italian patriots, in all their gradations and even their contradictions. Their cause was so much a part of his life, so primary both in his conscious and in his subconscious, that it determined many of his comings and goings, his professional decisions and his practical arrangements, as well as his moods and temporary capacities, the character of his music even on the remotest subjects. When his very name became the symbol of Italian unity and freedom, as it did in 1859, it was only the recognition, by a quirk of the people's genius, of something which was fundamentally true: V.E.R.D.I., as they chalked it on the walls, was what they meant it to be, simply Italy.[1]

A poor boy growing up in a tiny village, cursed by the determination of genius, could have had no chance to develop any particular sense of "politics." He was too busy trying to earn his own way, from the age of ten, and to acquire the rudiments of his own chosen trade, the making of music. His parents, who could not read or write, must have been unmoved by the arrangements of Talleyrand, Castlereagh and Metternich at the Congress of Vienna, and yet these arrangements really governed much of Verdi's life. The village of Le Roncole, where he was born, and the town of Busseto, where he had his early training, were part of the French Empire in 1813: the "kingdom of Italy," which Napoleon had invented to keep Milan quiet, did not extend to the Parma regions, which were organized into the "*départements au-delà des Alpes.*" Verdi's birth certificate is in French—he was an "*enfant du sexe masculin*" with the names Joseph-Fortunin-François—and his baptismal record in Latin.

The Congress of Vienna, the Hundred Days, the Congress of Vienna again: the duchy of Parma, Piacenza and Custoza was made into an independent principality for Marie Louise of Austria, Napoleon's wife. A debate of some acerbity took place over this detail: the powers were not quite at one over what to do about the lady. Louis XVIII, with a salutary shudder at the very name of Bonaparte, objected to giving her anything, but the Czar Alexander I, mindful of the fact that she had been an empress and therefore belonged to his own exclusive profession, insisted. Louis XVIII ("la vieille pouffe," as his family called him) seems to have cared more about this detail than he did about things far more important, and when the combined power of Russia, Austria and England was too

[1] Debate in the Italian parliament in 1957 revealed that monarchist clubs of young men in the universities, vowed to the cause of the "young pretender," Victor Emmanuel, are now called "Verdi" clubs. The old acrostic of a century ago is now being used for a different purpose but it still means Vittorio Emanuele Rè d'Italia.

much for him, he stuck to one point: Marie Louise might have Parma if they all were bent upon it, but her son (Napoleon's son) could have no rights or status, could not inherit, was not involved. The child, the "King of Rome," was then made "duke of Reichstadt" by his grandfather, the Austrian Emperor—they handed out these honorifics lavishly at the time—and Marie Louise took Parma, Piacenza and Custoza for herself. She was an indolent, good-natured fat woman, who was quite content to live with her lovers (successive, not simultaneous) and her illegitimate children in the charming little Italian town which was the capital of her state. At the sound of a far-off musket she fled (as she had already done from Paris when she was Empress of the French) but cowardice, stupidity and self-indulgence were much too common to be called faults in her environment. She was Verdi's sovereign; he actually owed his musical education in Milan to her (the scholarship fund was largely hers); and when they met later on they seem to have been at least able to talk; we shall see that he even sent her his "Mameli hymn," with a dedication—the hymn he wrote at Mazzini's request, for the Italian patriots! Such contradictions at the time were endless.

Marie Louise, however, was only a minor wart upon the cancerous skin of Italy. The infamous Ferdinand had been restored in Naples—now the Two Sicilies—and after the Congress of Vienna the Bourbons could resume their depredations upon the inhabitants of the south with greater power and immunity than before. The Holy Alliance had as its principal purpose the suppression of popular movements—"revolutions"—wherever they might appear; particularly in Italy and Germany, but also in Spain, Hungary or anywhere else. Even the Bourbons of Naples could benefit by this carte blanche: if they got into trouble (as they did), they could always call upon the Austrians (as they did). The Papal States were fortified in absolutism, and the degree of tyranny depended upon the whims of individual popes. Minor Hapsburgs were given minor thrones here and there—Tuscany, Modena—and the Savoy family, which had not yet discovered that it was Italian, reigned over the conglomerate domain called Sardinia, part French and part Italian, which went from Nice to the Alps and over to the Milanese border, including (incidentally) the island of Sardinia. Lombardy and Venetia were combined as a "kingdom" with the Austrian emperor as its king.

That was Italy in Verdi's childhood and youth—a poverty-stricken peninsula chopped up into slave states to be exploited mainly by foreigners. There were no communications worth mentioning, and the Holy Alliance—Russia, Austria, Prussia and France, but in practice it meant only Austria, only Metternich—would never have permitted the construction of a road to link up these abject territories. Cholera and famine were frequent; banditry was extremely common everywhere except in the flattest plains—almost everywhere except in the Po valley where Verdi was born. If anybody today wishes to get an idea of what travel in Italy was like then, he might well read Washington Irving's *Tales of a Traveller* —so urbane and good-humored, so full of the joy of life, but nevertheless permitting a view, and rather a sharp view, of what it was like to get from, say, Florence to Rome. The louse, which has now practically disappeared from Italy, was at that time the chief part of the population, rivaled only by the flea. There was no drinking water, except from wells or springs, and the magnificent waterworks of the Romans had been plundered for their materials by the Popes or left to the attrition of the centuries. Baths were unknown except in palaces, where, in their heavy gold and marble, they were for ostentation rather than for use. The heavy odors of unwashed and diseased bodies were, it was hoped, disguised by even heavier scents, oils and powders. In the lower orders no such disguise was attempted, and foreign travelers made a practice of carrying aromatic salts constantly in the hand. Every traveler who could afford to do so took his own bedding with him, even his own linen and silver, for fear of disease or discomfort. Rich travelers, like Lord Byron, had not only a retinue of servants and guards but also enough material to furnish a house. The roads were the worst in Europe except for some parts of Spain and the Balkans. Many areas in the hills were without roads at all. The police, customs inspectors, frontier guards and other officials of the petty tyrannical states were often worse than the bandits. Bribery was not only common but universal, and it was necessary to be provided with gold coins, preferably of France or Austria, to satisy the guardians of the law.

Those who lived in these slave states made their earthly pilgrimage under a load which can hardly be imagined today. The gravamen was spiritual or psychological, more than material, and weighed equally heavily upon the subject whether he happened to live under a relatively enlightened despotism or under a bad one. The best states, so far as ordinary administration in peaceful times was concerned, no doubt were Parma (where Marie Louise had kept a good deal of Napoleonic law intact) and the Austrian kingdom of Lombardy-Venetia, in which there were established institutions and procedures of ancient date. The worst were Naples (or "the Two Sicilies"), an unrelieved despotism in which no institution could stand against the decree of power, and the Papal States, governed by priests alone (no civilians), in which the admixture of Roman law, Church law and the vagaries of the administrator left the subject without any clear idea of what the law might be. Verdi, as may be seen, was lucky to be born in the state of Parma and to spend his youth in the Austrian kingdom of Milan-Venice, but we can be absolutely sure that he did not think so. It was better to be a Parmesan or a Milanese than it was to be a Roman or a Neapolitan, but the overriding fact which obsessed every man of feeling during all those decades was that it was a terrible misfortune, civically speaking, to be an Italian at all.

It is to that, essentially, that I refer when I call these states tyrannies. They were not tyrannical in the systematic and relentless manner of modern times. Tyranny, such as we have known it in the twentieth century, when one man, a Hitler or a Stalin, can put millions of helpless subjects to death, was never known until our supremely mechanized century. The lazy, corrupt, dirty and incompetent governments of the little Italian states were not capable of efficient tyranny. They had appalling jails and kept them full; but the death sentence was not frequent and every public execution caused a wave of horror through the people.

No: tyranny on our advanced scale had not yet come into being anywhere. But there was no citizenship, there were no real rights, there was no rule of law, and the heavy load of which I have spoken—that which weighed upon every Italian from birth to death—consisted in being thus deprived of any element of civic pride or collective self-respect. Curiously enough the great tyrannies of the twentieth century have inculcated an enormous amount of pride into the masses they govern: anybody who has ever seen or talked to a soldier of the Third Reich or of the Red Army —not necessarily a Nazi or a Communist; merely a soldier—knows how successful this inoculation has been. It has succeeded so well that untold millions of Germans under Hitler, or of Russians under Stalin and his successors, have been substantially unaware of their own slavery, accepting as a patriotic duty the sacrifice of every conceivable freedom. Such people cannot move, think, speak or feel as they wish, but they are taught, and ostensibly believe, that they are lucky to move, think, speak and feel as their masters wish. It is this wholesale conversion of masses to a positive acceptance of their tyrants which distinguishes our efficient modern despotisms—that and their equally efficient methods of destroying dissent. For both processes, positive and negative, the mechanical powers of a very high technology are prerequisite.

Thus the words "tyranny" and "despotism" as they were used by the makers of modern Italy do not mean what we mean: they mean nothing so integral or so intense, nothing so methodical or efficacious, nothing so devilish. An absolute monarchy, responsible only to God—which is the meaning of "legitimacy," the one guiding principle of the Congress of Vienna and the Holy Alliance—might not be devilish at all; it might be enlightened and benevolent, promoting the welfare of its subjects by every convenient means, kindly rather than cruel and generous rather than exigent. It would still be a tyranny and a despotism as the men of that day, including Verdi, understood the terms, because it robbed the human being of his self-respect, his collective pride and his patriotism. Instead of a fatherland, it supplied a sovereign; and the two, although they may occasionally coincide by accident, are not at all the same thing.

The load of which I have spoken was, therefore, constant. It had to be borne in good times or bad, under good government or bad. What it did to the Italian character has been described, by Italians themselves, in language a foreigner might hesitate to use. After three hundred years of patchwork despotism there really was no such thing as an Italian any more. For some fifteen years Napoleon revived the idea and the expression, but Metternich abolished it again. The educated, who were very few outside the nobility and clergy, lived by the favor of princes. Italian character had become servile, flattering, obsequious: it may be seen in eighteenth-century literature, especially stage comedies, or in the shameless self-revelations of Casanova and Lorenzo da Ponte. The Italian *intrigants* in *Der Rosenkavalier* are a perfect example of this Italian character as it was known to the eighteenth century and the beginning of the nineteenth. The wandering Italian musician, teacher, secretary, "arranger" of festivals or designer of court regalia, the "*abbé*" (and an astonishing number of them took minor clerical orders, for practical advantages, thus becoming "*abbés*"), was a known figure in every country, familiar to the courts, princely houses and indeed every other establishment in which money was free and a good table was set. This pauperization of the Italian spirit galled whatever pride was left in Italy. A nation which had once been expressed in Dante and Michelangelo found itself represented in the eyes of western culture by fencing masters, dancing masters, music masters and court poets, not to speak of the less reputable professions. In the eighteenth century itself the revulsion against such a prolonged decadence began to grow stronger. It was at first difficult for writers, who generally find themselves expressing the thought of their time whether they so intend or not, to achieve enough independence of spirit to give this revulsion words. The writers of the seventeenth and eighteenth centuries had been organized into "academies," generally with some dilettante prince or other as their patron: such "academies," of which the one called Arcadia was the prototype, spent their time in the most elaborate neoclassical composition and recitation, poetastry of a rigidly involved metrical structure, a ridiculously high-flown vocabulary and a wealth of intricate "conceits," about as valuable to literature and life as an acrostic. It took courage to break away from a strait jacket which had been endured for three hundred years.

Giuseppe Parini in his odes and in the work called *Il Giorno*, a poem ostensibly composed for the instruction of a "young lord," had the honor of leading Italian literature out of Arcadia into a renewed and most fecund relationship to life. *Il Giorno*, a masterpiece of irony in its day, purports to tell the "young lord" how a nobleman's day is spent, and, in the course of so doing, contrasts that useless existence with the life of the working poor. It is divided into four parts (morning, noon, evening, night) of which the first appeared in 1763, and although those who read Parini for pleasure today may not be numerous, the historical importance of the work is great; we may well say that in 1763 the gates were opened. In the new freedom Vittorio Alfieri wrote his tragedies, most of them imbued with ideas of the French Revolution, and died (1803) before he had time to be disillusioned. To Italians at the beginning of the nineteenth century and even later, Alfieri seemed all fire beneath the ice, and if for our own part we perceive the ice rather more distinctly than the fire, it may be our fault. Certainly to his immediate successors Alfieri was not only precursor but awakener.

That, at all events, he certainly was. The early nineteenth century burgeoned with writers who, like Alfieri, vowed themselves to liberty and abominated the tyrants. When censorship became, so to speak, professional, when it acquired not only power but purpose and method, such work could no longer be performed on the stage. The writers after Alfieri were poets of the library—to which censorship did not yet apply itself so closely—or writers of novels and romances; they were almost all of them publicists as well, writers of pamphlets or essays or diatribes, not all of which could circulate freely. Italy probably owed most to Ugo Foscolo (1778–1827), the poet of *I Sepolcri*, although his exact contemporary, Vincenzo Monti, enjoyed much esteem at the time—more than most of us nowadays would give him either as a poet or as a man. The whole movement of Italian literature from Alfieri onward took more and more the tinge and sentiment of patriotic aspiration—that is, not merely toward freedom and against tyranny, but specifically for Italian freedom and, finally, for Italian unity and independence. By the time Verdi was a young man working in Milan, literature itself had become a part of the Risorgimento. The culminant figure of the process is Alessandro Manzoni (1785–1873), the author of *I Promessi Sposi*, whose hymns and odes, tragedies and prose writing, all impregnated with the spirit of the time, had profound effects in life as well as literature and thought. Verdi's worship of Manzoni (his own word for it) was not really different in *kind* from the feeling all Italy had; it was only more intense and, of course, more fruitful.

Foreigners contributed to the awakening very considerably indeed, through their influence upon these and other writers, even though their work could not reach the Italian public directly and was not yet translated. Goethe and Byron were first and strongest; they did not attain their power through being "lovers of Italy"—which they both were—but through being read at the right time by the right Italians (Manzoni, Mazzini). Goethe's influence, slower but more permanent than that of Byron, came first from his lofty ideas and only afterwards from his poetry, but it began to pervade Italian thought by the time the Risorgimento was in full development. It owed some of its curious power over Italians to a rather recondite circumstance of which most of them may not have been aware: it reminded them—that is, *Faust* reminded them—even though not at all explicitly, of the supreme Italian genius, Dante. There are no resemblances except sheer magnitude of vision and scope of attainment; otherwise the testament of the Middle Ages and the testament of modern man do not look much alike. But when an Italian is reminded, more or less willy-nilly, of Dante, and above all by a foreigner, an attention much deeper than ordinary ensues. Mazzini acknowledged that this somewhat nebulous affinity of Goethe to Dante was part of the German's power. With Byron it was "energy of expression," Mazzini thought, which commanded Italians who shared the same love of liberty—that and the poet's death at Missolonghi. We in our century know too much about Byron to believe, as Italians did in Verdi's youth, that he was heroically devoted to liberty or to anything else; that, however, is irrelevant if a whole generation of Italians sincerely thought otherwise.

There were other foreign elements in the fermentation. Obviously Voltaire and Rousseau had played their part; most of the Frenchmen of the Revolution (Condorcet, for example) had lasting effects on many Italian minds; Homer himself (in Monti's translation of the *Iliad*) aroused the freshest and most vigorous response in the 1820's and 1830's. What is vitally creative in this literary awakening, which preceded and helped to bring about the rebirth of Italy, is that everything contributed

to the same end, whether native or foreign: the end being the freedom
and unity of the Italian nation. You might find it difficult to find any
special pleading toward that end in Homer, and yet it was there. The
characteristic of such an age, stirring to thought and patriotic passion at
the same time, is that it reaches out for whatever it can get that will feed
its profoundest necessity and will contribute—in the moment of in-
candescence—toward the transition from thought to action. Thus Homer,
like Goethe and Byron, in the alchemy of time, helped to make the boys
volunteer for Garibaldi.

For my own part, I find the purest and truest expression of the feeling
which created the Risorgimento not in any of these writers, although it
is the historic fact that they did a great deal to create it. One reason why
I could never be a historian is that written history, if it is to have merit,
must give due weight to each several circumstance, element and fact,
whether the historian in the depths of his being feels it to be true or not.
Thus it must be said that Parini, Alfieri, Foscolo and Manzoni were the
great awakeners of the Italian soul. It is the *historic* fact. The influence
of Byron is another historic fact. But I cannot myself feel in any of these
writers the terrible, irresistible appeal, the appeal of the profound patriotic despair, which would make me shoulder a musket and trudge off
to the wars. That I find in one and one only, Leopardi. Perhaps it is
because he was so much the greatest poet of the age, perhaps because I am
not Italian and live a century and a quarter too late for the others, but
Leopardi alone, out of that period of travail, seems to cry down the
century with a voice to which it would be impossible not to respond.
Given some knowledge of the language and the circumstances, some
slight feeling for poetry and truth, nobody could resist it. I am sure that
if I had been an Italian youth in, say, 1848, and had just read the first of
Leopardi's *Canti* for the first or the fiftieth time, I would have run barefoot over the mountains to the nearest recruiting station for Garibaldi.

The *Canti* of Leopardi were published for the first time in Florence in
1831, a time of revolution, and they must have spoken to the youth of
Italy (or its most sensitive members) as nothing had done since Dante.
Indeed it is difficult to imagine how, at any time or place, a more penetrat-
ing melancholy could be expressed in words. This, I say, is the feeling
which gives birth to the Risorgimento—the cry of sorrow at the downfall of Italy. The first *Canto* contains by implication, as it winds its
majestic way toward Thermopylae and Simonides, that further cry essential to the Risorgimento: awake, take arms, die if you must, that
Italy may live again!

By implication, that is—translated into the terms of Simonides at Thermopylae—because a direct call to arms could never have been printed or distributed. It is direct enough as it is (indeed, one could hardly bear more), and the wonder in our minds is that it could be printed and distributed at all.

We might well pause to contemplate that beautiful poem—so beautiful that it almost breaks the heart for a moment. It is impossible to know Verdi without knowing the Risorgimento, and for me, as I suspect for many or most others, the literature which produced or helped to produce the Risorgimento is here at its freshest. A great deal which aroused storms of emotion in Italy during the 1830's and 1840's is dead and forgotten now. Leopardi, because he was a great poet and sang from the depths of his being, has survived all else, every change and whim of fashion, every vagary of time. The first three of the *Canti*, the patriotic ones, are early work; they were in fact written at Recanati, in his father's house, in 1822, although the first collection did not appear until nine years later. As early work they naturally contain some leftover baggage (elisions, inversions, personifications) from preceding poets, but there can be no doubt, from the very first lines, that an authentic voice is heard at last, a true immortal.

The second of the *Canti* is "On the Monument to Dante Being Prepared in Florence," and the third is addressed "To Angelo Mai, when he had found the books of Cicero *On the Republic*." Their subjects evoke the same mood as the first, although perhaps not quite the same exaltation. All were written at about the same time, in or just after the poet's twentieth year when the awareness of life had begun to press in upon him—of his own misfortunes and those of his country. His life was short and miserable, oppressed not only by physical illness but by an ugliness which he felt as deformity; like Keats, he seems to have thought that his name was "writ in water"; and yet our own time has found in him what (unfortunately) we can no longer discern in any of his contemporaries, a great, permanent, irresistible world-poet.

The greater part of Leopardi's work in verse and prose has nothing to do with the Risorgimento. That is, his subjects are in the main those of lyric poets since time began—youth, love, death, the setting of the moon, a shepherd on a hill, a funereal stele. One of his *Canti* is actually called "Risorgimento," without reference to the national movement: the word was in the air in those days and was most variously applied. Only the first three *Canti* are direct in their attack upon patriotic emotion, but they are so direct (the unbearable lament followed by the thrilling call to arms) that they must have been felt like an electric shock by all Italians who could read.

There were, however, not many Italians who could read, and those who possessed that accomplishment were no more secure in their taste than readers before or since. The shock administered by Leopardi's genius wore off; it must have done so, or his contemporaries would not have been content to admire so many of his inferiors. Probably the most lasting effect of Leopardi's poetry on the creation of Italy was the indirect one, that which is the inevitable effect of all greatness: Italians were proud that one among them could sing to the stars, and that pride (valuable to any nation) could help to stiffen the backs that had once been so servile. The revival of pride in Dante—as shown by the project of a monument in Florence, the subject of the second Canto of Leopardi—served the same purpose even among those who did not actually read Dante.

Any thoughtful observer of human events must have been struck, over and over again, by the fact that the direct appeal to passion in the midst of turmoil is most effectively made by inferior talents. What you want to stir the mass emotion in time of crisis is Kipling, not Shakespeare— John Philip Sousa, not Beethoven. (I have taken extremely respectable examples, since both Kipling and Sousa were masters in their own fields, but at least the distinction is clear.)

It was so in the Risorgimento in Italy. Leopardi may have galvanized many sensitive thinkers and dreamers who kept their own counsel; he may have created individual heroes for the barricades; but he could not bring to bear any direct power on the masses (like that of La Marseillaise). No doubt he would have fled from any such thing—and to be sure, it would be hard to think of the poor little count with his twisted body up before a mass meeting. Yet, as could be guessed, many "poets" did exercise direct power on the people in this period and even, occasionally, in the turmoil of the market place—what we call today a mass meeting. Gabriele Rossetti—the Neapolitan, whose long exile in London afterwards produced, among other works, his son Dante Gabriel, the Pre-Raphaelite—was one of these: in 1821 in Naples he was a revolutionary figure and once, by improvising a poem before an indignant mob, actually saved Ferdinand I from death or worse. His poetry was read thoughout Italy, and in Naples, at least, it had direct result in action. It is some of the most wretched patriotic doggerel ever strung together: today it is indistinguishable from parody. The reprinting of Rossetti's work in Italy (after freedom and unity) was undertaken by no less a littérateur than Carducci himself, probably for historical rather than aesthetic reasons, but it went unread and is totally forgotten. I know it only from the excerpts given by De Sanctis in his lectures at the University of Naples in the 1870's (they come in the volume called *Mazzini e la Scuola democratica*), and in citing his examples De Sanctis confesses that not even he has been able to plow through all of it. Yet, in its time— which was also Leopardi's time—this jingler-jangler had a strong response from the feelings of the people and thus helped to set his country free.

On a higher level, from any literary point of view, is Giovanni Berchet (1783–1851), greatly admired by Mazzini, some of whose poems in patriotic vein swept Italy more decisively, so far as the general reading public was concerned, than those of Leopardi. Berchet began and ended as a translator and imitator—he seems to have been easily influenced by any superior talent, first Parini and then Foscolo—but he had a brief moment, just when he went into exile in 1821, when a flame of true poetry was somehow ignited. There are seven or eight of these inspired pieces hurled by the poet from London, where he was earning his living by keeping up the mercantile correspondence of an Italian importer: they reached Italy and were read by everybody who could read. Three or four of them, De Sanctis thinks, are "immortal." In 1831 when revolution broke out again in Modena and Bologna—it was a year of many revolutions, but these two were Berchet's incentive—he wrote the hymn "All' armi! All' armi!" which immediately became known to every Italian and still is. It was his attempt at a *Marseillaise*, and to some extent it did serve its purpose, but it has not by any means the youthful vigor and freshness, the utter naïveté of the French prototype.

No more, and no matter. There were many writers. They reached the highest level with Leopardi, whose immediate effect was upon individuals rather than upon crowds; they taught Italians not only to feel their woes and grasp for arms to set them right, but first of all they taught (uniformly, every single one of them good and bad) the essential thing, which was the existence of an Italian nationality. That was what was new in the early nineteenth century and led inevitably to action, after three centuries of a singularly dark night. I have been at pains to show that some of the worst writers had the most direct influence; and I say so, in part, because Verdi himself was to go through a singular exemplification of the general truth. It was not his best work, but as a rule his worst, which aroused the people to patriotic enthusiasm. At his best he was Leopardi, at his worst almost Rossetti: like all these writers, he was a son of Italy, but the gods seem to have made him at birth a somewhat more comprehensive exemplar—a more "total" Italian—than any other.

3 "Men of action" have a theoretical difference from writers in that they are supposed to convert thought into deed, rather than word. It is their historic function, and by its accomplishment we know them. Most of them are, however, writers as well; in the Italian national movement they all were. The conditions of Italy did not permit action except under favorable circumstances as they occurred from time to time. Between these times the word, spoken or written, was the instrument of the Risorgimento. Mazzini, Garibaldi, Cavour—all were writers, the last-named under protest; all were also readers and knew their Dante and Leopardi as well as they did the current situations with which they dealt.

There were earlier revulsions than those of the writers, more primitive revolts than those of the "men of action." These are the half-expressed but instinctive movements, sometimes savage and cruel, always uncertain of their direction, which shook Italy in the early nineteenth century. Sometimes they remind us of those purely emotional outbreaks of poor against rich, downtrodden against oppressor, of which the Jacquerie in France and the Sicilian Vespers at Palermo were examples in a darker age. All Italy was in turmoil after the Napoleonic period, and the revolutions of 1821 (in Naples and Piedmont, with a velleity in Lombardy which the Austrians nipped in the bud) and 1831 (almost everywhere) were expressions first of all of that turbulent mood of the time, the *Zeitgeist*. We know that few of the men who rebelled against their oppressors in those days had any clear notion of what they wanted. They wanted to get rid of the Austrians (or the grand duke or the Pope) and create some kind of government by "constitution," by representatives of the people; they wanted most of all to get rid of the tax collector, the recruiting agent, the jailers and spies and police who ruled them; they wanted to lead better lives; they wanted "freedom." It was in both cases, 1821 and 1831, a violation of common sense to suppose that they could possibly obtain a result. The Congress of Vienna had established legitimacy as the only principle for government anywhere, and each revolution against a "legitimate" absolute monarch was bound to be opposed by the concert of powers. The Holy Alliance, by origin a mystical declaration on the part of the Czar Alexander I, became in the clever hands of Metternich a practical weapon for the suppression of any popular movement anywhere on the continent. It was signed at first by Russia, Prussia and Austria, but Louis XVIII, attracted more to its practical than to its mystical aspects, also signed and in fact used French troops to crush the Spanish revolution of 1821. How could a popular revolt in, say, Modena, against a petty Hapsburg despot, or in Rome or Bologna against the Pope, or in Naples against the Bourbons, have a chance against such power? Metternich already had strong Austrian garrisons not only in territory governed by Austria (the "kingdom of Lombardy-Venetia") but also at other points deeper in the peninsula—Piacenza, for example. It was easy for him to move his troops up and down. The Italian rebels were not only unorganized, inexperienced, without either military or political skills, but they actually possessed no force: mobs alone, unarmed, brought about most of their temporary successes, and whenever it came to actual fighting they ceased to exist. There was remarkably little combat, in any modern sense, either in 1821 or 1831. Few shots were fired and hardly anybody hurt. The killing came afterward! As a result of their military helplessness, their lack of organized force, the rebel elements in some areas, particularly in the Papal States, fell back upon political assassination as a weapon and also—at given times and places—took refuge in ordinary banditry.

The worst weakness of the popular revolts was their intense localism. In the height of the struggle the men of Bologna had not the faintest notion of what was going on in Milan and did not care. They did not call themselves "Italians," even. They revolted for certain abstractions (freedom chiefly), and in the name of the "people," but never tried to link up what they were doing, or trying to do, with the efforts of others elsewhere. Even in 1831, when a much greater degree of political literacy had come into being, Rome was still only Rome and Naples only Naples. There were no communications; the dialects—still strong now—were then practically separate languages; it was child's play for Metternich to defeat these isolated outbursts.

Giuseppe Mazzini was a boy in Genoa when the revolution of 1821 took place. He was going along the street one night with his mother and father (a doctor) when a gaunt specter came out of a shadow and asked for money to help the victims of the repression. His father (a republican by firm conviction) gave money and explained why. On another occasion, or perhaps several other occasions, the boy (then sixteen) saw the exiles and refugees piling onto the boats to go away to safety. He was then not much aware of the meaning of such things, but soon, when he went to the University of Genoa, he found out. The students were then, as always, more easily stirred than others, and the *Carboneria* found a good many recruits among them. In 1827, when he was twenty-two and a student of law, Mazzini joined the Carboneria.

This was a secret society with some vague resemblance to freemasonry; it had rituals, initiations, vows to secrecy and pledges to high ideals. There were secret societies all over Italy at this period and for decades before and after. Some were vowed to freedom and some to the established order (i.e., repression). The most famous were the Carboneria, whose members were called Carbonari, and the Santa Fede, whose members were Sanfedisti. They were, in their way, a symptom of the unrest of the whole country, the "cooking soul of the people," as Hitler called it (kochende Volksseele). The Sanfedisti were strong in Naples, Calabria, Abruzzo, Puglia, where in the reaction after 1821 they wreaked horrible vengeances with the blessing of the Church; the Carbonari were strong (or weak, whichever it might be called) all over Italy, which is to say that they had members everywhere. They were condemned by the Church and eventually excommunicated—not only the members of the society, but any other person who refused to give evidence or information against such members. Excommunication was a powerful weapon in politics in those days because many members of any family (the mother, sometimes the father, inevitably the grandmother, perhaps the sister) could be paralyzed by fear of it. What it meant in practice was that a mother was excluded from all the sacraments of the church, and must burn in hell forever, if she did not give over her son to be hanged by the Austrian or the Pope. The boys did not care, and joined the Carboneria by the hundreds of thousands, and yet the so-called "spiritual" weapons brought great misery to the country at large and untold confusion to the minds of the people.

These rough-and-ready improvisations, such as the Carboneria, could not really do much for Italy, and obviously from the start they were riddled by police spies and agents for the various despotisms. Mazzini at twenty-five was given a salutary lesson in such matters. The brotherhood charged him (a great honor) with initiating a new French member. While he was going through the rigmarole with the novice, a head was stuck through a curtain in the room; he was told that this was a "brother"— in itself also an honor, since they tried not to know one another. Well— the "new member" was a spy and the "brother" who stuck his head into the room was a policeman. Mazzini was sentenced to the fortress of Savona, where he had some time to think it over. He might have suffered worse—even death—except that the case against him reposed only upon the evidence of the policeman; the "novice"—the French spy—had fled.

The *Carboneria* was finished for him, and, as it happened, for Italy. It only lingered on in the Papal States for a while because that was where it was most savagely persecuted and, with a natural human response, it refused to die. Actually, its myriad absurdities had made it useless; if it served a purpose, aside from that of exhibiting—as all the secret societies did—a true unrest in the Italian people, that purpose was the accidental one brought about by its geographic extent. It had so many branches in so many Italian satrapies that it became an unconscious instrument, however feeble, toward the making of a nation.

Mazzini started upon his first exile—on release from Savona—with some food for thought, but he was not a man to digest slowly. From Marseilles in 1831—at the age of twenty-five—he launched his manifesto to all parts of Italy in the name of a new secret society, a new vow, more solemn and comprehensive than any before: this was *La Giovine Italia*. In substance he called upon the entire youth of Italy, regardless of where it might find itself, to unite for freedom and independence. The appeal was made to them as *Italians* and for *Italy*: in this respect it had no precursor or parallel. Years were to pass, indeed, before the words "Italy" and "Italian" could be officially used in a gathering of the powers of Europe: Cavour, who could not employ such words himself as the prime minister of a state concerned, exercised every talent he possessed (up to, I think, hypnotism and telepathy) to get somebody else to use them. So far as I can find out it was Count Walewski, Napoleon III's foreign minister—bastard of Napoleon I by Marie Walewska—who first said the word "Italy" out loud in public before representatives of the great powers, on April 8, 1856, in Paris. From the Congress of Vienna until that Congress of Paris (i.e., from 1815 to 1856) any use of the word "Italy" in public or in diplomacy was not only avoided but, in effect, forbidden. By the doctrine of the Holy Alliance Italy did not exist, and to imply that it did was an insult to Austria, Prussia and Russia, to the principle of legitimacy and, hence, to Almighty God. (Almighty God was the cornerstone of the Holy Alliance and is most favorably mentioned in the text of it.)

Mazzini in 1831, just twenty-five years before the word "Italy" was heard in diplomacy, introduced the idea of the Italian nation. *La Giovine Italia!* Young Italy. From the outset he had a few governing ideas which he never abandoned. *Dio e il popolo!*—*Unità e indipendenza!*—*Pensiero e azione.* God and the People; Unity and Independence; Thought and Action. He discarded the "liberalism" of his predecessors and sought a democracy, instead, which should not condescend to the inhabitants of the country or bestow benefits upon them, but involve them in their own fate. He had a wholly new definition of education, which was that the people must learn by doing—thus, of course, destroying the argument that the people were not sufficiently educated to govern themselves. In his endless juggling with the words "for the people, by the people, through the people, with the people"—there are variants and discussions of all these phrases—he was working toward the triad of Lincoln in the Gettysburg Address, the ideal American statement of democracy as a theory of government; that is, "government of the people, by the people, for the people." It is quite likely that Lincoln, well aware of the Italian struggle, had read Mazzini's work. (He offered Garibaldi an army in the American Civil War, as we shall see in due course.) If his triad came from Mazzini's ideas it would be only natural, since there was a kinship of thought between them and Mazzini had expressed himself in a kindred way.

We are all so jaded nowadays by doctrine of every kind that we may not realize how new this was, not only for Italy but for the world. "Liberalism" and "democracy" are concepts so different that they might even be called opposite. Everything, up to Mazzini, had been "for the people." Even the despots, when they were able to think or speak coherently, professed to be "for the people," governing for the good of the people. The Age of Enlightenment had made much of such liberalism even before the French Revolution: Voltaire's friends, Catherine II of Russia and Frederick II of Prussia, were "enlightened" despots, and certainly Joseph, the son of Maria Theresa, was not only enlightened but positively benevolent. The distinction Mazzini made between liberalism and democracy was this: both were "for the people," but liberalism operated *without* the people and sometimes *against* them. Democracy, in Mazzini's view, would govern *with* the people—"everything with and for the people" was another of his successful formulae.

Similarly, he discarded all the older generation of liberal thought from the time of the French Revolution, while paying due respect to its historical value. For the future, he maintained, "Liberty, equality, fraternity" were not to be considered as ends, but as means. Liberty was not the goal; it was a means to the goal. Democracy was the goal, first of the nation and then of all humanity. The nation, free, united and independent, was, however, indispensable, and once it had been achieved there could then follow the larger association of all humanity. For the immediate purpose of creating the nation he would accept the aid of liberals, including even—occasionally—princes, although he was scornful of the liberal naïveté which had been so deceived in them in 1821. The heirs of the northern and southern thrones, Piedmont (or Sardinia) and Naples (or the Two Sicilies), had enjoyed the confidence of the liberal revolutionaries and had betrayed them; was not this a clear example of how princes could be trusted?

All of these concepts came flooding out from Mazzini in France and reached, almost at once, an important element of Italian youth from the Alps to Sicily. He wanted only youth, and said so; the older men were no good; their ideas were no longer applicable. In the universities the new society, Young Italy, made such rapid progress that it soon drove out the old ones. It probably absorbed a good many *Carbonari* into its ranks, as well as other secret brotherhoods. It was at once more serious, more intellectual and more adult than its predecessors (rituals and initiations were abandoned; the Ku Klux Klan aspect, so to speak, vanished). It taught its members to think in terms of the whole nation, but to be prepared at any propitious moment to pass from thought to action; thought was incomplete without action, according to Mazzini. Thus Young Italy had to be, under the conditions then existing, a society of conspirators, waiting for the moment to act.

A later development of Mazzini's system of ideas, the mystical or prophetic superstructure suggested in the formula "God and the People," played little part in the 1830's when Young Italy was coming into existence. Mazzini's religious feeling was powerful but the form it takes hardly seems different, to us anyhow, from Protestantism. It postulates a direct relationship between man and God, with no intermediaries, and if this is not the central doctrine of Protestantism, what is? Yet Mazzini professed to abhor Protestantism as a system of thought, and above all the sectarianism in which it resulted. He obviously thought—and here the irrational begins—that the new religion of God and humanity must come from Rome; must, in a sense, be the new form of Catholicism or the substitute for it: only "the Eternal City," he believed, could so enlighten the world. Why? He gives no plain, comprehensible reason, and in fact he had none to give. It was an ultimate goal, in effect a world religion, and like most of his ultimate goals it remained in words only. Italians, no matter how anticlerical or how bitterly opposed to the temporal rule of the Church over Italian territory, never ceased to be Catholics, and one of the most agonizing experiences of the whole Risorgimento was the Church's refusal of the sacraments to its political opponents (whenever and wherever it was possible to refuse them; not always).

In all the immediate part of his teaching Mazzini had an instant and prolonged success. Young Italy was a reality; it ignited a great fire. For a good many years in the 1830's and 1840's the governing cliques at the various Italian courts did not understand this. They underrated Mazzini woefully; even Cavour seems to have thought him a half-cracked fanatic; they even kept on talking about the *"Carbonari"* long after those predecessors had ceased to exist or had been absorbed into Young Italy. Mazzini was a superb agitator, one of the most skillful in a century which abounded in them. He not only poured out the pamphlets in great quantity, with irresistible fervor and excitement, but he knew how to keep his followers in a state of expectation; they never fell asleep; they expected the revolution to break out any night or any morning. And he saw to it that some kind of revolution did break out every now and then, just to feed the fires. He did not really care whether it succeeded or not—indeed it is difficult to avoid the conclusion that in many of these cases he was assured in advance that they must fail. He believed in force. So did everybody else of his time. But he believed in something else even more than in force, which was *martyrdom*. He was firmly convinced that successive martyrdoms were historically necessary in order to awaken the Italians to the necessity of fighting for their existence. The martyrdom principle—"the blood of the martyrs is the seed of the Church"—was expressed by him most forcibly in many of his pamphlets, open letters and, as we may call them, encyclicals, those documents which circulated secretly from hand to hand throughout the Italian peninsula. Consequently he instigated many small, abortive and hopeless uprisings in which a few young men were killed and others subsequently became martyrs at the hands of the police, ever more active and more cruelly repressive in reaction. There is no doubt that the martyrs did stir up patriotic resentments and a determination to avenge them; but humane men of whatever category were inclined to condemn, if they understood, and to pity, when they did not understand, the cold-bloodedness with which martyrs were thus fabricated. (Cavour, at a much later date when Mazzini was still making martyrs, refers to the little uprising of June 29, 1857, as follows: "Mazzini has just made one of his insane enterprises in Genoa.")

Mazzini could call upon Young Italy for heroism and for martyrdom because the country knew he was, in his purity, poverty and devotion, a kind of hero himself; he was always ready to risk his own life and thus become a super-martyr, which, indeed, was narrowly avoided on several occasions. But the fatal defect of his entire system of thought as well as of his intellectual and moral character was that he was incapable of any change, any modification or accommodation to reality. Once he had stated a principle it was as fixed as the laws of the Medes. Revision, amendment, reconsideration, were utterly beyond him. He could learn nothing, it seems, after about the age of thirty. Even in his literary culture, as De Sanctis has pointed out, what he drew upon in his old age was what he had acquired in youth. Naturally the power of such a system as his arose from its few great fructifying principles when they were fresh, especially from the formulae in which they were capsuled. These few great principles, combined with skill as an agitator and courage as a conspirator, made Mazzini into a magical legend for twenty years. During the 1830's and 1840's no other name meant the same to the people. However, any reiteration may become a little wearying after twenty years. With the fall of his Roman Republic, he, too, fell, and the rest of his life is a decline from that height. He quarreled with anybody who deviated in the slightest from his own fixed principles—even with Garibaldi!—and, like all doctrinaires, found that life had eventually passed beyond him. In his later enterprises on the European scale he tried at one time to obtain leadership in the Socialist International, to be defeated very decisively by Karl Marx; only in the vague utopian field of international fellowship as between the exiles of Poland, Hungary and other countries—he, of course, representing the true Italy—he found some opportunity still to speak and write. Before he died all of the immediate part of his own program (unity and independence, at least) had been carried out by other men in ways of which he did not approve. Cavour, his bête noire, was the primary artisan of modern Italy, aided and abetted by Garibaldi, and there was a king—detestable word!—at the head of Mazzini's republic: a king, moreover, from the thrice-perjured and abhorrent house of Savoy.

Garibaldi was also born under the Savoy monarchy—at Nice, one of the oldest parts of its dominions—and had, like Mazzini, every reason to detest it. (We must repeat once more that the Savoy family was only another foreign oppressor in Italy for many centuries, and to Mazzini and Garibaldi no different from the Hapsburgs or Bourbons.) Garibaldi's mother wanted him to be a priest—which may account for his vehement language about priests to the end of his days—but he felt it more congenial to run away to sea. He was just two years younger than Mazzini (1805 and 1807 were the dates of their birth); he was three years older than Cavour, six years older than Verdi. They were all products of the same decade—subjects of Napoleon Bonaparte—and thus senior by a few years to the prince who was the chief single beneficiary of the struggle for freedom, Victor Emmanuel II of Savoy.

It was inevitable that a young man of Garibaldi's nature should have joined, first, the *Carboneria*, which was strong on the Genoa waterfront, and afterward Young Italy. Ardent, impulsive, handsome, intelligent, overflowing with words, ideas, plans, schemes and radiant possibilities, he had a galvanic effect upon other young men capable of understanding his aspiration, and even, sometimes, upon those who did not understand. (He often declared later that he had been unable to make real headway with the peasantry; they were terrified of their priests, he said; but the young men of the cities, university students, sailors, workmen, middle-class intellectuals and the like were susceptible to his influence from the beginning.)

In 1833, when he was twenty-six, his ship touched at Marseilles and he met Mazzini. The conversations between these two obscure, power-less youths must have contained a good deal more fire and fury than was characteristic of the time; after 1830 France was governed by the "liberal" monarchy of Louis Philippe, and Europe on the surface was tranquil. Mazzini and Garibaldi had in common the great, fundamental principles and each could recognize in the other the presence of that kind of deter-mination which refuses to be discouraged by defeat. Mazzini was now thoroughly—and permanently—disgusted with the house of Savoy and was set upon creating a revolution in its dominions, perhaps because it was his homeland (and Garibaldi's) but more probably because it was most accessible of all the Italian states by land and sea.

Mazzini had made one effort to call upon the head of that house for sympathetic action two years before. This was in his celebrated "Letter to Charles Albert," which circulated secretly all over Italy for a long time thereafter. (Many a student and workman suffered imprisonment for being found in possession of that letter.)

Charles Albert was the princeling who had been the hope of the Car-bonari during the confused and misdirected uprising of 1821. He was actually supposed, by most of them, to be a member of their secret so-ciety; it is now clear that this was never the case, although as late as the early 1870's (after Italy was united and free) such an authority as De Sanctis still said so in his lectures at the University of Naples. In 1820 Charles Albert was an ambitious and bigoted, but wavering and capri-cious prince of the cadet branch of the Savoy family (Savoie-Carignan). In the family chart, if you trace it back far enough, his ancestor Thomas of Savoy, first prince of Carignan, was own brother to Victor Amadeus I

(d. 1637), who was married to Christine de France, "Madame Royale," daughter of Henri IV and sister of Louis XIII. In fact, the Carignan branch set out on its career in fine style by opposing this lady as regent of the Savoy dominions when her husband died, and Thomas, with his brother Maurice (the cardinal), made a civil war against her: the war, no less, of the "*principisti*" against the "*madamisti.*" The "*madamisti*" won, of course (is this not a rule?), and the Carignan branch of the house of Savoy was never distinguished by wealth thereafter. One of their members (a cadet from a cadet branch) went penniless to Vienna and made up for the poverty of all his relatives: this was the great "Austrian" military commander, Prince Eugène.

But now, by the whim of fortune, the cadet branch was about to inherit everything from Nice to the Alps, including Genoa and Liguria as well as the older French dominions and Piedmont. The senior branch of the family died out; the last three of its kings were bachelor brothers (Charles Emmanuel IV, Victor Emmanuel I and Charles Félix), who successively abdicated (1802, 1821 and 1831), after reigns of no distinction or benefit to their country. They were stubborn, old-fashioned absolutists who kept the "Spanish etiquette" in their court at Turin, and after the downfall of Napoleon, when they were restored to their dominions, they operated on a rule book of 1798 that they had kept in their possession during their "exile" to Sardinia. (The name of their mottled kingdom was, and had been since 1720, Sardinia; but that poverty-stricken island saw its princes very seldom except when they were in need of refuge.)

Now (1831) Charles Albert of Carignan became king. The legend of his "liberalism" died hard, although he had done everything possible for ten years to discourage it. He had broken his oath in both directions a number of times, and perhaps the "liberals"—which in these surroundings was a portmanteau word meaning almost everybody except the king, clergy and highest nobility—thought that he only meant half his treachery, the other half. The house of Savoy itself distrusted him, and Charles Félix obliged him to sign a document swearing that he would never change any of the fundamental laws of the state; at this price (in 1823) he was permitted to go on being heir presumptive to the throne. It hardly needs to be said that it was Charles Albert, who had broken his word so many times, who finally granted the constitution (1848). Few princes have so deserved distrust and received it.

Mazzini, like most of contemporary Europe, thought the accession of Charles Albert might bring a change. It was his one failing in the direction of princes or monarchy. He composed the famous "Letter to Charles Albert" in good faith, or so he always maintained; in it he calls upon that new sovereign to take up the great crusade for the union of Italy and to become its king.

King of Italy! It might have bedazzled a younger or stronger man. What Charles Albert did was to make an alliance with Austria immediately after his accession and, in accordance with the principles of Metternich, to embark upon a reactionary course which soon filled the jails of his dominions. Those who participated in the uprising of 1831 felt a repressive violence which in this part of Italy (the relatively enlightened and prosperous northwest, half of it French) had never been known before. The police were given new powers, the tribunals were urged to haste, and the death sentence was used for political offenses more extensively than the conscience of the period could condone—although not, of course, on the scale of our century.

Mazzini thus had every reason to return to his natural detestation of the house of Savoy and to conspire against it. If we had not so many assurances to the contrary, we might even suppose that he had written the "Letter to Charles Albert" as a sort of trap, to elicit the response it received. At all events he never again deviated a hair's-breadth from his opposition to all monarchy and, in especial fervor, to the house of Savoy.

The conspiracy of 1833 provided for an invasion of Savoy from France and for an uprising in Genoa, the latter to be led by Garibaldi among others. A conspiracy in the army, which was to have exploded into action with these other plans, was discovered too soon (April, 1833) and was followed by repression of great severity. The "invasion" of Savoy by a column of just over a thousand men, *Mazzinisti* of one kind or another, not all of them Italians, was quickly defeated by the troops of Charles Albert. The insurrection in Genoa—Garibaldi's—never even took place (February, 1834). It was his first experience of a well-known phenomenon in such activities: he sprang to arms and found himself alone.

He was able to get away ahead of the police and stopped first in France before making his way to Brazil. He was condemned to death "in contumacy," as they called it, by the courts of Charles Albert; so was Mazzini. In fact Mazzini was condemned to death twice—first for the abortive insurrection in the army and second for the "invasion" of Savoy.

Garibaldi in Brazil developed into an organizer and leader among the Italians, and his dutiful letters to Mazzini reporting progress have been (some of them) preserved and published. It was not his natural work, however, and when the "Republic of Rio Grande" rebelled against the

Brazilian Empire, he discovered the most notable of his talents, that as guerrilla leader in rough country under difficult conditions. Later on, in Uruguay, he had further experience of the same kind, and by the time the events of 1848 called him back to Italy he was a hardened warrior of one distinct variety—the variety, as it happened, which was most needed in his native hills.

The third of our "men of action," Cavour, came to his political maturity also in the momentous year 1848, although he was not prime minister until three years later. For each of these three men, although quite differently, 1848–1849 were years of terrible trial and suffering, as they were for most Italians of heart and mind; it was both the high and the low point of the national movement up to then.

Cavour originated in a different social and economic environment from the others; his family (Benso by name) was an ancient feudatory of the house of Savoy and originated at about the same time, in the middle of the eleventh century or thereabouts. Humbert the Whitehanded, the founder of the Savoy dynasty (Humbert Blanchemain, comte de Maurienne), is supposed to have come into the hills of Savoy and Piedmont from Burgundy; the Benso family is supposed to have come from somewhere farther east, in Germany itself. Cavour was talking to his brilliant and indispensable Jewish secretary, Isaac Artom, on the subject one day and asked: "Do you believe that story? No? Well, neither do I!"

The Benso family held several fiefs from the house of Savoy, the marquisate, castle and estates of Cavour (1649) being the latest of them and highest in rank. (As a younger son of a marquis, Cavour was called, by custom, not law, count.) Another holding was the castle of Santena where many generations of Bensos are buried, which has just now (1957) become the property of the Italian nation through the extinction of the family.

It was a proud feudal house with many, many quarterings—as many as you can crowd in, I suppose. Cavour himself seems to have been a singularly free human being even from childhood, but if he had not had, innately and very strongly, this distinct individuality, he might easily have been smothered under the weight of feudalism. His extraordinary good luck, leading to his liberation, came through his mother's family: she was Adèle de Sellon from Geneva, daughter of a scholarly philanthropist whom the Emperor Joseph had made a count of the Holy Roman Empire. Her brother Jean-Jacques, comte de Sellon, was a philosopher of a sort, had a fine library, founded a "peace society" and conducted a large correspondence aiming at the abolition of the death penalty. One of the sisters was the duchess of Clermont-Tonnerre, who, with her husband, settled in Turin after the Orleanist revolution (1830) and remained there. As Dowager Duchess she was one of the greatest ladies of Turin, holding her court every night at ten o'clock, rain or shine, for many years; she occupied the ground floor of one wing in the Palazzo Cavour where Cavour was born. The less brilliant, but as it seems more charming, of the two sisters was the comtesse d'Auzers, who also lived there.

The Geneva connection and the ability to take flight to Geneva when Turin grew unendurable were of the highest value to Cavour and without them even his robust character might have succumbed. Turin was one of the most benighted capitals in Europe. Almost everything worth reading was forbidden; nothing worth discussing could be discussed. After the downfall of Napoleon and the return of all the monarchs to their thrones, Pope Pius VII had restored the Jesuit order, which quickly sprang into a stronger position than before, with, what is worth remark, an intact organization and membership after having been "abolished" for more than forty years. (Pope Clement XIV had abolished the order in 1773.) The Jesuits controlled not only education and morals in Turin (such as either of them were) but, within a few years after the restoration, almost everything else as well. Cavour's powerful old aunt, Madame de Clermont-Tonnerre, had to move heaven and earth to get permission to receive, from Paris, copies of that harmless but forbidden newspaper, the *Journal des Débats*. The atmosphere of Turin had always been stifling, ever since the French Revolution, partly because it was a favorite refuge for the most reactionary of the French nobles; there had been a qualified breath of air under Napoleon; now the eighteenth century was back in full control. The monarchy of Louis Philippe was looked upon as little better than red revolution, and that king's legation was not recognized by Cavour's relations. Turin society, French throughout, was "legitimist" beyond anything known in either Paris or Vienna.

The Italian language was used only to servants and the aristocracy of Savoy-Piedmont did not consider itself to be Italian at all; most of its members had no real knowledge of the language. The use of French had spread from the court and the aristocracy into the middle classes, the university, the intellectuals (such as they were) and even to commerce. This had been true for centuries, of course, but its result now was to make Turin a glaring example of that unpleasant situation in which all the possessing and ruling groups speak one language while the people in general speak another. Cavour's personal correspondence and his first efforts in writing are all in French; his love letters and those written to him (just published, in part, a few months ago) are in French. It seems certain that although he became bilingual in time, French was his native tongue until he was a mature man. We have many witnesses to the fact that the Italian language was never heard in polite society in Turin.

Nobody was to blame for the alignment of languages, which had grown up naturally over a very long period; to this very day the dialect of Turin has strong French elements, after such an impregnation of the native speech from above. It was, however, unfortunate that the court and the Jesuits actually encouraged French and discouraged Italian at a moment when all of Italy, including Piedmont, was beginning to discover its national existence. It added one more to the numerous divisive criteria shutting off class from class, state from state and even region from region. (Piedmont and Liguria, both dominions of Savoy, were linguistically divided at the base as well as in the upper classes.) What made Milan the intellectual and psychological capital of Italy all through the first half of the century was not only its size and wealth, but also the fact that it was *Italian*, speaking Italian in daily life in all classes and occupations.

This was the strange little outpost of Versailles in which Camille de Cavour was born and brought up. He had an elder brother and therefore no great prospects under feudal primogeniture, which was still the law in Piedmont. His father intended the older son, Gustave (who inherited the marquisate and the fiefs), for diplomacy; the second, Camille, was for the army, and entered the royal military academy at the age of ten. It was not really what we understand by a military academy, but it was at least a school leading toward military grade, and if it provided little classical or literary training, it was strong in mathematics: "Mathematics," said Cavour, "taught me to think." (If the Savoy had known this, they would have prohibited it!) At the age of fourteen Camille de Cavour was gazetted as page to the Prince of Carignan, heir to the throne.

The *corps des pages* was, as everywhere in Europe, a privileged group, and a page to the Prince of Carignan had access to the palace at all times, certain ritualistic functions at fixed times and a general duty (superseding all ordinary military duties) of attendance when required. It might have been the straight way to preferment, promotion and high favor. Carignan —Charles Albert—had only returned to Turin in May of that year (1824), after his extraordinary performance during the revolution of 1821 in which he betrayed both sides two or three times each. The King (Charles Félix) had considered removing him from the succession, in spite of the holy principle of legitimacy, in favor of his infant son Victor Emmanuel, the one who eventually profited by all these titanic efforts. Charles Albert had been housed by his Hapsburg father-in-law in Florence the while.

On his return to Turin the Prince was undoubtedly actuated by the desire to be more royalist than the King, not to say more papist than the Pope. At all events he threw himself into everything that could prove how utterly he abhorred "liberalism" or anything to do with "the people." He was immersed in "the congregations," as they were called, groups of the Société Catholique, almost the only association permitted at the time. He was, as you might say, working his way home. His new page boy took the most instant dislike to him and never lost a chance to be negligent and sullen. The boy was only fourteen and the Prince was thirty, but they seem to have taken the kind of vivid aversion to each other which is more usual between persons of the same age. Neither ever forgot it. Cavour was accustomed to refer to this ornament of the monarchical system as "the magnanimous Charles Albert," or sometimes, for short, just as "le magnanime."

(It may be noted that Cavour, Mazzini and Garibaldi were divided in many things, but their hatreds show a remarkable unison.)

All this was bound to come to grief. Camille de Cavour was a strong character, much too strong for courts, much too given to reading and thinking. We have no evidence, and must imagine for ourselves what caused the antagonism between the Prince and his page boy. Perhaps Charles Albert came upon him one day when he was reading a book. Almost any book except those by Joseph de Maistre and some others approved by the Jesuits would have been enough to bring down the royal disapproval. Or there may even have been some expression of opinion. Whatever it was, and even if no specific incident occasioned it, the antipathy was immediate and permanent. It very nearly made a republican out of Cavour.

In the Geneva atmosphere (talky and bookish, comfortable to the highest degree and at the same time easy, without rank or etiquette, a patriciate rather than an aristocracy) Cavour spent weeks and months throughout his life, early and late, learning an immense amount and solacing himself for all the miseries of politics and fate. He felt at home in Geneva. His third cousin, Auguste de la Rive, had in his opinion "one of the best organized brains in Europe," and his uncle, the comte de Sellon, certainly had one of the best libraries. Even from childhood he learned to meet all kinds of men there and talk to them freely, which was not possible in his own country. The Pastor Munier, a Protestant (which, in Turin, was equivalent to saying a devil), was one of these whose mind he valued and to whom he never ceased to send his regards. In the most terrible crises—such as the treaty of Villafranca in 1859, by which Napoleon III betrayed him and Venetia was lost for another seven years—he went as fast as he could to Geneva.

This is about the only element in his life which could help to account for his strength of mind in extreme youth under the pressures to which he was subjected. He had few friends in Turin to whom he could talk at all safely; none, so far as we know, in the military academy or the army. It is recorded several times on good authority that he declared, even when he was a child of eleven or twelve, that he was one day going to be "prime minister of united Italy." Where he got such ideas it is impossible to imagine, since they did not yet exist. The good, kind marquise de Cavour, the sweetest, it would seem, but the most self-effacing of the three sisters, must have regarded him as a changeling in the nest. The comtesse d'Auzers, his second mother, the most "elegant" and the most "noble" of the three, worried over him incessantly, but the duchesse de Clermont-Tonnerre adored him without restraint from birth and was always ready to defend him against all comers. The two aunts were childless women and lived in the Palazzo Cavour, so that some degree of concentration upon their nephews might have been expected, but Cavour had—as he once remarked—"three mothers." The most active and vociferous of the three was Madame de Clermont-Tonnerre. De la Rive, who knew them all well, has recorded it as his opinion that the portentous dowager loved her younger nephew as she had never loved any other person in her entire life. If this be so it must have been a mighty protection for the young man, who could easily, otherwise, have suffered an early eclipse.

At sixteen Camille de Cavour passed (first) in his examinations at the academy and became a sublieutenant of engineers; he had tours of duty in Turin itself and in garrisons, the last of which was at Genoa (March to November, 1830). It was in Genoa that he met the lady called "Nina," whose love letters to him have recently been published. She was Anna Giustiniani, wife of a gentleman who asked only that she "make no scandal." Cavour notes in his diary: "Nina never stops telling her husband that she adores me. I have advised her to choose a more suitable confidant."

What with this, that and the other thing, the young lieutenant was enjoying life in Genoa when, unfortunately, the popular uprising of July, 1830 took place, and he could not help feeling sympathy toward it. He was never accused of dereliction to duty, but at some time or place during this period he seems to have shouted out loud: "Long live the Revolution! Long live the Republic!" (Even this has been denied but De la Rive, who knew him well, repeats it as "an imprudence of words.") He was only twenty and his heart was too much for his head. For a young man with lesser family connections this might, indeed, have been a costly indiscretion, but Cavour got out of it with no more than the sacrifice of his military career. He resigned his commission, after some half-hearted attempts to save it, and left the service in November, 1831—that is, over a year after his "imprudence of words." No other course was possible since, in the meantime (April of that year), Charles Albert had succeeded to the throne, bringing with him an undiminished rancor toward his erstwhile page. The possibilities for a blond, high-spirited and impulsive cadet of good family, not well educated—by his own account, "illiterate"— and not in favor at court, were not, in the Piedmont of that time, very good: he could go into exile, join a foreign army, hang about the salons of Paris on a pension from his relatives, or—the preferred alternative in many cases—make a rich marriage based upon the brilliance of his heraldic quarterings. Cavour did none of these things. He went to work as estate manager on one of his father's properties near Alba, lower down in Piedmont; flat country with none of the Alpine beauty and grandeur, but good for farming. As he said himself, Cavour could never "do anything by halves." He threw himself into agriculture with his usual energy and intelligence; he was up at five in all weathers, he learned all tasks so that he could do them himself; he read everything he could get his hands on with any reference to the subject; he made practical experiments upon the basis of the chemical theories just then coming into fashion; he tapped his correspondents in all parts of Europe for information and suggestions (especially William de la Rive, then studying in Scotland with the celebrated Professor James F. W. Johnston, a pioneer in agricultural chemistry). Within four years Cavour had become so competent that he was placed in charge of a big enterprise which his aunt, the Duchess, had bought in partnership with his father some years before, a rice-planting estate long neglected and decayed. This was Leri, which he came to love in a peculiar fashion—perhaps as his own creation, his first brilliant success—more than all the other houses or castles of the family. Leri, an ordinary farmhouse, big enough and comfortable, but with nothing feudal about it, was in the midst of an apparently limitless plain of rice land, with no hill or forest to break the monotony or impede the flight of the malarial mosquitoes on their busy rounds. Here Cavour proved himself: he not only brought the rice crop into phenomenal production, but he varied the crops and introduced every improvement which his sound practical sense found worth adopting. Within ten years he had made himself one of the best farmers in Europe, both practically and theoretically, and it was through agriculture that he made his way at last into his natural domain of politics.

This success in agriculture seems to have been the result of character and intelligence, originally, rather than of inclination. At twenty-one, as a rather spoiled young officer, he could not have felt any irresistible inclination to leave the salons of Turin for the fields and stables.

He did not remain on the farm without respite; he had journeys to Geneva, France, England; in 1840, on his second visit to Paris, he met certain cabinet ministers and great men (the duc de Broglie, Guizot, Molé and others); he was welcomed in two of the great salons of Paris, that of the comtesse Boni de Castellane and that of his lifelong friend, the comtesse de Sircourt. His resounding welcome in Paris was due in the first place to the recommendations of his friend, the baron de Barante, who was Louis Philippe's minister to Turin during this period and always welcomed a conversation with the young Cavour even though both knew it was frowned upon by family and court. In Barante's legation at Turin one of the secretaries was the comte d'Haussonville, of later renown as politician and historian, who became one of Cavour's greatest friends. Thus Paris was prepared for him, but, upon acquaintance, liked him for himself rather than for his introductions. He seems to have admired the duc de Broglie (then no longer prime minister) almost to excess, and it was true that Broglie seemed to have every gift, skill and advantage; Cavour liked to think that the Broglie family came originally from Piedmont and, many centuries before, had been kinsmen of his own family. In London his reception was less *mondain*, less in the high world of government and aristocracy, but it was equally valuable in giving him the chance to talk to intellectuals, economists and agriculturists. Lord Althorpe, Sir John Boileau and Lord Leicester made it possible for him to study new agronomic methods on estates which, for their time (especially Leicester's), were famous as models.

The knowledge of the world acquired during the eight months of this second visit to Paris and London was invaluable to Cavour, reinforcing all he could learn from books and from his various sojourns in the beloved Geneva. His life was too busy to afford much time for travel; its only change was when it became busier. We are constantly being astonished by the amount he took in and really digested of all that was spread before him; his letters show not only a keen interest and perception, which we could have expected, but also a penetration which the older men of the world who were actually engaged in its doings did not always share. On the repeal of the Corn Laws in England, for example, young Cavour (then thirty) saw with uncanny clarity exactly what would happen and must happen. He did not hesitate to say of an English candidate: "He will not be elected," and the facts proved him right. For a young Piedmontese gentleman on his private travels, unfamiliar with the English language, this was not bad. From 1840 he was convinced that the Corn Laws would be repealed, *not* by those who had agitated in that sense for twenty years, but by the very party which had upheld them. This came in part from his comprehension of the character of Sir Robert Peel, whom he greatly admired (from a distance—he never met him). It is worth noting that Cavour, a born liberal in the precise economic, social and political sense— the correct sense—admired a number of great conservatives more, very often, than he did the men of his own persuasion. So it was with Pitt, Chateaubriand and Peel, all of whom seemed to him excellent in character and intellect; and we do not find him using the same language about others (such as Palmerston or Lord John Russell) who were his historical allies.

To return to Turin was a penance after such experiences, and although he could plunge into the estate work at Leri it was becoming insufficient for his energy and (above all) for his patriotism. The monarchy of Charles Albert and the Jesuits was going from bad to worse; it had now taken to banning all "associations" or "societies" even if they were of an industrial nature, such as the various companies set up to project or build railroads. Charles Albert was afraid of the railroad anyhow, as he was of newspapers (what would he have thought of the radio?).

Cavour wrote to Auguste de la Rive from Turin in 1843:

"Since I left you I have been living in a kind of intellectual hell; that is, in a country where intelligence and science are considered hellish things by those who have the kindness to govern us. Yes, my friend, for two months past I have breathed an atmosphere charged with ignorance and prejudice, and I live in a city where one must go into concealment to exchange ideas which are beyond the political and moral sphere in which the government wishes to enclose our minds. This is what they call enjoying the felicity of a paternal regime. After eight months of Presinge, Paris and London, to fall all at once into Turin; to pass without transition from the drawing rooms of the duc de Broglie and the marquess of Lansdowne to those where the retrograde spirit reigns without opposition: the fall is violent. One is left beaten down morally as well as physically. Do you

remember that uncle of Madame Laforge, who, after having been exposed for a long time to an atmosphere of ignorance, ended up by catching a cold in the intelligence? I am a little like that uncle, except that instead of a cold I have been stricken by a sort of paralysis."

On August 25, 1842, Charles Albert signed the royal brevet which sanctioned the creation of an Agrarian Association of Piedmont. This was an idea of Cavour's and he had worked on it for some time; the statutes of the organization had been drawn up chiefly by him, with the help of his friend, the Marquis Alfieri. The King had hesitated a long time. Any association was regarded as containing the germs of sedition, no matter what subjects it was formed to discuss; any meeting, of whatever nature, was deemed to be dangerous and was subject to police control. There were too many men of high rank and wealth in the project for it to be treated quite as others were, and, after misgivings, the government allowed the association to come into being and thereafter kept it under strict surveillance. It had strange vicissitudes (at one time the "democrats," lesser agriculturists, combined with the King and the government to remove Cavour from its control; he, the most advanced intelligence in Piedmont, was conveniently accused of being conservative and an aristocrat). At all events, it gave Cavour his first experience of practical organization and thus, by a natural transition, of politics. He was at the same time beginning to write a good deal, at first against his own will and under the urging of his cousin De la Rive, but afterwards with considerable ease. His earlier efforts were confined to subjects on which he had practical competence (agriculture, political economy) and to the French language.

The admission of this agrarian association was perhaps the beginning of the end for Charles Albert; it was the first of a series of such concessions made by the absolute monarchy, either through fear of the popular wrath or because the King was vacillating again. Cavour's agriculturists soon became an active political force and he himself became known in the country for the first time. In 1844 Charles Albert allowed orphanages and some municipal schools to be opened, thus robbing the Jesuits of their monopoly in such public instruction as there was. Massimo d'Azeglio, Vincenzo Gioberti and other liberals were allowed to come back from their exiles a year or so later, and Charles Albert indulged in a few expressions of outright Italian patriotism (as reported by D'Azeglio).

The real spark which set off the conflagration of 1848 came, however, from the last place in Italy where it might have been expected: Rome. The Pontifical States were reputedly the worst governed in Europe;

the population (which was one-third priests, monks or nuns) had declined, banditry flourished, commerce was dead and taxes could no longer even be collected from the despairing people. At the moment when the repressive policy of Gregory XVI seemed to have reached a dead end, that pontiff died (June 1, 1846) and the college of cardinals was sharply divided between those who favored and those who opposed his secretary of state as successor. As a result a most unexpected candidate, Giovanni Mastai-Ferretti, was elected pope (June 16) and took the name of Pius IX (Pio Nono). As soon as he was elected he proclaimed a political amnesty of wider range than usual on such occasions; newspapers were allowed to appear in the Papal dominions; rumors of the new Pope's "liberalism" surged through Italy and stirred up a tremendous new hope. Pio Nono was not, of course, a "liberal," but he was an Italian of strong national feeling, not fond of the Austrians, and disliked police rule and police spies by nature. His temperament was kindly enough, as shown in his previous governments (Spoleto and Imola), although he was subject to sudden and impulsive changes which, according to some authorities, might be traced to his epilepsy. During his first years he aroused such enthusiasm among Italians that even stern anticlerical republicans like Mazzini and Garibaldi would have been ready to follow if he had been ready to lead, and the idea of an Italian federation under the Pope's presidency (which Louis Napoleon cherished off and on for years) might actually have come to something. The transformation of Pio Nono into the most reactionary force in Italy was one of the oddities of the Risorgimento: eighteen years later, in 1864—although by that time it no longer mattered much—he issued the encyclical *Quanta Cura* (December 8, 1864) in which he condemned liberty of opinion and of the press, popular sovereignty, the legal supremacy of the State over the Church, and the neutrality of the state in religion, as well as religious freedom at large.

In 1847 the new Pope's reforms set Italy afire; he was creating a free press (that is, with a censorship board to which laymen were admitted as well as priests) and a constitutional government (a cabinet of ministers appointed by the Pope without a parliament or elections). There were demonstrations more or less everywhere and some of the petty sovereigns either abdicated or granted constitutions. Charles Albert, who had already dismissed his most antiquated ministers and granted a few reforms, proclaimed another batch of them before the year was out and also started negotiations with Rome and Tuscany for a customs union with Piedmont —a move which, in its suggestion of union for Italy, inflamed liberal hopes and passions still more.

There was certainly a germ in the air that year (winter of 1847–1848). It was afloat not only in Italy but in France, Austria, Hungary, Poland and more or less everywhere else in Europe. England itself, the stablest of the stable, had just undergone a formidable popular movement and was still blinking with surprise. How or why all the revolutions happened at once is a question I have not yet seen answered; although cogent reasons can be given for each separately, their coincidence in time—an element of their success—is as baffling to history as it was to the sovereigns.

So far as Italy was concerned nothing outside (nothing in Europe as a whole) brought about the decisive demonstrations, riots, insurrections and disorders which swept the country that winter. It was time for them to happen and they happened; the most that can be said for causation is that Pio Nono, by a few timid reforms, got the thing started. Milan rioted against the Austrians in early January; Sicily rebelled on the twelfth of that month and drove the army of the Neapolitan Bourbons out of the island, proclaiming their own old constitution of 1812; Naples itself came out into the streets toward the end of the same month and Ferdinand II was forced (January 29) to declare constitutional government. Smaller despotisms followed suit, and on February 8 in Turin even Charles Albert, after much fasting and prayer and receiving the sacrament, announced that he could not disdain the example of the Holy Father and that he, too, would give his people a constitution.

All these, and many other, events had taken place before Louis Napoleon, by the coup d'état of February 22, 1848, drove out Louis Philippe and proclaimed the Second Republic; it was March 13 before Vienna revolted and Metternich resigned. The events elsewhere (in Berlin or Hungary, for example) do not concern Italy so closely, but the downfall of Metternich and the rise of Louis Napoleon, occurring in the midst of this tremendous popular effervescence and patriotic optimism, marked a notable stage in the evolution of the Risorgimento. From now on all of its movements seemed larger and seemed to convey a deeper meaning; there were no more petty skirmishes and trivial episodes; whatever happened, even if small numbers were involved, had historic significance; everything moved to the same end. It was one of those periods in Europe when "the people," of whom so many speak without meaning much more than themselves, did actually seem to have a will of their own against which the combinations of tyranny could not prevail. In whatever happened, defeat or victory, the tide was set now and did not change.

4   When Verdi left the Scala in 1845 (after *Giovanna d'Arco*) he had contracts which gave the next three operas, in rapid succession, to Naples (*Alzira*—a failure), Venice (*Attila*) and Florence (*Macbeth*). By this time he was exhausted; he had been writing too much; his health or his imagination, for they were closely intertwined, made him want to retire from all activity for at least a while, to rest, to think. He knew that this work was not the best he could do. Indeed he judged *Alzira* very severely. And yet he had tried hard with *Macbeth*, his best up to that moment by his own standards, and the public had been as lukewarm as the critics toward the result. He had contracts in London and Paris which he had been putting off from period to period; now, in his exhaustion, he started staving them off with doctors' certificates, but at last (May, 1847) could dally no longer. He started off on his first journey to the great capitals with the faithful Emanuele Muzio in attendance. His Rhine journey, his experiences in Paris, London and again in Paris, belong to another category of ideas from those which now engage us; we shall see to them later. The point of immediate concern is that the *annus mirabilis*, the tremendous year of 1848, caught him on foreign soil and unprepared for it.

He kept up a steady correspondence with Italy during his absence—that is, from May to the end of the year 1847—and paid the closest attention to developments there as reported in the French and English press. He does not seem to have expected the Revolution of 1848 any more than others did. At the time he probably knew large numbers of patriots and republicans (all his friends were of the same way of thinking) but no actual conspirators, no members of secret societies or "actionist" committees. He met Mazzini in London that summer several times and they became friends; he also dined one night with Louis Napoleon, who was at that moment only a shabby conspirator like Mazzini and so many others. It is, however, out of the question to suppose that either of them would have told the fashionable composer, the successful maestro, anything about their plans. Verdi's anxiety over Italy and Italian affairs at this period comes, in my opinion, from the simple fact that this was his first journey of any length outside his own country and he was homesick. (He had only been to Vienna for *Nabucco*—a short, professional foray.)

Now, after the London venture, he was involved in Paris not merely with the Opéra (his first of several ordeals there) but also with Giuseppina Strepponi. She had left the stage and was teaching in Paris; their union, which was accomplished in the autumn of 1847 by taking a house together at Passy, was never to be broken again. Verdi was, we know, happy. His work was not good—*Jérusalem*, the Paris effort, one of the least good—but aside from his gnawing anxiety over Italy he was at peace, for once.

In the midst of this idyl came the news of the rebellion in Milan (March 18–22, 1848) which goes by the name of "The Five Days." As soon as he could get himself out of bed—he had one of his recurrent rheumatic fevers—he made haste to Milan, which he found in a turmoil of patriotic excitement. There he met Mazzini again; and Muzio, who had bought a rifle and fought in the streets, and dozens of other friends. Verdi was thirty-five, and men much older were shouldering the rifle just then. He clearly wanted to do the same himself, but all his friends told him what he himself also believed, that it was his duty to give music to Italy—martial music under the circumstances; music which called the nation to arms. He was already the most famous of young Italian composers; already some of his work—in particular, *Nabucco, I Due Foscari* and *Attila*—had aroused the popular passions; what Mazzini and Italy asked of him now was to do it again. In those perfervid hours of blind excitement he cast about him for a subject, for a librettist, for anything which might give him a chance to strike his own blow in his own way for Italian freedom.

He did not see Garibaldi at that time; he may not even have known any of the details of Garibaldi's campaign up the Lombard side of Lago Maggiore and over to Como; the chances are that he had only the most distorted and inaccurate view of what was going on. Milan had driven out the Austrians, for the first time in innumerable attempts, and that alone was enough to upset the equilibrium of every citizen. Charles Albert had taken the field; the Pope was on the side of the people; the monarchs of Modena, Tuscany, Parma, Naples, all were with the people; Italy was in flames; the Austrian was doomed. This, at least, was the general idea.

There were not, in 1848, enough common-or-garden tools (such as the post office) to correct the lurid guesses. Weeks or months might pass before even the most important news from a distant place became known. Just now, when more or less everything was happening at once all over Italy and Europe, no clear, steady view of the turmoil was possible and even a great city like Milan had to encounter its fate in the dark. Verdi, seizing upon the one thing he knew he could do, single-mindedly sought

for an operatic subject of such patriotic significance that it would aug-
ment or bring to fever heat the temperature of his countrymen. In this
case, at Mazzini's request, there was no unconscious creation and no
idiosyncrasy involved; he deliberately sought for a deliberate effect. Salvatore Cammarano, the poetaster who had already written the ill-fated
Alzira for Verdi, happened to be in Milan. In his opinion the most
patriotic subject that could be found in Italian history(!) was the
battle of Legnano, in May, 1176, when the troops of the Lombard League
defeated those of Frederick Barbarossa. According to Cammarano this
was the first time Italian troops ever defeated Germans. Verdi, in his
haste and fury, accepted the subject as soon as he understood it and
urged Cammarano to write it at once. He would then put it on—or ask
Ricordi to arrange for it—at the Argentina in Rome, where he had promised an opera, and where it would serve better, probably, than anywhere
else in the peninsula at the present moment. Perhaps Mazzini gave him
this idea; we do not know.

For the sake of clarity we might leave Verdi in this preoccupation
for a moment and see what actually was going on: after a century and
more we have a better chance than he had to find out. It was true that
Charles Albert had taken the field and made one last attempt to be a hero
or, failing that, to take a side and stick to it. (His greatest military activity
up to now had been as an officer in the French army in Spain, after 1821,
in the service of the Holy Alliance—that is, to stifle the Spanish revolution.) What led him to his decision, aside from the obvious excitement
of the whole people which he could observe for himself from his palace
windows, we do not know. He had just granted a constitution to his own
dominions after having pledged himself in writing to his predecessor not
to do so. He could have had no genuine feeling of dislike or distrust for
the Hapsburgs because he was more Hapsburg than anything else
(mother, wife, daughter-in-law were Hapsburgs, along with numerous
ancestors). He was not really Italian and could not speak the language
properly. The half-witted Austrian emperor, Ferdinand, who abdicated before this year was out, was married to a Savoy. Charles Albert really
dreaded and disliked the people, especially the Italian people, and his natural links of loyalty were to those families, in particular Bourbon and
Hapsburg, to which he belonged and whose ideas of divine right he
shared. His dominions themselves were by no means all Italian, although
his sons, being of their time, had already declared themselves to be of
that nationality and anxious for war in the name of "Italy."

Charles Albert was a terrible turncoat but my own feeling (for what it may be worth after the perusal of the evidence) is that there was a fundamental sincerity in his final escapade. It seems that the Pope's "liberalism," so-called, had given him a tremendous shaking-up and had convinced him that hellfire for all eternity was not the inevitable result of political change. In his actual declaration of war (which was made in the form of a proclamation to the peoples of Lombardy and Venetia, although the diplomatic paper was sent at the same time) he professed to confide in "God who has given to Italy Pope Pius IX." Privately (diplomatically) he assured the European powers that he was making war to shut out the republican revolutionaries, who otherwise, in the state of popular feeling, might take over northern Italy. The monarchical powers in general were ready to accept this explanation, which also, up to a point, had its vein of truth. (The exception was Russia, which disapproved and broke off relations with Charles Albert.) In all this tangle it is not easy to follow the reasoning of such an inconsistent, insincere, priest-ridden and cowardly man as Charles Albert, but for a guess from a distance, it might run like this: the penniless cadet had played both ends against the middle and almost lost his heritage, after which he acquired great fear of God and the Jesuits, but opened his eyes in wonder when at last the Pope himself spoke out in favor of the Italian people. The process from 1846 (the election of Pius IX) was extraordinarily rapid in Charles Albert and seems to me to have corresponded to some starved inner truth. The Pope inadvertently knocked some chains off his ankles. He was not actually under great immediate pressure to take the steps he took in 1847 and early 1848 toward liberalization; he was not even in any danger of losing his throne when he granted the constitution. He was obeying—at long last—the dictates of a nature which had never dared to be itself before. I think that when he said to Massimo d'Azeglio that he was prepared, at the right moment, to give everything he possessed ("my sons, my arms, my treasures, my army," etc., etc.) for the cause of Italy, he was simply and truly, at the end of his life, coming out of that cave of cowardice in which he had always lived. When Pius IX began one of his manifestoes (1847) with the words "Great God, bless Italy," a phrase which like everything else at the time produced wild excitement, Charles Albert at last received the highest religious authority for being, at long last, himself, which was an Italian. For, curiously enough, the final impression one gets (that is, if one is not vowed to the thesis of deep, dark treachery) is that in his final phase Charles Albert had discovered himself to be an Italian. He might not have been able to conjugate the verb "to be," and he certainly had not read Dante, but he seems to me to have felt in those fateful last months all the power of that emotion which Walter Scott expressed in the line we learned in childhood: "This is my own, my native land." Charles Albert was not in the least Italian by race or ancestry or language or anything else, but he was born in Turin.

When to this view (contested though it is) you add the obvious fact that the Savoy dynasty stood to gain everything by the gamble, I think it was sincere, humanly speaking, and as honest as Charles Albert was capable of being. The evidence that it was all treachery from the beginning never amounted to anything; the evidence that it was treachery at the end does not convince. He merely gambled and lost, but not for his children.

From the time Charles Albert granted the constitution, in early February, events moved very fast. (In this mysterious concatenation, by the way, the frequency of his visits to the confessional is not the least link; what sins could this man have committed from one dawn to the next?) France went two weeks later and Austria (along with Hungary and Prussia) in two months. The news of the insurrection in Vienna set off the insurrections in Milan and Venice; the "Five Days" of Milan had the astounding effect of driving trained Austrian regulars, under Marshal Radetzky, out of the city. Those "Five Days" really did the trick. Italy was already at the peak of hysteria; after the "Five Days" it began to take arms and move. Even in the Papal States it was not possible to keep the inhabitants from volunteering for "the war." There was, in fact, no war, but in the delirium of that moment hardly any Italian knew it. Delegations from Lombardy and Venetia pleaded with Charles Albert to intervene. The exiles were coming back from all over Europe (Mazzini in April, as we know, along with Verdi). Most of them were republicans and proclaimed governments of that complexion in the cities where they organized provisional regimes. Finally, on March 23, 1848, Charles Albert declared war against Austria, trusting (evidently) in God and Pope Pius, and set his troops in motion across the Ticino into Lombardy. His proclamation spoke of the "help which brother expects from brother, friend from friend." This was directed toward the republicans of Milan and Venice, who, by May of that year, found themselves in fervent, if incompatible, alliance with the King and the Pope. The Pope was embarrassed; he had permitted volunteers to form and march northward from his dominions and now he found that some parts of the Catholic world (German countries chiefly) did not like it; he took occasion to declare that he was the father of all the faithful and not of one group; but his troops were in action. The despots of Modena and Tuscany also had troops moving north to join Charles Albert. The king of Naples (Ferdinand II) was afraid of this avalanche; before long Charles Albert might be king of Italy at this rate; he had to send some troops for fear of his own populace, but he withdrew them as soon as he dared. Charles Albert with his two sons took the field regardless of what the other states might be doing and without counting too much upon the untrained volunteers who streamed north during April and May. The Piedmontese army, although not well equipped or prepared according to the standard of the great powers, was by far the best in Italy, with a general staff and cadre of some professional quality; the men in the ranks were chiefly mountaineers and peasants used to hardship and tough in adversity.

The successes Charles Albert attained with this army during the spring and summer were due chiefly to the fact that Marshal Radetzky, the Austrian commander, was pulling in his troops from all exposed areas to the small fortified tract called "the Quadrilateral," which had been constructed for this purpose. It consisted of the land between the four fortresses of Peschiera (on Lake Garda), Mantua, Verona and Legnano. In this compact and easily defended patch of territory he could afford to wait for reinforcements, for orders from Vienna, and for the unfolding of events—not least of them the Hungarian rebellion and kindred movements within the Hapsburg dominions. Charles Albert advanced more or less steadily everywhere, although more slowly than his critics considered necessary. (The accusation of treachery against him begins with these slow movements in May and June.) But the parochialism of the time, crumbling though it now was, still stood in the way of large movements: even when Charles Albert wanted to go fast and far, his own general staff opposed him. They could not see the point of any military operation beyond Lombardy—apparently Venetia was still, in their eyes, "foreign." In the same way the revolutionaries themselves in the full tide of their success (the Hungarians, the Poles, the Berliners) minded their own business in a way which showed how little they understood of the general movement; they had no sympathy with the Italian revolutions and even no interest. The Hapsburgs alone could benefit by this separatism among insurrections which ideally and materially ought to have been closely linked. The new "liberal" regime in Vienna which succeeded Metternich was thus able to defeat its enemies singly and consecutively, and it proceeded to do so.

The broad outline of the war became what, under such circumstances, might have been foreseen: successes for Charles Albert during the period while the Austrians regrouped, rearmed and received reinforcements;

then a steady retreat across Lombardy and (next year) a stinging defeat in Piedmont itself, at Novara. This was the end for Charles Albert. His abdication, exile and death in 1849 (within a few months) were equally beyond his power to prevent.

The Austrians were coming back everywhere, even in the duchies; the Neapolitan jackal was bound to follow suit, and Ferdinand reconquered Sicily that May. Reaction was apparently resuming full control of Italy in the spring and summer of 1849, just one year after that first great wave of hope and joy. The last outburst of the spirit of 1848 was in Rome, where it had taken its origin two years earlier, and it was in Rome that it was finally crushed. After these years of anguished effort there followed a whole decade of silence during which the despotisms returned in most states and Italy seemed, but only seemed subdued. It was a decade of grim, hard work on the part of those who were variously determined (that is, separately and with various systems of government in mind) upon unity and independence.

The Roman Republic of 1849 and its extinction by the troops of France, Austria and Naples was the last and most heroic episode of these troubled times. It struck the imagination of all Italy and, to be sure, of the world at large, as nothing else had done in the recurrent struggle. It made Garibaldi the hero of the nation and Mazzini a symbol of republican purity; it involved and concerned the troubled conscience of Louis Napoleon so that he could never again rid himself of a sense of obligation toward Italy; it changed Pius IX from the patron of the liberals into their bitter enemy; and, not least from our point of view, it involved Verdi in the most extreme musical demagoguery of his whole career, in which he became, for a while, the "Tribune of Music" for the Roman Republic. He never got so deep into the midst of the turmoil again, and it seems to me that the experience was salutary above all for his art as a composer. After 1849 his patriotism was as constant as ever, his anxiety and his fervor undiminished for years to come (they only began to dwindle along about 1866, when they were no longer necessary). Even so, he learned a few rather profound truths from the experience of 1849 in Rome, and the general development of his work from then on shows it more and more: 1849 was the climax but also the end of his effort to make music serve a cause other than its own.

5 We left Verdi in Milan with Mazzini, feverishly trying to find a subject for a patriotic opera. During those weeks Milan lived so to speak, on air and fine words; nobody could be sure whether the end was to be a Republic of Lombardy or union with Piedmont, but liberty was certain in either case. There was the shadow of the Austrians, turned into reality at the end of the summer, and those who did not spend their time discussing ultimate ideals were preparing to fight for the city. Among the eager youths who sat at Mazzini's feet, ready to man whatever barricade he might point out, was the poet Goffredo Mameli, twenty years old, author of "easy, inspired, spontaneous songs like the song of the lark at morning; beautiful, tender with flowers and scents like a woman, but resolute in everything that touched the patriotic faith he had embraced." (The words are Mazzini's.) This radiant youth, who died for the Roman Republic a year later, was more a promise than a fulfillment in literature, but we shall see that at least one of his poems—the one Verdi set to music—was the nearest thing to a national hymn Italy has ever had.

They all got out of Milan within a few weeks, long before the siege by the Austrians began. Verdi had left Giuseppina in Paris and sworn to return to her—her anxieties were incessant; and before going back he wanted to buy the property on which he had set his mind, the farm of Sant' Agata near Busseto. This accomplished, he could return to Peppina in June.

The Italian revolutions and uprisings preoccupied him all summer long, just the same, and he could not get the text he wanted out of Cammarano so that he could begin work on the new opera, the super-patriotic work. He fretted and fumed; his letters on purely professional subjects (such as the negotiation for an opera for the San Carlo in Naples) were short-tempered and touchy. He had only one real desire, which was to strike his blow for Italy now, in this year of 1848 when so many blows were being struck; he was quite incapable of thinking on other subjects, and if he did turn occasionally from the battle of Legnano (Cammarano's delayed libretto) it was only to muse on such themes as Cola di Rienzo, the Roman tribune, and others of the same kind. Before Cammarano—who had many other employments in his native Naples—could get the stage treatment completed, Verdi was already anxiously and imperatively demanding changes, both in scenes and in actual words. The correspondence between Paris and Naples was so slow that it racked the composer's nerves. It was not until the beginning of October that the third act of the play reached him and he could begin to compose, even though he was still demanding changes.

In the meantime Mazzini had sent him a poem by Mameli, asking him to set it to music in a popular fashion so that it could be sung by the people everywhere. Verdi had never tried his hand at anything of the kind, but it afforded an outlet for his restless and impatient patriotic feeling. He sent the music of the *Inno di Mameli*, Mameli's Hymn, to Mazzini on October 18, 1848, with a letter which began as follows:

"*Dear Signor Mazzini, I am sending you the hymn, and although it may be a little late, I hope it will arrive in time. I have tried to be as popular and as easy as it is possible for me to be. Make whatever use you like of it: burn it, even, if you do not think it worthy. If you should make it public, get the poet to change a few words in the beginning of the second and third stanzas, in which it would be good to have a phrase of five syllables having a sense of their own, as in all the other stanzas.*"

There follow a few more detailed suggestions to the poet which may make it easier to sing each of his stanzas to the same tune, as is essential in popular music. Then, at the end, Verdi says: "May this hymn, in the music of the cannon, soon be sung on the plains of Lombardy."

Many have supposed—and I, for years, among them—that Verdi's song was that "*Fratelli d'Italia!*" which generations of Italians have learned to sing in school, and which is now officially the national anthem. However, the version which caught the people's imagination and endured was not Verdi's. It was a simpler tune already current, which just happened to fit Mameli's words, and the composer's effort remains in the music libraries. Although he aroused the people with his operatic music, often without meaning to do so, his one attempt at a "national hymn" was a little too complex, and perhaps also a little too good, for its purpose.

Verdi wrote *La Battaglia di Legnano* at headlong speed because he, too, wanted to go to Rome and supervise its production in January. It was a blaze of patriotic emotion from the rise of the curtain: the very first words are "*Viva l'Italia!*" sung by a chorus of men. As may be seen, 1848 was in his blood; in a sense it always had been, but this was an unrestrained, uninhibited outburst, a really shameless display of passion. As such, it offended most permanent standards and would probably be unendurable today, but in its time and place it created such storms as no other opera ever did. It would not be extreme to say that this astonishing production helped to bring about the proclamation of the Roman Republic just thirteen days later. Mazzini's expectations were not disappointed.

Verdi arrived in Rome at the beginning of January to rehearse and produce his opera. Everything had gone badly for the patriots elsewhere; in Milan, for example, the Austrians had returned as conquerors, and Verdi's friends (Countess Maffei, Muzio and others) had fled to Switzerland. Rome had continued on the liberal course set by Pope Pius IX two years before; in fact, on March 14 the Pope had granted a constitution, somewhat against his own wish, and called for elections. His constitution (with a few special provisions preserving the theocracy) was like most of the others in 1848, modeled on that of Louis Philippe (1830): it provided a parliament of two chambers, the upper appointed and the lower elected by a restricted electorate; a ministry responsible to this parliament; juridical equality of citizens, freedom of the press and a civic guard. Ministries had succeeded each other in the few months of this system without making much progress, since the Pope himself was at cross purposes with them. Much as he had enjoyed his brief whirl of popularity, he did not really believe in freedom of any kind, either in politics, religion, opinion or the press, and had been carried much too far in that direction—by the rush of events and the strength of his own innate Italian feeling—before he knew what was happening. Now he tried, in vain, to curb the liberalizing and democratizing influences in his own government. When the effort seemed to him hopeless he left Rome in disguise (under the impression that he was in some personal danger, which he was not) and reached Gaeta (November 24, 1848), where he felt safe enough to disown his own government, dissolve the parliament and appoint a commission to govern in his name. Parliament refused to be dissolved, named its own governing council and called elections for a constituent assembly. The Papal States, forming a broad band across the middle of Italy from the Tyrrhenian to the Adriatic Seas, thus provided Europe with a spectacle containing every extravagance and contradiction characteristic of the time: the most backward of all European administrations and the most illiterate of peoples, in the most poverty-stricken part of Italy—a country where it was possible to send a man to prison for eating meat on Friday—an area where it was not safe to go into the city streets without a bodyguard after dark—suddenly set itself up in the vanguard of progress and became, for its brief hour, the hope of those who could still believe in freedom.

Verdi arrived during the first days of January and set to work at his rehearsals in the Teatro Argentina. The abnormal state of affairs in the city could not have made his task easier. He was already called "the Maestro of the Italian Revolution" by many and could hardly stir outside his rooms without collecting a crowd. As is usual in such tumultuous times, men had taken to neglecting their ordinary occupations—if they had any—for the sake of meetings and parades which kept up their courage. In no time at all the whole population of Rome—not above fifty thousand at the time, but swollen with patriots and exiles from other parts of Italy—became aware that La Battaglia di Legnano was a kind of operatic manifesto for the freedom and union of Italy. The theatre was besieged; long before the first night every seat had been sold for that and the subsequent performances. On the night of the dress rehearsal the mob stormed the theatre and filled it; there were not enough guards or police in Rome to keep them out; they made the ordinary work of a dress rehearsal impossible by paroxysms of enthusiasm. Even at the dress rehearsal this unruly mob, which had paid nothing to get into the theatre, insisted on repetitions of many separate pieces, so that the exhausted singers, musicians and stagehands were kept up half the night.

The official first performance, January 27, 1849, was a weird event, in which street crowds made it almost impossible for those who had tickets to use them. The patriotic delirium started with the first words, "Viva l'Italia," and grew more abandoned all through the evening. Practically every piece in the score had to be repeated, even though it could scarcely be heard in the pandemonium. The cheering and chanting in the audience ("Viva l'Italia!" and "Viva Verdi!" were incessant all evening) must have given the singers on the stage a difficult task, if, indeed, they really tried to deliver the words and music as written. It used to be the custom in Italy for enthusiasts to throw onto the stage anything they happened to have handy if it could serve as a present to the singers or an indication of pleasure—not flowers only, that is, but gloves or scarfs or almost anything else, including sometimes money and jewels. On the first night of La Battaglia di Legnano the objects thus hurled at the proscenium were of large number and many categories. An officer in the fourth row of boxes (afterwards subdued by the carabinieri and removed to cooler quarters) was so exalted that he threw his cloak, spurs and dagger on the stage and thereafter all the seats from his box (pretty high up) one by one.

These or similar scenes recurred at every performance of La Battaglia di Legnano, and the entire fourth act had to be repeated every night, as well as single pieces in earlier acts. No other opera held the boards in Rome at the time, and this one had been most deliberately put together for the occasion. Its effect upon the temper of its audiences, already flaring to wildness, was great. When we remember the power of opera in Italy as the primary art of the people, even now, and consider how much stronger it was a century ago, we can see how Verdi came to be called, in that short but glorious episode of the Roman Republic, the "Tribune of the People" for music.

He did not wait for that honor. The Roman Republic was proclaimed by the constituent assembly, in defiance of the Pope, on February 9, but by this time Verdi was back in Paris with Peppina, who was most disturbed over his every absence in this unsettled time. Just what day he left Rome is not clear to me. There is a letter to Piave from Paris under the date of February 1, but even if the composer had left Rome the day after his first night (that is, if he had left on the twenty-eighth) he could not possibly have reached Paris by February 1. The letter (I suspect) is misdated, but historically speaking it makes little difference, since the main fact is that Verdi got out of the Roman turmoil as quickly as he could and returned to Peppina. His letters for the rest of the year contain little but anguish over the political events, and not much of consequence about his own profession. He wanted to return to Rome as soon as he could wind up his affairs in Paris—or so he said—but it was not to be. The Pope at Gaeta launched an appeal to the principal Catholic powers, Austria, Spain, France and Naples, to occupy Rome, and only the French hesitated: the others, as the principal upholders of despotism in Europe, jumped at the chance. The French assembly, uncertain at first, authorized Louis Napoleon to move as a counterpoise after the Austrians had done so. Thus the Roman Republic was rapidly beset, besieged and overwhelmed by an enormously superior alignment of forces, and the Pope was returned to absolute power with only such qualifications as might be imposed by his gratitude to these eager friends.

The resistance of Rome under a triumvirate (Mazzini, Saffi and Armellini), with Garibaldi as commander of the defense forces, took up the whole spring and half the summer of 1849. It was a desperate and even a thrilling struggle which engaged the sympathies of a great part of Europe (especially in France and England). Garibaldi had hardly been known before in wide circles; when this heroic fight was over, his name had become magic not only in Italy but throughout the world.

He was in South America, of course, when the news of the first revolts in Italy reached him. He was off at once for Genoa, taking with him as many of his Italian Legion as wanted to return to the land from which many (like himself) had been exiled under severe penalties. His was the severest; he had been condemned to death; but he knew that in a time of emergency the services of an experienced fighter would not be disdained. He was, in fact, permitted to organize his own followers and call for volunteers for a campaign all his own—the government of Charles Albert was accepting volunteers from all directions, and his prowess in South America, which had been reported in Turin, overshadowed his past sins. His very first proclamations on his arrival in Italy after years of exile have the same flamboyance as his latest; this kind of language was native to him and (fortunately) to many young men who answered it. "To the Alps!" he would proclaim. "Let us show Italy and Europe that we want to conquer and we shall conquer!" This particular appeal (July 27, 1848) was made after Charles Albert had already been beaten and was in full retreat. His broadsides were addressed "To the Youth!" or sometimes quite simply, "Italians!" (In Rome, afterward, they almost always began with that vocative, afterward to become the daily rhetoric of Mussolini —"Italiani!")

Garibaldi had a handful of men; at most it is supposed that about seven hundred followed him in his campaign on Lago Maggiore and Lago di Como. With this small following he defeated larger Austrian groups several times, notably at Luino and Morazzone. His activities had no effect upon the outcome of the war but they greatly stirred the imagination of the youth in Lombardy and Piedmont, to whom he was in fact showing a kind of warfare suited to their own mountains, to their natural inclinations and to their lack of regular training. The guerrilla tactics, at which he was a master, had not been used against the Austrians up to this moment and although their successes were without practical result, they constituted the one moral comfort and psychological gain of the whole war for those who (like Garibaldi himself) wanted to fight. There were other moral gains for other kinds of men: the experience of even a few months of freedom, without an Austrian soldier in sight, was in itself tremendous. But for those who actually wanted to fight and thought of the liberation of Italy in terms of fighting, the war had been a lamentable humiliation throughout: these few small actions of Garibaldi's assumed disproportionate greatness. He escaped, at the end, into Switzerland, and his volunteers dissolved in the best guerrilla style, so that no Austrian could be sure whence they had come or where they had gone.

The Roman Republic was, inevitably, Garibaldi's next port of call. Mazzini commanded his allegiance then, as for years past and to come; the temporary accommodation made with Piedmont and monarchy was for the sake of winning the war, if possible. It was the kind of accommodation Garibaldi always showed himself ready to make (Mazzini never): for Italy or for the good of Italy, its ultimate union and independence, Garibaldi had accepted Charles Albert as he was to accept Victor Emmanuel later on, but everybody—including those kings—knew perfectly well that it was a temporary arrangement. Garibaldi put Italy before everything, but fundamentally his republican, antimonarchical and anticlerical feelings were unchangeable. He used to say, long afterward when the republican ideal had gone far out of fashion, "I have never met anybody more completely republican than I am," and it was probably true, even though Mazzini himself was implied in the comparison. Mazzini's republic was like that of De Valera: a state in which the people had no right to disagree with him. ("The people have no right to vote wrong," said De Valera.) Garibaldi's republic was one in which the people must rule, even though they might, temporarily, for brief periods, entrust their fate to a military commander as "dictator" (in the ancient Roman sense).

The Roman Republic lasted from February to July, 1849. From South America and from northern Italy Garibaldi had a nucleus of his own, personal followers, those who were ready to follow him everywhere and do his bidding to the jaws of death; this small band exhibited a valor and devotion seldom witnessed in warfare, and some of them were not even Italians. With this "Italian Legion" (or what was left of it) Garibaldi entered the service of the Roman Republic and commanded its own forces, untrained volunteers, throughout the period. The Austrians, the French and the Neapolitans converged on the city. There was very fierce hand-to-hand fighting, far more savage, really, than the great clashes of armed millions who (as in contemporary warfare) so seldom even see each other. The stories of heroism in the final days of the Roman Republic are numerous, and although it is natural to suppose that some have been embellished by patriotic imaginations, most of them seem true. Italy and Europe watched with awe; this Garibaldi, with his few groups scattered here and there, seemed to be holding whole armies at bay. Finally, of course, the sheer weight of power was too much for him. He extricated himself and his followers from the city and executed a skillful and daring retreat (fighting part of the way) through the mountains to San Marino, where he took refuge in the mediaeval republic. There again his followers dissolved and he escaped through Venice. Mazzini in the meantime had made his way to London, whence in a relatively short time the decline of his influence could be measured; the Roman Republic, which was in fact only the beginning for his disciple Garibaldi, had been the highest but also the last activity of Mazzini on the stage of enacted history.

The truth was that the Roman Republic in its sheer romanticism—its defiance of the material universe—was probably what young Italy needed most to give it both an ideal and a warning. Ideal, because there never had been in modern times such a brave fight against terrible odds in this peninsula. It really did have something of the quality of the Spartan three hundred at Thermopylae. There were enough heroic episodes in the defense of Rome to feed the nationalist youth for the next three generations. It remains the very highest point of physical or military courage in the whole story, since there was remarkably little fighting in most of the other episodes. But although the ideal was there, and the descendants of those who fought under Garibaldi will never forget it, there was also a plain warning for any man of common sense, to wit: if you want to give battle to immensely superior forces you must prepare very carefully and get everything you possibly can get on your side before you begin.

In a sense every great exemplar contains both positive and negative admonitions, but it seems to me that this, of the Roman Republic in 1849, had the plainest presentation and the strongest effect in modern Italy. We see the consequence: a whole decade during which none of these romantic defiances took place and the peninsula, on the surface, was quiet. We also see that in the same decade every force that was headed in the same direction (that is, toward the creation of Italy) was at work indefatigably preparing for the next day of trial. The lesson of the Roman Republic might not have been so incisive if the drama had taken place elsewhere (in Florence, for example); but in Rome, Rome itself, though it was only a flea-bitten slum with a hinterland of starving people hiding from priests, there was some ancient magic, some inextinguishable power of association, which made every Italian attend to its weal and woe with a serious mind.

And Cavour, of course, at the very outset of his short but incomparable career, had this set before him as the most vivid of all examples. He could never for one moment forget it; I think his respect for Garibaldi, which was profound although Garibaldi never truly understood it, and his scarcely veiled contempt for Mazzini, both come from the Roman Republic. At the time he could do nothing. He had presented his candidacy for the parliament at Turin in April and had been defeated; in a by-election two months later (June 26, 1848) he won in no less than four constituencies, or colleges, as was possible under the constitution, and chose that of the first Turin district, which he continued to represent until his death. He was known at court, unfavorably, and in the highest aristocracy; he was also known through the Agrarian Society, which had made it possible for him to be a candidate for office; but even the Savoy dominions in general did not know him, to say nothing of Italy as a whole. This year, 1848, was his first in politics and we know from his own papers how it made him suffer. He had come to the fore in 1847 by founding, with various friends, the newspaper *Il Risorgimento*, which made itself, so far as was possible, the spokesman for Italian unity in Turin; but since his contributions to the paper were unsigned and his interventions in parliament modest and few, he retained the anonymity of (as he called it) "a Piedmontese country gentleman." In the ill-fated war his nephew Auguste, nineteen years old and a sublieutenant in the Guards, was killed, and few events later or sooner seem to have grieved Cavour so deeply. He had seen in this boy (the eldest of his brother Gustave's children) a re- birth of his own feelings and opinions "under more brilliant, energetic form," as he said. The boy had willed to him a considerable fortune, in- herited from his own mother and grandmother, but Cavour refused it. He asked, instead, for the bullet-ridden uniform Auguste had worn when he was killed, and this, in a glass case against the wall of Cavour's study, remained a visible reminder ever afterwards.

The second legislature under the new constitution only lasted from January to July (1849) and from this Cavour was absent; the clerical vote had defeated him; but for the third legislature, chosen July 19, he was elected again from the first Turin college, which, during the succeeding storms, never deserted him again. He was becoming better known, and in March of 1850, in the debate on the abolition of judicial privileges of the clergy (including the "right of asylum" for criminals), Cavour made a speech which deeply impressed the chamber and the country. He was not an orator and never became one. His command of his subject was complete whenever he spoke, and his deliberate appeal was to the intellect rather than to the passions; in a subject of this kind, on which the priest- hood made use of every possible prejudice or emotion among the people, Cavour's intellectualism had a maximum effect. The law passed, and in the excitement that followed—with the hierarchy, supported by the Vatican, openly opposing the government—Cavour deepened the impres- sion he had made. In August of that year a cabinet ministry fell vacant by the death of Pietro di Santa Rosa, Cavour's friend (Agriculture, Com- merce and Marine). The Prime Minister, Massimo d'Azeglio, apparently knew very well that by admitting Cavour to the cabinet he was taking in his own successor, but did so (October) just the same. It could hardly have been avoided; but it should also be said that D'Azeglio, painter and poet and littérateur, one of the ornaments of the Risorgimento, was by this time rather bored with practical politics and not at all inclined to cling to power beyond the requirements of duty. Thus Cavour entered government, where he belonged by a natural talent of almost biological intensity, and within a short time his extraordinary energy and competence had given him a commanding position. To his own departments he added that of Finance in the following April, which (although it was supposed to be a temporary appointment) afforded him the opportunity for a brilliant analysis of the financial state of the kingdom and proposals for reform; in that same brief period he successfully negotiated and launched an international loan through the Hambro bank in London. In the following year, after a brief absence from office, which he spent in travel as usual, he became Prime Minister (November 4, 1852), taking the Finance Ministry as well. He held almost all the key ministries at one time or another, combining them with the prime ministership, and often was administering four or five such departments at the same time—not in an honorary or titular manner, but in full control and thorough knowledge. Although he was a convinced constitutionalist liberal and never infringed upon the rights of parliament, freedom of the press or assembly —indeed made it his business to extend them when he could—the government at Turin became Cavour's government in a direct sense. Life is full of paradoxes at any period and perhaps the mid-nineteenth century in Italy contained more of them than usual; but it was observed in the 1850's that the constitutional government of the Sardinian kingdom and Savoy dominions, liberal by definition and in practice, where every man could have recourse to law and no opinion was forbidden—this, the only government of its kind in Italy, was more *personal* than any absolutism. That is, the Pope and the King of Naples, in their absolute power, did not control their governments as Cavour did his. He was ready to resign whenever parliament wished him to do so (which it never did). While he was Prime Minister, however, he governed. It has often been said that Bismarck did the same, and the two men have been compared in many a history book (such as in the one I studied in high school: I well remember it). Bismarck, however, was not a liberal in the slightest degree, whereas liberalism was Cavour's most intimate conviction of the good and the true. Bismarck was a brute, really, as a human being, and never took the trouble to show ordinary politeness to most of those with whom he dealt, whereas Cavour was exquisitely human and humane, humorous and kind, with the manners which can never be taught or learned because they come from the heart. The two men are as different as chalk from cheese, and if by creating Italy and Germany they became "makers of modern Europe," as I seem to remember they did in my school textbook, all one can say is that modern Europe had an oddly assorted pair of fathers.

The decade of the 1850's is Cavour's decade. His goal was plain enough and nobody outside of Italy, that is at the courts of the European powers and in general opinion, had any doubt of it: he was going to unify Italy under his sovereign, Victor Emmanuel II, if it were at all possible for a human being to do so. Inside Italy the republicans in general, followers of Mazzini and Garibaldi, distrusted him on principle but also personally, as being too clever, too smooth, too aristocratic and (from their point of view) impenetrable or inscrutable. His admirers in the earlier stages of his career were chiefly outside of Italy, in France, in England and in Germany, not to speak of his beloved Geneva where all the thoughtful men of a very thoughtful society had early learned to know him. Napoleon III said to Cavour: "There are only three men in Europe—you and I and one other." The other, of course, was Bismarck. The man in Turin was not precisely understood, just the same, by those who so correctly estimated his aim and his powers; what they did not know was the pure patriotic passion which animated him, above and beyond devotion to the house of Savoy or its temporary chief. We know the strength and continuity of that passion through Cavour's letters, including a good many private ones which his contemporaries did not see. We know now that this man deliberately used the house of Savoy as his instrument in the creation of Italy. He had, so to speak, a going concern in his hands: the Savoy monarchy with its hotchpotch of territories was the only half-way modern government in Italy, and if it could be strengthened and made more modern it was the best means to the desired end. The end (as with Garibaldi) was Italy. Cavour's passion for union was a good deal like Lincoln's; if you remember, Lincoln was prepared to save the union with slavery, if he could do so, or without slavery if he could do so: his supreme aim was to save the union. Cavour's supreme aim was to create it.

It is in this respect that posterity has a great advantage; we know Cavour cared little for the house of Savoy as such, and perhaps nothing at all. His contempt for court ceremonies, uniforms and usages was unreserved. It is possible that some remnant of ideal republicanism, which he had certainly experienced in youth, was never extinguished in him. When William de la Rive asked him what kind of garments he had to wear when he was page to the Prince of Carignan, he said scornfully: "What do you expect? The livery of a lackey." Intimately as he had known the

Savoy family in critical as in ordinary times, he could scarcely have preserved for them any of the childish awe by which monarchies profited in
that century. He knew that no prince of Savoy had enough brains or
education to take the place of one of his own secretaries, even for a
day or a week. Only by assimilating the cause of the dynasty within the
cause of united Italy—by making an ultimate identification, one actually
becoming the other—could the loyalty of such an intellect as Cavour's
have been commanded; but once it was commanded, it was irrevocable.

I have mentioned only what was understood and what misunderstood
by his friends; for Napoleon III, Bismarck and the English liberals were
all, for various reasons, his friends, and the Italian republicans—no matter
how much they opposed him—were not really enemies. They would not
have taken his life if they had had it in their hands. His enemies, who
included all the despots of Europe and of Italy in particular, misunderstood far more widely and thoroughly, as is the way of enemies. They
thought of him as a man without principle or conscience, personally
ambitious (through his sovereign), who had, in defiance of his ancient
feudal house and native loyalties, espoused the "liberal" cause in order
to rise to power and exercise it. He was a sort of Lafayette, a "traitor to his
class," but he was also touched by the devil's wing in that his anticlericalism was unwavering from the beginning to the end. It is highly
probable that Pope Pius IX regarded Cavour as either an incarnation of
the devil or a highly trusted representative. The Church as an organization and an army—the Church Militant—was still intellectually be-
fuddled by the strange desire to govern (theocratically!) a little patch of
land across the middle of Italy. No compromise was ever possible between
this "temporal power," as it was called, and the unification of Italy, but
the question was political, not religious. The Church's effort to make it a
religious question not only failed, but glowingly demonstrated the common sense of the Italian people: they knew that there was no reason why
the priest, because he was "minister of God," should collect the taxes
or control the courts. The true religious miracle of the age took place
against Pius IX and the entire machinery of the Church: it was that the
Italian people could oppose the Church in politics, systematically and
steadily for two or three or four decades, and *still* remain devoutly, over-
whelmingly Catholic. It is only in recent times that the Vatican has
shown the slightest comprehension of what a true miracle this was, or
a trace of gratitude for it.

The formula under which Italy was created was Cavour's: "a free
Church in a free State." He did not come to this simple, irresistible solu-

tion until toward the end of his life, but its enactment in history (a high achievement of liberalism, as new in Europe as Jefferson's "Statute of Religious Liberty" was in America) was not long delayed. In this, as in the more practical steps, his was the work.

Those more practical or material steps may be only indicated: he built up the Piedmontese army and strengthened the finances of the Savoy kingdom until, in the Crimean war (1854) between Russia on one side and France and England on the other (in defense of Turkey), Cavour was able to engage as an ally and send troops. Piedmont, as it was increasingly called—it seemed nonsense to keep on calling it Sardinia because its king's title came from there—did well in the war and entered the council of powers of Europe. The action was much criticized then and since; we are all reluctant to approve, nowadays, of a war deliberately declared for motives of aggrandizement, especially when the direct interest is so slight. Cavour's mind saw it as one battle for Italy, and in the long run, harsh though this might be for the dead and wounded, it proved to be so. It was clearly in the interest of western civilization (and therefore of Piedmont and Italy) to keep the Russians out of the Dardanelles. Russia had also been Austria's main support six years before— had crushed the Hungarian revolt and released many Austrian troops for the reconquest of Italy—so that there was a score to settle. In the Congress of Paris, which brought this war to an end, the French Foreign Minister Walewski used the word "Italy" publicly for the first time in forty years as indicating a country or a nation, not merely a peninsula.

The interval between Cavour's triumphs in this respect (as an ally of France and England; as a member of the council of the powers) and his war against Austria could be measured by opportunity only. Every man of sense inside or outside of Italy knew that this was the next step. A foolhardy nationalist would have forced the pace, but Cavour, anxious though he was, made as sure as he could—as sure as the character of Napoleon III would permit—that he was well supported before he undertook it. He then had to maneuver the Austrians into starting the war, since his alliance with Napoleon only applied in case Piedmont itself was attacked. All of this enabled Cavour's enemies to piece together their version of his character: intrigue, duplicity, no moral conscience whatever. It was, to say the least, a very contrived and stage-managed bit of human history, but it reposed upon the sound thesis that the Austrians had to be driven out of Italy if there was to be an Italy. Cavour's crime, therefore—if it was a crime—consisted in choosing the best moment for his own country to make a war which could never have been avoided anyhow.

If he could have had the English with him he would have been delighted, but their sympathy did not extend to direct military action, to which they were not obliged by treaty. The aid of Lord John Russell, of Palmerston and of their minister in Turin, Sir John Hudson, was valuable in a great many other ways; they did not promise the earth, moon and stars, as Napoleon III was inclined to do in his more expansive moments, but what they promised they fulfilled.

Cavour's bargain with Napoleon III (at Plombières, July 20–21, 1858) provided for an Italian kingdom to be created at the end of the war with Austria, which, it was understood, would be provoked at the right time. Cavour was to give Napoleon III the French (or mainly French) dominions of the house of Savoy, but in exchange Victor Emmanuel would be king of Italy from the Alps down to and including the Romagna. (Everything, that is, but the Papal States, exclusive of the Romagna, and the Kingdom of the Two Sicilies.) Jérôme Bonaparte, the Emperor's cousin, was to receive a Savoy princess (Clotilde) in marriage—characteristic of Napoleon III to think of such an embellishment: it would make the Bonapartes more "royal"!—and King Victor Emmanuel and Napoleon were both to make significant remarks at the beginning of 1859 to help bring on a crisis. (How polite they all were by modern standards! Napoleon merely said to the Austrian ambassador at the New Year's Day reception in the Tuileries: "I am sorry our relations with your government are not as good as they were in the past." It was enough to precipitate a diplomatic crisis.)

The Austrians fell into the trap by taking alarm and demanding the disarmament of Piedmont. Disraeli had then come to power in London (with Derby) and intervened with a proposal for general disarmament, which Cavour was obliged to accept on paper, but the Austrians were not satisfied and demanded the isolated disarmament of Piedmont. This, in the form of an ultimatum, Cavour could quite properly refuse. It was then up to the Austrians to make war if they wished. They crossed the Ticino river—invaded Piedmont—April 29, 1859, thus automatically bringing Cavour's alliance with Napoleon into effect.

It was what Cavour wanted, and what, up to the last moment, he had feared the Austrians would be too wise to do. There is a famous anecdote of how he received the longed-for news of the Austrian invasion.

Verdi's *Trovatore*, for some reason, had made a deep impression on Cavour in the earlier part of this decade. The Prime Minister never had time to hear an opera all the way through and did not care for music anyhow. It is said that he could not carry a tune and knew very few bits of music well enough to recognize them. On that momentous evening in Turin when he was waiting to know what the Austrians were going to do—and to his mind the whole fate of Italy depended on it, as we know —the poet Giovanni Prati, who told the story afterward, was received by Cavour for some purpose. A secretary entered with a telegram which the Prime Minister opened at once. Prati and the secretary both stood silent as Cavour's face lighted up with an ungovernable excitement. The Prime Minister said nothing. What could he say? Most of this was secret. He gazed at the other two and then went to the window of his office, flung it wide open and bellowed into the night a tremendous phrase (we do not know which one) of *"Di quella pira,"* the *cabaletta* for tenor which ends the third act of *Il Trovatore*. Nobody connected with this story knew enough about the music to tell us what Cavour actually sang, and my own guess is that he did not sing much of the piece (it is too difficult). He probably made a rough, loud stab at the ending, which is exciting enough for any such occasion: it works up to the final declamation, on three high C's, of *"All'armi!"* ("To arms!") In some way this piece was associated in Cavour's mind with the life-and-death struggle for Italian unity, even though it bears no such meaning in the opera. He used to refer to Verdi as "the author of *Il Trovatore*," and did so in the letter pleading with the Maestro to enter the first Italian parliament.

Cavour, then, made war; Napoleon moved into Piedmont with a hundred thousand men; the Austrians were decisively defeated at Magenta and Solferino. It could have been—should have been—the end of Austrian power in Italy. Cavour admitted the republican Garibaldi as a general in the Piedmontese army and authorized him to raise volunteers for the Cacciatori Alpini, with which Garibaldi moved up to Como and subsequently Bergamo and Brescia. Again, as eleven years before, Italian hope went sky-high. It was during this year that the word *Verdi*, written on walls throughout the Austrian dominions and other despotisms, became the recognized symbol of Italian unity and independence. (It was only the name of a composer of operas—what could the police do?)

The victory at Solferino by Franco-Piedmontese troops commanded by Napoleon, over Austrians commanded by the Emperor Franz Josef, marked the end of the war for the French. Napoleon III was disturbed by the attitude of Prussia and the German Confederation and by the unpopularity of this war in France itself (especially among Catholics). Russia, too, showed its dispeasure and could not be disregarded. Napoleon therefore came to terms with Franz Josef in the so-called peace of Villafranca (July 11, 1859). Of his fine promises and honorable oaths he remembered only one: he took Lombardy from Franz Josef on the understanding that he would pass it on to Victor Emmanuel. Otherwise Austria was to return to the duchies (Parma, Piacenza, Modena, Lucca, which had their own republican governments by now) and was to retain the Venetian provinces. The only thing Louis Napoleon did for his lacerated conscience was to hold the Austrian emperor to some lip service toward the notion of an "Italian federation" under the presidency of the Pope.

The treachery of the French was so quick and so complete that hardly anybody could take it in at first. The French had done it before and were to do it again on this precise ground: Napoleon I, in the peace of Campoformio, had been equally treacherous, but his obligations were less precise and his period less advanced. The one Italian leader who knew beforehand that Louis Napoleon could not be trusted was Mazzini, who said so loud and long. He experienced a brief interval of influence again in central Italy on the basis of this melancholy prescience.

Cavour was as nearly heartbroken as a man of his tough and resilient nature could be. By now he had hardly any personal life left; everything was for Italy in a gathering intensity which almost makes one wonder if he knew how short a time remained to him. He refused to sign, approve or condone the agreements of Louis Napoleon and Franz Josef, resigned as prime minister and made his way to his refuge, Geneva, dusty and broken and sore at heart, for a period of retirement which, although it lasted only five months, may have given him the strength to go on the rest of the way. There were countless other Italians without his responsibility or deep involvement who felt an equal passion of grief, Verdi among them. The outbursts of horror and sorrow in his letters are well known; they show a frame of mind in which it was almost impossible for him to do his normal work. In his case an obstinate predilection for Louis Napoleon, dating from over a decade before, made it more difficult to accept or understand the perfidy of the French.

The autumn of 1859, just the same, showed some mitigations of the gloom: Austria found it very difficult to get back into the duchies and Tuscany without a military campaign which might have brought Napoleon III down again. Napoleon stuck to one of his principles, that of "non-intervention," which made it impossible for Austria to move. This principle stated that action by one power would free the other to do likewise if it chose. Emilia and central Italy (even the Romagna) voted for union with Piedmont and asked for Prince Eugène de Carignan as regent in the name of Victor Emmanuel. Piedmont did not accept, and could not, but in the meantime the ex-Austrian territories all the way down the present main railroad line from Milan to Florence and Rome were organized as republics and combined under the leadership of Ricasoli, Farini and others. This was a very great step toward unity, although nothing could make up for the loss of Venetia. Even before the betrayal at Villafranca the government in London had changed, the Derby-Disraeli cabinet of Tories giving way to the Palmerston-Russell cabinet of Liberals. Lord John Russell was a determined, consistent friend of Italy; with this assurance the English and French were now sufficiently in agreement to quell any Austrian impulse toward adventure.

The circumstances made it possible for Cavour to resume the prime ministership on January 21, 1860, and to retain it until his death eighteen months later. He had very soon to decide what to do about Sicily and Naples, which were in a state of sporadic revolt, and to which the unquenchable Garibaldi was determined to bring aid and leadership. The red-shirted hero was getting together his men and ships in Genoa, under the eyes of Cavour's police. Should he be stopped, ignored or encouraged? It appears now that Cavour took all those courses progressively: that is, he tried to oppose the expedition at first, until he saw how determined Garibaldi was; then he tried ignoring it so as to have a suave diplomatic response to questions; and, finally, throwing caution to the winds (caution including the Emperor Napoleon III but not, we gather, Lord John Russell), he allowed the Garibaldi expedition to proceed and gave it actual assistance and protection from the navy in Genoa.

This was the famous "expedition of the Thousand." The Thousand were Garibaldi's volunteers, the red-shirts, young men of almost every class and character, not all of them Italians, some of them the hero's personal followers even from his South American days. They made a sort of triumphal march through Sicily, acquiring a considerable number of Sicilian boy volunteers, the so-called *piccioli* (little ones), but encountering small resistance. The triumph was due in part to Garibaldi's exceptional skill in maneuver—a guerrilla genius—and in greater part to the low spirits and general dilapidation of the Neapolitan troops opposed to him. The Neapolitan troops, who shared Sicily's detestation of the Bourbon tyranny, had nothing whatsoever to fight for; they were not even paid up to date or decently equipped; they were only peasant conscripts themselves. Garibaldi's treatment of the situation was masterly: he made these troops (greatly superior in numbers if in nothing else) vanish before him. His proclamations and orders of the day in Sicily were of high interest and could be a textbook of such warfare if a similar situation arose again. The people of Sicily (who were unanimous in his support) were to harass the Neapolitans in every way possible, cutting their communications, interrupting their supplies, frightening them when nothing better could be done. The instructions about bonfires are of special interest: the Sicilian peasants were to set big fires alight on every hilltop visible from the Neapolitan encampments, so as to increase the enemy's nervousness, give him an exaggerated idea of his dangers and accelerate his retreat. This (the war of the bonfires) was remarkably successful. Another curiosity of the Sicilian campaign, as pointed out later by Garibaldi on several occasions, was that in this case he had the peasantry with him; the *piccioli* were almost all farm boys under twenty. The priests, themselves Sicilians and opposed to Neapolitan tyranny, did not employ the sacraments for political purposes as they did elsewhere in Italy. A number of them actually joined Garibaldi.

The triumph in Sicily was followed immediately by an equal triumph on the mainland: Garibaldi was dictator of the south. He had consented to move not only in the name of Italy, but in that of Victor Emmanuel, and in his case there never was any pretense of loyalty to that prince— when he said "Italy and Victor Emmanuel," he meant simply Italy with Victor Emmanuel as the immediate and convenient instrument. He would not proclaim the annexation of the south to the northern kingdom, although Cavour did everything to precipitate it; Garibaldi said the kingdom could be proclaimed only in Rome, and Cavour, foreseeing international difficulties, knew that Rome could not be taken just yet. The Savoy troops hurried south to the junction with Garibaldi, which involved the occupation of the Papal States from Perugia to the Adriatic. There were plebiscites in the theocratic areas and in Naples, resulting in overwhelming popular votes for union under Victor Emmanuel. The Piedmontese king proceeded on south and was met at Teano on October 26 by Garibaldi, who hailed him as "King of Italy" and accompanied him on his triumphal entry to Naples (November 7). Two days later Garibaldi retired. All of Italy except the Venetian provinces (still under Austria) and a small rump theocracy in and around the city of Rome was now united. If Garibaldi had had his way Rome might well have been included also. The entire process had taken less than six months (May to November) from the time the "expedition of the Thousand" landed in Sicily.

Cavour had innumerable diplomatic preoccupations through those six months, however, and although he could swiftly and cleverly take advantage of Garibaldi's victories after they had occurred, he was unable to support the hero in advance or assume responsibility for any of his acts. France, Russia, Prussia and Austria had all protested, separately and together, and the Piedmontese monarchy was not strong enough to defy all of Europe. The gravest danger was that the whirligig mind of Louis Napoleon might induce him to send another expeditionary force (to "protect the Pope" could have been the pretext), which, of course, would have legalized a similar action on the part of Austria, thus probably undoing all the work of the past two years. Against this ever present danger Cavour worked indefatigably, and there is no doubt that it was his persuasion that dissuaded Napoleon III from intervening. When, afterward, the French Emperor decided to "protect the Pope" by a garrison force in Rome itself, it did little harm, since the Roman question was left in abeyance for the moment and the Pope was in no danger.

The Palmerston-Russell government in London had proved its friendship for Italy at the most critical moment by issuing a diplomatic circular (October 27, 1860) propounding the right of all peoples to self-determination. (The word used was "autodecision" in continental languages—*autodécision, autodecisione*—and "to decide for themselves" in English.)

Speed, caution, authority, security, diplomatic skill, military firmness, popular support and constitutional processes all had to be combined now, and Cavour was the only man in Italy capable of the combination. He pushed the new laws through the two houses of the Piedmontese parliament during February and early March of 1861, meanwhile keeping the whole peninsula in line behind him and the powers of Europe relatively quiet. On March 17 Victor Emmanuel signed the law and became King of Italy. Cavour's formula, also new, was "by the Grace of God and the Will of the Italian People," which combined the principles of legitimacy (or "divine right"), dear to the old monarchical houses, with the new principles of nationalism. At the end of March a full-dress debate took place (by Cavour's arrangement) on the subject of the capital for the new kingdom. Not much disagreement appeared: Rome was the obvious capital of Italy. Cavour, in his masterly speech, his last great effort, produced the formula of "a free Church in a free State," and said that Rome could not take its appointed place as capital of the nation until the Sovereign Pontiff and the Catholic world were convinced that other guarantees than those of temporal power were sufficient for the seat of the Church. (The "Catholic world" included Louis Napoleon, whose troops were now the Roman garrison.)

If Cavour had lived, it is just possible that a negotiation with Pius IX might have come to something. The Pope was stubborn and deeply prejudiced against new ideas, but Cavour was almost incomparably skillful. However, two months after the proclamation of the Italian kingdom, the great man who had piloted it into port fell ill, and on June 7 he died at the age of fifty-one, in that Cavour Palace in Turin where he was born.

6   Verdi's part in the whole national movement was deeper and stronger than he ever could know, but it was of a kind not to be estimated precisely, even by the most astute of his contemporaries (such as Cavour) or by posterity with all its advantages of evidence. Whether the composer was deep in the struggle, as in Rome in '49, or far away from it in Paris or at Sant' Agata, it was never for long absent from his mind. We can trace its effects in his music with ease. No other category of external experience—not even love itself—had such a direct translation in his creative moods. After the orgy of patriotism which his character made inevitable in 1848, the worst was over, as we have already said; his artistic conscience would never again lead him into musical demagoguery. La Battaglia di Legnano, of which it has been remarked that you could cut out a piece anywhere and it would be the Italian national anthem, was a dead end, and no man of Verdi's deep, sure and steadily maturing aesthetic sense could have gone through those mob scenes in Rome without realizing that such frenzy had nothing, really, to do with music. His very next subject was the Kabale und Liebe of Schiller, a domestic drama of almost bourgeois character, which became his opera Luisa Miller, a forerunner (at least in tenderness and intimacy) of the exquisite Traviata. Then came the "romantic trilogy" or the "popular trio" or the "middle triptych" —it has borne the first two names and we may as well add the third— of Rigoletto, Il Trovatore and La Traviata itself, in which it would take considerable ingenuity to find any reference to Italian nationalism. Those works (the first in 1851 and the others in 1853) bore only such political implications as the ears of their listeners might choose to hear, but nobody nowadays could hear them. Les Vêpres Siciliennes (1855), on Scribe's

French text for the Opéra in Paris, reverts to an Italian revolutionary sub-ject but without the contemporaneity which had clung to earlier work on such themes. *Simon Boccanegra* (1857), a turgid melodrama of Genoa in the Renaissance, and *Un Ballo in Maschera* (1859) exhibited the matur-ing powers of the composer, his search for new expressive frontiers; but neither one could have stirred political feeling.

Verdi, therefore, passed the entire decade of the 1850's—the decade of Cavour—without making any attempt to influence the patriotic evolution of his countrymen. It can be guessed that he made a deliberate effort to avoid themes likely to do so. This was not because of any decline in his own interest; his letters are full of politics. It was, rather, through the in-stinct of the artist. He knew what was *musicabile,* in his own most prac-tical theatre sense, but he was also beginning to feel more deeply and securely what was *music.* Loud patriotic shouts were most unlikely to be music under the best of circumstances, and when they were drowned under louder shouts and cheers from their audiences they became down-right useless: something like this, we may imagine, was the course of his internal progression.

He was frustrated in his desire to purify and isolate the creative transac-tion by three circumstances of imperious power. The first was his own mind and character, which responded so swiftly, simply and strongly to the ups and down of Italy's story that it was reflected inevitably in his compositions. A glaring example is *Don Carlos,* which derives its prevail-ing gloom not so much from the subject itself as from Verdi's anxiety and depression over Italy. Every once in a while a flare-up of the Italian col-lective passion can be heard in works unrelated to it—such as the tenor *cabaletta* in *Il Trovatore* which meant so much to Cavour. Verdi, in short, did not know what he was composing all the time (no good com-poser ever did), and it was beyond his power to keep these emotional waves out of his work.

The second circumstance was, of course, the aforementioned tendency of his listeners to hear what they wished to hear, whether he had put it into the music or not; and the third—obvious by the 1850's and impos-sible to cancel or change—was the plain historic fact that his name itself was a symbol of patriotic passion, aspiration and struggle. If he had com-posed a Mother Goose suite (like Ravel) or a fairy tale (like Prokofiev), it would have made no difference to the Italian public. Whatever he wrote and whatever reached the stage under his name aroused the loyalty and (whenever possible) the public demonstrations of the patriots. To be pro-Verdi was to be an Italian patriot; to be against Verdi, or even to

dislike part of his work, was a betrayal of the national cause. The con-
notations of his name went far deeper than the mere acrostic VERDI, so
as to align the public for or against him on a basis remote from any reasonable consideration of music or the theatre. It was rather like what happened to the same name two decades later, when all Wagnerians were
ipso facto anti-Verdi and all Verdians were under the same automatic
compulsion to be anti-Wagner.

There then arose the problem which few artists have to face in life
and none has ever integrally resolved. That is, how much political responsibility should the artist accept and how far should it go? If he has taken
a side in a great struggle, has contributed immeasurably to its successes
and (no doubt) sent many brave young men to their death, as was
demonstrably Verdi's case in the 1840's, can he withdraw to his so-called
tour d'ivoire, herein understood as a comfortable villa in the country near
Busseto, and wash his hands of the consequences?

Following the law of his own being, Verdi had never had a chance to
escape this dilemma, because his early work was electrically charged with
the emotions of his countrymen. Now, as he grew older, all he wished to
do was to compose opera for the theatre, and no longer by any means
in the same vein: between Nabucco and Falstaff there is an interplanetary
distance and he was about halfway along it. The demand that he "represent" his own people in some way or other, as a member of parliament,
a senator, a member (even) of government, a public speaker, a maker of
public appearances, recipient of this, that or the other honor—many
such clamant and suffocating intrusions—began to occur toward the end
of the 1850's and never died down again no matter what he did and no
matter how tightly he locked himself into his refuge at Sant' Agata.

His first appearance in the unwanted public character which he found
so unsuitable to a "gypsy" (his word) was in 1859, when the vote of the
plebiscites had united central Italy (between Lombardy and the Papal
States) to the kingdom of Piedmont. Already, on the occasion of this
vote itself, he had a foretaste of what was coming.

The voting in Busseto took place in the church of Santa Maria degli
Angeli. For a people who had never voted before it was a solemn historic
occasion and the entire populace was out in the streets. When Verdi arrived in his carriage from Sant' Agata he was met at the boundary of the
little town by the band, which preceded him into the center through the
crowds, playing music which we can only suppose must have included
the Chorus of the Hebrew Slaves. It was the high moment of the day
when Verdi arrived and cries of "Viva l'Italia! Viva Verdi!" filled the air.

The applause was apparently continuous, even in the church—since Italians are not afraid of churches—and the tears were copious. Verdi dropped his vote into the magic urn—the first voting apparatus ever seen in those regions—and we can be sure that his own eyes were not altogether dry, either.

All Emilia and Tuscany, as we know, voted for union under Victor Emmanuel, and the various "republican" dictators (combining under Farini for the duchies and Ricasoli for Tuscany) held the fort for the King during the time when he could not take possession of his new territories because of the armistice. Busseto wanted Verdi to represent it in the assembly of the Parmesan provinces, which he accepted: then that assembly wished him to represent it in presenting their allegiance to Victor Emmanuel, and he could hardly refuse.

Verdi—forty-six, vigorous, handsome, hair and beard brown without a gray hair—was flanked in this expedition to Turin by the other most famous citizen of the state of Parma, Jacopo Sanvitale, an octogenarian poet who had spent years in prison and in exile for the cause of freedom. They became great friends on the journey and agreed to write the national anthem of the new Italy together (another national anthem), which, of course, they never did.

The delegation arrived in Turin at noon on September 15, 1859, and was received by Victor Emmanuel at three in the afternoon. He is supposed to have said something of this kind: "I know that I don't understand music, but also I know how, and how much, your sublime songs have brought out the love of the fatherland in the hearts of Italian people from 1842 until 1859."[2]

Verdi's primary wish in Turin, just the same, was not to meet the King—his republicanism left obstinate traces for years—but to meet the great man of Italian union, Cavour. It was during that interregnum when Cavour had resigned office in indignation over the Villafranca armistice; Rattazzi (who was afraid to accept the allegiance of Emilia and Tuscany, by the way) was struggling along as Prime Minister; Cavour at the moment was in retirement at Leri, his rice-planting estate in lower Piedmont. Verdi asked Sir John Hudson, the English minister in Turin, whom he met on that first day, and Hudson arranged it immediately. On September 17 the two of them took a train early in the morning to Livorno

[2] Gino Monaldi, *Verdi aneddotico*, p. 47. The words sound awkward as transcribed, but the King probably said something along those general lines. Monaldi might have had his version from Verdi or might not. His anecdotes are of uncertain authority on the whole.

Vercellese, a few kilometers from Leri, where Cavour's carriage met them; when they got to the farmhouse the count himself was out in front with open arms. (During these hours the rest of the delegation from Emilia was making a pilgrimage to lay a wreath on the tomb of Charles Albert at Superga—an insincerity of which Verdi could hardly have been capable.)

The meeting with Cavour moved Verdi deeply; the only other encounter in his life to compare with it was that with Alessandro Manzoni a decade (almost) later, but Manzoni was an immensely old man and Cavour was a contemporary—not only a contemporary but in some respects, for an Italian patriot, *the* contemporary. The public demonstrations in the streets of Turin, the official greetings, the King's flattering attentions, all put together, did not equal for Verdi the conversation by the fire in Cavour's big living room. For Cavour, too, it was an encounter unlike others. He knew little of music and cared less, but he regarded Verdi as one of the true makers of the Italian revolution and furthermore found his own heart touched to a kind of response, musical or not, by some pieces of Verdi's. His reverence for Alessandro Manzoni—their elder by some thirty years—was equal to Verdi's, and he had once met Manzoni, at Stresa in 1850. The integument between these three was not much short of mystical, since no single one seemed to have been equipped by nature to understand the other, and yet (originally through the Italian aspiration) they came to a rare degree of special awareness and special comprehension between them. We cannot doubt that Cavour found in Verdi's utter honesty and simplicity a species of splendor; it was outside the experience of a man in public life; whereas to Verdi the spirit and humor of Cavour, his instinctive kindness and his bonhomie were, altogether, more than he could have imagined possible for such a great man. Verdi—without a trace of affectation—wrote to Cavour afterward almost as a peasant would write to a prince. Cavour was wise enough to know how great must be the source of such humility.

On that day the city of Turin made Verdi an honorary citizen (it took Milan thirty more years to do the same). The delegation returned to its native regions through Milan, where there were more public demonstrations, street scenes and patriotic outbursts. When Verdi got home again (September 21) he wrote his letter to Cavour—his "bread-and-butter" letter, we might say—which reads as follows:

"*Let Your Excellency excuse the extra work and boredom which perhaps I inflict with these few lines. I wished for a long time to know, personally, the Prometheus of our nationality, and did not despair of finding* an occasion to satisfy this lively desire. However, what I should not have dared to hope was the frank and benign welcome with which Your Excellency deigned to honor me. I went away moved. Never shall I forget your Leri, where I had the honor to shake the hand of the great statesman, the supreme citizen, the one whom every Italian should call the father of his fatherland. Receive with kindness, Your Excellency, these sincere words of the poor artist who has no other merit than that of loving and of having ever loved his own country."

It was shortly after this, under the pressure of the time's uncertainty, that Verdi bought 172 rifles from Genoa to equip the Civil Guard in his town of Busseto. The British Minister in Turin, Sir John Hudson, tried to help him at first, and he got them eventually through the conductor Mariani; all men were of all trades in time of stress.

But Cavour returned to power in January of 1860 as we have seen, and there was no further danger that foreign bayonets might come into the states of Parma and the rest of Emilia. There followed all the stirring events of 1860 which we have touched upon. There was no thought in Verdi's mind of composing music or producing anything in a theatre. He thought of Garibaldi, of the Thousand, of the union of Italy. "Those are the music masters," he said, "with the cannon." Of Garibaldi: "By God this is a man to go on your knees before." In April, just before Garibaldi and his Thousand went to Sicily, Victor Emmanuel came to central Italy on a visit to his newly acquired provinces (which he, or Cavour, had now accepted). Busseto presented him with a cannon, mounted, drawn by two horses—chiefly paid for by Verdi's money.

During this year of hope and fulfillment Mariani came to Bologna for the first time as conductor of the Teatro Comunale in its opera season and wanted to open with Verdi's most recent work, *Un Ballo in Maschera.* Bologna is not far from Sant' Agata. The conductor hoped to get the composer for rehearsals and productions: not a remote chance. Verdi was only interested in the war in the Romagna, wanted to hear nothing of opera or theatre, and upbraided Mariani: "Where is the King? You who are in the midst of everything, why don't you write to me about the war in the Romagna?"

There was not much likelihood that the unification of Italy, as it now might be called even with Rome and Venetia left out, could take place without involving Verdi in some fashion. Cavour it was who decided: Verdi must be a member of the first Italian parliament. With Verdi in the Chamber of Deputies and Manzoni in the Senate, the two most famous of Italian artists, or most Italian of famous artists, would lend the luster of their presence to the great meeting; they would help to make it national and not simply political.

Sometimes we are inclined to wonder if Verdi's marriage to Giuseppina (August 29, 1859) was not in some way connected with the political activity which his friends wished upon him in that and the next year. Peppina had been united to Verdi for twelve years by then. There never had been any subterfuge about their relations; they lived together as man and wife and might at any point have become man and wife; there were no real obstacles. In August, after the plebiscite in which central Italy joined Piedmont, and just two weeks before Verdi's mission to Turin and his visit to Cavour, they went to a village in Haute-Savoie (then still Victor Emmanuel's dominion) and were married by the Catholic rite. When we turn, and soon, to Peppina's whole story, we may speculate a little more fully about the time and manner of their marriage, but in this connection it is enough to say that the arrangement of the dates is suggestive. Some of Verdi's friends may have helped him to realize that Peppina's position, in the event of any public or national duty on Verdi's part, might be distinctly awkward. By this time it was almost as embarrassing to get married as to stay unmarried; it was all done as quietly as possible to avoid notice; but at any rate during the next few years when Verdi was trying—like a fish out of water—to sustain life in an alien element, Peppina could at least go along with him. Life in Turin might have been difficult, to say the least, if they had not taken the trouble to get their marriage lines.

It was the town of Busseto, again, which put forward Verdi as a candidate for parliament without his own consent. He was ready to support another candidacy and had already given his word when Cavour publicly declared (January 10, 1861) that Verdi belonged in the new Italian legislature. At this news the composer took himself off to Turin to see if he could avoid the unwelcome duty. "Don't be surprised to see me in Turin," he wrote to Mariani. "Do you know why I'm here? In order not to be a deputy." In a capital crowded with men trying to get themselves into the new parliament he was, as he said, doing everything possible to get out of it. It was in vain. When Cavour got his letter and sent for him it was seven in the morning of January 18, bitter cold.[3] The composer had prepared a set speech giving his reasons for refusing this honor—his unsuitability in every way for parliament, his occupations, his terrible impatience, which he feared would make him unable to listen to the long

---

[3] Verdi remembered it as being six in the morning, and in December. (The letter to Piave, February 8, 1865.)

speeches customary in the Chamber, and other arguments of the kind. Evidently poor Verdi spilled it all out in haste, as he confessed in a letter years later, so that it seemed like a schoolboy's excuse, memorized word for word. Cavour listened gravely until the part about the long speeches, at which he burst into a tremendous peal of laughter. (His own patience was none too secure.) He then proceeded to knock down the composer's excuses, one by one, in a courteous and deferential manner, producing in their stead some reasons which seemed to him to make Verdi's presence necessary. The musician then accepted on condition that he could resign later on. Cavour accepted the condition, provided that Verdi would consult him before taking any such step.

Verdi did have some hope that he might be defeated in the election: he had received a flattering offer from St. Petersburg and was about to "take up his pen once more," as Peppina said. (She was greatly in favor of the journey to Russia.) The voting took place only a week after he got home to Sant' Agata and he was elected. Parliament was summoned for February 19. Instead of the mild winter in Genoa, to which he and Peppina had grown accustomed, they must now pack and depart for the cold mists and sharp winds of Turin. Mariani again, from his vantage point in Genoa, obtained the "passport" for "poor Loulou." (Conductors had various jobs with Verdi, it seems.) "Poor Loulou," the spaniel, accompanied the composer and his wife wherever they went at that period.

Verdi took his duties as a parliamentarian seriously. He attended all the sessions of the Chamber and tried to keep his mind on the procedure and the speeches. When it came to voting he did whatever Cavour did. "This way I know I'll never make a mistake," he said. He did not speak or take any part in the politics of the corridors, but his opportunities in conversation with the Prime Minister were not neglected. He set forth to Cavour his favorite scheme for the reorganization of the great conservatories and opera houses of Italy, which he would have had the government support in the three great centers, Milan, Rome and Naples. (The government was to pay chorus and orchestra in each of these theatres.) Evening schools for singing, full conservatory courses for instrumentalists and singers, were to be open, free, to all the people, who could thus supply the "choral and instrumental masses." Soloists were not difficult to find, but the "masses" in any theatre were a problem. Verdi himself had more consistent dissatisfaction with chorus and orchestra than with any other element in the opera house, and ten years later when he presided over a commission to put reforms into effect he gave them chief attention.

Cavour accepted the plan and took steps to get it going.

During the four months of the parliamentary session Verdi was much in the company of his lifelong friend, Count Arrivabene, an aristocrat from Mantua whose culture in all directions, particularly music, was valuable and whose character as a patriot and a man—as well as his devotion to the composer—made Verdi's esteem for him high and permanent. Arrivabene had another quality rare among their contemporaries: he never committed the treachery of dying, at least for a very long time, and was able to mitigate the solitude of the composer even at an age when most of the others had gone. With this spirited mentor, who knew all the kitchens of politics (he was a journalist, too, and wrote for *L'Opinione*), the musician was saved from some of the errors he might have made in his innocence of a new world.

The one person we might have expected him to meet in Turin during that momentous session was his idol, Alessandro Manzoni, but it could only have happened by accident and the accident never occurred. Manzoni had taken his place in the Senate, like Verdi in the Chamber, because Cavour put it as his patriotic duty. The two were extremely aware of each other—they were the prize ornaments of the parliament, for one thing; they were Cavour's special jewels; they admired each other inordinately; each of them had a host of fervent adherents, even in a cultural desert like Turin, and many of these must have been the same. (Among the Manzoniani there must have been many Verdiani, and vice versa.) How an accidental meeting failed to happen, or why, indeed, somebody did not contrive it, we do not know. Verdi had a morbid horror of forcing himself upon anybody's attention, and he was most of all fastidious about "intruding" upon the great old man whom he so deeply revered. Manzoni knew this—all of Verdi's idiosyncrasies were famous; everything in connection with him, including his little dog, was by this time household knowledge in Italy—and he, too, was unwilling to take a step. They probably did glimpse each other occasionally, at court, for example, or in some diplomatic reception; both were friends of Sir John Hudson, for instance; both were devoted to Clarina Maffei; it is odd that somebody did not overcome their separate and combined delicacies enough to bring about a meeting. Clarina would have done it, as she eventually did, but she was never in Turin.

The new parliament voted the kingdom of Italy, under Victor Emmanuel; it passed Cavour's resolution calling for Rome to join Italy as the natural national capital; it went through a dozen new and stirring ceremonies. This was a time of ardor and sentiment, but we may be sure that nobody in Turin was more deeply moved by it all than the amateur deputy from Busseto. Still he wrote to Mariani: "What beautiful things they all say, and what a waste of time it is!"

It was a waste of time for him in particular because the Imperial Opera at St. Petersburg was getting impatient. Verdi, too, who had written nothing for two whole years (indeed a record in his life up to then), was anxious for pen and ink. Peppina wanted to "freeze her nose" in Russia, as she made clear. Politics and parliament, we may conjecture, did not mean much to Peppina. The only subject Verdi had in mind for an opera was *Ruy Blas*, on the Victor Hugo text, which he had been considering off and on for twelve years, but the Imperial Opera refused; there then followed the usual despairing search through dramas old and new to find a subject. Verdi was in a slight huff with the Russian censorship for refusing *Ruy Blas* and did not try very hard—"he is much more occupied with the Chamber than with the Theatre," says Peppina. In the midst of this unpromising situation an emissary arrived from St. Petersburg (the son of Tamburlick, the leading tenor there) with a sort of unconditional surrender on the part of the Imperial Opera. Verdi could write *Ruy Blas* or anything else he chose to write, under whatever conditions he chose to name, "so long as he did not oblige the Emperor Alexander to proclaim the Republic in Russia." (Peppina's words). Verdi hemmed and hawed. *Ruy Blas* no longer appealed to him, nor did anything else. In the course of the discussions he remembered something he had once read; it might do; but of course it could not be found in Turin; somebody had to go to Milan and institute a search. It was, or became, *La Forza del Destino*, and Peppina began to make over all her clothes for a cold climate. It was May, but she embarked with enthusiasm on a program of "*foderare, adattare, impellicciare vesti, sottane, corpetti e camicie*"—padding, adapting, befurring the garments—for the succeeding winter. It was in this mood that they left Turin, at the end of the session, for Sant' Agata and the tranquillity of their own garden.

Before parliament rose—in fact, soon after the vote on the resolution to make Rome the capital—Verdi went to Cavour and said that in his opinion the time had come to "say farewell to these benches."[4] Cavour objected: "No," he said, "wait until we go to Rome." Verdi: "Are we going to Rome?" Cavour: "Yes." "When?" Cavour: "Oh, when, when —!" Verdi: "Well, in the meantime I'm going to the country." Cavour: "*Addio*, take care of yourself, *addio*." These were the last words he heard Cavour speak.

The news of the death (June 7), so inopportune and early, of a man

4 Verdi's own account in a letter to Piave, February 8, 1865.

whom Verdi regarded as the father of his country was a blow unlike any other he had endured or was to endure. It was especially cruel because it did not seem possible that anybody else could undertake the work that still remained to be done. All Italians felt bereft on that day (except, perhaps, Mazzini and Pope Pius IX, the two extremes). It was harder for Verdi than for most because he had felt Cavour's spell, had known it on close terms, had put his faith in this luminous intellect and firm purpose. He knew every Italian of eminence in his time, but none ever made the impression upon him that Cavour did: the idol Manzoni, so old and great with his summit in the clouds, was not at all the same thing.

"I have not the courage to come to Turin," he wrote to Arrivabene. "Nor could I be present at the funeral of that man."

He stayed at Sant' Agata in one of those seizures of gloom which were a torture to him and to all who came near him. The town of Busseto had a memorial service to the Prime Minister, as most towns did, and Verdi told Arrivabene about it.

"The clergy performed gratis," he said sourly, "and that is no small thing."

(Cavour had received the last sacraments from a pious and devoted Franciscan, Padre Giacomo, a friend of many years, afterward summoned to Rome and punished by losing his parish and his right to administer the sacraments; to many patriots, as we have seen—including Santa Rosa—the sacraments had been refused on their deathbed by order of Pius IX.)

Verdi had to keep on as a member of parliament because he had no recourse, but after Cavour's death he lost interest. For most of two years he was not present at the sessions and when he did go he took no part. As he said in the famous letter to Piave which gives his own account—erroneous, as we have seen, in some details—it could have been said of the Italian Chamber of Deputies: "The 450 are truly only 449, because Verdi as a deputy does not exist."

He went to Russia and came back, a journey resulting not only in the opera La Forza del Destino but also in some exceedingly funny photographs of himself befurred in the snows of the north; he worked at his revision of Macbeth and then entered upon the heavy, heartbreaking labor of Don Carlos, the last work of his middle maturity. The wild, passionate Verdi of other days was no more. In one sense it may have died with Cavour: that is, never again was he capable of a patriotic outburst or one which could be interpreted as such. The "war" music in La Forza del Destino is little more than a joke, and for my own part I have always considered that Verdi wrote it as such. His concentration upon Italian unity and freedom never slackened but it was turning dark, getting a little sour. He detested all the circumstances of the war of 1866. He wanted Venetia, yes; every Italian did; but to take it at the hands of Napoleon III, after an attack upon an already defeated enemy—Austria was shattered by Prussia before Italy even moved—was repellent and ignoble. His anxieties over this war and its results colored *Don Carlos* and gave it at the same time its somber grandeur as music and its failure with the frivolous public of Paris. Only four years more, and the Prussians, swollen with pride at the humiliation of Austria, turned on France. Napoleon III was compelled to withdraw his garrison from Rome and the Italians immediately occupied it, bringing to an end the temporal power of the Church and putting the capital of the nation where it belonged. This, too, was according to Verdi's lifelong hope and prayer, but he could not rejoice in it sufficiently because it was accompanied by—indeed caused by—the victory of the Prussians over the French. The composer saw, as every man of sense must have seen, an omen of tragedy for Europe and the world in this triumph of brutality over civilization.

The last years of the unification of Italy, after Cavour's death, were in fact anything but heroic. The two big steps were made against no opposition and cost nobody anything: they were the kind of bargain-price bravery in which Mussolini indulged when he declared war upon France in 1940, after Hitler had already won. Verdi felt the events of 1866 with indignation, fury at times, and even with shame: he thought Italy should refuse to accept Venetia under such ignominious conditions. Garibaldi, the only Italian commander who had won victories against the Austrians, was ordered to retire from the ground he had gained in the Trentino: he replied with the celebrated word, "*Obbedisco*," (I obey), and tried to redeem the honor of the kingdom a year later by attacking Rome, but was frustrated by Napoleon III. From that conflict (Mentana, 1867) until the Prussians invaded France in 1871, Napoleon kept a strong garrison in Rome. Garibaldi himself was at the end of his military career, which he crowned after Napoleon's downfall by a generous and effective contribution to the defense of republican France as a volunteer.

These public events were profoundly different in moral essence from those which had engaged Verdi's heart and mind throughout his first fifty years. The Italy of struggle and sacrifice, the Italy which was saturated with the blood of heroes and martyrs—at least ideally speaking; in material fact there was little blood and less martyrdom—the Italy of Homeric dreams, now turned into a workaday country like any other, in which the politicians took advantage of everything that seemed likely to produce a result, the stock market was more important than ideas, and a whole new set of oppositions (capital and labor; socialist parties; colonial ambitions) came into being. Verdi's progressive disillusionment was shared by most of those who had striven to create this Italy: some of the expressions he uses about it are similar to those used by Garibaldi. The makers of Italy were not pleased with what they had made. It is easy to say that " 'twas ever thus"; the pain is no less each time.

Cavour's untimely death was in 1861; Mazzini, steadily denying that the new Italy was the true product of the Risorgimento, died in 1872, Victor Emmanuel II in 1878 and Garibaldi in 1882. All together in their various ways, often at cross-purposes, these men had molded the nation. Alessandro Manzoni, greater than any of them, as Verdi came to think, had gone his way in 1873, when he was nearing ninety. The composer survived them all into a world in which not one of them (except perhaps Cavour) could have made his distinctive fight for life, the life of the individual and of the species, against what seemed a welter of bourgeois greed and a stifling of the spirit. Verdi's distaste for the stock-market culture of prosperous, successful and united Italy shows in many letters of his old age. He gave himself no political label, detested the party organizations, was as distrustful of the "left" as of the "right," and never shared Garibaldi's final belief that a return of what they had all known in their youth (the spirit of Risorgimento) might come through socialism. (Garibaldi's socialism, with an anarchist tinge, came through such personal influences as Bakunin, Alexander Herzen and Louis Blanc; the old red-shirted hero really knew next to nothing about it.)

The composer may have come to think of the most fiery passages of his youth with some regret; he never said so. It was not in his character to deny the past. The rigidity with which he now stayed aloof from every movement, position or undertaking which might be called "political" or be suspected of a political tinge was statement enough. Once Italy had been at last united (Venice, 1866; Rome, 1871), there was no artist in Europe who more ferociously minded his own business and told the rest of the world to let him do so. The last composition he ever made which was of a "public" significance or could be given such significance over and above its musical content was the "Hymn of the Nations," on a text by Boito, for the London Exposition of 1862. The work (for high voice, tenor or soprano, with chorus and orchestra) was Italy's contribution to the musical part of that great Victorian display, and Verdi felt its composition to be another form of patriotic duty. Arrigo Boito, the talented boy of twenty whom he met in Countess Maffei's house, produced a poem dedicated to peace, freedom and love between the peoples of the earth. The misadventures of this cantata in London may be of interest in another connection, but as regards the Verdi of "public" life it counts chiefly as a farewell. "These pieces for occasions (*pezzi di circostanza*) are, artistically speaking, detestable things," Verdi wrote to Arrivabene.

The world's affairs never ceased to interest him, no matter how deep his retirement from them. His feelings were often harrowed; his opinions seem to grow more trenchant as he grows older. Much of what he had to say contained the wisdom of the peasant and the intuition of the artist, a combination far beyond the powers of most politicians. Perhaps it is not surprising, therefore, to find that his views stand the test of time better than those of almost all the "statesmen" who were so industriously going from bad to worse. For a case in point we might mention his grasp of the elements involved in Napoleon III's downfall. Verdi had had a long experience of *Hassliebe* with the French, whose natural, unconscious arrogance drove him into fits of anger. He had suffered greatly at the Opéra. As an Italian, he had raged at the heartless whimsicality of Louis Napoleon—or at his uneasy and changeable conscience, whichever it might be called—and the French Emperor, whom he had known and liked, seemed to him a villain and traitor in 1859. Never had he suffered more from French frivolity, superficiality and unmusical or antimusical standards than in 1866 and 1867 with *Don Carlos*. His soreness and rawness whenever France and the French were mentioned can be seen in many letters of the late 1860's. Yet there was much in his own life that was involved with Paris, where, after all, he had discovered the permanence of love (the "*sortilège mystérieux de la vie à deux*," as Alphonse Daudet once called it—not marriage, but "life in twain"). The French culture and life in general had once seemed very good to him, and as soon as the disasters of 1870 came along he remembered that, too. Above all, as an Italian and as an European, he was aghast at the downfall of what, for better or for worse, had seemed the capital of western civilization. To his Neapolitan friend Cesare de Sanctis (August 10, 1870) he writes from Genoa:

"*I have lived too much time in France not to understand how the French make themselves insupportable by their insolence, their morgue and their fanfaronnade. But whoever thinks seriously, and whoever feels himself to be truly Italian, must be above such pinpricks, and we must remember that Prussia has declared on another occasion that 'the sea of Venice and Trieste belongs to Germany.' . . . Prussia victorious means: the German Empire definitively constituted, Austria destroyed and pushed into the frontier of Europe, the Adriatic sea to the German*

Empire up to the Adige. The rest of Italy, think for yourself what it would become! . . . This is what we have to fear later on and what frightens me now. . . . I am still hoping. I hope in the valor of the French soldier, even though I fear the strategic knowledge of the German."

To Arrivabene, September 13, 1870:

"I am saddened by the events of the war and deplore the misfortunes of France; I fear a terrible future for us. . . .

"I should have liked, for my part, a more generous policy in our government, and I should have liked for us to pay our debt of gratitude. . . . I know it can be answered: 'What, a European war?' But the European war will not be avoided, and if France were safe we should also be safe."

To the Contessa Maffei, September 30, 1870:

"This disaster to France puts desolation into my heart, as in yours. It is true that the blague, the impertinence, the presumption of the French were, and, in spite of all their miseries, still are insupportable: but after all, France gave liberty and civilization to the modern world. And if she falls we must not illude ourselves: all our liberties and our civilization fall, too. Let our writers and politicians sing the knowledge, science and even (may God forgive them!) the art of these conquerors; but if they looked a little bit within, they would see that in their veins there flows the old Gothic blood; that they are of unmeasured pride, intolerant, scornful of everything that is not Germanic, and of a rapacity that knows no limit. Men with heads but no heart: a strong but not a civil race. And that King, who has God and Providence always in his mouth, and with their aid is destroying the best part of Europe! . . . The antique Attila (another missionary idem) stopped before the majesty of the capital of the ancient world; but this one is about to bombard the capital of the modern world, and now that Bismarck wants to announce that Paris will be spared, I fear more than ever that it will be, at least in part, ruined. . . ."

In this letter he says that perhaps a hundred thousand Italians might have been enough—thrown into the battle in time—to have saved France "and ourselves." That, of course, is debatable, but he believed it. The occupation of Rome, which was the only action taken by the kingdom of Italy during the crucial year, left Verdi cold (his words). He could not imagine the constitutional liberties of the Italian state existing alongside the Inquisition, or a parliament reconciled to the College of Cardinals. "I can't see Pope and King of Italy together even in this letter," he says.

We have observed that he gave 10 percent of his first Aïda money to the Paris hospitals; later on, after Napoleon III's death, there was a proposal to put up a monument to him in Italy and Verdi subscribed money for that, too. Many old republicans and patriots were shocked. The composer shocked them still further by saying that he believed Napoleon III had been instinctively and naturally a friend of Italy. The posthumous pardon has more weight, as a result of reflection, than his angry words in 1859.

There is good evidence for Verdi's strong dislike for colonialism: Italo Pizzi, an Orientalist who knew the composer only in old age—from *Otello* to *Falstaff*, so to speak—used to go to Sant' Agata every year in the autumn and take notes of what the old man said. Upon Verdi's death these notes were worked into a brief book called *Ricordi Verdiani* (1901) which are valuable in several contexts. One day in September, 1896, the aged musician got started talking about India, which at that time had not yet achieved a national movement or a national leader. According to Pizzi he said:

"Here's a great and ancient people given over as prey to the English. But they will regret it! Peoples allow themselves to be oppressed, vexed and maltreated, and the English are sons of bitches.[5] Then comes the moment when the national sentiment is aroused and nobody can resist. That is what we did with the Austrians. Unfortunately we, too, are in Africa now playing the part of tyrants; we are wrong and we will pay for it. We say we are going there to bring our civilization to those people. A fine civilization ours, with all the miseries it carries along with it! Those people don't know what to do with it, and moreover in many ways they're more civilized than we are!"

In these and other formulations of his views, right to the very end, we see in Verdi a direct, honest and essentially unchanging independence. It made him a rebel until his ends were achieved; but contentment, acceptance, the capacity to go along with the tide wherever it might go, were not in his nature. The union of Italy, by releasing him from any need to work for it any more, did him an immense good: it allowed him to forget it. The height of his achievement—*Aïda* and the Manzoni Requiem, *Otello* and *Falstaff*—came only after Italy was free, as we observed earlier. There may be an interdependence, a partial relation of cause and effect; it is at all events a fact which suggests its own explanations. In the first of these great final works, the "liberated" works as we may call them, patriotic passion does have its part, and *Aïda* would be a different and much weaker creation without that element. Afterward it vanishes, never to be heard again.

[5] Literal translation of the dialect expression *fioeui de can*.

7   The old man going home in the night in Rome might well say, "Find me another libretto!" In moments of expansion he must have felt that his powers were still with him; they had never yet played him false. His sense of the body's decay was active, but then, to tell the truth, it always had been; he was forever weighing himself and counting his hours of sleep and experimenting with his diet, even many decades earlier. Now, in this last farewell to Rome, after the intoxication of *Falstaff*, which he knew to be good, and true, and beautiful, he may have briefly dwelt upon the possibility of another recourse to that eternal spring from which he drew his strength. In the morning it would be different (*"triste, triste, triste!"*), but on this night of nights there was still the distant voice of the siren, youth, calling upon him to be up and doing. He could show himself, late as it was, to the crowds in the street, and wave his withered hand, and sigh: this was Rome, the Rome of 1848 and of all the anguished years, the Rome that had gone to the barricades shouting *"Viva Verdi! Viva l'Italia!"* Just as they had shouted tonight— just as they had shouted tonight.

In spite of all the disillusionment of the dream fulfilled, there must have been a great, fixed clarity in that last Roman night, a vision of what could last out a life and had already lasted out many. It was the vision of Rome itself as ideal, as an undying center of light. He had given much; others had given more; and here it was, before him. In saying farewell he must also have made his salute to the dream of which these moon-drenched stones, old and new, were the counterpart on the earth of men. *Vale*, yes, but *Ave*, too. For Mazzini, Garibaldi and Cavour; for all Italians past, present and future: *Ave, Roma immortalis!*

3

Peppina's Paris

1   Peppina liked Paris.

The broad, deep and permanent character of Peppina was that of the human female. It preceded, sustained and survived all of those other personal and exceptional characteristics which made her for decades unique in Europe. She was, in the familiar simile, like an iceberg, a pleasantly warm iceberg, with the submerged part of her invisibly joined onto other and larger realities. In old-fashioned Freudian language, she was a woman.

There was never the slightest doubt of what Verdi would do about his invitation to Paris in the great year of his final triumph, the year which is the theme of this book. He would go. He would go not because he wanted or needed to go, and not because it would be of any advantage to art, history or human welfare, but simply because Peppina wanted to go. Through all the long story of Verdi's negotiation with the outside world, that negotiation which is the artist's livelihood as well as his sorrow, the Paris transaction had always been the worst, the most painful, the one which gave least aesthetic satisfaction for most hard work and anguish of spirit. He suffered more in Paris than anywhere else, before, during and after; he resisted going there; he regretted having been there. Aside from French composers, of whom the best were failures in their own capital, only the Italian opera composers of the early nineteenth century (Rossini, Bellini, Donizetti), along with a few Germans willing to shed their own skins for another, such as Meyerbeer, could make the necessary submission to French standards. Wagner's disastrous attempt to do so has—fortunately for us—left one gorgeous fabric of orchestration, the *Tannhäuser Bacchanale*, but remains in other respects a ruefully sad and funny piece of musical history. If Wagner and Verdi are today, and permanently, a part of the Paris repertoire, it is only because the French themselves, always stronger and braver than their mentors, have enforced their will upon an administration inimical to art.

Peppina wanted to go to Paris simply because she liked Paris. Like all women, she bought dresses and hats there. She had a fondness for the amenities and elegancies of a life which, after all, must be seen—even now —to have no parallel on earth for those who wish amenities and elegancies. Just as French champagne is quite beyond comparison to any imitation which has so far been made of it in any country, so life in Paris is now, as in Peppina's day, much more sparkling and unalloyed by thought. No milliner can compare with a Paris milliner; no dinner is like a Paris dinner. Domestic servants in Paris are deft, comprehending, skillful, abounding in forethought and forgiveness for error; the washing of clothes is better than anywhere else on earth; silver is polished even better than in England; it is not necessary to explain to these domestics any of the ordinary habits of comfortable people. Peppina, poor dear, must have had a great deal of trouble making it plain to her country servants in Italy about baths; these ideas have even yet not penetrated far into the Italian people outside of the great cities and hotels. Neither the French nor the Italians take baths regularly, of course, but the French regard bathing as a normal procedure on the part of those who can afford it; the Italians think it abnormal. Peppina's stipulations for the baths, the kitchen, the cooking, the changes of linen and all the rest of it (as we have them in several of her letters demanding accommodations in various hotels) are those of a woman who has had a great deal of trouble obtaining what she wants and must have. In Paris she could get it all by a wave of the hand.

Peppina loved comfort, cleanliness, warmth, the surroundings of life which material prosperity can so easily provide. The chances are that she found it out first in Paris, since these conditions scarcely existed in Milan before she went away. She also quite obviously liked society; that is, the companionship of human beings who could exchange remarks with her, and this, also, must have been a Paris discovery. A cultivated woman of good sense and good taste, capable of wit upon occasion, Peppina may have been naturally superior to all but a very few of the Milanese countesses in social grace; she may have been kinder, prettier, better dressed and livelier in every way; and certainly she had no need to feel of lesser account than they on moral grounds. Aside from her early liaison with the manager Merelli, her life seems to have been completely monogamous by even the strictest Victorian standard (matrimony excepted). None of this made any difference: she could not be received in the rather limited number of aristocratic or semi-aristocratic houses which constituted Milanese society. Few, very few, were the theatre artists of any kind, among women that is, who escaped the general taboo: those who did were so fantastically famous (like the dancer Taglioni) that curiosity annihilated the barriers, or else they made grand marriages and entered the salons, if they wished to do so, as duchesses or princesses but not as theatre artists. Milan was small, provincial, stiff-necked; it had been governed, socially speaking, by an Austrian court for a very long time, and a Spanish court before that; it had "die Spanische Etiquette," like Vienna. And there are plenty of witnesses now living who can testify that no theatre artist could have been normally "received" in a great Vienna house before 1914.

Paris was totally different. It was not only bigger, richer, gayer, more cosmopolitan and consequently less hidebound, but its own most interesting social intercourse took place on precisely the plane where Peppina felt most at home—among artists, writers, musicians, painters and members of the aristocracy and bourgeoisie. There did exist a rigidly enclosed aristocratic society which Peppina would never see—the so-called "Faubourg Saint-Germain"—but this, apparently, was so antiquated and so deadly dull that already by the 1840's it was being deserted by its younger members, excepting always the young girls. (Until they were married they remained in the treadmill, and that tendency still prevails in many families.) By and large, however, "Madame Strepponi, the Italian opera singer," had not the slightest difficulty finding friends in Paris, especially after she had united her life to that of an enormously successful composer. There were a great many houses where she and her admired friend were constantly welcomed, and a great many men and women of intelligence who were delighted to be asked to her house. This was not the demimonde—far from it: it was as remote from the half-world Balzac so vividly described as it was from the Faubourg Saint-Germain. Peppina in Paris need never be bored by the stale grandeurs of aged duchesses, but neither need she be shocked by the sight of a young man drinking champagne out of a slipper. Her natural taste for decorum (akin to Verdi's, and perhaps each brought it out in the other) was thus gratified by a social life in which her "irregular situation," as it was called in Victorian language, played no visible part. Such things might have been less important, of course, if her situation had not been, in fact, irregular; but since it was, she valued the good manners and prosperous respectability of her Paris world as much as she did its intelligence, gaiety and wit.

In addition to all these attractions, Paris possessed one other of special merit to Peppina: it spoke a language she knew well. She not only talked it with little accent, fluently and correctly, but she had an excellent command of French in writing and in reading as well. This made her more valuable to Verdi in Paris than anywhere else; made her, in fact, indispensable, since he never overcame his difficulties in that respect. He had learned the language late and imperfectly; his youth had given him no time for studying French; and as for English . . . ! There is not much doubt in my own mind that the main reason (aside from climate) why he refused to settle in London, in spite of great financial inducements, was that he would then have become totally dependent on Peppina for everything. As we shall see, she, too, perceived this, and would not have been at all averse to such a decisive move: she already could read and write English well enough and with her talent for language would soon have mastered the speech.

So, all in all, what with comfort and social consideration, a life agreeable to her tastes and her self-respect, with much more to do for Verdi as translator and secretary than she ever had to do in Italy, Peppina had all the usual feminine reasons for liking Paris and a few added ones of her own. She was not a sentimental woman, really, at least in her maturity, but she certainly could never forget that it was in Paris that she and Verdi had first openly united their lives. Her "*Mago*" as she called him, her "wizard," was hers for the first time in the eyes of the world when they took that house out at Passy and lived there, in the 1840's, happier, probably, than ever before or afterward, without thought of marriage (so far as we know), without either pledges for the future or regrets for the past. Free and still young, deeply in love, Peppina in her early thirties must have regarded herself as one of the luckiest of women, and the Paris in which all this came to pass was a sort of paradise.

Over the tremendous vista of their years the glow of Paris never faded for her. Sometimes she had to conceal this from her "wizard," because his sorrows as an artist were too often connected with the fair city of her predilection. She learned to complain about Paris weather, taste, manners and Philistinism, almost word for word as Verdi did, but her heart was not in it; left to herself she always showed her eagerness to grasp at any excuse to go there. Through the long period—almost half a century— which elapsed between their first and their last days together in Paris, there is a perceptible tug-of-war between Peppina and Verdi on this subject so long as it remains open to discussion. Once they have arrived in Paris, she joins him in condemning it, but up until they get there it is Peppina who wants to go—avidly and sometimes insistently—and Verdi who would rather not. She had an incomparable feminine technique of bringing him around to the decisions she wanted him to make. She could mention it in all sorts of ways at all times of day, gently and by indirection. Her gay, amusing letters on the subject of St. Petersburg reveal how she worked her wiles, and how helpless Verdi was in the long run against a beloved woman whose mind was made up on a course of action (*his* action).

It was natural that they should have had this lifelong tug-of-war because, after all—and we can see it plainly although they could not— Paris meant quite different things to them. Paris—and we may as well take this as meaning the whole world outside of Italy—was boundlessly exciting and interesting to Peppina anyhow, and would have been so under any circumstances; she loved travel, change, new faces, the theatre of life and art, just as much as she enjoyed luxury and society. To Verdi every visit to Paris was an aesthetic ordeal because it involved the agonizing preparation of an opera against difficulties unknown elsewhere, with results which never once compensated for the suffering. (They compensated financially but in no other way.) The very first time he heard an opera in Paris he judged its musical standards correctly; he never had occasion to change his opinion. Politics, too, meant at least half of life to Verdi, and perhaps more (nothing at all to Peppina, we think): and in this realm of his being he could scarcely ever feel warm toward the French until their decisive catastrophe in 1871—until, that is, they lost the power to vex and impede their neighbors. Peppina did not have to struggle for eight or ten hours every day in the opera house with musicians who refused to understand what the composer wanted them to do; Verdi did. Peppina was evidently not exposed to the attitude which Verdi so fiercely resented, that of French superiority to all others in the theatre—the intolerable pretension, as he felt it to be, that they knew more about his own music than he did. It is also most probable that Peppina never felt the artistic shortcomings of the French orchestras, choruses and singers so deeply as Verdi did: sometimes she seems to see success where he saw failure, or at least an acceptable result where he found only hopeless inadequacy. It is possible to surmise that the external trappings, including the large payments in gold francs, may have weighed more with Peppina than they did with Verdi. He was a shrewd peasant and wanted every gold franc that was his due, but he was also a supreme artist to whom bad musicianship was torture.

Then, to be sure, they were not only man and woman, a categorization involving many differences, but they were also country-bred and city-bred. At a much earlier stage of this examination I mentioned how very hard this was on Peppina during the long, snowy winters or the rainy seasons in the country when she had nothing whatever to do except order the meals and try to keep warm. Verdi was locked in his study, writing black pothooks on white paper, for many hours every day, and for many other hours he was out tramping the fields in the mud: these were two adventures in which she was unable to accompany him. It was *morne* and it was *triste* for her (her own words), and the Villa Sant' Agata, beautiful and eminently comfortable as it may seem to us, only came to life for poor Peppina in the good weather, which, on that vast plain, means the summer months with a bit added at each end. It might have been different if she had had any neighbors to whom she could talk, or if she could order the carriage and go calling on somebody; these ordinary pursuits were barred to her in the beginning by her "irregular" situation and, afterwards, by the stern and haughty refusal which the Maestro presented to every neighborly advance. What it came to was simply this: for a good few years the neighbors would not speak to Peppina, and thereafter Peppina was not allowed to speak to the neighbors. This may all seem hopelessly inconsistent or illogical, but we shall hope to understand better as we go on; and anyhow, as all know, logic and consistency seldom prevail in matters of human passion. This entire business of Verdi and Peppina, their nonmarrying and their marrying, their relations with their country environment and with their city environments, their very carriage routes when they went out driving, involved a network of human passions, stupidities and weaknesses which, however regrettable, were only the particular form of a condition general to all of us.

Now, in 1893, with the Maestro about to have his eightieth birthday and Peppina only two years behind him, you might have thought all this tangle of pride and prejudice must be over. In one respect it was: that is, nobody in their country or city neighborhood, anywhere they chose to go, would treat them with less than reverence. But by now a wall of habit had shut them in: by now they had formed whole systems of existence, collocations of time, movement and response. Certain persons regularly visited the villa and stayed for a few weeks without ever setting foot in the nearby town of Busseto; this was their society, as it had been for many decades, and by now they wanted no other so long as they were at the Villa Sant' Agata. Inside the walls of their garden and park they were inviolable, and the compromise reached years before was that they should take to a gentler clime—the Palazzo Doria in Genoa—in bad weather. Peppina's dream of Paris had come true again and again during the past half-century. It was to come true once more before the end.

Verdi's year of apotheosis was bound to bring offers for a *Falstaff* production in Paris. There were such offers from almost every great city possessing an opera theatre; the difference was that Paris, because of old ties and a closer general relationship, claimed the Maestro's own presence for the rehearsals and the first three performances of the work. Carvalho, director of the Opéra-Comique, was eminently shrewd in this: it was Verdi himself who had startled the world by producing such a youthful masterpiece at the age of eighty; and for a Paris audience the composer's presence would greatly add to the excitement of the occasion. (In other and more brutal words, the curiosity aroused was as much about him as about his work.) Gailhard and Bertrand, co-directors of the Opéra, felt disinclined to be left out of the party, and proposed to put on *Otello* at the "big shop" while *Falstaff* was going on at the "little one." If their scheme had worked out, something like a Verdi festival might have been the result in the following winter or spring.

There were difficulties which came from the old Maestro himself. After the *Falstaff* première in Rome he and Peppina went back to Genoa for a while until it was warm enough to go to the country, and, both from Genoa and afterwards from Sant' Agata, Verdi imposed his conditions in a series of letters to those concerned. He was (as always) concerned about casting, scenery, chorus, orchestra, conductor. The idea that these two productions, one at the Comique and one at the Opéra, constituted a very rare tribute to any composer, or that they had been conceived with any such purpose, never seems to have crossed his mind. All he wanted was for each of his final works to be presented properly. Gailhard and Bertrand had thought to please him by making their *Otello* production (the first in France) with an Italian cast, chorus and orchestra and in its original language. To this Verdi strongly objected, on the ground that such a thing would be so strange and unusual that the audience at the Opéra, accustomed to French texts, would resent it. For both *Otello* and *Falstaff* he wanted French texts prepared by his own indispensable Boito with the assistance of Du Locle. When Gailhard and Bertrand dared to suggest some changes in text, this, too, was barred. It became evident that the *Otello* production could never be made ready for the following spring and must be held over for another season. Gailhard and Bertrand, looking for a new work of similar importance to take its place, hit upon *Tristan und Isolde*, which, although by now a quarter of a century old, had never been performed in Paris. Then, when the enormous success of *Falstaff* at the Comique threw them back on their original idea, Verdi was reluctant again. He did not feel that the directors of the Opéra could very well juggle in this manner with Wagner and Verdi productions, especially such mature works as *Tristan* and *Otello*, since those who expected the one would resent the other, and the public in general might resent the whole business. Thus, as it turned out, *Falstaff* went on in the spring of 1894 and *Otello* in the autumn (after considerable difficulty); and, in spite of all his hesitations, objections and forebodings, Verdi was present at both. Peppina's wishes in the matter must have played their usual part, even though we find no precise proof in the letters; she could hardly have failed to run true to form in such a conjunction. Verdi's fears were

quite unfounded, since no Wagnerian "animosities" (his word) arose
on either occasion; nor did the public of Paris object to the rare honor
done to a foreigner by two such premières within a short time in the national theatres. That Verdi could have dreamed of resentments, animosities and failures for his two supreme masterpieces indicates—to me at
least—not only his unconquerable fear of the Paris public and his distrust
of it, but also a certain bone-deep humility of spirit which fame and
fortune could never change. As a practical man he knew that his dominion in the opera theatre was unique, and he once said to his friend Arrivabene: "When you go to India and the heart of Africa you'll hear
Il Trovatore." In spite of this state of affairs he went through the same
trepidation over each work, up to the end, and especially in Paris.

The Verdi ménage moved in 1893 in its usual orbit: Genoa, Sant'
Agata for the summer, then Genoa again; and in the spring of 1894 it
was in Paris for April (*Falstaff* at the Comique, April 18), then back to
Genoa and Sant' Agata. In October, the last visit to Paris: *Otello* at the
Opéra (October 11). It was the day after his eighty-first birthday.

2   There were two strands or elements in Verdi's Paris career as a
composer: one was made up of his own experience in writing
work directly for the Paris theatres, rehearsing it, directing it for its first
production, or, in a few cases, rewriting work which had already been
produced elsewhere and going through all the struggle of a première.
The other was the less painful but more normal procedure by which his
work reached Paris after having seen the light elsewhere. The first thing
that strikes us in comparing the two is that the work he did directly and
originally for Paris was less successful in every respect to him and to the
public. When he was not thinking of Paris at all, or only in the most indirect sense (as he must have been in *Aïda*), his work took Paris by storm.
It almost seems, on the face of it, that his "bad luck" in and with the
Paris theatres arose when he was there himself, trying very hard, failing
and bemoaning his fate. When others took charge, there was a long
record of triumph.

This may be shown clearly by the list of works he wrote directly for Paris. This is:

Jérusalem, a rewritten version of the earlier I Lombardi, to the French text by Royer and Vaëz: Opéra, November 26, 1847.

Les Vêpres Siciliennes, original, to the French text of Scribe and Duveyrier: Opéra, June 13, 1855.

Macbeth, rewritten to the French text by Nuitter and Beaumont, considerably changed from the earlier Italian work of eighteen years before: Théâtre Lyrique, April 21, 1865.

Don Carlos, original, to the French text of Méry and Du Locle: Opéra, March 11, 1867.

None of the four, not even the admirable Don Carlos, can be heard today except in rare revivals; the first has totally disappeared and the others, when they are produced at all, have gone into an Italian text. There is little doubt that Verdi did not feel at home with French words, however well he might know their sound and meaning; he was not at ease in the language and never became so. He was inclined to attribute some of his other Paris failures—such as Luisa Miller, at which he was not present—to the inferiority of the French translation. But the general vexation and ultimate failure of his personal experiences in Paris came from another source, and we have already indicated it: he felt strange there and was constantly resenting what he felt to be unfounded pretensions. He had a good deal of incidental trouble connected with Paris productions, as well—Victor Hugo's objections to the operas made from his plays; the litigation over the rights to Le Trouvère (a French version of Il Trovatore) and other such annoyances, all of which contributed to his very peculiar and touchy attitude toward the French even in political matters. When it came to writing Aïda, as we have already seen, he refused to consider a French text: after Don Carlos and its heartbreak he would not attempt that language again.

As against these few harrowing failures, there can be set a long list of Verdi operas which were instantly successful in Paris and many or most of which have continued to be performed there to the present day. That list began with Ernani (in spite of Victor Hugo) and went right on through all the most familiar Verdi works to the end. There never has been a time when the romantic trilogy, Rigoletto, Il Trovatore and La Traviata, altogether disappeared from the Paris theatres, and Aïda is as essential to Paris as to other capitals. All of these, ending now in his extreme old age with *Falstaff* and *Otello*, came to Paris after productions elsewhere, after the period of trial and error was over. True, Verdi himself did preside over the rehearsals of both the final works, but with far less trouble than in his earlier days: their premières were over and their styles were set; moreover, some of their singers were familiar with the Italian productions; it was altogether a different problem. Nothing like the amount of work was required of him now, in all his prestige and power, as had been demanded in his youth. He, who was accustomed to prepare an opera and put it on the stage in twenty days, found when he first went to Paris that the average at the Opéra was five months for a new work! All that was over now.

There still remains a strong suggestion that Verdi's suffering in Paris and the unsatisfactory results he obtained there may have been in part (although only in part) his own fault. The hardest case to understand is that of *Don Carlos*, a beautiful work to which he gave the best he had to give; it had a mediocre success in Paris, or what he preferred to call a failure, and the moment it got into Italian it was rapturously received. There may be innumerable and complex reasons, but the simplest of all is language: this most Italian of composers probably should never have been working with French words, singers, orchestra and managements at all. There were veils upon veils between him and them. He had to try because all his predecessors had tried, most of them with glittering results, and because the highest emoluments for a composer were in Paris. After several trials he ended by taking the emoluments—which were his anyhow, in good gold francs paid to the Rothschild Bank—and staying out of Paris.

The last return, in 1894, was one long triumph in two sections: the first in the spring and the second in the autumn. We may see in this something very characteristic of Verdi's life as a whole, its long, long progression toward a high peak seldom reached in any art. The inadequacies (his own and those of others) were forgotten now. *Otello* and *Falstaff* made a sort of living miracle out of this composer, whose earlier work had evoked acid criticism in Paris even when it was most popular. Now it was roses, roses all the way, and never a thorn among them. The clamor over *Falstaff* at the Comique in the spring was equaled or eclipsed at the Opéra in October. The President of the Republic (Casimir-Périer) was present at the first *Otello*, sent for the composer at the end of the first act and presented him to the cheering public from the imperial box. He kept Verdi with him throughout the second act and bestowed on him the

Grand Cross of the Legion of Honor. In accordance with Paris custom, the composer took bows from the stage at the end of the evening. He and Peppina were the guests of honor at a presidential luncheon in the Elysée Palace on October 18. After the third *Otello* they went back to Genoa.

3   All this was a story different not only in degree but in kind from Verdi's entire previous acquaintance with the capital of the West. We have already seen how he hesitated, in those far-off days before 1845, to leave Italy. He could have kept on composing for the Italian opera houses without a moment's rest: indeed, he had already done so, with an effect on his own nerves and health which his friends deplored. He had never been outside Italy at that time except for one flying trip to Vienna (for *Nabucco*). Before the age of thirty-two, he could very nearly name his own terms in the Italian theatres, and the offers which came from London and Paris were less attractive than they might have been otherwise.

But, as we know, in those years he was growing steadily more disillusioned with the capacity of the Italian theatres (especially La Scala) to give good performances of his work. He had quarreled with Merelli. In the end he said he would not produce at the Scala again, and did not do so for many years. In all this it is difficult to disentangle the personal from the impersonal, the private motives from the artistic ones; was the Scala really as bad as he said? Only three short years before he had been delighted with it. Were chorus and orchestra, scenery and management and public, all in such a rapid state of decay? Perhaps not. Perhaps the young Verdi, overworked and dissatisfied, was like many young men simply tempted by new fields and thought (like many another before and since) that the far-off hills might be greener. If this were his motive he certainly concealed it well, for the amount of postponement, reluctance and tergiversation he put into his correspondence with the foreign managers (chiefly Lumley of Her Majesty's in London) showed that his mind was not clear. He was in bad health, and this alone might have contributed to an infirmity of purpose. I believe, however, that the secret of the matter was Peppina.

The truth of the triangle formed by Merelli, Peppina and Verdi cannot be known because the written evidence—which becomes so lavish later on—does not exist. Letters, diaries, memoirs and the tangle of cross-references which enable the curious to establish almost everything in the lives of Wagner, Cosima, Bülow and King Ludwig are not in this case available; if they existed, they were destroyed. In the Wagner circle it was customary to keep scraps of paper and copies of scraps of paper (even telegrams): such became the custom in the Verdi circle later on, but not in the early days when Verdi first set out for Paris and London. We do not know precisely when Peppina left Merelli's bed and board, or when Verdi's quarrel with the manager reached its height; all we can conjecture is that the two events were not far apart in time and not unrelated. By the time Verdi at last consented to leave Italy and carry out his postponed contract with Lumley of Her Majesty's in London, Peppina had already migrated to Paris and established herself there as a teacher of singing. If she wrote to him—and it would be surprising if she had not; she was an indefatigable letter-writer—nothing remains to prove it. He certainly knew where she was, and one of the curiosities of the story is the hesitant and roundabout way he took of rejoining her, which he did not do until almost two years after her own departure from Milan.

He had, of course, numerous engagements, of which one—the Macbeth score for the spring of 1846 in Florence—enkindled more enthusiasm than any other of the period in Verdi: he thought it best of his work up to then, and went so far as to dedicate it to his revered and beloved father-in-law Barezzi, the benefactor of his youth. In this homage to Barezzi we may perhaps discern a hint (which may not have been consciously intended) of feeling that his relationship to Barezzi might soon change—some premonition, that is, of an alteration in his own life. All the uncertainties of these years (1845–1847) are uncharacteristic of Verdi, who generally found little difficulty in making up his own mind. It is quite possible that he felt himself drawn to Paris and Peppina by a force beyond control, but at the same time dreaded the possible results upon his "own" family, that of his first wife, which stood in a relation to him which was stronger than the ties of blood. A remarriage, or even a union without marriage, must in some way wreck the most valuable connection he possessed; so he seems to have thought a little later on; and it took him a very long time to outgrow the strange, shy and powerful sense of guilt toward his dead Margherita and all her family. Of all this there is ample evidence during the next few years, and to a man of Verdi's clear intelligence it cannot have been unforeseen; he knew himself. I am not suggesting that he left Milan, the Scala and Italy on a prearranged scheme with Peppina, or that there was any element of deliberate plan involved. In the absence of direct evidence the supposition is too strong. What is much more probable, as well as more in the natures of all concerned, is that he felt himself drawn toward Peppina and Paris but reluctant to yield; as a composer of opera he must go abroad sometime, and his contract for London could not be indefinitely postponed; he had a tender conscience about Barezzi; he hated Merelli by this time, and between the two there had been unpleasant episodes even after their final quarrel (that is, professional disputes in which they did not meet but the public and company at the Scala were involved). The situation in London just then made his manager, Lumley, more insistent than ever on the contract, for a rival opera house, Covent Garden, was beginning its career with a number of the most popular singers and Verdi was needed.

Verdi finished his London opera—*I Masnadieri*, which was Maffei's version of *Die Räuber* by Schiller—toward the end of May, 1847, and set out on his travels. Accompanied by his devoted Emanuele Muzio, who reported their doings in copious letters home, he made his way from Como through the St. Gotthard pass to the Lake of the Four Forest Cantons, Basle, Strasbourg. There he decided not to go direct to Paris: the stagecoach was not ready and, by a most uncharacteristic whimsicality, he chose to alter his route and go by way of the Rhine and Brussels. It was a devious but rewarding journey. He and Muzio went to Baden-Baden, Karlsruhe, Mannheim and down the Rhine by boat in the most exquisite season of the year. Diversions were rare with Verdi; he had done nothing but work for most of his life; the Rhine and all the sights and sounds were a joy to him. At Brussels he and Muzio got the stagecoach for Paris, saw "that monument" (Waterloo) with "great regret," and tried on their arrival to push on at once for London.

If they had done so, it would be pretty well established that he did not meet Peppina again at this time. However, he was met with unexpected news which turned out to be unfounded, but it delayed him two days in Paris: it was said that Jenny Lind refused to learn any new parts and consequently would not be available for his opera in London. Verdi sent Muzio on to London at once to find out the truth of the matter. If he could not have Jenny Lind (the *prima donna assoluta* of Lumley's theatre), he would not go to London at all. Léon Escudier was able to assure him that Mademoiselle Lind was not only ready but anxious for her part in the new opera, and after this brief pause Verdi followed Muzio across the Channel.

During his two days in Paris he refused to go anywhere or meet anybody, although Escudier wanted to drive him about the city and introduce him to useful friends. In this behavior (getting rid of Muzio by sending him ahead; refusing Escudier's good offices and immuring himself in his hotel) Verdi may tempt us to suppose that he was providing himself an opportunity to meet Peppina again. We are at liberty to suppose it; we shall never know. The only thing on record is that he went to the Opéra and wrote: "I have never heard worse singers and a more mediocre chorus." On June 5—after all this travel in about ten days—Verdi arrived in London.

Muzio had already seen the apartment reserved for them by Lumley: three rooms at five pounds a week with ten shillings extra for the servant. The loyal pupil had been horrified at this expenditure and quickly knocked off part of it by introducing a divan-bed for himself into the sitting room; there would thus be one room less. On arrival two days later Verdi promptly restored the more extravagant arrangement. He was very late for his engagement and was told that the management of Her Majesty's Theatre was on tenterhooks. Said he: "The impresario may complain; but if he says one word to me that goes against the grain, I will give him ten in exchange and then immediately go back to Paris no matter what happens."

There were, in fact, no complaints. Mademoiselle Lind—as she was always called at the time—a phenomenal Swedish soprano now twenty-seven years of age, had just stunned England by her vocalism only a few weeks before, as she had previously stunned Berlin and other cities in Germany. She had an extraordinary purity of tone and a dramatic talent to go with it in her own particular parts (wide-eyed and innocent characters like Agathe in *Der Freischütz* or Amina in *La Sonnambula*). She was already beginning to have grave moral doubts about the propriety of appearing on the stage, at least in opera or any form of dramatic entertainment, and was soon—within two years—to give up the theatre for good, to sing afterward only in concert or oratorio without the frivolities of paint, powder and costume. Mademoiselle Lind's puritanism found an echo in that of Queen Victoria, whose favorite singer she rapidly became and remained.

Jenny Lind is such a familiar name in the social history and legends of her time that her qualities as a musical artist, aside from the fact that she had a rare voice, are obscured. She seems to have been, aside from everything else, a remarkable musician, and in the task of preparing a new opera for presentation Verdi probably found this the first and most welcome quality, as it was (among singers) the least expected. But aside from everything else—everything she had to give, great as it must have been—the immediate and overwhelming effect made by Mademoiselle Lind was that of unreasonable, inexplicable fame, magical and limitless celebrity. She was one of those women whose mere presence in a city was enough to cause the assemblage of crowds difficult for the police to control. Her American tour two years after this, a landmark in the social and cultural history of the United States, was managed by P. T. Barnum, who had a reputation for exaggerating such things or superinducing them by artificial means; yet it certainly must be observed that she had had the same effect on the Germans and had been having just the same effect on the Londoners for about one month when Verdi first saw her. At this moment, when Verdi met her, she was fleeing the attentions of her admirers; it was next to impossible to get a ticket, at any price, when she sang at the opera; she had created an excitement in London which seems to have been more intense and unreasonable than any similar craze of the Victorian era. Those who gathered to cheer her or even to catch a glimpse of her had never heard her sing, for the most part. She had that kind of fame which seems to be almost independent of its own cause; that is, whether she sang or not, the people had somehow elected her as a focus for their joy and wonder.

Verdi, of course, was only human, and also he was a composer; it was no small thing to him to come to London with a new opera for the star of all stars. As he often remarked, he was a boy from Busseto, "excluded even from the geographic charts." As a poor peasant boy from the town that was not even on the map, as an Italian who had never been in London or Paris before, as a young man whose only knowledge of polite society was very recent, he may have been afflicted by a good many misgivings during these first weeks in London, and Mademoiselle Lind was probably at the center of it all (more even than Queen Victoria herself). Yet, after he had met Mademoiselle Lind and had heard her sing, he could write to his friend Giuseppina Appiani in Milan: "I am always the type of fidelity. Do not laugh, by God! or I shall fly into a rage."

These words, as applied to Mademoiselle Lind, may be interpreted as one wishes. The composer evidently admired without surrendering. For one thing, the virgin musician from Sweden probably spoke no Italian, although she sang it exquisitely; Verdi spoke no English or German; they were undoubtedly obliged to get along in their contrasting varieties of bad French. Nor was Mademoiselle Lind beautiful to an Italian eye, in spite of the raptures which had been lavished upon her. But most of all, these enigmatic words—"*io sono sempre il tipo della fedeltà*"—seem to me to refer to Peppina. Professor Gatti in this connection has inquired: "Faithful to whom? Or to what?" He leaves his own question unanswered but it is evident that he, too, thinks it must have been Peppina, whether Verdi had seen her again in Paris or not.

At all events, our ever trustworthy Muzio gives us the best account of Mademoiselle Lind, and since he never had an opinion that varied much from that of his Mister Master, we are safe in assuming that what he thought, Verdi also thought. This is a literal translation of Muzio's letter to Barezzi on the subject:

"*She can read any piece of vocal music at sight. Her voice is a little harsh in the high notes, weak in the low ones; but by means of study she has succeeded in making it flexible in the high part so as to overcome the most abstruse difficulties. Her trill is unapproachable, she has an agility without equal, and, in general, in order to display her virtuosity in singing she sins by ornamentation, shakes and trills: things which pleased in the past century, but not in 1847. We Italians are not accustomed to this style, and if La Lind came to Italy she would abandon her mania for embellishments and would sing simply, having the voice even and flexible enough to sustain a phrase in the manner of La Frezzolini. Her face is ugly, serious, and there is something Nordic in it which makes it antipathetic to my eyes; she has a great big nose, big hands and feet the same; I wanted to look her over well on the sly, as they say (this is what one must do with all celebrities, one must look at them very well). She leads a most retired life; she receives nobody (and she is quite right, because she won't be bored). She lives for herself; she hates, or so she told me, the theatre and the stage; she says she is unhappy, and will experience contentment and a little pleasure when she no longer has anything to do with theatre people or with the theatre itself. On this point she is greatly in agreement with the Maestro, who also hates the theatre and cannot wait for the moment to retire from it.*"

Aside from Mademoiselle Lind, the great world of London scarcely existed for Verdi because he refused almost all invitations. He dined once at Lumley's house to meet Prince Louis Napoleon, then an exile from France but so soon to become its president; this strange personage, who afterward played such a part in the affairs of Italy and consequently of Verdi himself, seems to have made, initially, a good impression on the composer—an impression which evidently survived decades of political ups and downs, since Verdi subscribed to his monument. More than once, with Italian exiles, he met Mazzini. These (and Queen Victoria!) were the historic monuments that came his way. Otherwise he devoted himself to the orchestra, the chorus and the singers of Her Majesty's Theatre as soon as the ink was dry on his score of *I Masnadieri*. (The instrumentation came last, as usual in this period, and was not even begun until the end of June.)

I Masnadieri was performed for the first time, by the Queen's command, on July 22. It was the last day of Parliament, and, as usual, Victoria intended to repair to Scotland immediately afterward; if she were to hear the new work it could be no later. Verdi might have liked a little more time—he had, in fact, only a week with full cast and orchestra. As it turned out, nothing would have made much difference. Under great urging the composer himself conducted the first performance, an effort he rarely consented to make at any time in his life. Mademoiselle Lind at the height of her powers and, what is more, at the peak of her phenomenal novelty, gave the central part great brilliance. The Queen, the public and the newspapers all responded with enthusiasm—and the opera itself fell dead, deader than all but one or two others in Verdi's profuse early work. It had been written, says Gatti in excuse, upon "a drama false in concept and artificial in expression." It had aroused in Verdi no flight of inspiration—nothing, in fact, but his professional skill and a certain vividness of expression which could never desert him for more than a few pages at a time. Beyond a doubt the psychological uncertainties, the hesitations and reluctances which afflicted him during this period in life itself, causing him to be more unsure of his own course than was natural to him, must have permeated the whole work. At all events it had only three performances in all, the last of them conducted by Michael Balfe (of *The Bohemian Girl*). Jenny Lind's magic could have given it more repetitions if it had been ready for production on time, but Verdi's slowness (which he himself calls "laziness") kept it from the boards until the final gasp of the London season. In those days, after the Queen had gone to Scotland it was not worth-while keeping the doors of an opera house open. The work has disappeared for a century, as it apparently deserved to do. Verdi summed up its practical results as "enough success to procure many thousands of francs for me."

Just the same, London was keenly aware of the composer and he could have made himself quite a downy nest there if he had so desired. Lumley offered him a contract for ten years as conductor and composer; he was to prepare and conduct all the works and contribute one new one of his own each season, which at Her Majesty's meant February to August. Terms: 60,000 gold francs a season, with lodging and carriage provided. No practical man could turn down such an offer without serious thought.

Verdi left London for Paris after his second performance of *I Masnadieri*, and it was in Paris, under quite different influences, that he had to make up his mind. Surveying all the elements (including those which we are obliged to guess), it seems that the London climate was another deterrent. For a man with a throat, even if it were only a psychological throat, that climate is never highly recommended; and for a valetudinarian like Verdi, constantly fussing over temperatures, diet, weight and the like, it was a source of misery. His letters dwell upon it more than on any other subject. "If I can carry off my bones from London this time it will be hard for me to come back," he wrote to Countess Maffei. "London is a marvelous city, the surroundings are stupendous, but the climate is horrible."

Muzio, keeping Barezzi fully informed on the Maestro's state, says (even at the end of June, when the weather should have been at its best): "The heavy and humid air reacts upon his nervous system and makes him more moody[1] and melancholy than usual."

Paris in August was, like London, deserted by the great world, and Verdi seems at first to have thought he could treat his stay there as a period of rest and recuperation. He would pause a while, "quiet, free, away from all annoyances, seeing neither managers nor publishers." He treated Lumley's offers coldly, although at one moment he did contemplate the notion of taking a London contract for three (rather than ten) years. In the meantime Lumley's eagerness vanished; the rival management at Covent Garden had come to grief and there was no longer such urgent need for Verdi as a counterpoise. That scheme, before long, went off into thin air and we hear no more of it, but within a very few weeks the Paris managers had discovered their guest and laid siege to him, with, in spite of all his previous declarations, a quick and easy conquest.

What had happened in those first few days or weeks in Paris to change Verdi's mind so completely? He had met Giuseppina Strepponi once more —we do not know precisely when—and had renewed with her a relationship which, whatever it had been before in Milan, very quickly became the most indissoluble of human bonds in his existence.

There is no reason for adult human beings to doubt that Peppina and Verdi had been lovers from about 1842 or 1843; everything suggests it and nothing precludes it; the extreme propriety or reverence of certain

[1] In Italian, *lunatico*.

biographers leads them to gloss it over or even to ignore it, owing to the fact that she was still (at that period) the official mistress of the manager at the Scala, Bartolomeo Merelli. Aldo Oberdorfer solves the difficulty by saying, upon no evidence adduced or indicated, that by 1842 Peppina had passed from Merelli to Verdi and that their great "love affair" was the matter of the next three years or so in Milan.[2] We could hardly expect older authorities, those close to the family and friends, to be more specific than this, or even so specific in the absence of proof. None of Verdi's love letters exist and even Peppina's are of a considerably later period, after their union had long been public.

Where all is guesswork and (unless some forgotten documents come to light) must forever remain guesswork, one makes one's own version of events, based upon such study, contemplation, sympathy and comprehension as one may have had for the persons involved. It seems to me beyond question that the loves of Peppina and her Verdi began in Milan in 1842 or possibly even earlier; there are strong suggestions (to me, anyhow) that she fell in love with the composer the moment she met him, and at what precise point he reciprocated enough to become her lover matters little, although I should guess earlier rather than later. Verdi was not by any means difficult to entice into a lady's bedroom; according to the legend of the time, the difficulty was to keep him out. The loss of his wife and children had perhaps left him—after the tragic coma of many months had passed away—freer than most men in such ways, less reckful of the consequences, more dispersed and unquestioning in his habit. If Peppina were, as I think, madly in love with him, she would have thought nothing at all of the necessity to deceive her lord and master Merelli, nor would she have given overmuch thought to the further fact that Verdi was simultaneously the intimate friend of other ladies of Milan. In other words, I see the origin of this lifelong attachment in *une affaire de boudoir* (using these words in the way they would have been used in the 1840's or in Balzac) which involved no concept of union or fidelity on either side. I believe Peppina was in love and Verdi not, or less, or intermittently. His other connections, the talk of Milan at the time, went on during these same years. It may seem to be a scented, lascivious and unworthy inception for a wonderful human union, and yet can any grown person with knowledge of the world deny that such evolutions do occur? The amount of deception, subterfuge and pretense, the number of downright lies, which must have been involved in such a relationship would, in many cases, have brought it to an abrupt and painful end. Pep-

2 G. Verdi, *Autobiografia dalle Lettere.*

pina's love, which was the truest strand in the web—we cannot read a single one of her letters without feeling it—was what turned the *affaire de boudoir* into a serious, lifelong union more admirable and more enviable than almost any other marriage of the century.

How strange it is—we cannot help thinking—that Verdi and Wagner ran in such parallel and related lines! If there is such a thing as the *Zeitgeist*, it must be a matter of air waves more subtle and delicate than any yet discerned, but every student knows that human thought and feeling, and consequently human behavior, tend to show these lateral concomitants or echoes or concordances throughout history. Wagner's prolonged intrigue with Cosima, the wife of his friend Bülow and daughter of his friend Liszt, did not begin until years after Verdi and Peppina had solved their problems by open defiance of the world. Wagner never really defied the world; he hoped, instead, to deceive it, to envelop it in a "big lie" which it would be too stupid to reject. He lived for a long time in the kind of *affaire de boudoir* which kept Verdi and Peppina (more honest characters at bottom) prisoners for only about three years. Wagner and Cosima denied their own union for ignoble reasons, lest the infatuated young King of Bavaria should cut off their money and the beclouded Hans von Bülow proclaim a divorce. They even falsified the paternity of one child (Isolde, the third one), not because of the putative father, Bülow, whom they treated with contempt, but because the adoring young King, homosexual and half mad, could not have endured the thought of a sexual relationship between his confidante, Cosima, and his idol, the friend.

In August, 1847, Verdi and Peppina must have reunited with rapture and a certain decisive finality which both felt to the depths of their souls. They had been through the worst, and she (above all, she) had won out. She had thrown over not only her rich lover Merelli and all his corrupt world, but she had foresworn the theatre itself, its paint and powder and disguises, for the honesty and simplicity of a life which was henceforth to be devoted entirely to Verdi. I have not the faintest doubt that this was in her mind from the moment she left Milan (and Merelli) for Paris. I cannot read her letters without understanding that this woman truly gave up the world for Verdi; and if you tell me that going to Paris is a peculiar fashion of giving up the world, I must reply that her woman's wisdom told her that this was the one place where she would most certainly attract him and regain him.

He was thirty-four and she was thirty-two. He was a handsome young man, in spite of his big nose, and she was an extremely presentable young lady in spite of her equally big nose. She had not found the slightest difficulty in obtaining pupils for singing lessons, and not little girls with adenoids and mammas, but actually persons with some talent to be developed. She had a house, a clientele, a considerable array of acquaintance. It must be remembered that for ten years she had been highly successful in the leading opera houses of Italy, and always in leading parts. Her certificates from the Milan Conservatory were of the first class, with praise (that conservatory to which Verdi could not obtain admittance and which now calls itself by his name). Thus Paris had not been difficult for her and by August, 1847, after a year of activity, she was in a position to act more or less as hostess to Verdi, showing him the sights and introducing him to persons of interest. She may have been a little frightened about Mademoiselle Lind. Who, in that world in those days, was not? She may even have thought that London with its pounds sterling and its lords and ladies might have spoiled her uncouth young composer, whom she had, after all, rescued from the fleas and the straw. She may have been terrorized by her own past, as she evidently was for a number of years thereafter, and she could hardly have forgotten for one moment that curious cloud or shadow which clung about him, the phantom of his dead wife and children. There were regrets and anxieties in the air, apprehensions, feelings of guilt, but above all there was a love that cut through everything like a sword. ("Ah, my magician, my wizard!" she was wont to write only a few years later in the earliest of her letters that we possess, "I detest you and I embrace you!") From August to November, a matter of three months at most, their relation passed from that of a secret intrigue to that of a public union. Madame Strepponi and Monsieur Verdi were, in the language of Paris, "together." Unto death.

Verdi entered upon a period of peculiar happiness which we should be at pains to define if we could find the words. It was not love's young dream; he and Peppina had lived through that under quite different circumstances; and it was scarcely romantic love in the most headlong style (Romeo and Juliet). Gratitude and affection were too much mixed in with it—wonder, too, at the capacity for love in the soul of a woman; wonder at the goodness of a woman who was not (according to peasant standards as he had learned them in his village) a "good" woman. Partly because of his phantom wife and her still living relatives, partly because Peppina was not a "good" woman, partly because of reasons too deep for him to recognize (reasons buried in the amalgam of race, religion, nation and *Zeitgeist*), it never seems to have occurred to Verdi at this period or for long afterward that he might actually marry Peppina before God and man and let the dead past bury its dead. He was happy with things as they were, and in his mind, in some mysterious way, a soft music was beginning to gather about her devoted head.

If I have understood anything about the arcana of composition either in music or poetry, it is that the composer first has vague intimations scarcely more tangible than clouds drifting across the consciousness. It takes something very tangible to bring it all into focus; that is, to make the clouds and sunrises, the half-apprehended and half-perceived, shudder into intelligible form. In this case the final result, after a series of such kaleidoscopic metamorphoses, was the tender, elegiac composition which crowns his youth, *La Traviata*. We are now in 1847, and the novel *La Dame aux Camélias* did not appear until one year later; but the actual story or theme supplied by the Dumas novel (and, four years later, by the Dumas play made from it) gave Verdi the framework for the most intimate and personal of his inventions, a music distilled from his inner being at that moment when youth is saying its farewell.

Peppina as the lady with the camellias is not to be taken too literally, of course, although almost everybody who has studied Verdi at all sees the connection. That is, the actual characters and events in the Dumas story cannot be read into Verdi's own experience. We may be quite sure that he never threw handfuls of banknotes into Peppina's face or called her names in public; he was scrupulously deferential to her at all times and exacted from others every mark of respect; nor was his father-in-law Barezzi in the least like the old bore who comes into the novel, play and opera. Peppina never at any time led a gay life, a courtesan's life; she was a busy musician and a woman of culture; her admirers, if she had them, would never have dared to bid against each other for her favors. Furthermore—and perhaps most important—Peppina was a perfectly healthy young woman without a germ or a cough in her system, and until she got rheumatism long years afterwards she never had a serious illness. In short, characters and story, as supplied by Dumas, were for the theatre and Verdi used them for the theatre.

When we ask what attracted him to this story we come near to the secret truth. When we examine what he *did* with the story we feel this truth in its essence. His web was spun from within because here, for the first time, he actually felt the drama at his heart's core. Most of his earlier work exhibits the stamp of his own genius at some point or other; your true Verdian (such as the late Franz Werfel) will find the pulse in more places than could you or I; the distinctive emotional expression which is Verdi, which did not exist before or after him, occasionally surges up in such pieces as *Ernani*, for example, strongly enough for all to hear. But it was not until the sudden outburst of the early 1850's (*Rigoletto, Il Trovatore, La Traviata*) that the "absolute" Verdi, if we may so describe it, comes into existence and can be heard from first to last in integrated compositions for the opera stage. By "absolute" I mean, of course, the completely uninhibited but controlled expression of individual genius. Regardless of good, bad and indifferent (all of which may be found in these three compositions), they are Verdi throughout, fully and completely; nobody else who ever lived could have written them. In this sense they are just as "absolute" as the G Minor Quintet of Mozart. There is, in fact, no other sense in which the word "absolute" is intelligible in aesthetics.

The three popular or romantic works are not the best but they are, in the sense I have emphasized, the first. If Verdi had not himself surpassed them by later inventions they might remain today as the utmost of which Italian opera was capable in the way of emotional expression. They "ring true." He meant every word and every note, with the exception of a few set pieces stuck into each opera for conventional reasons; his taste was not yet sure of itself and he had not yet acquired the courage (or the arrogance) to disdain and ignore what was inimical to his own best talent in the operatic requirements of his time. Thus two of the tenor's airs in *Rigoletto*, the cabaletta for tenor in *Il Trovatore* and the tenor's air in Act II of *La Traviata* (not to speak of the baritone's), seem false, unfelt, untrue—stuck into their respective places because the rules said the tenor must have an aria, the baritone an aria, etc., etc., to exhibit their voices; otherwise competent singers could not be obtained to sing these parts. Verdi was already, in these three works, breaking dozens of rules: he was by no means ready to break them all. It is quite fair to say, I think, that the worst passages in each of these pieces (the "trashy bits," as a friend of mine calls them) come not only when the composer is weary but when he is yielding to external force—the force of public expectation, operatic tradition and convention. He is best when he is most himself; it might be said of anybody; but self-realization is much harder for some artists than for others, takes longer, costs more. In the case of Verdi it took eighty years and cost him his life.

The great step forward which occurred after his union with Peppina was not immediate—in fact the first work done in his new-found happiness was the French opera *Jérusalem*, less than useless—but we are able to discern the evolution, during the next few years, of a composer increasingly sure of himself and steadily more determined to do his own work in his own way. He had a good many things to get out of his psychological corpus. There was that mighty patriotism, for example; a passion with which we have already dealt at length: he had to express it to the utmost limit (*La Battaglia di Legnano*) before he could get rid of it as an obsessive element in his aesthetic universe. Patriotism, so useful to second-rate artists, seldom contributes much to the power of the great; we may find it in *Henry V* but not in *Macbeth* or *Lear*. The revolutionary events of 1848, following immediately upon Verdi's love-compact with Peppina, deflected his mind and work completely. For quite a long time he was scarcely even permitted to realize his own happiness, his personal adjustment to existence: he was too anguished over Italy. Peppina was always there in Paris, holding him when she could, pulling him back when she could not forfend a temporary departure; but the chances are that Verdi felt guilty a good part of the time in 1848 and 1849 because he was not more actively engaged in the turmoil of Italian rebirth. His union with Peppina took place on the eve of an immense national and international drama, and two or three years had to pass before the fact of that union and the sense of fulfillment it gave—even the sense of permanence which it must at least faintly have adumbrated after the first two or three years— pervaded his consciousness. The romantic trilogy, *Rigoletto*, *Il Trovatore* and *La Traviata*, unrelated in subject matter but evolved more or less simultaneously, came out of the new breadth and depth of feeling released in Verdi's own being by that *sortilège mystérieux de la vie à deux*. It would be superficial indeed to attribute the sudden efflorescence to happiness alone, since each of these pieces contains also much unhappiness; but life with Peppina, complex as it was and filled with strands of guilt, jealousy, remorse, awareness of the past and distrust of the future, was what fructified and released the talent which, until then, had shown signs of lassitude or even of exhaustion. The three romantic works not only crowned Verdi's youth but pushed it well into the past, so that all his work from now on—however flawed, however imperfect by his own developing standards—was that of a mature artist struggling toward ultimate expression.

   La Traviata is commonly supposed to be the most "autobiographical" of Verdi's work—or, as Aldo Oberdorfer says, his "only autobiographical" work. Two remarks must instantly be made: first, that any sincere work of art is autobiographical in the true sense, whatever its subject matter. Goethe defined art as a form of autobiography, which it indisputably is. Second, *La Traviata* as a story—or rather, *La Dame aux Camélias* as a story—bears no resemblance to the characters, circumstances or evolution of Verdi's life with Peppina. If both these preclusive conditions are borne in mind, there is no doubt that otherwise—in mood, color, feeling, in the general *tinta* of the work—a powerful personal element has taken over, an original, a deeply authentic genius is beginning its journey toward the birth-death of fulfillment. To some degree this is also true of the companion-pieces, *Rigoletto* and *Il Trovatore*, which also contain autobiographical elements, if you wish to call them so—personal feeling powerfully expressed out of emotional experience—but in those works the failures of taste and judgment are more frequent, the artist's control is less complete, the sheer exuberant vitality of the talent sometimes runs away with its owner, like chariot horses maddened by the circus. In all three pieces emotion—not heroic at all, but human, common in all human experience—expresses itself with new vigor and freedom, as if Verdi himself had learned a new language: the humiliation and horror of the crippled jester, the brooding of the half-mad gypsy woman over her changeling son and her visions of the stake, the love and sacrifice of the dying courtesan, although they have special dramatic or theatrical circumstances just as they have costumes and scenery, are in fact aspects of common experience and are so recognized through the phenomenon called listening to music. We are not all crippled jesters, at least not constantly; we have not all had our mothers burned at the stake and our children exchanged for those of others; we do not die each day of love and tuberculosis; yet when the emotional content or residue of these situations and characters is poured forth with Verdi's untrammeled sincerity, we recognize them at once (in the mysterious transaction from ear to heart) as our own—they have become universal. What makes them so is nothing our eyes can see, nothing the spoken stage drama could possibly evoke in the same way or to the same degree: the music has transcended its text and pretext. As Marcel Proust said, *La Traviata* lifts *La Dame aux Camélias* into the realm of art.

4 Verdi's first work in Paris was undertaken at the request of Duponchel and Roqueplan, who wanted a new opera to French words in the "grand" style of the Opéra. Verdi had written in August that he would never write for this theatre, which, said he, "is in a state of incredible decadence, and no composer could get out of it with honor." When the proposal was made, so very soon afterwards, he promptly accepted; in the brief interim his world had changed; Peppina undoubtedly wanted him to stay in Paris and work there, which he did. It was only a short time afterwards that they took a house together out at Passy and openly began their united life.

The work he undertook, to be ready for production in November, was a French version of *I Lombardi alla Prima Crociata*, considerably retouched musically as well as in language. He took out some pieces and put in others; he rewrote sections, rescored bits for orchestra, introduced the all-important ballet music without which nothing could be performed at the Opéra. It was the sort of cobbling and patching which, only a few years afterward, he would have disdained: for, frequently as he did rewrite passages in later work (even in *Falstaff*, between the first production and the printing of the score), it was always to satisfy himself, not on demand or order. As a result, his *Jérusalem*, as we have already said, was the deadest of his early work, although *I Lombardi* itself, the original opera, does occasionally receive a performance.

Verdi did not mind much; he had his new-found happiness, the garden at Passy and, a little later, the engrossing excitements of 1848 and 1849; the Italian revolutions, those of France and all Europe. We have dwelt upon his journeys to Milan and Rome, his effect upon the patriotic crowds in the cities, his quick, if somewhat guilty, returns to Paris and Peppina. It should be useful to list the four operas of these years, of which only *Luisa Miller* has survived into our own time: forgotten as they are, they had their triumphs when they were new. We have already indicated the excitement which surrounded *La Battaglia di Legnano* in revolutionary Rome; *Il Corsaro* was by no means a failure, and *Luisa Miller*, although in an unfamiliar vein of almost bourgeois intimacy, made a deep impression. Of the four, only *Stiffelio* was a downright failure; Verdi tried to salvage it several years later in a revision under the name of *Aroldo*, but without result, so it falls historically into the same limbo as *I Masnadieri, Jérusalem* and a few others. By noting the theatres where Verdi produced these four works we may see how busy he was— how substantial were his journeys away from and back to Peppina. They are:

Il Corsaro, *three acts, text by F. M. Piave (from Byron). Teatro Grande, Trieste, October 25, 1848.*

La Battaglia di Legnano, *four acts, text by Salvatore Cammarano. Teatro Argentina, Rome, January 27, 1849.*

Luisa Miller, *three acts, text by Salvatore Cammarano (from Schiller's Kabale und Liebe). Teatro San Carlo, Naples, December 8, 1849.*

Stiffelio, *three acts, text by F. M. Piave. Teatro Grande, Trieste, November 16, 1850.*

It was Peppina who induced Verdi to move out to Passy in the first place, urging upon him the beauties of the flowers, the trees, the birds— all those adjuncts to a dilettante's countryside—which he had scarcely had time to notice since his laborious childhood. From a number of later documents, in particular a letter to Countess Maffei written twenty years afterwards (June 4, 1867), we are entitled to guess that Peppina sometimes had reason to regret her "conversion" of Verdi to country life. The garden of their house at Passy, which was her idea of country, must have been much like that which is shown in Act II of *La Traviata*, an affair of some well-clipped hedges, disciplined beds of flowers and graveled walks between, with an oak or an elm for shade. From this trim *villeggiatura*, in which, if a lady picked up her skirt ruffles and carried a parasol the while, no ill effects might be suffered, it was a long way indeed to the determined plunge which Verdi was so soon to take into his own native countryside. Peppina gives her version in the letter (since celebrated and much reprinted) to the Countess:

"*Many years ago (I do not dare to say the number), loving the country very much, I asked Verdi with considerable insistence to leave Paris and go to take, under the pavilion of the open sky, those salutary baths of air and light which give as much vigor to the body as calm and serenity to the mind. Verdi, who, in the likeness of Auber, had almost a horror of country visits, consented, after many petitions, to take a little house a short distance from Paris. So far as pleasure is concerned, I dare say that this new life was a revelation for Verdi. He fell to loving it with such a love and such a passion that I was conquered and overgratified by his love*

for the bosky deities. He bought the property of Sant' Agata, and I, who
had already furnished one house in Milan and one in Paris, had to organize
a pied-à-terre in the new possessions of the illustrious Professor from Le
Roncole. . . ."

The rest of her tale of woe can await our visit, in the next section, to
Sant' Agata, Busseto and Le Roncole. For the moment we rest our eyes
on Peppina at Passy, elegant among the roses and geraniums, waiting for
Verdi's return from his visits to Rome or Naples or Trieste, greeting him
with the utter sincerity and devotion which shows in all her character,
but unaware, poor she, that by giving him a patch of land and a blade of
grass she had aroused the deep obsession of his innumerable ancestors for
the earth and the fruits thereof. Between operas, sick of the grease paint
and the gaslight (for by now gas was beginning to come in at all the
leading theatres), he would hurry back to Passy as fast as the stagecoach
could carry him over the Alps. We have already remarked that he made
startling speed from Rome after the 1849 revolution and the Battaglia di
Legnano; he did the same from Naples at the end of the year. The chances
are that Peppina's garden in Passy gave him an abrupt, unexpected perception of what his own country heritage might mean to him. He had
worked so constantly, since the age of ten, that he could scarcely have
noticed the countryside even as he toiled through it (as he did from Le
Roncole to Busseto, on foot). He had lived in Milan too long to know the
seasons as they are known on a farm, or to realize how things grow in
their time appointed, or how the birds do sing. These discoveries hit him
very hard, as everything else did, and before long Peppina found, to her
astonishment and discomfort, that the "country," and country indeed,
was what he wanted: no suburban gardens within easy reach of the
Opéra but a working farm on the flat plain of the river Po where he was
born.

Verdi was himself no doubt unconscious of the extremes thus set up
for their life in common—at least, let us say, he did not realize for some
years the extent of the gap between the Opéra and the cow shed, and
we may be sure his insistent preference for the cow shed was a sort of
revulsion so natural as to be almost unaccompanied by thought. He may
not have seen quite what a big jump it was from Paris to Busseto, since
he had made it so gradually, so painfully, in the inverse direction. He had
bought a little land near Busseto as early as 1844; it was a farm near Le
Roncole, his birthplace, and although he never had time to go there it
is to be assumed he thought of it.

Now, in the great year of 1848, while Italy was alive with revolution—

just after he left Mazzini in Milan, just before he returned to Peppina in her garden at Passy—he went to Busseto and bought the property of Sant' Agata. It was a piece of land which dominated a great part of his life thereafter, and the growth of the property, its houses, outhouses, gardens, park, lawns, crops, livestock, machinery, occurring by natural processes bit by bit, without plan or scheme or general coherency, over the space of half a century, was at least equal in vital significance to him— occupied at least as much of his consciousness—as his life in art. The deed of transfer for the original property at Sant' Agata, between Verdi and a family called Merli, is dated May 1, 1848. In this deed Verdi transfers the little farm he had originally bought (four years earlier) to the Merli family in exchange for the new property, and makes a substantial cash payment as well as assuming some obligations. These were as nothing to the amounts the Sant' Agata villa and property would cost him in the next fifty years.

In less than ten years Peppina was to write—from Sant' Agata to Paris, to the trusted Escudier—these sad words:

". . . *son amour pour la campagne est devenu manie, folie, rage, fureur, tout ce que vous voudrez de plus exagéré. Il se lève presque avec le jour pour aller examiner le blé, le maïs, la vigne, etc. Il rentre harassé de fatigue, et alors comment trouver le moyen de lui faire prendre la plume!*" (July 4, 1857).

"Mania, folly, rage, fury"—these are the words she uses to describe that "love of the country" which she had herself brought to life, as she believed, in the first years of their union out at Passy.

Well, that was long, long ago: when they returned to Paris in the year of the apotheosis did they think of it again? Perhaps not: they would have remembered the pictures themselves, the golden summer of 1848 when the poor man was fretted between love and patriotism so that he could do no work, but Peppina, as we can discern, was happy: the bright flowers, the parasols and the atmosphere of *fête champêtre*—in fact, the second act of *La Traviata*.

It was in that year that the Dumas novel made its appearance, with an immediate success on the largest scale. It is not at all fanciful to suppose that Verdi and Peppina read it together out at Passy. It was their custom to read the new books together, especially since her French was so much better than his; she also read aloud; it would have been rather strange if they had not read *La Dame aux Camélias*, the most popular and the most talked-about book of its day. References begin to appear, not long afterwards, to a work of an "intimate" nature (*Luisa Miller* was such a work, of course, compared to most operas) which Verdi would like to try. We know that he had picked up and put down, more than once, the beautiful prototype of the Dumas book and so many others, the *Manon Lescaut* of the Abbé Prévost. This story has a freshness denied to all its successors, and in many ways we may regret that Verdi never found a librettist who could give it to him, ready to put into music: it would have suited him at that period of his life, and whatever he had done with it would have been honest and true. When the story eventually reached the opera stage, in French with Massenet and in Italian with Puccini, it was no longer naïve—it had become too knowing for credence. Since we have *La Traviata*, of course, we are not entitled to complain, but one's imagination is tempted by the thought of what Verdi at that period of his aesthetic existence might have made out of *Manon Lescaut* if he had been given the right text.

What did Verdi and Peppina, between them, find in *La Dame aux Camélias* which appealed so much? Is it not possible to suppose that they felt their own situation (especially as reflected in the second act of the play and opera) gazing back at them, all transposed and weirdly different but emotionally recognizable? If we suppose this (as most Verdi students do), we are led to the further supposition that Peppina must, at some point along in 1848 or 1849 or 1850, have made a conscious and deliberate sacrifice, giving up the idea of marriage to her adored "wizard" out of deference to his phantom Margherita and the Barezzi family. Something of the kind there must have been, for when Dumas fils produced his theatre version of the novel later on at the Vaudeville—as a play with songs—Verdi and Peppina were prompt to attend (February, 1852), and quick to order from Escudier a copy of the play as soon as it was printed. Within the year, that same year in which he was also working on *Il Trovatore*, the composer had written *La Traviata* and was rehearsing it at the Fenice in Venice.

During these five years (1848–1853) Peppina had made her first, discouraging acquaintance with Busseto, with Verdi's native heath, his family and friends. When he bought the property at Sant' Agata there was much to be done in the way of building, planting and gardening before the Verdi ménage could move there; in the meantime he took a spacious apartment in the Palazzo Orlandi, in the town of Busseto, and a good deal of the work on his triumphant middle trilogy was done there. It may have been rash of Peppina to move with him into the heart of a small provincial town where all of his first wife's family still lived—where everyone knew everybody else and nothing was private. Even today the presence of a very celebrated composer with an unmarried companion in such a town would cause a great deal of comment; in 1850 it must have been a source of consternation to the inhabitants. Furthermore, everybody in the town had known Verdi as a penniless, barefoot peasant boy, and to see him come back now with a train of servants and a "Parisian mistress"—for Peppina, a good Milanese born, carried the aura and name of Paris with her—was difficult of realization. The unpleasantness that ensued, the small hurts and slights and irritations, were impossible for Verdi to forget thereafter, but for a great deal of his time he was plunged into work and impervious to his surroundings; for Peppina it was very different indeed. We are not surprised to find that she longed to get back to Paris and never lost an opportunity to do so. During this period their journeys back and forth (not always together) were numerous and need not be detailed; they were not yet in a position to call any one place "home," but it is quite comprehensible that during these awkward years Peppina felt more at ease in one of the Paris houses (either out at Passy or at 13 rue de la Victoire in the city), while the composer himself was feeling more and more drawn toward his native countryside, no matter what he felt about its inhabitants.

Rigoletto was written in forty days in the Palazzo Orlandi at Busseto; its first night (Venice, March 11, 1851) was a memorable triumph and it had made the tour of European capitals within a year. *Il Trovatore* (Rome, January 19, 1853) met with the same glittering fate; only *La Traviata* (Venice, March 6, 1853) was a failure in its first production, but quickly righted itself and went on to unending effectiveness in all the theatres. These three works, coinciding with a rather unsettled period in Verdi's own life—a period of "gypsy" wandering, as he called it—made him rich and famous as never before: henceforth he had only to choose his opera house and name his own conditions for any work he wished to produce.

The romantic trio had as much success in Paris as everywhere else, during the next few years, although Verdi's difficulties on copyright and author's royalties did not notably increase his good humor toward the French; he had a particularly tangled and acrimonious dispute over the *Trovatore* production at the Théâtre Italien. (*Rigoletto*, now at the Opéra, was originally at the Italien and had a hundred repetitions in its first year; *La Traviata* was at the Opéra-Comique.) No composer of the day, not even Meyerbeer, had more operas running at the same time as Verdi did in the late 1850's in Paris, but before he reached such heights of glory he had to go through one of his most painful Parisian experiences, the writing and staging of *Les Vêpres Siciliennes* at the Opéra.

This was cursed by all the usual bad luck, delays, impatience, intrigues and disputes which seemed to befall Verdi's efforts in French and with the French. The Opéra made its proposal to him in the winter of 1851–1852 and the contracts were signed in February, 1852: Verdi was to write an opera in four or five acts on a French text to be supplied by Scribe, provided he approved of this libretto or at least of its preliminary "scenario." The draft was to be submitted to him by June 30, 1852, and was to be completed by December 31, 1852, at the latest; he would then write his music and be ready to go into rehearsal by July, 1854, for a production in late November or December. All this ponderosity and deliberation, although characteristic of the Opéra, was alien to Verdi's nature and may have helped to make things difficult for him. It seems that he actually worked better, at this period, when time was short (*Rigoletto* in forty days!). The prospect of a work to be turned out in two full years, with a year and a half for the music and five months for rehearsals, may have been altogether too "mastodontic" for him. (He used that word more than once in referring to the Opéra.) In Italy he was accustomed to putting an opera on the stage with three weeks of rehearsal.

Scribe chose for his libretto a subject about as inappropriate for the occasion (the great Paris Exposition) as anybody could wish: the Sicilian Vespers, that lurid patriotic uprising in Sicily in which the French invaders were massacred. Of course, he had a text already prepared in his inexhaustible kitchen, and Verdi had to make do with it. He and Peppina took yet another house (this time at Enghien) for the summer of 1854 and, after delays, discouragement and misgivings, the opera was more or less ready; the casting had been completed and rehearsals with piano had begun. At this point Sophie Cruvelli, the leading soprano, having become enamored of some young man who did not wish to share her with the Opéra, disappeared from the surface of life for an entire month. Rehearsals stopped; there was a general uproar involving even the imperial court; the director of the Opéra (Roqueplan) had to resign and another take over. Madame Cruvelli (actually a German by birth, named Crüwell) had been the first Gilda in *Rigoletto*, and in one of his letters Verdi cautiously says he understands her to be "a good singer but a crazy woman." On her return to Paris she was better than ever and both the imperial court and the general public had no trouble forgiving her, but she added greatly to Verdi's burden. The amount of underground skulduggery that accompanied all these events could fill pages, for the direction of the Opéra was then, as generally, a political post and a center of intrigue. Verdi knew some of the seamy side, particularly as regards the director, Roque-plan. What he did not know for almost thirty years was that Eugène Scribe had palmed off an old piece of work as being a new one, merely changing characters and setting. Scribe had made a fortune out of the Opéra, and wrote so many librettos that he could dig up an old one at a moment's notice; in this case he took something he had written for Donizetti (called *Le Duc d'Albe*) and rebaptized it *Les Vêpres Siciliennes*. Verdi was never satisfied with the piece, but he never actually knew the truth of the matter until the original came to light in 1882.

Worst of all for Verdi, during these apparently endless months of rehearsal, all this senseless expenditure of time and money on stage machinery and effects, was his feeling that his opera itself was suffering. He was unable to get any work at all out of Scribe, whose *"souveraine indifférence"* was the most irritating thing in the opera house. The quarrel over the libretto went on more or less all year and Verdi was reduced to wishing that he had never left Italy. The first performance did take place, at last, on June 13, 1855, with a tremendous fanfare of a semi-political nature (the alliance made by Cavour with Napoleon III for the Crimean War had brought victory; many Italians came to Paris for the *Vespri*, for the Exposition, or for both). The opera was well enough received at first, but did not last long at the Opéra or anywhere else in its French version. It did better afterward in the Italian translation which Verdi himself supervised, although the censorship compelled him to move the plot from Sicily to Portugal and tinker with the plot in such a way as to render a wretched libretto even worse.

Such, indeed, were his experiences in Paris—painful to an honest man who was steadily, constantly enlarging his horizons as an artist. Such they continued to be for the twenty years (1847–1867) during which he and Peppina were so frequently obliged to be there three or four or six months at a time. Aside from the four productions made by himself at the Opéra during those years, there were others for which his services were demanded and sometimes given. A revival of *Les Vêpres Siciliennes* at the Opéra in 1863 detained him there a long time, for example, on his way home from St. Petersburg and Berlin. What is more, Paris at that time was a more or less indispensable way station between Italy and any other country. If it had not been, Peppina's taste in the matter would have made it seem so. Thus, although nowadays nobody going from Italy to Spain, or Italy to Russia, would consider it strictly necessary to go by way of Paris, this was the way Verdi always took. During those years in the middle of the last century the stagecoach was disappearing and the railroad rapidly taking over, with its general historic function of accentuating the importance of big centers. All these various visits to Paris, some of them occupying the better part of a year, were regarded by Verdi as stern necessity, although in one of his letters to Arrivabene he does say: "I leave for Paris tomorrow. And why? I don't know." The chances are that this was one of the occasions when Peppina's wishes prevailed, although the excuse at the moment was a production, which he never made, of *La Forza del Destino*. To get to the Pyrenees, for example, where he and Peppina took the cure at Cauterets, they went to Paris first, as also for his Madrid engagement.

The professional challenge of Paris was not a small thing to Verdi: nothing in his profession seemed unimportant to him, and Paris, which had been the scene of ultimate achievement and recognition for almost all his predecessors in Italian opera, had very special claims. From the time of Louis XIV Italians had been dominant in the French lyrical theatre and French music in general: Cherubini above all, and at a later period Rossini, exercised dictatorial powers over French musical taste. In the rapid decline of the Opéra after the Revolution, the principal interest for the capital in such matters came to be the Théâtre Italien, and even after the restoration of the Bourbon monarchy this enterprise, which was outright Italian, root and branch, performing only works in the Italian language, commanded more patronage, and more respect, than the official French houses. Rossini became director of the Théâtre Italien in 1824 and brought it to a peak of popularity: his own final theatre works were, however, produced at the Opéra (including *Guillaume Tell*), which gave him, in a manner of speaking, one foot on each side of the street. Bellini's last work, *I Puritani*, was written for and performed at the Théâtre Italien (1835); so was Donizetti's *Don Pasquale* (1843), during the last period of sanity in the composer's life. The Opéra and the Opéra-Comique had also brought forward a number of works by these and other Italian writers to French texts; Donizetti's *Fille du Régiment* (1840, Comique) and *La Favorite* (Opéra, same year) were among the most successful. As the acknowledged successor to all of these composers it was more or less incumbent on Verdi to have some kind of Parisian career, and this alone —aside from, or in addition to, the substantial fees involved—was enough inducement to him to try. He was always in favor of following custom and tradition when possible.

Even so, the evidence of his discomfort in Paris is too great, too consistent and invariable, to allow for doubt in the matter: he had, must have had, powerful private and personal reasons for spending so much time there. We see it as the tribute of his love to Peppina, which—although not necessarily accompanied by strict fidelity at all times—was the most enduring emotion of his life and the one which rewarded best.

5   Peppina's skill in getting Verdi to do what she wanted him to do is shown about as well in their Russian venture as in anything else. She was always a partisan of journeys, but there was something particularly alluring about the notion of the imperial Russian winter, the sleighs and furs and champagne, the lavish expenditure and otherworldly glitter of St. Petersburg. Verdi himself had seen about all he wished to see of this earth by 1855. That was the year in which he had squandered an immense amount of energy in trying to protect his rights of authorship in France and England; he had no time for any other work. A new law in England would copyright a foreigner's writing only if that foreigner produced it himself for the first time in England—which would rob Verdi of payment for anything he had ever written except the unsuccessful *I Masnadieri*. At this moment both *Il Trovatore* and *Rigoletto* were new and had stormed every citadel in Europe: their extremely large earnings would be denied to Verdi (and to Ricordi) under the new English law and an even more complicated French one. It was suggested to the Maestro that he could solve the difficulty most simply by taking citizenship in either France or England; those countries had a reciprocal treaty on copyright and he would thenceforth be protected in both. His own country—the duchy of Parma—had no standing, did not maintain embassies abroad, and could not protect him in any way. It scarcely needs to be stated that he refused: "I remain what I am," he said. But he had an enormous deal of trouble in getting the payments due him for the popular operas, and as a result he could not do his own work at all. His next two operas were for Venice and Rome, where at least he knew that he would not be cheated of his royalties: they were *Simon Boccanegra* (Fenice, Venice, March 12, 1857) and *Un Ballo in Maschera* (Apollo,

Rome, February 17, 1859), works of unequal inspiration but extraordinary quality, in which the growth of his creative power could be distinctly perceived. For many reasons he would have been happy to remain in Italy more or less forever after that. One of these reasons, of course, was the steady progress made toward unification, and his own part (willy-nilly) in public events. As we know, in 1859, on the eve of his brief trajectory through public life as a member of Parliament, he and Peppina were married.

Why they waited so long is a question to which no sure answer can be given. They had been living as man and wife for twelve years by this time, and could quite easily have married at any point along the line. We know the phantoms that afflicted his mind; we can imagine the sacrifice she made to them; but by 1859 they had been together so long that many persons supposed them to be married anyhow. We know that neither of them ever forgot an affront received because of the "equivocal situation" of those twelve years, and we wonder in vain why they did not put an end to it sooner or else ignore the world and its quaint prejudices altogether.

The world is difficult for its inhabitants to ignore, however, even at Sant' Agata, and furthermore the marriage of Verdi and Peppina (August 29, 1859) took place at a moment when the unification of Italy was at hand. In this unification Verdi had played an important part; he was, whether he wished it or not, in many respects a public man; he was world-famous; he was going to be called upon quite soon to carry out some duties of a public or political nature. Probably his intimate friends, such as Count Arrivabene, had found ways of suggesting to him that he might "regularize" his domestic situation before the inevitable occurred. The wedding took place just two weeks before Verdi's visit to Cavour at Leri.

Now, as Signora Verdi, Peppina's part in their life together was different. There had never been anything in the least furtive about their union, but in deference to general opinion in such matters Peppina had avoided public attention. She did not accompany him on the journeys involved in the production of a new opera; she went from Paris to Sant' Agata and back again. She could not have accompanied him to Turin when he went there as a member of Parliament; now, as his wife, she could go with him anywhere and everywhere, and did. Some parts of the new role evidently interested her more than others; it is not difficult to guess, for instance, that she was bored by politics and barely able to keep her interest going at a politely intelligent level. So lively, kindly and charming, full of good humor and good will, she would have had no difficulty in any society, but the indications are that Turin, parliament and politics were not naturally congenial to her. (They were not to Verdi either, in reality, but he was bent on doing his duty as Cavour understood it.) It was the most natural thing in the world for Peppina to welcome a chance of escape from this round, especially if it promised to gratify her taste for travel and novelty.

The first proposal from the Imperial Opera in St. Petersburg reached the Verdi household at Sant' Agata early in January, 1861. There is some possibility (we only suggest it) that Peppina was originally responsible for it: she had placed a friend of hers, Mauro Corticelli, as secretary to the celebrated Italian tragedienne, Adelaide Ristori, who had the same sort of international position then as Eleonora Duse and Sarah Bernhardt half a century later. Ristori took a company to Russia that winter, with Corticelli in her train; the tenor Enrico Tamberlick was singing at the opera in St. Petersburg; Italian artists then, as now, tended to get together for meals and talk. Tamberlick was the go-between, Corticelli the confidential correspondent, during the earlier stages of the negotiation between the Imperial Opera and Verdi. (Madame Ristori seems to have been a sort of guinea pig in the affair—food, weather, clothing and such were judged upon the standards set by her.) Peppina's first letter to Corticelli on the subject is dated January 17, 1861, from Sant' Agata, which at that time of the year was never bright or pleasing to her. Verdi was in Turin, but had already seen the imperial offer with its profuse inducements spread over many pages.

"Verdi will answer directly as soon as he returns," Peppina wrote, "in what terms I do not know, but from certain words he has let fall he does not seem to me so very adverse to taking up the pen again."

She shows her own wishes in the matter at once in her remarks on the Russian temperature in winter, which was, as always, the most startling thing to Italian travelers.

"If I were not afraid of committing a falsehood," she says, "I should be glad to correct that imposing number of twenty-two below zero, which will make his eyes pop out in fright. As for me, when I read that figure, I took refuge almost underneath the chimney piece, as if all the ice of Russia had fallen on my shoulders."

Every difficulty considered, she still wanted to go and made no bones about saying so, even at this early date. Her vague but eager willingness for new places and new faces may well have been expressed to Corticelli before—and to Madame Ristori herself—as I have ventured to suggest.

"There's another little thing not too attractive," she says, "and that is the ruble which one spends as if it were a franc! At all events, however bad an advocate I may be, I shall muster up for this occasion the best scraps of my eloquence so as to persuade him to subject his nose to the danger of freezing in Russia. If I don't succeed with eloquence, I shall go to work by a method which, they assure me, succeeds even with the illustrious St. Peter at the frontier of Paradise: that is, insistence, *nagging*, until the result is obtained. It's true that Verdi isn't as patient as St. Peter, but anyhow if he tells me to go and sleep it off it won't be the first time . . ."

Verdi's consent, in principle, although not in detail, was obtained by these or other means, and he suggested for the Czar's opera house no less a subject than the *Ruy Blas* of Victor Hugo. He had been drawn to this play, with all its antimonarchical and revolutionary implications, for some years past, but it seems a strange topic to dangle before the most absolute autocrat on earth. The Verdi couple then proceeded to Turin (February 15, 1861) for the opening of the first parliament of the Kingdom of Italy, and remained there four months. Petersburg promptly refused to have anything to do with an opera on the *Ruy Blas* subject—as ought to have been foreseen—and the negotiation simmered.

"Verdi," his wife writes to Corticelli, "has read through dramas ancient and modern without finding anything which pleases him as much as that one. The libretto will be the most serious obstacle; in fact, the only obstacle which may impede this business. Verdi is not the man to write music for *n'importe quoi*, and he had a tremendous lesson in Naples in [the dangers of] not coming to a very clear understanding beforehand with that shadowy thing called the censorship."[3]

Telegrams passed between the tenor Tamberlick in Petersburg—speaking for the Imperial Opera—and Verdi in Turin. The composer was, by this time, in no real need of money or engagements, and fame had ceased to interest him (if it ever had done so); the only thing he wanted was a subject, a libretto, a theatre piece which he could set to music without losing his mind or his self-respect. He wrote to Petersburg on March 5 releasing the Imperial Opera from any obligation, real or imagined, in the matter, since he could not find a subject and did not wish to keep them in uncertainty.

"On my side," he writes, "nothing could induce me to sign a contract

---

[3] *Un Ballo in Maschera* was written originally for the San Carlo in Naples, but even after drastic changes (during which it became something called *Vendetta in Domino*) it could not pass the censorship in the Bourbon kingdom there in 1858; the whole brawl ended in the law courts and Verdi took his opera to papal Rome instead, where the censors were a trifle more civilized.

which might, later on, force me to compose in all haste on a subject which might or might not be to my satisfaction."

Peppina and her friend Corticelli, meanwhile, were exchanging their merry but useful remarks about vegetables, furs and hotel rooms in Russia, until there came a point when even the cheerful Peppina despaired of making the journey. In mid-April the Imperial Opera sent an emissary to Turin: Achille Tamberlick, son of the celebrated tenor. He was, according to Peppina, "a cultivated young man, distinguished, and with such patience—ah, such patience!" He set to work paying court to the composer.

Here is Peppina's account of it:

"*Tamberlick's son arrived, saw that the field was not well disposed, and swore to win in spite of the fact that Verdi, taking advantage of the veto on his subject inflicted by that famous telegram, was far more preoccupied with the Chamber than with the theatre. So he gave a sweet beginning to his mission by correcting the error of that telegram, and declaring with the utmost calm that he (Verdi) could compose Ruy Blas or anything else he wished, since he (Tamberlick) had instructions to grant every possible condition that could be demanded, excepting that of obliging the Emperor Alexander to proclaim the Republic in Russia. Verdi scratched his head and observed that for Ruy Blas there was such-and-such a difficulty; that for other dramas in prospect there were such-and-such others; that a certain piece he had read some time ago had pleased him, but it was not possible to find it. . . . Enough, enough! . . . As soon as the title was known here we were all roaming the bookshops, to bouquiner Turin, leaving not a corner unexplored. Nothing: not to be found. Finally it was given to Verdi—who, to be just, had bestirred himself like the rest of us, since he could find no convenable way of escaping it—it was given to Verdi, I say, to seize a certain man by the hair, a man who was going to Milan, where alone it might be possible to find the drama, and from which, in fact, it was received in twenty-four hours; to the great consolation of Tamberlick, who, although he affirmed with the greatest joy in the world that he loved Turin and would be glad to stay a month, even so, as soon as the Gordian knot was cut, started out running and never stopped, I think, until he got to Paris. Now, therefore, it's 90 percent sure that Verdi will write for Petersburg. In this probability I have already begun to get things lined, befurred, altered . . .*"

In this letter to Corticelli she sends her best wishes ("*mille cose gentili*") to the young man who, no doubt under her expert tuition, had brought about the desired result. She calls him "the illustrious whale-

lover, Signor Achille Tamberlick," by which we may gather that in her
late forties our friend Peppina had put on a bit of weight. She also asks
Corticelli to tell the young man (who was barely in the twenties) that
the "Noble Father" commends himself *alla sua graziosa memoria.* The
whole correspondence, or that part of it which we have, shows Peppina as
a delightfully shrewd and expert feminine wire-puller who, on the whole,
knew what was good for her man as well as for herself; for nobody could
deny that it was better for Verdi to be writing operas than to be sitting
silent in a verbose parliament. It was her consummate art (as it was also
in her relations with various ladies who had engaged his interest) to
conceal this art. He unquestionably thought that he alone had conceived
and executed the Russian project.

In June, when the Verdi pair had returned to Sant' Agata, Cavour's
death fell like an axe across all the composer's political existence. There
is no doubt that he lost every shred of interest in practical politics from
then on—and, except for Cavour, he never had much to lose. His patriotism was of the indestructible sort, but much of it turned to gloom thereafter, as we have seen. Under the circumstances it was not easy to take up
his own work again, but he knew in his heart that nothing else would
make life possible—and he had Peppina at his elbow.

She wrote again to Corticelli (July):

"Dearest friend, the Petersburg affair was almost arranged as I wrote
to you in my letter of April 17, after Tamberlick had come to Turin; now
it is definitely signed and I am surprised that you didn't know about it.
Therefore we, if the Devil doesn't take us off first, shall all find ourselves
in the perpetual sherbet of Petersburg. Verdi says he was an idiot to sign
this contract because it will make him work and, thus, to sweat too much
in the summer and then cool off too fast in the winter. We'll need quite
perfect tagliatelle and maccheroni to get him into a good humor in the
midst of the ice and the furs! In the meantime, to avoid every storm, I
propose to say he's right about everything from the middle of October to
the end of January, foreseeing that during the labor of writing and rehearsals there will be no means of persuading him that he might be wrong
even once. When everything seems too dark I can take the air . . .
Gently! I'd forgotten that the air in Russia freezes one's nose! Then I'll
go to bed, the one place where I believe one can be comfortable in those
boreal regions. By the way, if La Ristori thought she could conquer,
predominate, by her tagliatelle, Verdi counts on eclipsing her with his
risotto, which in truth he does cook divinely. And therefore if you—in
spite of all your pilgrimages and the entourage of so many Big Lilies—

have kept yourself what you always were, an excellent friend, we shall happily profit by your offer and ask you to make a few provisions for us, too. We shall stop in Russia for about three months, that is from the first of November through January, 1862, and we shall be four to feed, two masters and two servants. If the interpreter is indispensable, and if it is the custom to feed him also, we shall be five instead of four. You can obtain for us in proportion to the number (that is, making your rule the number of persons) the provisions you get for La Ristori in the following categories: rice, maccheroni, cheese, sausages and those things which you know cannot be found in Russia or are found at an exorbitant price. As for wine, here is the number of bottles and qualities Verdi would like:

> "100 small bottles of Bordeaux for meals
> 20 bottles of fine Bordeaux
> 20 bottles of Champagne.

"Perhaps it would be less inconvenient for you to provide more abundantly for La Ristori and pass on to us the portion superfluous to her and necessary to us. I shall straighten out the accounts with you on arrival in Petersburg, having risen from the rank of singer to that of housekeeper, a rank far dearer to me—as you who know me will have no trouble believing, since you know how little I loved the stage. Don't accuse me of being prosaic! You must know that there can be as much poetry in these modest and, so to speak, solitary, domestic occupations, as in that species of delirium which one feels and sometimes communicates from the stage to the excited audience."

Madame Ristori was, of course, the most famous actress in the world, and had with her a large company and a train of attendants; Peppina evidently remembered these facts and, contrasting them with the simpler conditions of a composer and his wife, hastens to add:

"Let's understand each other, Don Cappellari.[4] If there is any difficulty in getting provisions for us, don't let us speak of it at all, because just now it occurs to me that perhaps La Ristori may have obtained some privileges which we don't have, and which Verdi would never think of procuring."

The drama to which Verdi turned in this hot summer of 1861—the piece for which they had all searched so frantically through the bookshops of Turin—was a highly romantic composition in the style established throughout Europe by Victor Hugo. It was the work of a Spanish

---

[4] "Don Cappellari," one of her nicknames for Corticelli, refers to his willingness to be of service.

aristocrat called Don Angel de Saavedra, who afterwards became Duke of
Rivas, and was written during that gentleman's exile to France during
the Carlist civil war. The play seems almost like a caricature on the
romantic movement when it is inspected with the eyes of the mid-twen-
tieth century, but in its own time it was extremely successful in France
and Italy as well as in Spain, where it was produced as soon as its noble
author had returned from exile. It is cloak-and-sword, blood-and-thunder,
to a degree which subsequent taste could never accept if it had not been
clothed in some of Verdi's loveliest music (as well as some of his worst).

He liked this play because of its "color," in particular—its light and
shade, strong contrasts, violent passions. He found it "certainly outside
of the common run." In fact, at this stage of his development, it may
very well have suited some obscure and complicated needs of his creative
intelligence: it went to such extremes that he could hurl his entire talent
into it, like an entire stable full of race horses. Here, for the last time in his
artistic career, he seems to have let everything go, and although the result
is an amazing jumble of styles, moods and achievements, ranging from
the abyss of banality to an ethereal beauty, as a whole *La Forza del
Destino* contains too much genius to be forgotten for long at a time.
This year, almost a century since it was written, it can be heard in the
principal opera houses of the world, although the greatly overpraised
works of Meyerbeer and Halévy (to which it was hesitantly, and with
great daring, compared!) have gathered the dust of decades without a
performance.

Verdi had difficulty getting his work onto the paper during that boiling
hot summer of 1861, and it was late November, instead of the first of
October, when he and Peppina set out from Sant' Agata for their journey
to the north. Even so, he had apparently not completed the instrumentation, for we find him working on it long afterward, after the winter's
plan in St. Petersburg had gone awry.

It went awry because of a single artist: Verdi, who never stopped insisting on the importance of casting a work ("certain operas for certain
artists, certain artists for certain operas," he said), would not take any
of the sopranos offered him in Russia except one Madame Lagrua, who
was obstinately ill from the moment he arrived. He asked the Imperial
Opera for permission to produce his new work in the next season—that
is, the autumn of 1862—and returned to Paris in mid-February, anxiously
on the lookout for a soprano who could sing Leonora. He and Peppina
had been a little over two months in Russia on this first visit, of which
some delectable photographs have survived—peering out from their furs,

in their sledges and sleighs, in the deep snow, they look like frightened animals strayed from their habitat. They were able to visit Moscow (as they did also on the next visit) and saw the treasures of the Kremlin; both of them were indefatigable sightseers, in their different ways—Peppina always eager to go anywhere, Verdi reluctant but, once he got there, determined to miss nothing. By March they were back again at Sant' Agata but in mid-April they took to the road again: this time for London.

Peppina was responsible again this time—or, if not wholly responsible, she did her best to make Verdi go. She had been studying English for a long time and had a good reading and writing knowledge of the language. Every opportunity to see the world (and get out of Sant' Agata!) was welcome to her, and she was particularly anxious to get a glimpse of English life. A few years earlier (in 1857) she had wanted Verdi to accept a London contract for *Luisa Miller* and *Il Trovatore* at Her Majesty's; Verdi refused because the money Lumley offered was less than he was getting elsewhere. Now, for the great Exposition of 1862, in the Crystal Palace, it was proposed to give a mammoth musical display of an international character—one of those things indigenous, apparently, to England, with vast numbers of participants. Meyerbeer was writing a piece as Germany's representative, Auber was producing one in the name of France, and Sterndale-Bennett represented England. The Exposition authorities had originally wanted Rossini to write something as a representative of Italy, but the old man (only seventy, but lazy) would not do it. Verdi had no desire to fill the breach but was urged for patriotic reasons to do so. He detested what he called *pezzi di circostanza*— pieces for special occasions—and constantly refused to attempt them, but this seemed difficult to avoid, especially with Peppina prodding him the while. He took a text from a very young man (twenty years old) who was to play an enormous part in his ultimate creative life: Arrigo Boito, a protégé of the Countess Maffei. This, a poem of elevated aspiration on peace, brotherly love, the association of nations and the rights of man, was Verdi's *Inno delle Nazioni*—Hymn of the Nations—which, although not often performed in the past century, was filmed and recorded by Arturo Toscanini for the American government during the last war, and thus has the singular honor of being Toscanini's only visible monument: that is, the only music in which future generations will be able to see what he did, as well as hear it.

The *Inno delle Nazioni* is perhaps not a major work from a composer of this magnitude; for a lesser man it would have been judged effective and at moments very moving. It was composed for a soloist (originally tenor) and chorus with orchestra, and the instrumentation was of a distinctly "festival" character—good and loud, with plenty of brass. When Verdi and Peppina got to London they discovered that this cantata could not be performed in the Crystal Palace because one of the rules of the Exposition was that the work should be instrumental only. Meyerbeer, Auber and Sterndale-Bennett had all written festival overtures in march style. In fact, Verdi and Auber had met by chance in Paris some months before and Auber had said he was going to send in a march; whereupon Verdi concluded, in his usual practical way, that it would be best to do something different. Now there was an unholy row in London over whether the Verdi cantata could or could not be performed at the Exposition. Verdi himself did not care, although he resented having it said that he had not sent his piece in on time; and in the good, healthy style of English debate on all questions, Londoners took sides for or against the performance of the Verdi work. (There were, as usual, other intrigues: Michele Costa, director of Covent Garden, was an anti-Verdian; moreover, he had the tenor Tamberlick under contract, so that the solo part in the cantata had to be readjusted for soprano.) In the end, the Hymn of the Nations was performed at Her Majesty's Theatre four times in a week, to crowded houses and with general acclaim. It seems that to Verdi and above all to Peppina the whole episode of the Great Exposition was notable chiefly for a chance to see London and to travel a little; they took a charming little house in the Regent's Park, with a garden, and were also able (while the argument over the performance was going on) to journey up to the lake country. Soon after the Hymn had its last performance the Verdi pair returned to Italy.

It was only in this summer (not the preceding one) that Verdi seems to have completed *La Forza del Destino*, with instrumentation, in the form in which it was presented at St. Petersburg, Madrid and Rome (the original version). He wanted to avoid the Russian winter this time, or at least the deepest part of it, by putting on his opera as early as he could; therefore he and Peppina arrived in Petersburg by mid-September and the work went into rehearsal at once. Every resource of the Imperial Theatre was at the composer's disposal, and the Czar Alexander II even offered him the male chorus from the guards regiments. The theatre directors spent 200,000 gold francs (or $40,000) on the stage alone, scenery and costumes, which at that period was an extravagant sum and equal to much more today. The opera reached its first performance on November 10, 1862, and although two distinct cabals—the pro-German and the Russian nationalist—were aroused against it, the imperial court and the public gave it a tremendous reception. Between November 10 and December 3, when Peppina wrote to Corticelli giving an account of the matter, there had been eight performances, which would seem about the maximum that could be crowded into three weeks in any opera house. The Czar was prevented by a sore throat from going to the opening night, but recovered in time to be present, with the Empress, at the fourth performance, sent for the composer, lavished compliments upon him and soon thereafter made him a commander of the order of St. Stanislas. What mattered considerably more is that fees, expense money and the like were on an imperial scale—what the jealous press in Paris called "myriads of rubles"—and even Peppina was forced to say that "the indemnification for having come to Russia two times was most convenient."

Just the same, before they had left Russia that December the composer was already deeply dissatisfied with some aspects of the work, especially its confused, bloody and violent ending—violent almost to the point of being ridiculous. The librettist, F. M. Piave, must surely have been one of the worst poets in any language, and in *La Forza del Destino* he outdid himself. Quite aside from grotesque absurdities in the plot, the words themselves—the actual single words—are of that weird variety which exists in no spoken language. Verdi worried over it for some years, and eventually—seven years later—produced at the Scala the revised and considerably improved version which we now have. It was, as we have seen, the instrument of his reconciliation with the beloved theatre of his youth.

Peppina, at all events, got a good deal of sightseeing out of this opera, even though Verdi's misgivings kept it from many theatres which wanted it. He refused to let the Opéra in Paris touch it because there were no tenors or baritones in that company fit for the principal parts; and he would consider no dealings at all with the Théâtre Italien which, under Calzado, had cheated not only him but every other composer or artist in sight for a number of years. (The Théâtre Italien, with powerful support at the imperial court, won lawsuits against both Victor Hugo and Verdi during this period, although both were obviously entitled to royalties.) Two opera houses, those of Madrid and Rome, already had contracts for it, and he was obliged to yield it to them; in Madrid he was himself engaged to make the production.

We feel that this journey to Spain was one in which Verdi needed no undue prodding from Peppina. He had had a lively curiosity about Spanish plays, novels, Spanish themes in general, for the greater part of

his professional career: the "color" was what appealed to him, the violence of the dramatic situations, the highly theatrical scenes and costumes
in which Spanish heroes, heroines, villains and saints worked out their
destinies. The whole romantic movement from Victor Hugo onward
(even from Byron) felt this same pull toward Spanish extravagance, and
although what they made out of it was more extravagant than Spain itself,
it satisfied some need of the troubled age for melodramatic expression.
We may smile today (or, in fact, laugh out loud) at some of this strutting
and ranting, which often makes both hero and villain seem outside the
limits of dramatic interest or human character. The fact remains that the
pseudo-Spanish dramas of the romantic period, with their insane jealousies, their passions of pride and remorse, do bear some kind of relation to
Spanish reality: no theatre setting could be more "romantic" than a
great many Spanish landscapes; no fiction ever invented surpasses Spanish
history for blood-and-thunder; a Madrileña with a mantilla on her head
and a rose in her mouth, swinging her haunches on the way to the bull-
fight, is about as theatrical a vision as ever struck human eyes, and yet
nobody can deny that she is real. Furthermore—as has happened in many
countries with this exaggerated differentiation from others—the Spaniards
responded eagerly to every foreign discovery, with the effect of further
accentuation: that which was theatrical enough already took on the
further light-and-shade of self-consciousness. Victor Hugo and Verdi
were immensely popular in Spain—as, indeed, is *Carmen*—and the
Spanish imitators of Hugo (counting Saavedra, author of *La Forza del
Destino*) were numerous and esteemed.

Verdi and Peppina arrived in Madrid from Paris on January 11, 1863.
(They had spent a month in Paris refusing proposals to produce *La
Forza del Destino* there.) The Madrid production went well, with an excellent cast, and two days after its first performance (February 23) the
Verdi pair started on their tour of Andalusia, which was not easy or comfortable. They visited Seville, Granada, Cordoba, Cadiz, Xeres (whence
the composer sent home a choice bottle of sherry) and left Spain for
Paris on March 14. Verdi was keenly interested in everything he saw, and
was at the same time reading Spanish plays, or seeing them performed,
with the idea of finding a new subject. Spain, like Russia, was so much
outside the ordinary existence of this composer that he broke a good many
of his rules in both countries. In Petersburg he accepted invitations into
high society, which he refused to do elsewhere; and in Spain he was
willing to undertake great fatigues and discomforts for the sake of sightseeing. To us his emotional resentment of the Escorial is perhaps the

most revealing note. He writes to Arrivabene after his return to Paris (March 22, 1863): "The Alhambra *in primis et ante omnia*, the cathedrals of Toledo, Cordoba, Seville, merit the reputation they have. The Escorial (forgive me the blasphemy) I do not like. It is one mass of marbles, there are very rich things inside it, and some of them very fine, among which a marvelously beautiful fresco of Luca Giordano, but all together it is lacking in taste. It is severe, terrible, like the ferocious sovereign who built it."

Some adumbration here of his musical picture of Philip II may be seen (and all Verdi students do see it), although we must also realize that the characters of Philip II and Don Carlos had engaged his imagination even before he went to Spain; the Escorial may only have confirmed, rather than originated, his ideas.

The journeys which devolved about *La Forza del Destino* (two to Russia, one to Spain), with the prolonged stays in Paris which clustered about them, and along with these the months in England which came in the middle, were high points in Peppina's married life. She had not been "Signora Verdi" for very long and on these journeys she enjoyed a certain liberty of expression and movement which—in spite of all their advantages—she could not attain during the years of their unmarried union. Indeed, on one previous occasion Verdi had refused an excellent offer from Madrid because it was intimated to him that his companion would not be welcomed: rather than shock the Madrileños, he did not go. Their life in Paris was the best Peppina had known, but as "Signora Verdi" she entered upon a new dignity and the sprightliness of her surviving letters shows that she enjoyed it. The St. Petersburg experience, with its fashionable evenings in the highest of Czarist society, evidently touched them both. Even Verdi enjoyed his meetings with the Russian aristocrats, whose "truly exquisite *politesse*, so different from the impertinent Parisian *politesse*," struck him in particular. Peppina, as she owed to her time, sex and character, showed a certain *sensiblerie* about the sufferings of the Russian people.

"Only think, Count," she says to Arrivabene (in the first letter she ever wrote to him), "that many coachmen remain whole days and part of the night fixed on their boxes, exposed to a fatal cold, awaiting their masters who are guzzling away in warm, splendid apartments, while some of those unhappy ones perhaps may be killed by the cold! These atrocious cases occur every year! I could never accustom myself to the sight of so much suffering."

Peppina had undoubtedly heard, as all visitors to Russia did, about the

ORPHEUS AT EIGHTY

princess who sat in her box at the heated and scented French Theatre of
Petersburg, weeping her eyes out over the sorrows of La Dame aux Camélias, while her coachman slowly froze to death outside. That story, true
or false, runs through a great deal of nineteenth-century literature from
Balzac to Tolstoy, and it must have had some basis originally. The Verdi
couple could have seen little of the Russian people during their few
months in Petersburg and Moscow, but the winter, at least in their first
visit, was enough to give them an idea.

6   Once more, and once only, did Verdi attempt to meet Paris on
its own terms. That was in 1866 and 1867 with Don Carlos, the
most mature musical composition of his life up to then, rich in invention
both for voices and for orchestra, with an instrumentation deeper than
he had ever dreamed of trying before, and yet built—with all the skill of
a highly trained and experienced theatre man—for the needs (real or
imagined) of the "grand opera" style. It was his last French opera and
he never even for one moment considered trying to write another, although the offers poured in upon him ever afterwards. His Italian operas
all eventually got into French versions (after the Théâtre Italien no
longer existed, the custom of putting on opera in the Italian language
ceased in Paris) and in their French disguises most of them did very well
indeed. The Opéra, Opéra-Comique and Théâtre Lyrique relied heavily
upon Verdi's operas, as they do to this day, no matter how badly they
may perform them; but it is the Italian works they perform, not the
French ones.

   The Verdi couple continued to pay their visits to Paris afterwards,
but in hotels. They went there in the 1870's for various reasons (Aïda
was one) but generally not for work in the theatre. An exception was
the 1876 visit, when Stolz and Waldmann—Aïda and Amneris—were also
with them, and it seems to have been a particularly happy one. We may
be sure that by that time Peppina, getting into her sixties and in excellent
control of all elements in her life, was not in the least disturbed if Verdi
spent a little time of an afternoon talking to Madame Stolz, or cooked a

little risotto for Madame Waldmann in the evening. Peppina had more actual interests in life—the search for a certain kind of hairnet, for instance, or for an Italian translation of Darwin, or for a length of Chinese silk—than Verdi had. His own requirements, although despotic, were few, and after he stopped composing for the theatre—that is, after Aïda— they were fewer still. During the sixteen years which passed between Aïda and Otello he would have been happy to stay at Sant' Agata all the time, good weather or bad, playing a little music for two pianos if any guest came along who could do it with him, or merely walking with his dog. The outside world—that is, Paris and all it represented, including Petersburg, London, Madrid, Cairo, and the rest—never really meant anything much to him except the opportunity to work. It meant so many things to Peppina, as he could realize without fully comprehending, that the journeys continued even when their pretext had gone. Neither Genoa, where they spent every winter for many years, nor Milan with its magical theatre only two blocks from his hotel, could have enticed him away from Sant' Agata if it had not been for Peppina's wishes. And nothing but the incredible wizardry of Arrigo Boito, that persistent young man who would not leave him in peace, could have dragged him back to the theatre again after the final renunciation.

All this must have been much in their minds during the final visits to Paris, for *Falstaff* in the spring and *Otello* in the autumn of his eighty-first year. The camellias of long ago may have been fresh in their minds from time to time, in spite of the rheumatism. Oddly enough, Verdi seems to have felt little or no pain during his triumphal parade through the opera houses of Milan, Rome and Paris in the year of apotheosis, and even Peppina was in good health and spirits. It had been necessary in Rome to insert an apologetic note in all the public press, to say that the Maestro Verdi was physically incapable of accepting invitations to dinner or to receptions. No such thing was necessary in Paris because the French government and official theatres protected him; the French—who can be so civilized when they put their minds to it—made up in the end for everything they had ever said or done to cause him discomfort. They atoned most handsomely for *Les Vêpres Siciliennes* and *Don Carlos*, even for the Emperor Napoleon III, even for that orchestral conductor at the Opéra who had once said to Verdi (one of the horrors of his life) that the orchestra had "other things to do" besides rehearse. All this was forgotten, wiped away, in a consensus of appreciation and esteem. Verdi's old admirers and defenders—Théophile Gautier, Catulle Mendès, even

Reyer, those Wagnerians who somehow also managed to be Verdians—
and his rivals or colleagues of another day, were alike departed and a new
generation filled the theatres. Far more than the fading of the camellias
(for who can remember last year's camellias?) was the fact that Monsieur
and Madame Verdi, before leaving Paris, were the guests of honor at
luncheon with the President of the Republic in the Palais de l'Elysée.

4

Home

1 In the great year, as for so many before it and for the few that still remained, Verdi's fixed base and preferred place of abode was the flat plain where he was born, and precisely in the house, garden and park he had made for himself at Sant' Agata.

The plain of the Po river in just that region—between Parma, Cremona, Piacenza—gives an illusion of limitless monotony. It is not really vast, of course; nothing in the Italian peninsula is; but actually it suggests great space and its flatness is unmitigated, so that the effect is akin to that of the greater prairies and steppes of America and Russia—the Kansas-Nebraska immensities or the Kuban Cossack lands. Nowadays, with good roads and a considerable advance in agriculture, with the almost inevitable grace of an occasional village and its church tower, the landscape does not seem altogether as mournful as it did for so many decades to Peppina; but even today it is not yet rid of its old enemy, the mosquito, or its harsh extremes of temperature in winter and summer. On my last visit, which was in March, other parts of Italy had already begun to soften and bud with the coming of spring, but the wind cut across that plain of the Po just as sharply as it had in December. Nothing in Verdi's life or work seems more stubbornly, unreasonably rooted in blind natural force than this passion he had, and never lost, for the few square miles of flat earth on both sides of the town of Busseto.

Italy is blessed beyond almost any other European country by a lavish variety of landscape and climate. Lakes and mountains, rivers and seas, engage in a sort of conspiracy of loveliness, and even the most ordinary village along the road in many provinces (Tuscany, for instance) can surprise and delight. There are also violent ravines and towering cliffs for the romantic, and there are grim or even terrible landscapes in the Apennines, or in Calabria, or in many other regions. It is not all beautiful and smiling by any means, but generally speaking (except in highly industrialized districts where the factory dominates everything else) it manages to be, in all its great variety and contrast, a country where our interest is commanded and held by nature as well as art. That is, not only the Italian people and their astonishing history, their inconceivable accumulation of creative work, but actually the physical conformation of this peninsula has special attributes not to be found elsewhere and consequently has engaged the active interest of all the generations for centuries without number. Indeed, much of Italy's history arises precisely from this, that the country always possessed a powerful attraction for foreigners, who endlessly endeavored either to conquer it themselves or to dispute its possession by others.

In view of these celebrated facts, so well known to every child in school, it seems strange to relate that the Verdi countryside is about as uninteresting as any to be found in the whole of Italy. Verdi's own friends and contemporaries found it downright ugly. Some tree-planting has been done in the present century and is being done today, but it is still a thoroughly deforested prairie for the most part. The Po river as a rule either has too much water or not enough, and there is nothing of natural interest along its flat banks. Its uncertain margins have encouraged the mosquito ever since that little beast came into being, no doubt, and in the nineteenth century the nature of the endemic fevers was not even understood. ("Malaria" literally meant "bad air," and the fever by that name was supposed to be caused by the bad air from the swamps in hot weather.) A deforested plain is a playground for the winds, of course, and the bleakness of the winter in those regions is equaled only by the dead heat of the summer. As against such deficiencies in climate and natural beauty there has to be set the excellent response of the soil to almost every cultivation; it is good land for growing most crops of the temperate zone, and was valued for this reason long before Verdi's birth, as, with greatly improved methods and materials, it is today. By and large, it is a region of fairly well-to-do peasants around the small market town or minor city of Busseto, which, because the land is prosperous, also flourishes.

Verdi was born three miles from Busseto on the road to Parma (that is, to the southeast) and built his villa three miles from Busseto in the other direction (this is, to the north). If the word "home" existed in Italian, he would have said that this patch of earth was home.

Few artists with his almost unlimited freedom of choice have felt such obstinate attachment to a bit of soil. His Italian predecessors (Rossini, Donizetti, Bellini) showed no similar proclivities; once they had gone to Paris they stayed, although it is true that Donizetti's doctors took him home to Bergamo to die. Verdi's own contemporaries in his own profession, notably Wagner, were ready to live where they worked, which has been the musician's lot for centuries; Wagner built himself a shrine and called it home, but it might have been almost anywhere so far as he cared. It was the deity within the shrine that mattered to him, and not its surroundings. Even if we leave the guild of musicians, who have ever been a wandering race, and glance at other kinds of artists in the nineteenth and twentieth centuries, we find few so devoted to their native heath as was our Verdi. Occasional exceptions (Flaubert, Tolstoy) only point up the general observation that artists are not much attached to the land or to their own origins, and for many or most of them success in life—fame and fortune—means a chance to go somewhere else. *Les déracinés*, as Barrès called them, the rootless ones who make the particular culture and tone of every capital, number among them a huge proportion of the time's best artists.

Verdi's ferocious attachment to his dull, unattractive native area is easy enough to explain as he did himself, on the ground that he was a "peasant born." So have been a considerable number (although a distinct minority) among his tribe. He could have been a peasant equally well, perhaps better, somewhere else—in some more pleasing countryside, in other and more amiable surroundings. He had all Italy or, in fact, all the world to choose from. What rooted him to the neighborhood of Busseto was not ancestral memory or tradition, not sentiment, and certainly not the joys of memory from childhood. It may have contained those elements in the beginning, faintly and subterraneously, but most of all it was sheer stubbornness that anchored him—a stubbornness of peasant quality, it is true, hard and strong as an oak, but based upon resentment and anger rather than love, power of will rather than of desire. He had lived through such a dour and acrid series of dramas on these few square miles of land that he felt in the law of his own being a necessity to surmount them, to assert his right to live, to assert, in a word, *himself*, there as nowhere else on earth.

Put in one way—as, for example, the barefoot boy and charity student who grows up to build the biggest house in the neighborhood and keep the neighbors out with a high wall—it may seem that this lifelong transaction between Verdi and Busseto was an example of the "inferiority complex" at work. The threadbare expression hardly seems to fit the case; the true pathological example of "inferiority complex" is rather that which would avenge itself upon a superior—as, for example, if Verdi in his riches had undertaken to drive out the ancient feudal lords of Busseto, the Pallavicino family, and install himself in their palace. He did nothing at all of a pathological or vengeful nature, unless you call a demand for privacy pathological; but he did determine very early, with all the authority of an unbending will, that he must have his own house and acres precisely here and in no other place. The more difficult life became the more determined he was to conquer it, not on the vast and glittering stage of the world, which was for him so easy, but here in the flat, ugly land of his birth, amid the sour, suspicious peasants who were his own people, and who never could quite forgive him for the pennies—repaid a thousandfold —that had gone to make him great. Choosing life at Sant' Agata on these terms was what he did, because with his nature he could do no other. It is power, yes: but at times a power so hard, so unrelenting, that we think it must have been a burden to its possessor as well as terrifying to the beholder. The kindly, warm-hearted Verdi, so just and frequently so generous in every aspect under which we see him elsewhere, becomes stern as fate itself when we observe his life at Busseto, and in particular the half-century he spent at Sant' Agata.

2   The birthplace at Le Roncole and the villa at Sant' Agata are in sharp contrast, and because they are so near together—one on one side of the town, the other on the other—the contrast becomes dramatic. Many great men have been born in small houses and lived (or died) in large ones. At Busseto for many years now the ordinary "Verdi tour" which every visitor takes leads him almost straight from the birth-place to the large, comfortable country house in its beautiful park and garden at Sant' Agata. By the merest glance one can see the whole trajec-tory from rags to riches, the drama of the poor charity pupil who attained fame and fortune. What is more, everywhere we look, coming and going, we see the name of Verdi. The main road to Parma, right out through the countryside, is called Via Verdi; so is the main street in Busseto; the square is Piazza Verdi; here is the Verdi Theatre and there is the Verdi Museum; signs at various crossroads inside and outside of the town direct the motorist to one or the other of the notable Verdian sights. What is more, nowadays the big motor-road is so built that it is possible to skirt Busseto, without going through the center of the town, and thus get from the birthplace to the Villa Verdi in about ten minutes.

The birthplace at Le Roncole is a strongly built cottage, half-timbered, which stands just off the main Parma road on a minor crossroads. It was an excellent situation for a shop and tavern, since every traveler from Busseto to Parma had to pass that way. (The motor-road of today is built over the old high-road.) There was a stable for the horses on the other side—primitive enough, but still shelter—and the ground floor of the cottage was divided between the kitchen and shop on one side and the tavern and sitting room on the other, with a hall running between which had outer doors at each end. These, of course, are small rooms, and we can imagine that the little Verdi was not restricted to any one of them, but roamed as much through the shop and tavern as in the kitchen and living room. Upstairs, by means of very exiguous little boxed-in stairs, we reach the attic bedrooms, of which one, set crosswise under the sloping roof, has more space than the others and boasts a ceiling. This belonged to the Verdi couple, Carlo and Luigia, and it was there that their children were born. These were Giuseppe himself (October 10, 1813) and three years later his sister Giuseppa (March 20, 1816). Giuseppa, whom Verdi loved tenderly and greatly mourned, never grew in mind after childhood and was frail of body; she was little over seventeen when she died. It is upon this gentle, beloved half-wit that Lombroso and his followers relied to support their theory of the connection between genius and insanity, to which otherwise the example of Verdi might have been a glaring contradiction, and much too near at hand to be ignored.

The Verdi parents were both illiterate, both of farm-laborer stock from the same small region, and had never traveled beyond it. Verdi's birth certificate, in Latin and in French, describes his mother as a "sempstress," which did not mean much more than housewife in that time. The village of Le Roncole, a dependency of Busseto, belonged to the French *département* of the Taro in 1813, toward the end of the Napoleonic empire, but was soon to become part of the duchy of Parma.

Generations of visitors have gasped over the simplicity and humility of Verdi's birthplace, the poverty to which it bears witness, the narrowness of circumstance and outlook which must have fenced in his childhood. A few observations should be made for the sake of common sense. In the first place, the house is a peasant cottage, true enough, and quarters must have been fairly cramped, but it is by no means a hovel. It is very solidly built and must have been comfortable in the hard winter of that plain; it is larger than a great many cottages in its neighborhood even today. I should say offhand that it was bigger and better than the contemporary English cottage up above Grasmere where Wordsworth and his sister Dorothy used to live, for instance—in which, as I remember, I had to bend almost in two to get through a door—and certainly it must have been superior to most peasants' houses at the beginning of the nineteenth century in any country. Le Roncole at that time was only about a dozen little huts and hovels gathered about a crossroads and a village church: in those surroundings the Verdi house was in all probability the biggest and most comfortable habitation.

In the second place, although the parent couple were illiterate, poor and hard-working, they must have had considerable industry and enterprise to be running even a small shop, and to have built such a sturdy little cottage with their own earnings. They no longer worked in the fields; from agriculture to commerce is quite a step and was a much bigger one in the early 1800's. Carlo and Luigia Verdi were respectively twenty-eight and twenty-six years old when Verdi was born: they must have worked and saved from an early age.

And, in the third place, the amount of movement and excitement to be found in a shop and a wine-tavern, however small, was greater than could have been afforded a child in the ordinary house of an ordinary peasant. The child Verdi saw travelers come and go, heard them talk, helped to sell them bread and sausages, and even though they may only have been peddlers and journeymen craftsmen they had tales to tell. For an imaginative and sensitive child the horizon, in those surroundings, must have begun to lift fairly early.

Le Roncole today has grown apace, and especially recently, so that dozens of new houses, many of them in the "California" style, all pink or yellow, have changed its look. The village may have as many as a thousand inhabitants today, I have been told, some of them quite prosperous persons with offices or business establishments in Busseto or elsewhere. Some of the houses look large and comfortable, as well as modern; they are, in fact, villas. (One house of pleasing aspect, far from small, belongs to the celebrated novelist Guareschi, author of *Don Camillo*.) With autobus, motor truck and car, Le Roncole is only a small jump from Busseto today, and in Busseto anything a comfortable household may need can be bought: the whole character of the village has changed.

Verdi's birthplace, spick and span and beflowered though it is, a national shrine and a place of pilgrimage, does look humble today next to its "Californian" neighbors, but we can be sure it looked different a hundred and fifty years ago to the wayfarer who, trudging across that dreary plain, sought for a place of shelter and rest.

The church is directly across the way from the Verdi house, on the same side of the highway about a hundred yards farther toward Busseto. Here is where Verdi was baptized (the baptistery is nationally protected, like all the rest of these sites, and cannot be altered in any way) and where he made his first acquaintance with music. Up a cramped and twisting stairs which I could barely crawl into or ascend, we reach the tiny organ loft where the child played the organ. The instrument itself with its ancient brown ivories gets its wind from electricity now but otherwise has not been changed (it is also a national monument and bears its inscription). I touched a chord or two, only recently, and can testify that the tone is still clear and sweet.

The bell tower of this village church is the scene of a very early Verdi legend, also commemorated by its inscription. The story goes that in 1814 when Napoleon's empire fell and the Austro-Russian armies, a marauding and lawless mob, were pouring across northern Italy, Luigia Verdi took refuge at the top of the campanile with her infant (Giuseppe) in her arms. The commemorative stone (placed there in 1914, the centenary of the event) says that by so doing she "preserved for art one sublime archangel," which is eloquent enough. The story was kept alive by oral tradition for a hundred years and may well be true, although Verdi himself seems to have known nothing about it.

The birthplace, like all the Verdi sites, like everything that concerned his story, comes under the law of national monuments and cannot be touched, improved or changed in any way except by order of the Department of Fine Arts. This has been the situation for many years now, but it is of some interest to observe that the very first inscription stone on the front of the cottage—the first of several—was placed in 1872 by the Marchese and Marchesa Pallavicino of that day. The Pallavicino family reigned as sovereigns in Busseto for over two centuries and remained the feudal lords for long afterward, under more distant sovereigns; their palace is the principal architectural monument of Busseto; but it was they who first thought of paying honor to their peasant genius. Verdi was very much alive in 1872, and only a few miles away on the other side of the town (in fact, he had just written *Aïda!*) but we do not know exactly what he thought of this memorial stone. Judging by his attitude to inscriptions, statues and monuments in general, it probably infuriated him, but by never going outside his own garden and park he could avoid seeing it, and the Pallavicino family had a right to do as they pleased with property which had (by this time) reverted to them.

The statue of Verdi which now stands in front of the cottage is a conventional monument, like those which rise in the public squares of almost every Italian town today. Several stone plaques with inscriptions, in addition to the original one placed by the Pallavicinos, have been authorized by the Department of Fine Arts. One of these (the most recent) was put up on the fiftieth anniversary of the Maestro's death by the choral societies of the country, and seems to me to contain a truth, although not all the truth, about this composer. It says:

> Pura espressione dell'anima popolare italiana.
> Pure expression of the soul of the Italian people.

3   The first music the child Verdi ever heard was, according to legend, the serenade of some strolling musicians on the night of his birth. This story—another oral tradition which the Maestro himself always ignored—says that some of these strollers, who were particularly likely to come to the tavern on Saturday night and on Sundays between mass and vespers, predicted that Luigia's coming child would be a boy, promised to play a serenade when he arrived, and in fact did so. Whether this is so or not, it is well established that such wandering musicians did come to Le Roncole—as they did to every village in Italy—and specifically to the Verdi tavern where, although it looks much too small for such activity, there was frequently dancing and singing on Saturday night and Sunday. The child Verdi from the earliest age took an interest in every musical instrument and every tune that came his way, and with those good-natured strollers he had a chance to try his hand at most of them.

The other source of musical interest, also from the earliest age, was the church across the way, where the same rather complicated three-manual pipe organ did duty then as now. (Its stops, which you have to push and pull, are an astounding array, filling a large instrument panel on the right side of the organ, so that the organist's right hand must have developed quite a stretch.) The organ was played by Pietro Baistrocchi, an old man who also taught the village school. The child Verdi—then called Beppino; from the time he was grown nobody called him anything but Verdi—served mass when he was old enough, took lessons at a very early age (perhaps at five) from Baistrocchi, and unquestionably listened to the music in church at a still earlier age, when most children would be pipe-dreaming or half asleep. There is plenty of evidence that his musical aptitudes declared themselves extremely early and in no uncertain terms, so that his parents, neighbors and elders were downright bewildered. His father Carlo, a frugal man, actually went into the town and bought him a small table-shaped spinet when he was (we think) in his sixth year. By the time he was eight he could play this tinkling little instrument so well that a conscientious artisan who was called in to tune it refused payment and left a document—signed Stefano Cavaletti, anno Domini 1821—to certify the fact; the document is preserved. By the time he was ten, surely a good five years after he started his musical career, the child Verdi was playing the organ in church—an organ which offhand you might say no child could physically manage, since it demands so much of the arms and legs as well as fingers: a really adult and properly built pipe organ, with none of the mitigations and conveniences of modern instruments.

And by that age, of course, he had learned all there was to learn either in the village school or from the village music master.

He was probably four or five when he first attracted old Baistrocchi's attention by playing—on various instruments, those of the strolling musicians who came to the tavern—popular tunes, marches, dances, opera airs, and all by heart, since of course he knew no music. Baistrocchi took the child in hand and we must assume that it was shortly afterwards that father Carlo went to Busseto and bought the spinet. It was a much-used instrument, by the descriptions, and probably came very cheap, but such expenditure on the part of a poor man indicates that Verdi's talent had convinced his father, even then.

This must, of course, have been a true spinet (false ones, or miniature pianos, were far in the future). That is, it was a harpsichord, with strings plucked by a crow's quill; only instead of being spread out wing-shaped like a harpsichord, it was packed, for space saving, into a rectangular box which could either stand on legs or be put on a table. On this instrument, even more tinkly than the larger harpsichord, the child Verdi toiled day and night for the first and evidently the formative years of his first acquaintance with music.

There is ground for saying that one might have guessed him to be a harpsichord player to begin with, if for no other reason than that his taste in keyboard music remained classical throughout his life. Even when he had two Erard grand pianofortes of his own, what he liked to play on them, if he could get an accomplice, was Corelli and Bach. The harpsichord was incapable of loud or soft, naturally, and the spinet of Verdi's childhood must have been one uniform tinkle at all times; so that what could be learned on it had to be (aside from manual dexterity) line or form, the actual structure of music. "Expression" could not exist. And it is worth noticing that the great expressive pianoforte composers, such as Chopin and Liszt, hardly seem to have existed for Verdi. He played piano by himself for work, but for pleasure his chief delight was in playing with somebody else. The counterpoint which he may have come to know, dimly and unconsciously, from his childhood years at the spinet, and which he slaved upon afterwards through his student days ("fugues and canons, canons and fugues in all the sauces"), was long afterward to surge back upon him in his final masterpiece, *Falstaff*. But well before *Falstaff*, when he was himself composing everything in simple harmony, his choice of piano music, at home and for pleasure, was largely polyphonic. In fact, he never got far on this side of it where the pianoforte was concerned; Beethoven was about as modern as he chose to go when he was playing for his own pleasure.

Anyhow, whether this theory holds water or not, he did play upon his wretched little spinet with such preternatural assiduity for so many hours out of the twenty-four that he came to have some kind of technique (even if it was, as afterward discovered, unorthodox) and for more than to astonish the neighbors; it enabled him to pass without much difficulty to the greater exertions of the organ; and, most of all, it brought him to the attention of the great patron of his youth, Antonio Barezzi.

Barezzi, a well-to-do merchant in the town of Busseto, furnished wines and liquors to Carlo Verdi's shop and tavern; it is only natural that Carlo, on some occasion, should have mentioned to him the bewildering musical talent of his little boy. Carlo knew nothing of music and we may be sure that the thought of having brought a "prodigy" into the world made him somewhat uncomfortable. Barezzi, however, was a great musical amateur, played several instruments, was president of the Philharmonic Society of Busseto, and would certainly be able to tell whether the musical obsession of the Verdi child arose from talent or moonshine. On some occasions, more than one in all likelihood, he heard the child play spinet or organ or both. His interest was aroused from the start and he saw that this gift had nothing more to learn in Le Roncole: he urged Carlo to send him to school in Busseto.

Busseto was better equipped with schools, libraries and churches than most towns of its size; it had benefited for many years by the lavishness of the Pallavicino family, who founded a library there in the fifteenth century, a hospital in the sixteenth and the Monte di Pietà in the seventeenth. For a town which, in Verdi's childhood, could hardly have counted more than six to seven thousand inhabitants, the opportunities were prodigious.

There was a cathedral with four singers, organ and string quartet, and there was a music school created by the commune to supply players for the Philharmonic Society. The Gymnasium dated from the end of the sixteenth century, and in the eighteenth—the century of Arcadia—the little city had no less than two "academies," one for Italian and one for Greek poetry. There was a school of painting and design which has left its mark on the whole region. And, most surprising of all in such a town, there was a rabbinical "university"—that is, a Jewish community with its own educational institutions, officially recognized.

Into this hotbed of culture the boy Verdi was thrust one month after his tenth birthday—November, 1823—when he entered the Gymnasium as a pupil in its lower grammar school, under Don Pietro Seletti, a canon of the cathedral. There is not much doubt that Seletti counted on making a priest out of the clever and gifted child—and the probability is that the Verdi parents wanted the same thing. Against this destiny there was set not only the child's natural passion for music but also the influences of Antonio Barezzi and the town's music master, Ferdinando Provesi. The priests and the musicians fought over the boy from an early date (later on they came to blows), but the outcome could never have been very doubtful if we consider the innate obstinacy and iron will which were born into Verdi. It seems that he did his work for the Gymnasium with exemplary results, but he had brought his battered spinet with him from home and if school work gave him no time to practice it, he took time from his hours for sleep.

His father had installed him as a boarder in the house of a cobbler named—or nicknamed—Pugnatta, which in the dialect of the region means the pot that hangs in the fire, the pot-au-feu into which anything there was to eat in the house was thrown. Food and shelter under the cobbler's roof cost thirty centimes a day, roughly six American cents, and even if this sum be multiplied by five (or more) to give its real value in purchasing power, it was still a barely visible sum. The oral tradition in Busseto—and Professor Gatti talked to some old people there forty or fifty years ago who repeated it—was that little Verdi used to eke out his rations from the pot by roasting slabs of corn meal (polenta) in the fire kept by a neighbor who sold roast chestnuts. This polenta he must have earned himself by his labors at the organ in Le Roncole.

For just at this time, when he was beginning his real studies, old Pietro Baistrocchi died and there was nobody left to play the church organ in the native hamlet. Le Roncole was used to the child organist by now—he had substituted for Baistrocchi frequently—and the villagers were already rather proud of him: they called him the *maestrino*, the "little master." It was not difficult for the boy to get the appointment as organist, at thirty-six francs a year (roughly seven dollars, to be multiplied by five or more for real value). What was difficult was to hold it, to fulfill his obligations in it, which he did for some years. This meant walking from Busseto to Le Roncole and back every Sunday and feast day, three miles each way in weather usually severe and hours too early or too late for comfort. We have already gathered, however, that Verdi in his childhood and youth was scarcely even aware of comfort (to which he paid so much attention later on!). It was his burning desire, against which nothing else counted, to learn music, and in this desire he could withstand any fatigue and all weathers. It is curious that we hear nothing of any illness during these hard years of childhood—it was not until much later, after, indeed, his first successes in the theatre, that he began to be plagued by so many ailments real and imaginary.

While the feud over his destiny was going on between Seletti and Provesi, the priest and the music master—accompanied by epigrams and satiric poems which they hurled at each other—Verdi was in fact making extraordinary progress. He could now read instrumental parts so well that he could be employed in copying them; he did so originally, it seems, for his own pleasure (as did the boy Toscanini long years afterwards) but subsequently for the Philharmonic Society. He made the acquaintance of the pianoforte at Barezzi's house and was allowed to play on it even before he had begun regular lessons with Provesi. He taught himself the pianoforte by means of a printed "method" he found somewhere. Professor Gatti says the instrument was a real pianoforte from Vienna, a "Fritz a coda," that is, an instrument by the celebrated Barthold Fritz in the open wing-shape of the "grand" piano. However, Barthold Fritz, who made his best claviers from 1721 to 1757, did not work in Vienna, but in Brunswick, and never made a pianoforte so far as history relates; his instruments were mostly clavichords (which, like the piano, had strings hit by little hammers) as well as some harpsichords (with plucked strings). If Barezzi's instrument at home was a Fritz, then it was not "a coda" (with tail) and was not a pianoforte at all but a clavichord, and even so a tremendous improvement over the tinkling, expressionless spinet. However, there is no reason why a well-to-do musical amateur like Barezzi should not, by the year 1823 or 1824, have had a real pianoforte in his house, and if Barezzi did not have one the Philharmonic Society certainly must have. The pianoforte in a somewhat more primitive form than that known to us—with an all-wooden frame, a total range of five octaves, a rather weak bass and no pedals—was predominant over all other keyboard instruments by about 1800, rapidly assuming the position it attained in the nineteenth century and in ours as primary among instruments. A little town like Busseto would not have had the most up-to-date pianoforte such as those being made just then in Vienna, London and Paris, but even an instrument made twenty years earlier would have been a revelation to Verdi: without being the thunderous piano of our own time (a whole orchestra in a keyboard, so to speak), it was at any rate a real pianoforte, capable of wide ranges of expression and tone.

He was also allowed to experiment with playing on other instruments, as well as copying music for them. At what moment he began to compose for them himself we do not know precisely, but he probably made a good many attempts in private, for himself alone, before he was officially admitted to the position of Provesi's prime pupil, disciple and assistant. At that time, when he was fourteen, he was already known as the best pianist in Busseto, an excellent organist, a good performer on a few other instruments and a skilled copyist and arranger of music.

All this advance was not accomplished without many sharp exchanges between the priest and the music master. It is said that Don Pietro Seletti, himself a musical amateur and an acceptable violinist, put obstacles in the way of Verdi's lessons with Provesi and finally arrived at the point of saying that the boy must choose one or the other, either the Gymnasium or the music lessons. Probably through fear of his own parents he began to work less on his music, which Provesi perceived, and, the truth coming out, the music master volunteered to teach both the ordinary Gymnasium courses and music as well. (This must have been in about Verdi's twelfth year.) An accident fortunate for Verdi brought the painful feud to an end and convinced even Seletti, finally, that the boy belonged to music.

The organist for some church ceremony, a certain "Captain" Soncini, failed to appear one day and Seletti turned to young Verdi, half in joke and half as a test, to take his place. The boy improvised with such brilliance—having no music there—that the listeners were amazed and Seletti gave in. From now on there was no question as to Verdi's future; although he finished his prescribed course at the Gymnasium with honor, and evidently did particularly well with Latin, Italian literature and history, henceforth nobody tried to entice him into the priesthood. Considering the strength of his anticlericalism later on, the good fathers were well advised even from their own point of view.

At fourteen, when he began to give his entire time to music as Provesi's assistant, Verdi had probably learned everything Busseto had to teach him, or at any rate most of it; the rest of his activity there until he was eighteen consisted in endless exercise of his faculties. (His weaknesses, such as in harmony and counterpoint, or in the placing of his hands at the pianoforte, were probably beyond Provesi's power to correct even then, and required a stronger or harder discipline.) At all events he began teaching others from the moment he became Provesi's assistant, and with whatever help the music master could give him he was already launching upon a period of indefatigable composition. Evidently he composed everything—marches, songs, religious music, overtures, variations, pieces for separate instruments, for the whole Philharmonic Society, for the church organ—and we can be sure that he had a good deal of such work already behind him when his first orchestral composition, an extra overture for Rossini's *Barbiere di Siviglia*, was triumphantly performed in his fifteenth year. From then on the compositions poured out in what seemed an inexhaustible flood. He regarded all these childhood efforts with contempt and would not allow them to be published afterward, but some of them aroused great enthusiasm among the listeners. There was a sort of cantata on Saul's delirium (*I Delirii di Saul*, to Alfieri's words) written for full orchestra with baritone soloist, in eight sections, which Barezzi thought very good indeed; it was written when Verdi was fifteen. Aside from studying counterpoint with Provesi, teaching other students, many older than himself, and tirelessly composing every kind of piece as well as practicing the pianoforte, the *maestrino* also copied orchestral scores, helped rehearse the Philharmonic Society in parts and as a whole, played the organ at the cathedral for Provesi when required and even helped Barezzi in the wholesale wine and liquor business (chiefly, it seems, with the accounts). He had become a member of the Barezzi family, in all but name, by the time he was seventeen. Long before then he had been having his meals with them and haunting their house; Barezzi had taken to regarding him as another son from a much earlier age. Now, at seventeen, he moved into the house altogether, because Signora Barezzi—alarmed by a deed of violence in the neighborhood—thought his habit of composing all through the night would make him an excellent watchman.

The Barezzi family consisted then of three daughters and the son Giovanni, with the infant son (Demetrio). The eldest daughter, Margherita, of Verdi's age, was gentle, pretty, fond of music; he was a remarkable boy with a shock of hair and blazing eyes to go with his fiery genius, his indefatigable industry and his voracity for music. An attraction between them, under the circumstances, would seem almost inevitable, and was probably going on full tilt before either one of them, inexperienced as they were, knew what had happened. When Barezzi, in every respect a beneficent and superior intellect so far as we can tell, heard or saw what was in prospect, he was delighted; far from taking fright at the thought of his daughter becoming entangled for life with the barefoot boy from Le Roncole, he saw this as a stroke of good fortune for her and for her whole family. Not many prosperous bourgeois of the time and place would have been capable of thinking the same way.

Verdi at eighteen, Barezzi saw, needed to get out of Busseto. He needed the disciplines and advanced instruction of a good conservatory of music; he already knew more about music than his own teacher and had composed more copiously and effectively in a few years than many a man in a lifetime. His proficiency in instrumentation had particularly startled his patron; some of Barezzi's notes on the subject have been preserved from the time when Verdi was only fifteen. Barezzi had a plan: he proposed to Carlo Verdi out at Le Roncole that the boy should now be sent to Milan to study for four years at the great Conservatory. On his return he could probably take Provesi's place as music director of the Philharmonic, head of the music school and organist at the cathedral, all three; Provesi was of the same opinion. He could marry Margherita, if they still wished to do so, and have a very dignified and relatively prosperous position in Busseto. If old Carlo would apply to the Monte di Pietà for a scholarship—twenty-five gold francs (five dollars, to be multiplied by something like ten for real value today) each month for four years—he, Antonio Barezzi, would supply whatever money would be needed in addition.

We know how that worked out: Carlo Verdi applied for the scholarship, which was eventually granted (thus establishing Busseto's never ending claim upon Verdi for gratitude, a claim which grew into an appalling irritation with the years). Barezzi anticipated a year's scholarship payment in advance and the boy wonder of Busseto, the prodigy of genius, went to Milan—only to be refused admittance to the Conservatory. The shock which that news sent through Busseto must have been almost as great, although less permanent, than Verdi's own anguish. We have seen him through those Milan years and know what he suffered as a student and even, after he had finally won his musical appointments in Busseto

and married his Margherita, what a dire ending their story had: death for
Margherita and both children within a few months of each other, black
misery for Verdi. Here we are concerned only with Busseto and its neighborhood, the flat, black land to which some power rooted him for all his
life, as if it were the only reality and the rest (the whole world outside)
a kind of dream.

4 Antonio Barezzi never lost faith in Verdi's genius and, what is
more to the point, never doubted the validity and power of his
character as a human being, its essential rightness, honesty and justice.
The point is worth making not only because some stories to the contrary did circulate, and because Verdi's enemies made the most of any
suggestion there could be in this direction, but also—for us, chiefly—because Verdi's delicate and peculiar sense of guilt might so easily mislead
us. Verdi did feel guilty toward his "other father," his beloved patron,
without whom, it is quite possible, he might have been quenched in childhood. There exist letters which indicate that Verdi thinks Barezzi might
be annoyed or irritated about money matters—though there is not one
scrap of evidence that it was ever true. Barezzi was repaid in full for every
penny he ever spent on Verdi, but we know that he always expected to
be—he always knew it would come back. From all the evidence he was
never ill at ease over Verdi's debt to him and never hesitated to increase
it in case of need.

Nor did he take other men's judgment on the talent of his protégé.
When the Conservatory of Milan turned Verdi down, Barezzi thought
it was the fault of the Conservatory. When, later on, an opera failed to
please the public—or, as in the case of *Un Giorno di Regno*, lasted only
one disastrous night—Barezzi blamed not Verdi but the circumstances of
the production, the accidents of taste: in a word, the public and not the
composer.

Finally, it was not in Barezzi's nature to expect Verdi to remain a
perpetual widower, and the union with Peppina would neither have
surprised nor shocked him, with or without marriage, if Verdi had not

chosen to come with her to Busseto and install the ménage, with five servants, in the most ambitious house in the little town. At that time, when Busseto as a whole pretended not even to see Verdi, when no right-thinking person would have called upon the composer's companion or bowed to her in the street, Signora Barezzi was still alive and inclined to regard the whole business as an insult to their dead Margherita. Indeed even now, more than a century later, Verdi's behavior in 1849, when he took Peppina to Busseto and installed her in the Palazzo Orlandi, is almost impossible to understand. Of all scenes whereupon he might have chosen to parade his recent but highly unofficial happiness, his union without benefit of clergy, this narrowly ingrown town which had known him as a child was the worst. It contained, within a small compass, every memory of his youthful struggle: there was hardly a cat or a dog in the town that did not feel itself to be part-owner of the Verdi fortunes, because that niggardly scholarship of five dollars a month (repaid in full) had come from the municipal funds of the Monte di Pietà. Anybody who has ever lived in a small town, no matter in what country, knows what Verdi and Peppina had to face. The town was no better and no worse than innumerable others in western Christian civilization, but it felt a corporate duty (no matter what its members might think as individuals) to disapprove of unmarried unions. It was conventional, but it was also, by virtue of its very smallness, curious, deriving pleasure and excitement from the contemplation of that which it condemned. The situation in its various aspects would have appealed to Flaubert or Ibsen or Sinclair Lewis, for the simple fact was that the Verdi ménage lived more respectably, if more comfortably, than any other in Busseto, never going out, never indulging in the slightest excess of behavior. The town had to invent reasons for being shocked, since—aside from the initial circumstance of having no marriage lines—Peppina and her Verdi behaved as properly as any bishop.

Verdi must have known in advance what would happen. He knew Busseto. His bare, practical reason for settling temporarily in the town— to supervise the work being done on his villa at Sant' Agata—was not imperative enough to overrule every social and humane consideration. He must have been, we think, in one of his most extreme moods of rebellion against the old Italy in which he had grown up, the Italy of petty princes and clerical tyranny, small minds in small frontiers. He had just been through the tremendous excitements of a year of revolution and the tumult of the Roman Republic of 1848. I do not find it hard to imagine that in such a time of political daring and individual assertion, with young men dying on the barricades while they sang scraps of his music, Verdi felt bold and bitter; he must have been contemptuous of the bourgeois standard of values; he may have experienced a certain exhilaration, as of one who strikes a blow for freedom, in affronting the censorious eyes of Busseto. What he did not foresee, of course, was the aftermath, the long aftermath lasting to the very end of his immense life, the state of martial law, of siege, which he was thereby setting up for himself and for Peppina.

For, of course, the small town won, as it always does. Verdi and Peppina found it impossible to live in Busseto. The resentments which they (chiefly he) cherished thereafter colored a large part of existence for them for the rest of the century, long after they had regularized their situation by matrimony, respectability and a relentless blaze of world-wide success. Nothing ever made things right again between Verdi and the town of Busseto in spite of innumerable well-meaning efforts. He lived the rest of the nineteenth century out at Sant' Agata, just three miles from the town, in a state of siege, with a running stream like a moat in front of his park and a high wall to discourage the importunate.

Barezzi must have suffered during the 1849 episode as much as anybody concerned, perhaps more. Verdi could not have suffered too much, since at just that period he performed the astonishing feat of writing *Rigoletto* in forty days, complete to the last drum-tap. Work was always his refuge. Peppina's suffering, which we can well imagine, had many compensations—she had her Verdi and her own perfectly secure sense of superiority: she could forget Busseto in thinking of Paris, and she had resources in the way of books, music and correspondence which lifted her completely out of the little town. Barezzi, however, had a two-edged suffering, for his adored genius son and for his beloved town, which was by now so much a part of him that he and Busseto were indistinguishable. It must have cost him a brutal anguish to obey his wife's wishes and stay away from the Palazzo Orlandi while the Verdi couple lived there. No decent person in Busseto would have anything to do with them, and Antonio Barezzi was the most eminent, the most respectable of the citizens. He had to do what he did; we can see that in reality, in the life he led, there was no choice. But we must also see that it almost broke his heart.

The relations between Verdi and his "other father" were reproduced in lesser degree with the whole Barezzi family, more particularly with his brother-in-law Giovanni (Giovannino, or Nino). They were his friends and followers after their father had ceased to be his benefactor. The Demaldé family (Signora Barezzi was born Maria Maddalena Demaldé) was in almost the same position of intimacy and devotion, and many of the details of Verdi's early life come from the *Cenni Biografici del Maestro Verdi* (1853) by Giuseppe Demaldé. A third family, interrelated with the other two, was that of Angelo Carrara, Verdi's lawyer and friend for the whole last of his life, who later married Verdi's adopted daughter and heiress (*"la cuginetta Maria"*). These three families must have formed an extremely powerful clan in the upper bourgeoisie of Busseto, and we can have no difficulty in perceiving that Verdi's behavior in 1849 imposed a severe strain upon all of them. Young Carrara alone (perhaps because he was already beginning to take care of Verdi's business affairs and legal papers) seems to have managed, somehow, to keep on good terms both with Verdi and with the town of Busseto. He would have been forgiven for calling occasionally at the Palazzo Orlandi if he were going there for business reasons, and he was just then assuming a number of tasks for Verdi which had, a little earlier (in happier times), been executed by the Barezzi father and son.

After Verdi and Peppina went back to Paris, the "scandal" of 1849, if it may so be called, simmered down, only to be revived in less acute form after they began to live at Sant' Agata. We then behold the transition—slow at first—from the town's disapproval to its inordinate and boastful pride, its desire to claim Verdi as its own and make his fame serve its own purposes. After the Verdi marriage in 1859 and his advent to parliament, his friendship with Cavour, his public importance in the life of the new Italian kingdom, the town was beside itself with frustration and bewilderment to discover that he would have nothing to do with it. He gave it money and on at least one occasion he paid some of its urgent debts, but he would not allow it to institute "Verdi festivals" or exploit his name for the sake of vain shows and false attractions. The misunderstanding persisted, decade after decade, and the more the town tried to avail itself of Verdi's prestige to attract visitors and enhance its importance, the less he would have to do with it. The amount of trouble taken on both sides, decade after decade, was immense, but Verdi stubbornly refused either to be exploited or to move away. He could not prevent the town from building a theatre and calling it by his name, but he could stay out of the theatre, which he did, and out of the town also. He reached the point at last when he would not set foot inside of Busseto and would permit hardly anybody from the town (aside from Carrara and a few others) to set foot inside the villa at Sant' Agata. When he came from Genoa, Paris or Milan, he got out of the train at Borgo San Donnino—the junction nowadays called Fidenza—where his carriage waited for him; he then drove to his villa without ever going inside Busseto. For the same reason he refused to allowed a bridge to be built over the Ongina river, the little stream in front of his villa—it served, like his wall, to shut out the nearby town and its inhabitants.

This weird, obstinate civil war, or state of siege as I have called it, lasted for half a century and may have been the longest such engagement in military history. What satisfaction Verdi got out of it is impossible to know with any assurance today. He was much too proud to put his feelings into words on most occasions. With regard to his "other father," Antonio Barezzi, the strained situation in 1849 caused them much grief and was ended in a few years, happily for both, giving way to a renewed friendship which filled the last part of Barezzi's life. The old man died in Verdi's arms (July 25, 1867) and the composer was inconsolable. In view of this long devotion, which, as we can see, was as rewarding to Barezzi as to the child of genius he had once found in a wine shop, Verdi's well-known letter of 1852 is worth quoting at length. It was written from Paris on January 21, 1852; that is, a year after the triumph of *Rigoletto* in Venice (at which Giovannino Barezzi had been present as the family's representative). This (1852) was the year in which the composer wrote *Il Trovatore* and *La Traviata*, and the letter to Barezzi was written about a month before Verdi and Peppina saw *La Dame aux Camélias* performed at the Vaudeville. It comes nearest, of all the Verdi documents known to us, to showing what he really felt in the drama of his own life in and near his native town and with the friends of his youth.

"*Most dear Father-in-law*," he writes—a form of address he never abandoned, although Margherita had died twelve years before. "*After waiting a long time I did not expect to receive from you such a cold letter, in which, if I am not mistaken, were some very pungent phrases. If this letter had not been signed Antonio Barezzi, that is to say my benefactor, I should have replied with considerably vivacity or should not have replied at all: but, carrying that name which it must ever be my duty to respect, I shall try, by any means in my power, to persuade you that I do not deserve reproof of this kind. To do so it is necessary to go back to things past, to speak of others, and of our town, and the letter will become a little prolix and boring, but I shall try to be as brief as I can.*

"*I do not believe that you would have written, under your own inspiration, a letter which you knew could not help giving me pain; but you live in a town which has the defect of meddling often in other people's affairs, and of disapproving everything which does not conform to its own ideas;*

I have the habit of not taking part in the affairs of others unless asked to do so, and precisely for this reason I demand that nobody should meddle with mine. Hence come all the gossip, the murmurs, the disapproval. That liberty of action which is respected even in the least civilized countries, I have the right to demand in my own. Judge for yourself, and judge severely, but coldly and dispassionately. What is the harm if I live in an isolated way? If I do not see fit to pay calls on those who have titles? If I don't take part in the festivals or pleasures of others? If I administer my own funds as I please and because it interests me?—I repeat: what harm is there? In any case, nobody can be damaged by it.

"With this premise, I come to the phrase in your letter: 'I understand very well that I am not the man for your business, because time for me has already passed, but for little things I could still be capable. . . .' If by this you mean to say that I once used to give you heavy responsibilities and now use you for little things, alluding to the letter you included with your own, I cannot find an excuse for this, and, although I should do the same for you in similar cases, I cannot say anything except that the lesson will serve me for the future. If your phrase means a reproof because I have not put you in charge of my affairs during my absence, allow me to ask you: How could I ever be so indiscreet as to put such a heavy load on you, you who never set foot on your own country properties because your business concerns are already too much for you? Should I have put Giovannino in charge? But isn't it true that last year, during the time when he was in Venice, I gave him a full power of attorney in writing, and he never once set foot in Sant' Agata? Nor do I reprove him for it. He was perfectly right. He had his own things to do, important enough, and could not take care of mine.

"Thus my opinions, actions, will, life are unveiled, one may almost say, publicly, and since we are in the way of making revelations I have no difficulty in lifting the curtain which hides the mysteries enclosed within four walls, and tell you about my home life. I have nothing to hide. In my house there lives a lady, free, independent, loving a solitary life as I do, with a fortune which shelters her from every need. Neither she nor I owes an accounting to anybody for our actions: but, anyhow, who knows what relations exist between us? What are our business affairs? What our ties? What rights do I have over her, or she over me? Who knows if she is or is not my wife? And in this case who knows what are the particular motives, what the ideas, in keeping it from the public? Who knows if this is good or evil? Why could it not also be a good thing? And even if it were an evil, who has the right to launch the anathema upon us? Furthermore I *must say that in my house she is entitled to equal, or I should say greater respect than I, and nobody is allowed to fail in it for whatever reason; and finally that she has every right to it by her own conduct, by her mind and by the special courtesy in which she is never lacking toward others.*

"With this long palaver I only mean to say that I claim my freedom of action, because all men have the right to it, and because my nature is rebellious against following the ways of others; and because you, in your own so good, so just [sic], and with so much heart, should not let yourself be influenced into absorbing the ideas of a town which—it must be said!—long ago would not deign to have me for its organist and now chatters wildly about my doings and my affairs. This cannot go on; but if it does, I know what to do about it. The world is so large, and the loss of 20 or 30 thousand francs would never keep me from finding a fatherland somewhere else. In this letter nothing can be offensive to you; but even so, if anything displeases you, let it be as if never written, because I swear to you on my honor, I have no intention of bringing you pain of any kind. I have always considered you and do now consider you my benefactor, and I make an honor out of it and boast of it."

The threat in the last paragraph was one Verdi never seems to have considered putting into effect: in all his wanderings he was not attracted toward any one place enough to live in it, and the idea of *una patria altrove*, a fatherland somewhere else, was quite outside his scheme of things. That he should have mentioned such a possibility only shows that he must have been deeply hurt and saddened either by the tone of Barezzi's letter (which has not been preserved) or by some remarks made in it. His frame of mind, as shown in this letter more distinctly than in most others, was perhaps unrealistic, and may cause surprise for that reason, but it was not insincere. He honestly did think private life could be kept apart from public interest, and it took him a long time to accept the bitter truth that for his kind there could be no real privacy on earth. Again and again, until very late in his life, we find the same revolt against the world's intrusion. Almost thirty years after this (October 18, 1880) we see him breaking forth in a rage because some confidential letters of Vincenzo Bellini— then forty-five years dead—had been preserved and published in a book of memoirs. "These poor little-big celebrated men pay dearly for their popularity," he writes to Arrivabene. "Never an hour of peace for them in life or in death." He thought "a music master's letters, written in haste," should never be submitted to public judgment in the form of a book. He evidently did not suspect that all of his own correspondents for many decades kept his letters carefully, or that the very friend to whom he made this outburst, Count Arrivabene, had accumulated a treasury of them. Peppina's secretarial efforts—for she kept letters too, and usually also copies of those she wrote for Verdi—may not have come under his close attention: they worked in separate rooms and the correspondence was more and more her exclusive concern. In the outburst about Bellini's letters in 1880, as in the letter of 1852 which we have given in full, what we see is Verdi's natural desire for privacy—which he erroneously called "solitary life" or "solitude," a very different thing—asserting itself irresistibly to the detriment of his common sense. He ought to have known, and probably did know in his calmer moments, that from mid-century onward any privacy he might ostensibly attain in the arrangements of life (by building high walls, etc., etc.) was illusory and theoretical. It provided no barrier whatsoever against local curiosity, since his own household servants—of whom he had ten at one time—were all from the neighborhood and had relatives all over the town and the nearby villages. It constituted no real obstacle to the curiosity of the world, which has never hesitated to invent when information was lacking; and nothing he could do would protect him against the interest of posterity. All of these things his sound common sense must have told him, but his stubborn nature ("peasant," if you like, or as he liked) never stopped insisting upon his right to shut the door and be alone when he so wished. This particular chord remained suspended, unresolved: he never worked it out. His great contemporary, Wagner, attempted the resolution of the chord by deliberately arranging the documents (and, when necessary or desirable, falsifying them) for the benefit of both contemporaries and posterity. In more recent times we have had examples (Mahatma Gandhi and Bernard Shaw were such) of persons for whom it was assumed that privacy was neither possible nor desirable, and every act of life was absolutely public: the door was never shut. Neither of these solutions was possible to Verdi. He had to go on struggling, right to the end, for his right to shut the door, even though he must have known in his own very lucid intellect that it was ultimately a hopeless endeavor.

5   After Peppina and Verdi took to living a good part of the year at Sant' Agata behind their walls, with such friends as they chose to invite from Milan or Paris or Rome, the town of Busseto felt extraordinarily bereft, not to say cheated. A good deal of the siege warfare for two or three decades consisted in the town's efforts: (a) to break into the villa somehow; and (b) to get the inhabitants of the villa out into the town. The first failed except on the most formal occasions, when representatives of the municipal bodies were received by the composer by appointment and their requests considered. Otherwise callers from Busseto (always excepting the members of the Barezzi and Carrara families) found the gates closed and the Maestro occupied, not to be disturbed, or out.

In the second effort, to involve the Verdi ménage in the life of Busseto, a more complicated and prolonged transaction took place. As a result, physically speaking, the Villa Verdi became more separated from the town than ever before, and through sheer self-defense (as he considered it) Verdi took to avoiding the town altogether. But before he got to that extreme there were many wearisome altercations and exchanges. It was only natural that a little town should wish to borrow some rays of glory from its most famous citizen; that might have happened anywhere. Considering what opera means to Italy—and that it meant more to the Italy of the nineteenth century than ever since or before—one cannot lift an eyebrow at the extravagances which marked the behavior of the Busseto citizens in the 1850's and 1860's. They would have trotted him out on Sundays, high days and holy days, without compunction or mercy; they would have used his name to entice famous musicians to the town, and with them a golden cloud of visitors; they would have had him handing out diplomas, making speeches, distributing prizes, opening bazaars and dedicating statues to himself. It was absurd and he was right to rebel. Some of their requests were, from the point of view of anybody who knew the world, quite monstrous—but of course they did not know the world, and the most monstrous of their demands were also the most naïve. They thought the Maestro could ask renowned singers and instrumentalists of the day to come to Busseto and play or sing for nothing; and of course, in sober fact, he could have done so; they would have come. But how could he bring himself to ask of them any such sacrifice, and for what reason? A woman like Adelina Patti, whom he adored and who adored him (without personal intimacy) would never have refused. Patti was in demand throughout the Western world, at the most exorbitant fees, and her time was subjected to detailed contracts for years in advance. Verdi could not possibly ask her to cancel New York or St. Petersburg (at two thousand dollars an evening!) for the sake of coming to the little town of Busseto and singing *La Traviata*, even though he was well aware that she would do it for him. In this and similar cases we are not startled at Verdi's recalcitrance, which seems only natural, but at the extraordinary stupidity of the town of Busseto in making such requests.

Therein lies the most wounding element for Verdi: that Busseto could think itself *entitled* to demand such things of him. Verdi was always generous toward the town of Busseto and the hamlet of Le Roncole, and neither ever hesitated to ask him for money. The hospital of Villanova (which still operates successfully) was one of his enduring gifts to his people at a time when they were scarcely able to appreciate it. He and Peppina not only gave their money but actually worked hard to build, equip, endow and perpetuate that hospital, which was completely their creation. He was at all times ready to contribute to any scheme for draining swamps or improving the conditions of health for peasants in the Po valley. He was constantly giving sums of money for local improvements, for talented boys, for the aged poor, for public works, in addition to those sums which he gave throughout the national struggle for patriotic purposes. When the municipality of Busseto got into a hopeless entanglement of debt over the building of a bridge, he paid off their obligations for them without a question. In all these transaction for fifty years, right up to his last will and testament, he was largely and nobly aware that these were his people and that he owed them something for the gift of life. (On November 10 of each year thirty lire, or six dollars, to be multiplied for actual present value, were to be given to each of fifty poor people in the village of Le Roncole; agricultural scholarships of four years each for two boys willing to study both theory and practice, one from Busseto and one from Villanova, were endowed in perpetuity; trust funds were established for the Villanova hospital and the orphanage, etc., etc.). Nobody could possibly contend that Verdi failed in his duty toward his native town or its people. The extraordinary bitterness with which his benevolence was accompanied was due, most of all, to the bad manners of the Busseto people and their lack of tact, but also, regrettably, to the all-too-human weaknesses of all concerned.

It was just this attitude—"we own him; we paid for him"—that Verdi could not endure. It was as infuriating for him in later years as the hostility

toward Peppina had been in 1849. Somehow, the two things merged, became one: he shut his door against those people. They could have his
money but they could not have him. It was rather like his attitude toward the Conservatory of Milan when it wished to adopt his name:
"They wouldn't take me young and they cannot have me old." Needless
to say, Busseto did not understand and never really gave up trying, although after the 1870's—that is, after Aïda and the virtual retirement of
the Maestro from the world—the town was somewhat overawed. By that
time (after years of frustration) it began to see that some other system of
values prevailed in this case. I have no doubt that the citizens of Busseto
in the 1880's and 1890's in general were content to say that the Maestro
Verdi lived near at hand but was too queer, too strange and antisocial to
be regarded as a human being. The moment he died the town had its
revenge: it plastered the name of Verdi over every conceivable or inconceivable object in the neighborhood.

The high point of this struggle between the town of Busseto and Verdi
—that is, of the town's effort to exploit him, the second of its two efforts
as I have named them—came in the 1860's, culminating with the opening
of the Teatro Verdi in 1868.

As early as June, 1845, some of the Busseto citizens had proposed the
building of a theatre to be named after the composer, who at this time
was thirty-two and had produced three really popular operas (Nabucco,
I Lombardi, Ernani), along with his failures. He protested violently and
the project was abandoned, only to be resumed periodically thereafter.
In the summer of 1865—that is, twenty years later, after La Forza del
Destino but before Don Carlos—the burghers started the same agitation
in a more serious and determined manner, and evidently the mayor of
the town informed the town council that the plans could be carried out
without consultation with Verdi, whose financial, moral and artistic support was automatically assured.

A vote of the town council had authorized this theatre in 1857 and
work upon its construction began in 1864. It seems to have been assumed
that Verdi would write a new opera for it and would ask the most notable
singers in the world to come there and sing in it. The mayor and town
council also assumed that he would give them some money for it—as
he had already done for their legal debts.

Verdi's minute on the subject is preserved in the archives at Sant'
Agata and has been reprinted by all the Verdi scholars (Gatti, Luzio,
Oberdorfer, etc., etc.). It says:

"How? Are they to dispose of me, of my means, and without speaking

to me, without consulting me? But this is more than an inconvenience: it
is an insult. It is an insult because this way of doing things signifies:
What's the need of talking to him? Oh! He'll do it. He will have to do it.
By what right do they behave like this? I know very well that many, speaking of me, go about murmuring a phrase which is either ridiculous or unworthy, and it's hard to tell which: We made him ourselves! Words
which hit my ears the last time I was in Busseto eight or ten days ago. I
repeat that this is ridiculous and unworthy. Ridiculous because I can
reply: 'Why don't you make some others?' Unworthy, because all they
did was to execute a legacy.[1] But if they throw this benefaction into my
face I can still answer: 'Gentlemen, I received four years of a scholarship
at twenty-five francs a month, twelve hundred francs in all. That was
thirty-two years ago. Let us count up the capital plus all the interests and
I will pay it all off.' There would remain always the moral indebtedness.
Yes. But I lift my head and say with pride: 'Gentlemen, I have carried
your name in honor through every part of the world. That is well worth
twelve hundred francs.' Bitter words, but just! See to what a point things
are reduced when one does not sufficiently weigh words or use the modes
of courtesy. I should never have wanted, and should have given I know
not what to avoid, these scandals; the proof is the conciliatory propositions which I offer by means of Dr. Angelo Carrara to the Commission
and to the Administration. Whatever may be the result this is an affair
of which I never wish to speak again."

The "conciliatory propositions" made by his lawyer, Angelo Carrara,
were that he would accept the dedication of the theatre to him and
would contribute 10,000 lire to them for its expenses if they would release
him from the other imaginary obligations they had wished upon him—
that of writing an opera for them, obtaining the most famous artists in
the world to sing in it, conducting it himself, and all the other fantastic
notions which the Busseto citizens had evolved during the course of their
lucubrations. It would have been brutal of Verdi to refuse them his name
for the theatre after they had already voted its cost and begun to build
it; and as the most prominent citizen of the town he could hardly refuse
them a gift for this purpose; but to turn the whole thing into a sort of
Verdi circus or festival was beyond his power to contemplate. He deplored
it from the outset and said so loud and long—it was "useless" in his view,
the worst word he had for any undertaking—but he could not prevent it.
All he could do was to refuse to have anything to do with it. He was most

[1] The scholarship of the Monte di Pietà, five dollars a month, was from a legacy
which cost the citizens nothing.

of all embittered by the fact that the town was not at all solvent, and had only recently come to him to help out with its legitimate debts; why it required an opera house at this point he could not understand and he refused to condone the movement.

Later on he was asked to accept the honorary presidency of this, that or the other worthy local society, which he refused with considerable anger. The opera house, the Teatro Verdi, may have been in origin an attempt on the part of the town of Busseto to use the composer for commercial purposes, but it was certainly also an effort to pay him homage. This part of it was obscured for Verdi by his unpleasant experiences with respect to his domestic life and all the petty incidents that clung in his memory; he could not see that underneath their astounding ignorance and stupidity the burghers of the little town really did reverence his genius. Ten years after the *minuto* which has been quoted, the Maestro wrote to his friend Arrivabene (1875): "You know I am a sort of pariah in this town. I have committed so many sins against them!!! They never have forgiven me because I didn't write an opera expressly for the opening of their theatre, because I gave them at that time 10,000 lire (which they nevertheless accepted!) and because I didn't bring them La Patti, Fraschini, Graziani, etc., to sing (it's history!). How the devil was I supposed to grab those artists by the neck and force them to sing in Busseto? You'll understand from this that I take no interest in the affairs of Busseto and when they yell I let them yell. . . ."

The theatre was built in spite of him, and stands today—Teatro Verdi —at the upper end of the Piazza Verdi, facing the statue of Verdi and adjoining the Via Verdi.

It was completed and opened in 1868 (September) with a performance of *Rigoletto*. Verdi had dreaded this event, which clashed not only with every instinct of his being but also with the specific gloom of his soul after *Don Carlos* and the annexation of the Venetian provinces. There is scarcely any time in his life when his melancholia was more profound: nothing, either in art or life or history, seemed to have justified the hopes which had sustained him up to this point. We know from all the letters how he railed against his erstwhile friend the Emperor Napoleon III, how he felt the dishonor to Italy, how he would even have refused—or thought he might have refused—the gift of Venice and its fair provinces, how he regretted, more than ever, the death of Cavour. (Cavour had carried with him into the grave, he said, all the brains and all the luck of Italy.) The "black year" of 1867 with its supreme aesthetic disappointment, the unrealized or insufficiently realized *Don Carlos*, combined with these lacerating impressions of fate on the new kingdom of Italy, made Verdi quite willing to die. We may all be glad that we did not have to live in the same house with him as Peppina did, during 1867 and 1868, when he was for days on end unwilling to speak. In this abysmal mood—combined, as usual, with a good strong dose of hypochondria—he had to face the intolerable imbecility of the "Verdi festival" and the "Verdi theatre" in his own native town, within spitting distance, as you might say, and all tricked out with bunting and fireworks. He could not endure it. We may well suppose that the anguish over *Don Carlos* was the most powerful element in his suffering, because he was, first and last, an artist. *Don Carlos* in its somber, grandiose integrity was by far the most intense effort he had ever made, and he knew very well that its general lines were incomparably beyond those of *Rigoletto*. Verdi, like the Lord, remembered his children; he never disowned any of his own work. But he knew perfectly well that *Rigoletto*, a spurt of genius composed in forty days, was not in the same category as *Don Carlos*. The dark splendor of that flawed masterpiece had been misunderstood, had, in his view, failed of its aim, only a few months before, while the town of Busseto was putting out its red carpets for a festival performance of *Rigoletto*. This, by my feeling in the matter, was what gave Verdi his sense of utter frustration at the time of the opening of the Teatro Verdi. He went away. Visitors came from all parts of Europe but the Maestro was not there.

He did not go far: only to Tabiano, in the foothills of the Apennines, to wait for the storm to blow over. On September 15, 1868, he wrote to Léon Escudier in Paris: "I am here in a village at the foot of the Apennines which takes the place of Cauterets and has spared me the theatre of Busseto. Fine consolation! Pay 10,000 francs and be exiled from your own house! So it goes! Tonight, however, the theatre is closing and I'll be able to get back to Sant' Agata tomorrow for lunch."

All these misunderstandings were of some years' date, since the argument had continued for so long; but when, in the end of all, he actually ran away and would not even be present at the opening, Busseto was not only enraged, which it had already been at frequent intervals for years, but completely obfuscated. Barezzi, who might have helped to explain or to serve as a buffer, had died the year before. There was nobody in the town who really understood Verdi's point of view except the lawyer Carrara, whose professional duties put him into a separate pigeonhole and impaired his persuasive powers with his fellow citizens.

And Verdi seems to have been almost equally obtuse, in that he did not understand the town's wish to borrow gorgeous plumage from its only peacock. The mayor and corporation of the little town (which by now had grown to over 10,000 inhabitants) wanted, just as plainly as any small town in the American Midwest or in California, to be "put on the map." That was what it was in origin, a desire for corporate recognition, for consideration and esteem above other towns, for special (if mysterious) advantages. Verdi himself, who claimed to be a peasant from a town "which was not on the map," should in common humanity have understood a little better how his fellow townsmen did want to achieve that dubious advantage. They could not possibly understand that in the long, long struggle of the past two decades—almost twenty years separate *Rigoletto* from *Don Carlos,* as you can hear with the unaided ear if you listen to the music—a tremendous process of deepening and widening had taken place in the creative consciousness of the composer. There is hardly any way in which Busseto could have understood Verdi in 1868, and obviously Verdi—who had been perhaps too much alone for too many years—no longer understood Busseto.

The whole affair, decade after decade, can only arouse pity or compassion among those who consider it in retrospect. The Busseto townspeople were never as rapacious or insensitive as Verdi so often considered them to be—many of the stupidest things they did were done out of sheer admiration for him, nothing else. Some men, quite possibly most men, would have harnessed this admiration and exploited the exploiters. It would not have been difficult for Verdi to make of his native town a sort of shrine for Italian opera and for his own operas in particular, just as Wagner did with Bayreuth a short time later. The stupidity of Busseto consisted in not being able to see that this self-glorification was utterly beyond his capacity even to imagine: he could have turned himself into a goat or a rattlesnake as easily as into an idol at a shrine. He wanted to live there, yes, because so far as I can make out he never really felt at home anywhere else in all his life, but he wanted the town to ignore that he lived there. It was an impossibility, of course, and it poisoned much of his existence, but nobody could deny that it was a perfectly natural desire for a man of his character.

The twenty-five years of pain and venom—I put them from 1849 to 1872 or 1873, ending roughly in the period after *Aïda* and before the Requiem—were succeeded by a long afternoon in which the siege or civil war went into an inactive stage. That is, the town finally learned that it was not welcome at the villa; it also learned that the Verdi family had no intention of visiting the town except under direst necessity. Relations never grew better and there was never a moment when the villa was altogether safe from an attempted intrusion, but there never again was quite such an outburst of agitation and acrimony as went on in the 1860's over the question of the theatre. During the 1880's and the 1890's life at the Villa Verdi was pretty much as the composer had wanted it to be— that is, comfortable and secluded, not "solitary" at all, even though he persisted in using that word, but restricted to his own family, servants and friends. Certain friends such as the orientalist Italo Pizzi, from the National Library in Florence, came for a fixed period every year (generally two or three weeks in September), as, of course, did Arrigo Boito after he had hitched his wagon to Verdi's star. The Ricordi family and some others were annual visitors. Giulio Ricordi frequently brought pilgrims, such as the young conductor Arturo Toscanini at the end of this period. Madame Stolz, Madame Waldmann and some other friends of theatre days were familiars. It was not at all a "solitary" life but it was at least private and the town (by now somewhat overawed) allowed it to exist. That was perhaps the most that could have been attained under such conflicting aims or views.

But before we leave the subject of the painful period, the active siege, candor compels us to say that Peppina was never a peacemaker in the affair. She was anti-Busseto, anti-Sant' Agata and anti-countryside in every dispute or altercation of which we have evidence. Sometimes she threw herself into good works for the people, as she did in the creation of the hospital at Villanova, but that was for Verdi, and by his side. In her own letters to others we see that her attitude toward the town and neighborhood was that of a permanent and hardly veiled bitterness. She had suffered more than he, and more intimately, from that disastrous 1849 visit. We are not surprised that she resented the town and egged Verdi on to greater severities toward it. She was convinced, or so she said, that her beloved dogs (she was speaking of Loulou at the moment, but it would have been just as true of Loulou's successors) were far nicer and better than the inhabitants of Busseto, and she professed herself unable to understand how her "wizard" Verdi could have been born in such a place. If he had ever felt inclined to make his peace with his surroundings she would, we may be sure, have managed somehow to prevent it.

6   Life at Sant' Agata behind the high walls of the villa became agreeable indeed when the Maestro's conditions were approximated. That may have taken a long time but it was certainly brought about sometime in the 1870's—let us say, after the Requiem. Without making any pompous farewells or public pronouncements, Verdi had, in effect, retired from the world.

Much of Verdi's time during these fifteen years went into work on the garden, the park, the house, the farm. His little lake, which he called "the mud puddle," his avenue of elms, his maze of walks, the running stream and the grotto—those things which are now glibly exhibited to the tourists and form the subject of many picture postcards—were all his doing, much discussed before, during and after. Peppina was in particular charge of the flowers.The house, very large and comfortable, settled into an aspect of permanency along about the middle of the 1870's and has not been much changed since then. The Maestro's study and music room, on the south side, with its two pianos, its books and scores, was the heart of the house for him during many hours of every day, even when he was not composing. He had often said that he could not take in music through the eye, and he discouraged Ricordi from sending scores to him, but at the same time he had a considerable number of scores, some of which (such as the *Lohengrin* we have mentioned) were profusely annotated. For everything which concerned the lyric theatre he preferred to form his impressions in the theatre itself—which is, we must see, the perfection of good sense: an opera is such a combination of elements that it cannot possibly be judged or appreciated from a printed page. In other music—aside from opera—Verdi obviously did read scores; he could not otherwise have formed his reasoned opinion of symphonies (Beethoven's, for example) or of the polyphonic compositions of early masters such as Palestrina. Performances of such works were not frequent enough then to give him a first-hand acquaintance otherwise. His famous advice to the young, "go back to the antique and it will be progress," was based upon his reading of scores. To this very day, in spite of a vast amount of scholarly editing and resuscitation, the work of Palestrina is seldom heard even in the greatest musical capitals, such as Milan and Vienna, and never anywhere else. Verdi's insistence on the study of Palestrina and other early masters, all through the last three decades of his life, could only have come from the performances he gave in his own head with the scores under his eyes.

When he played the piano for himself it seems to have been mainly Corelli, Haydn, Mozart and Beethoven (at least these are the scores kept in his workroom). We know that he played the Beethoven sonatas up to a very advanced age. We also know that he was delighted to play two-piano compositions with any visitor who was able to do so, but that the visitor was also expected to bring the scores. Actually Bach, Haydn, Mozart and Beethoven seem to have constituted the staple fare in that music room for many decades, as they have in innumerable other music rooms everywhere, and under the circumstances it seems a little strange that Verdi should have let himself go so far in opposition to "foreign" influences on Italian youth. We realize that he was thinking chiefly of Wagner and that his fear was that Italian music, which he felt to be primarily and essentially vocal in its genius, would be led astray—into sterile imitation and futility—by the so-called "symphonic opera" and the "music of the future." He was eminently sensible in this thought and in this fear; not a page of the Italian music composed under directly Wagnerian influences has survived; and if Italian music persists in getting itself written, it is far more in Verdi's spirit than in Wagner's. Even so, there seems a certain inconsistency in the fact that Verdi went right on playing the Beethoven sonatas at the very time when he was spitting rage at all the musical youth of Italy for yielding themselves to German influences. The true battlefield of his aesthetic being, which was in his own soul, had its physical or external counterpart in that workroom on the south side of the Villa Verdi at Sant' Agata. There he spent the sixteen years of silence: silence, that is, so far as the theatre was concerned. Gradually the scores multiplied, and we are told that in the final phase (the 1880's and 1890's) there never was a time when some score did not lie, opened, on the music stand in the middle of the room. The Maestro who had once said he could not "take in" music with the eye was now reading all kinds of scores, good, bad or indifferent. He was battling with himself, of course, and very often what he said in letters or in print was an intellectualization of some attitude he had already in his heart of hearts abandoned. Not that he was in any way dishonest: he was always stating his truth, but since he happened to be a gigantic genius the truth he stated had sometimes already been left behind by his swift, silent and irrevocable evolution.

Thus, during the sixteen years when he stayed out of the theatre, the inconsistencies multiplied. He had been bitter and scornful over the formation of the "quartet societies" in Milan and other Italian cities; he thought chamber music was a German fad or fancy, so far as Italians were concerned, and could only dull their natural gifts. He even thought orchestral concerts were un-Italian. He was sharp indeed over such young men as Boito, Faccio and others who were active in such matters and welcomed the music of the north. And what do we find, during this very period, at the very time when his hostility to such innovations is so manifest? He composes a string quartet (1873), which, although somewhat conventional and scholastic, is far from insignificant and shows his full acquaintance with the form; he writes some sacred music for voices with orchestra and gives it to Faccio to be performed in a symphony concert in Milan (1880); he accepts the belated homage of Brahms and some other non-Wagnerian Germans and apparently studies some of Wagner's orchestral scores; at Wagner's death (1884) he deplores the irreparable loss to art! These are inconsistencies, if you like, when they are placed alongside of his frequent pronouncements on Italy's need to remain Italian in music. It would be more accurate to characterize them as symptoms of the mighty struggle which was going on in the very depths of his being and which, finally, resulted in *Otello* and *Falstaff*—the two works in which Italian genius, remaining vocal and supremely Italian, nevertheless confiscated and employed "symphonic opera" to its own purposes without for one second following the dictates of Wagner. This evolution is unique in the history of art and it took place during those sixteen years of silence, the titanic struggle in that workroom on the south side of the house.

When you go to Milan nowadays and see the array of good music which is performed during any winter season (the season traditionally called "Carnival and Lent") you may be misled into thinking that this was always the case. Nowadays chamber music and recitals are frequent, choral and orchestral works are performed in regular subscription series, every sort of instrumentalist can be heard in every kind of composition, ancient and modern; the level of performance is extremely high and the range is great. This activity was only beginning when Verdi was about sixty. During all the first half of his creative life music was opera and opera was music: there was nothing else in Milan. A symphony orchestra was unknown; a chamber-music society was a German innovation of the 1870's. Even singers, who abounded then as now, practically never sang anything but opera. The recitals of German songs (Schubert, Schumann, Wolf, Strauss) which are so regularly enjoyed in Milan today with exquisite artists from beyond the Alps, such as Mesdames Schwarzkopf and Seefried or Mr. Fischer-Dieskau, would have been regarded as utterly incomprehensible in Verdi's time. Wagner had not yet invaded the Scala and even Mozart was rarely performed. Rossini, Bellini and Donizetti dominated that stage (along with Verdi himself) throughout the nineteenth century, aided and abetted by the most secure foreign works by Meyerbeer, Gounod, Bizet and a few others. Aside from freakish phenomena such as Liszt, who could fill any theatre in Europe, individual virtuosi seldom appeared in Milan: the city had fallen into the strange delusion that there was no music outside of opera. Mr. Jascha Heifetz packed the Scala to its limits last winter for two violin recitals, and could have done the same for two or three more if his time had permitted; the chances are that in Verdi's middle period he would have found no audience. The old, traditional relationship between Milan and Vienna, which has been revived in our own time, had also lapsed by 1850; those fruitful exchanges, now valued in both cities, were a victim of politics and their absence helped to create the musical vacuum in which opera, and only opera, seemed to survive.

Verdi was certainly no intellectual. He abhorred theory and rationalization: from the beginning to the end we find him proclaiming that nothing matters but music (i.e., opera), no matter on what principle it may be constructed. So long as he lived in the theatre he had no time to think and no desire to do so. It was only by means of this withdrawal to Sant' Agata, to the workroom on the south side of the house, that he was freed to be himself at the fullest. He had finished his formal education at the age of twenty-two and plunged headlong into the composition of operas for the theatres of the day, according to the taste of the day, under the financial, commercial and artistic standards and customs of the day. Much of his work was not worth preserving in any serious sense and he knew it himself by the time he was forty. Of the misbegotten work called *Alzira* he said: "*Alzira!* Now that's really ugly" (*Proprio brutto*). He seldom went so far in condemning his own earlier work, but we know what he thought of it, not only by implication from phrases in his letters, but also by the internal evidence of his later compositions. (That is, the composer of *Otello*, complex and profound under all its brilliance, cannot have thought too much of *Nabucco*.) An unconscious, ineluctable process had driven him through the years from a relatively simple, sincere tunefulness, such as we find in *Nabucco*, to the gathering clouds on the higher peaks. The climb from *Nabucco* to *Aïda* is vertiginously steep and high and long. Then, with *Aïda*, the composer suddenly feels that he does not want to make music for the stage ever again. He is not tired—not at all—as will be amply proved—and he has too much common sense to believe that growing crops, building hospitals or planting trees will fulfill everything there is in his relentlessly creative nature. If we were forced to be specific, we might say that his mind was drawn most of all toward a return to polyphony (the Palestrina obsession) and to sacred music. The Requiem (1874) was the first great fruit of his turn from the theatre to the church, although the final sacred pieces (especially the *Te Deum*) may be even more beautifully a proof of it. I am not referring, however, either to the Requiem or to any other concrete result of the process, but rather to the process itself, which I believe to have been incomplete—an aspiration, not a fulfillment. If I am guessing reasonably, the composer's revulsion against the theatre was strong and deep enough to lead him into quite another direction, and if it had happened earlier—or if he had been given an added decade or two of creative power in an already fabulous life—we should have had from him a new kind of music which his very last pieces only adumbrated: that is, contrapuntal and sacred, probably in the form of Masses. He was already headed in that direction when the irruption of Arrigo Boito into his life hauled him, willy-nilly, back into the theatre; and after *Falstaff* he returned to his counterpoint and his sacred texts. What he had in mind would have been, eventually, as different from all of his other work as those symphonies which Wagner intended to write after *Parsifal*.

For, of course, Verdi kept on composing music all the time, even during the silent years when little or nothing was published. Fugues, madrigals, canons, all kinds of contrapuntal exercises, although he kept them for himself, are known to have preoccupied him for many years. It stands to reason that his instrumentation (already highly evolved by the time of *Aïda*) was also enriched by the long years of reflection and work alone. He used to advise the young to "compose something, even if only a little bit," every day, and even if that little were not for the public; he followed his own advice. All this work, combined with the reading of scores and the consequent examination of numerous novelties, made his long retirement one of the most fruitful of which we have knowledge: when he did return to the world it was not as a stranger indeed (he was always fundamentally the same Verdi) but with mightier forces than ever.

The polemical discussions, in print and in correspondence, were frequent during all this period, and we can have a look at them later. Their general characteristic as defense of Italianism against Germanism we have already noticed, and along with this is a natural sense of personal affront when Italian music was attacked: Verdi and Italian music were by now almost synonymous. We should have to be stupid, deaf, or both, not to discern, just the same, that he was actually devoting considerable study to that which he attacked, and absorbing from it whatever parts his nature as a composer could usefully take. His last two works are "continuous opera," speaking simply of the voices—that is, set pieces no longer exist and everything flows with the drama. He had always tended in that direction at high moments of dramatic action ("This is no time to stop and sing," he said to Cammarano once, even in *Trovatore* days). But only at highly dramatic moments: otherwise his works right up to and including Aïda are composed in the traditional aria-recitative-duet-trio-quartet forms, far freer that those of his predecessors—and far freer in his later works than in his earlier ones—but still within the old framework. Furthermore, his last two works are "symphonic opera" in one very real sense, in that the orchestra is supremely important, rich in instrumentation and dramatic significance. He kept the voices on the stage primary (as a general rule, anyhow) and in this was sharply different from Wagner and the Wagnerites, but he demanded of the orchestra a contribution which the Verdi of only a few decades before would have regarded as monstrous or insane. In these two respects, as "continuous opera" and as "symphonic opera," *Otello* and *Falstaff* prove far more in the history of the art than Verdi's theoretical or polemical pronouncements. His theories or principles (at least as we have them in print) were frequently left behind by his own practice, and he was in this long period of study and reflection actually taking from his opponents—his "enemies"—anything they had which might be useful to him, so long as it was germane to his own genius.

We are reminded of one of his own sarcastic outbursts of years before (1864) after the performance of Rossini's *Petite Messe Solennelle* in Paris. Rossini had been silent for many years and the "little mass," performed in a private house to a choice audience of musical critics and theorists, was received with great acclaim. The learned Dr. Filippi—Milan's Beckmesser—who had already infuriated Verdi many times by his articles in the magazine *Perseveranza*, wrote a review of the work in which he said the old Italian master, who was already seventy-two years old and not far from his death, had "studied a great deal" and had "made great progress." This patronizing comment, combined with the implied slight on Rossini's youthful work of genius, caused Verdi to write to Arrivabene (from Sant' Agata, March 3, 1864): "Rossini just lately has made *progress* and has *studied!* Auff! Studied what? For my part I could wish for him to unlearn music and write another *Barber.*"

This point of view, practical or empirical, was in accord with most of Verdi's prose writing—he never felt that anything mattered but the music itself, and all notions of erudition, scholastic classification or analysis aroused his scorn. It is ironic to reflect that he lived to prove that an old master could indeed "study" and "make progress," for if he did not do so in the 1870's and 1880's then no man ever did.

The dramas of Sant' Agata, internal and external, were over by the year of *Falstaff*, and even Verdi's own secret struggle had ended in victory. The whole countryside, overawed for decades past, grateful for the very existence of the composer—who never ceased to be a source of benefit—knew how to leave him in peace, and the months spent at Villa Verdi each year passed without disturbance, the garden grew older, the park grew more bosky and umbrageous. There was one more ordeal before the end, one more tragic circumstance if not exactly a drama. Peppina died on November 14, 1897, in her bedroom adjoining that workroom or music room in which he also slept. (Gatti relates, no doubt on family evidence, that he used to wake her up in the middle of the night to hear or look at something he had just composed, or to obtain her opinion on a new idea.) The only way in which Peppina failed him in the fifty years of their union was by preceding him to the grave.

She had been ill for some years past; aside from simple old age and rheumatism she had suffered from a tumor and undergone an operation; now, in the late summer of 1897, she had an attack of bronchitis from which she recovered, although it left her very feeble and with an obstinate cough. She still intended to pay her annual visit to her sister Barberina, at Cremona, after which the two of them would go to Milan for fifteen days and then back to Genoa for the winter. On November 11 she was attacked by acute pneumonia and at four in the afternoon of the 14th she died.

Verdi obviously expected it: that same spring (April 17) he had written to the Prefect of Piacenza, the province in which Sant' Agata now was, asking permission to construct two sepulchers (*sepolcreti*) in his chapel at the villa. However, as soon as Peppina's summer illness began to foreshadow the end, he wrote to the Mayor of Milan and asked for two places in the great city cemetery there (the Monumentale). It is evident that the thought of Peppina buried in the chapel of the house, while he might have years yet to live, was more than he could bear. The Mayor and inner council (without consulting the larger body) granted his request at once so as to keep it out of the newspapers. Even this was to be temporary, for he had already in mind the idea of burial for both of them in the House of Rest for Musicians, whenever it could be finished.

Peppina's will, which left a large part of her income to fifty poor families of Sant' Agata, asked that she be buried at dawn without flowers, "representations" or speeches. She was carried from the villa at half past six on the morning of November 16, a foggy and wintry day like so many of which she had complained for many years, and on down the road, beside the Ongina river, for her last visit to Busseto.

The whole town turned out for her funeral.

5

Heroes and Hero Worship

1   The advent of Arrigo Boito into Verdi's life was providential, a stroke of destiny, an act of God. Many points in the matter are arguable. It can be contended that a man of Verdi's powers would never have been able to remain in retirement—that his nature would have called him back to the theatre, or, if not, would have driven him more imperatively than ever into sacred music and back to the "antique." It is a plausible hypothesis, but without Boito what could he have written for the theatre? As the libretto-furnisher, Boito made a contribution to Verdi's fulfillment which may have been all-important: there might have been no fulfillment without him. So much is generally recognized, and it is quite common to read in musical literature that Otello and Falstaff are "the perfect libretti" for which the old composer had waited in vain all his life.

And so much is, I think, obviously true, but it does not take account of the dynamic or incendiary element in Boito's own talent, which could inflame the genius of the old man. Before all else, Boito had to re-create the creator: this was his most difficult task as a human being. He had to "reactivate," as they say, an extinct volcano. Subsequently he had to keep it going, and he had to subjugate to this task every part of his separate being, talent and ambition. Aside from this self-immolation, which, in a man of Boito's intellectual stamp, was clearly realized and deliberate, there was a day-by-day devotion of much humbler spirit: neither woman nor friend nor dog, we often think, could have surpassed Boito in the small anticipations and responses of life. (Example: as soon as he knew Peppina was dying he hastened to Paris to arrange the performance of Verdi's last sacred pieces, aware that only some artistic preoccupation could take the old man's mind out of overwhelming grief.) In all these ways put together —and we count the "perfect libretti" first, of course, but only as one of many elements—Boito can reasonably be said to have kept Verdi alive, in the truest sense, for over twenty years, and to have extracted from him the highest and best he had to give.

Many must have wondered (and I among them) about Verdi's acceptance of a devotion so very great and rare. Fiercely reticent, proud, resentful of intrusion—rébarbatif in French, and how rébarbatif he was!—Verdi after sixty was no easy nut to crack. Why, then, did he, after a struggle, accept Boito? Aside from high talent and wide celebrity, neither of which was novel to Verdi, what did Boito have to offer which made him able to work his miracles on the old man? The special thing he had to offer, I suggest, was pure hero worship, and the reason why Verdi was able to understand and accept such a phenomenon was that he had experienced it himself in an intense form.

Verdi's capacity for this exalted emotion, this reinforcement of belief in life by a growing exemplar, is known to us already in a number of cases: Mazzini to some extent, Garibaldi certainly ("a man to go on your knees before," he said), and of course, most of all, Cavour. The political or patriotic passion which governed so much of Verdi's view of the world during the decades of the Italian struggle for freedom needed personification. It is difficult to have a national movement at all without some such process. (Thomas Masaryk used to say: "For a national movement you need one old man and a hundred thousand young ones.") Verdi was like other Italians in personifying his patriotism; but the difference is that he actually did know all these men; he was not merely putting flags around daguerreotypes. If he had been looking for feet of clay he could have found them. His vision, however, aimed at higher levels, and what he saw in Cavour was the highest level of patriotic effort, combined with the true, the indispensable, magic of prowess, without which the hero does not come into being at all.

None of these, not even Cavour, was the complete exemplar for an artist. Verdi was Italian, he was peasant, and he was artist, but as he grew older this last fatality overwhelmed the others: he grew to be all artist, one is tempted to say, except that he never lost a certain fundamental and pervasive humanity and was not, therefore, subsumed into an abstraction. As an artist, the hero of his election was Alessandro Manzoni, in whom he found prowess and power, purity and elevation of spirit, all at once and in all the fields where his own soul had longed to roam. Manzoni was not only art and history, poet and patriot: he was also Italy, and he had the immense advantage of being twenty-eight years older than Verdi.

The difference in age between them was almost the same as that between Verdi and Boito.

2   From the birth of Manzoni (1785) to the death of Toscanini (1957) is an expanse of time in which the whole history of Italy, as Italy, may be comprised. There was scarcely a notion of Italy before. A concatenation of heroes and hero worship stretches through all that time, one hundred and seventy-two years, between men of genius who variously struggled for their land and people, passing on from elder to younger, or from father to son, an aspiration which was inextricable from their life effort and gave it meaning. There are many such chains of recognition. They can be found in other countries and other periods, and of course in legend too: it is Greek, it is the passing of the torch, and it may even be the succession to the priesthood of Diana, but it is at all events a known phenomenon in all times and places. The particular segment of interest to us is that which includes Manzoni (1785–1873), Verdi (1813–1901), Boito (1842–1918) and Toscanini (1867–1957). Boito and Toscanini were in the relation rather of elder and younger brother—both, that is, as sons of Verdi—than of an extra generation in descent, but here, too, the same magical reverence and comprehension obtain. And it was to Toscanini that Boito owed such justice as he has received for his own last work. What seals the relationship between them all in a formal, historical sense is the product of the final Verdi period: that is, the Requiem, *Otello* and *Falstaff*. Verdi wrote the Requiem for Manzoni; Boito went to Verdi largely because of the Requiem; for Verdi and from Verdi he somehow struck forth *Otello* and *Falstaff*; Toscanini, last of the line, rescued these and earlier Verdi works from the incrustations of every kind of abuse the late nineteenth and early twentieth century could evolve. Owing to Toscanini's tireless efforts throughout the world, and to the mechanically recorded evidence of them, it will never again be possible to treat the best of Verdi, or even the second-best, with the carelessness which obtained forty or fifty years ago. Each of these men *understood* his predecessor. Hero worship without understanding is an adolescent ailment.

Verdi himself was most explicit on the subject in the letters which describe his meeting with Manzoni. He was not without an assortment of idols in art and history: Dante, Shakespeare, Michelangelo, to which there is added the odd but highly characteristic choice of George Washington. These, from far away and long ago, cast their benign shadows across his imagination throughout his life. Cavour made him believe that such exalted characters were possible even in the prose of daily existence, here and now, but it required an artist to arouse in Verdi the full torrent of enthusiasm which was there to be tapped. By 1868, we might say, Verdi was in a state of readiness for the summation: that is, what he revered and admired in Cavour and a few others, commingled with abstract notions of greatness, needed a focus and received it. On June 30, 1868, as we know, he met Manzoni at Clarina Maffei's house.[1]

One of several letters he wrote on the subject gives a picture of his state of mind which may resemble that of all hero worshippers. It is his letter to Camille du Locle, in French, dated July 10, 1868. I have translated the pertinent passage as follows: "There I paid a visit to our great Poet. Poor old man! If you saw what simplicity, what naturalness! I could have thrown myself on my knees because that one is truly a serious writer, who will remain not only as the first of our time, but among the greatest of all time. He leaves a great book, a true book, the most beautiful of our lyric poetry and some sacred Hymns, such as the Prophets have not written better. And all is perfect. What would you have? When I find something beautiful and good (we have so little of them!) I remain in ecstasy, contemplating it."

Leaving aside Verdi's estimate of Manzoni's work, which the taste of our own century might consider excessive, the letter to Du Locle shows not only the depth of the impression Manzoni made, but also—more important as regards Verdi's state of mind—the generic situation in which he found himself. In a manner of speaking, Verdi seems to have been at this point a worshipper looking for a hero. He had the wish to admire, venerate, esteem: he wanted a personified ideal, and a nature like his could not very well have found it in a man of action. An aged poet (Manzoni was eighty-three at the time) whose work had commanded his love for decades, but who had also powerfully contributed to the national Italian rebirth, was qualified to command his allegiance as nobody else in Italy could since Cavour's death. This is not to say that Verdi seized upon the famous old poet as a personification or abstraction—as an excuse for the Requiem!—but only that he did meet Manzoni at the right time. Countess Maffei, perspicacious woman, understood all this: she knew Verdi had made a sort of idol of Manzoni in his own mind for decades past and that he had never had the courage to bring about a meeting.

Peppina herself put an end to this situation by going to see the Countess in May, 1867, at her house in Milan, without telling Verdi. The opportunity presented itself naturally enough. It was Peppina's habit to

[1] Cf. page 59.

visit her invalid sister Barberina, in Cremona, once or twice a year, and at that time their mother was also living. It was natural enough to go on from Cremona to Milan and attend to some business matters for Verdi; she also had to buy some furniture both for the villa at Sant' Agata and for the new apartment in Genoa. Verdi, remaining at Sant' Agata, did ask her if she wanted a letter of introduction to the Countess Maffei, who would be able to help her with the furniture; Peppina said it was not necessary. As soon as she got to Milan she called on the Countess, who received her with rapture and had probably been wondering how long she would have to wait for some such chance. The two women took to each other at once, and were calling each other "tu" before they had gone far in their first conversation. Both must have felt, for years past, how awkward it was for them to remain strangers; both welcomed a chance to get out of the unnatural situation, which only fear of Verdi's displeasure had kept them from terminating before. Peppina, having gone so far, did not hesitate to go further: she asked the Countess to take her to see Manzoni (around the corner), which Clarina did at once. The old poet was touched and grateful for Peppina's visit: he, too, who had been repeatedly assured of Verdi's immense regard for him, must have been wondering how long it would be before this ice pack of diffidence would break. Countess Maffei, his greatest friend, had never ceased telling him how Verdi thought of him, but years had passed without a sign. Now he gave Peppina a little photograph of himself, at her request—perhaps she wanted it as evidence!—on which he wrote: "To Giuseppe Verdi, glory of Italy, from a decrepit Lombard writer."

The whole episode has a conspiratorial look: all these gentle and beneficent souls, Peppina, Clarina and the old poet, were trying to help Verdi conquer his humility, his excessive reverence. They were also trying to lift him out of the terrible melancholy of that year, 1867—he called "the black year" or "the accursed year"—in which the disappointment over *Don Carlos* in Paris, only two months before, had been a crucial point. Verdi's own father had died in January while the composer was in Paris ("I wish I could have closed his eyes for that poor old man," he wrote to Arrivabene.) His other father, Antonio Barezzi, was incurably ill and died two months later. The behavior of Napoleon III in making peace with Franz Josef as if Italy did not count at all—as if Italy were an unconsidered vassal of the French—played its full part in all the accumulation of melancholy. Peppina knew these black moods of Verdi's, to her own sorrow, and must have become fertile in expedients for struggle against them. She could hardly have chosen a better one at this moment than to strike up a friendship with Clarina Maffei, which gave Verdi deep pleasure and relief, but also by the brilliant courage with which she actually called upon Manzoni and talked to him. The consequences—that Countess Maffei would at last come to Sant' Agata and that Verdi would at last meet Manzoni—were obvious: they must have been Peppina's objectives before she started.

When she got home to Sant' Agata Peppina wrote to the Countess, in part, as follows:

"I said to him with affected indifference: 'If you should go to Milan I would present you to Manzoni. He expects you, and I went to see him with you [i.e., with the Countess] the other day.' Pouff! Here the bomb was so strong and unexpected that I didn't know whether I ought to open the windows of the carriage to give him air, or shut them for fear that in his paroxysm of surprise and joy he might jump out! He got red, then white, and broke into sweat, he took off his hat and manhandled it so that it was almost reduced to a pulp. Furthermore (and let this be between us) the severe and ferocious bear of Busseto had his eyes filled with tears, and both of us, moved, convulsed, remained for ten minutes in complete silence. Power of genius, virtue and friendship! Thank you once again, my good Clarina, for Verdi and for me. From Sunday onwards, in this solitude, the name of the saint and your own are repeated every moment, and with what concert of praise and affectionate words I leave you to imagine. Now Verdi is worried over what to write to Manzoni, and I laugh, because if I was so confused, stammering and foolish when you obtained for me the great honor of finding myself in his presence, I am pleased that also those who are much more than I feel a little embarrassment, pull at their mustaches, scratch at their ears to find words worthy to say to the colossus."

The scene Peppina describes evidently took place in the carriage on the way home from the railway station at Borgo San Donnino (the present-day Fidenza). Some allowance must be made always for her rather hifalutin manner of expression, which is just as stilted in Italian as it is in English, and for a little exaggeration to make a good story for her new friend. Even so we find Verdi himself, so sober in his language, writing thus to the Countess on May 24, 1867: "I am still open-mouthed at Peppina's account of what happened between you and with you."

In this letter he sends the Countess a photograph of himself to present to Manzoni. On the back of the photograph he had written: "I esteem and venerate you as much as one can esteem and venerate on this earth, both as man and as true honor to this our motherland forever in travail. You are a saint, Don Alessandro."

The letter says, in part:

"*How I envy my wife for having seen that Great One. But I do not know whether, even if I came to Milan, I could have the courage to present myself to him. You know well what and how much has been my veneration for that Man who, according to me, has written not only the greatest book of our time but one of the greatest books that ever came out of a human brain; and it is not only a book, but a consolation to humanity. I was sixteen years old when I read it for the first time. Since that period I have read many another, upon which, in rereading, advanced age has modified or canceled out (even among those of greatest reputation) the judgments of youthful years; but for that book my enthusiasm endures, ever the same; or even, on knowing men well, has grown greater. It's that this is a true book; as true as the truth. Oh, if artists could once understand that true, there would be no more musicians of the future or of the past; no painters puristic, realistic, idealistic; no poets classic or romantic; but true poets, true painters, true musicians.*

"*I send you one of my photographs for him. I did have the idea of accompanying it with a line or two, but my courage failed me, and furthermore it seemed to me a pretension which I cannot have. If you see him, thank him for his little portrait, which, with his name, becomes for me the most precious of things. Tell him how great is my love and my respect for him.*"

On this occasion Verdi no doubt disappointed all of the benevolent conspirators because he did not even write a letter to Manzoni—which would have given the old poet a chance to reply—and because he did not seize the opportunity to go to Milan and pay the expected visit. Every word he says in this letter is transparently sincere. Yet he had vowed to stay out of Milan, and he was a remarkably stubborn man. He must have known, at some level of his consciousness, that powerful interests—the Scala theatre, the House of Ricordi, the municipality of Milan itself—were friends of the Countess Maffei and quite conscious of his friendship for her; he may have had some remote concept of the importance which Milan attached to getting him back again; he perhaps glimpsed, out of the corner of his eye, the probability that he would go back. None of these things rise to the surface when he considers the "saint," Manzoni. When he speaks of Manzoni it is of the old hero-poet, not of all the layers upon layers of other circumstances involved.

Well, of course, we know what happened. The women got around him

—so did the municipality of Milan, the House of Ricordi, the Scala theatre; so, also, did Boito in due course.

Countess Maffei did not press her advantages—she was much too clever for that—nor did she immediately accept the invitations of her new friend Peppina. From May, 1867, when they became friends, a whole year passed before the Countess at last drove through the gate of the villa at Sant' Agata. She and Verdi had not met for twenty years, in spite of their indefatigable correspondence, and perhaps Clarina, too—who was but human for all her wit—may have felt a little afraid of the meeting. So much can happen in twenty years! Verdi might have changed: she, too, was she not older and sadder in every way? And how would dear Peppina be in her own house, as hostess to another woman from another world, sharing—for this was the fundamental problem—the attention of her "Mago"?

However they did it, the two women managed very well, and if there was a single moment of awkwardness the "Mago" never knew it: the visit was a great success. Countess Maffei had brought with her a formal, definite invitation this time: she wanted Verdi to come to Milan and meet Manzoni in her house. This, sanctioned by the old poet in advance, was impossible for Verdi to refuse, and by the joy which shows in his letters we may suppose that he had hoped to have his hand so forced.

The Countess stayed at Sant' Agata for eight days, exercising all her magic in a circle smaller than she had known for decades—a circle consisting of Peppina and Verdi, their servants, their dogs and horses. The composer (in his letter of June 7th to her, a letter of thanks for her coming) hoped the time had not been "too boring for you," because for him and for Peppina it had been "a blessed eight days, so happily passed." No doubt she took the right amount of interest in every bit of irrigation or cow-breeding, every flower bed, every one of the incessant improvements and embellishments. This was about the period when the *laghetto* —the little lake which Verdi generally called the "mud puddle"—was new and the Lombardy poplars were beginning to look old. He may have played sonatas to her in the evenings (he had a new Erard grand just at this time) and they must have talked a good deal of friends they had once had in common, before he abandoned Milan.

He went to Milan on June 30, 1868, and drove straight to Countess Maffei's house in the Via Bigli, where Manzoni was waiting for him. It was his first visit to the metropolis of his youth since the great year of the uprising and siege, 1848, when he had sat in cafés with Mazzini and agreed to write music for the national revolution. His emotion at seeing the Scala again we must imagine: he does not tell us. What he felt at seeing the revered "saint" in the flesh is much more fully reported in his letters. Aside from the letter to Camille du Locle in French which has been quoted, making a sort of general declaration of a hero worshipper's attitude, he wrote to the Countess soon after his return to Sant' Agata on July 7: "What can I say of Manzoni? How can I explain the new, sweet, undefinable sensation produced in me at the presence of that Saint, as you call him? I could have gone on my knees before him, if one could adore men. They say that we should not, and so be it: however, we venerate on the altars many who had neither the talent nor the virtues of Manzoni, and who were indeed the pink of scoundrels. When you see him, kiss his hand for me and tell him all my veneration."

The streets through which he drove on this brief visit have changed their names since: the main one is now called the Via Manzoni, and the one alongside the Scala, leading into the Piazza, is called Via Verdi, and there is a bronze plaque on the front of the Countess's house in the Via Bigli.

The Countess wrote back on July 9th:

"*After dinner I shall go to my Saint, I will tell him what both of you have written me for him, he will cover his face with his hands and I shall seize that moment to carry out your charge, Verdi, and kiss them. I knew, Verdi, what a mass of emotion you would experience in his presence; he is great in every moment of his precious life, as in every word of his writing: since I have had the honor of being near him and possess the treasure of his benevolence, I feel more than ever the responsibility of my conscience, because He is the true personification of the True, the Beautiful and the Good. Neither a book nor any other artistic impression has left upon me such a complete impress as some of his talk, so simple, clear, illuminated and felt.*"

A year later we find Verdi writing to the Countess, from Genoa, that he envied her a visit Manzoni had paid her in the country; he also envied "that busybody Petrella" for having received a letter from the old poet; and he confesses that he has never yet (1869) had the courage to write a letter to the Sainted Man for fear of obliging him to a reply.[2] He says, however, that he will repair this omission soon so that he, too, can have an autograph. [He never did.]

In 1871, also from Genoa, telling the Countess as usual to kiss Manzoni's hands and express his veneration "in words I could never be able

[2] Enrico Petrella, an industrious but uninspired composer, wrote an opera on *I Promessi Sposi*.

to say," he adds: "It's strange. I, once very timid, now no longer am; but before Manzoni I feel myself so little (and please note that I am as proud as Lucifer) that I can never or scarcely ever find a word."

The death of Manzoni on May 22, 1873, five years after their meeting, filled Verdi with sorrow, although at such an age—the poet was then eighty-eight—it must have been no surprise. He refused to go to Milan then because, as he wrote to Giulio Ricordi, "I have not heart enough to be present at his funeral." To Countess Maffei he wrote: "I was not present at the funeral but very few on that morning could have been sadder and more moved than I, however distant. Now all is over. And with him ends the purest, holiest and highest of our glories."

However, even in his grief on the day after Manzoni's death, Verdi was able to think of what he was going to do. In that same letter to Giulio Ricordi he says:

"I shall come soon to see his tomb, alone and without being seen, and perhaps (after ulterior reflection, and after having weighed my forces) to propose something to honor his memory.

"Keep the secret, and do not say anything at all about my coming, because it is so painful to me when the newspapers speak of me and make me say and do things I do not say and do."

The funeral took place on May 29th, with everything the city of Milan, the people and the government at Rome could do to make it imposing, and Manzoni was buried in the Cimitero Monumentale. There Verdi went on June 2nd to carry out his intention, and remained a long time at the poet's tomb. He had come to Milan in all secrecy—he had discovered the Grand Hotel by this time and had its management and staff as most willing slaves—and sent a note to Countess Maffei nearby: "I am in Milan but I beg you to tell nobody, nobody. Where is our Saint buried? . . . I will come to your house tomorrow after ten o'clock."

Between his meeting with Manzoni and this solemn visit in June, 1873, five very momentous years had passed for Verdi. From the time he saw Milan again it was certain that he would go back into the theatre and would once more belong to the life of the city. The mere sight of Milan on that first revisit excited him, and he thought everything new was wonderful—even the Galleria was "artistic." He returned to the Scala to supervise the production of his retouched *Forza del Destino* (1869), but he returned most of all, triumphantly and forever, with *Aïda* (1872), soon after its première in Cairo. The success of *Aïda* surpassed anything that had been known at the Scala—or indeed elsewhere in Europe—for many decades. As a result Verdi could hardly get in or out of the city without arousing too much attention from the public and particularly the newspapers: hence his conspiratorial air on this occasion when he wanted to be alone with his grief.

But what we do know is that his hours at the tomb of the hero settled his doubts. He may have discussed the matter also with the Countess or with Giulio Ricordi or both, since both knew he was in Milan. What he had in mind was the *Messa da Requiem*, in memory of Manzoni, nowadays usually known in English as the Verdi Requiem, or, sometimes, as the Manzoni Requiem.

3 Back at Sant' Agata, thinking it over, Verdi came to a decision unlike any other in his life: he would make the Requiem into a solemn commemoration on the first anniversary of Manzoni's death, and he would make it as official as possible by entrusting it to the city of Milan.

For a man who could scarcely be persuaded to take any decoration or honor, who despised the authorities in general and was bored to a coma by public ceremonies, this was a strange idea. We know that he did it for Manzoni, not for himself—for himself he had never solicited any support or patronage except that of the public, and never would. But he had been disgusted and angered by the tone of some newspaper essays or evaluations of Manzoni at the time of the poet's death; he read all he could get, a rare thing for him, and found nothing that suited his sense of the immensity of the loss, the grandeur of the departed soul. Worse: there were even some criticisms. "What a brute race we are!" he wrote to the Countess. He then proposed to the mayor and council of the city of Milan to write a Requiem for Manzoni and give it to them for a memorial a year later, if the city would decree "solemn honors" for the occasion.

Giulio Belinzaghi, mayor of Milan, accepted the proposal, but not without a certain amount of discussion in the city council. There were councilors who opposed the idea, probably on the ground of unnecessary expense. The city had already given Manzoni an extremely pompous and costly funeral only the week before: what was the need of a memorial a year later?

At this point up rose Arrigo Boito, the young genius of the avant-garde. He was then thirty-one and a council member, but had been known to Milan in one way or another since before he was twenty. In the discussion on Verdi's proposal Boito astonished everybody by an impetuous defense of the composer himself and of the proposal to honor Manzoni in this way. By this time the Wagner-Verdi argument, which seems so foolish today, was taken very seriously and had already caused a deal of disturbance in Italy; Boito was supposed to be a leading Wagnerian; and yet in this speech at the council meeting he made a passionate tribute to Verdi as the great Italian composer of the day and to Manzoni as poet. He was carried away by the Philistinism of his fellow aldermen, and may even have said more than he really meant; but it was all repeated and reached Verdi's ears in due course. An early step in the process by which Boito became not only Verdi's one true collaborator, but the staff of his old age, his more-than-son, may be seen in this incident.

To the mayor, in reply to a grateful letter accepting the proposal, Verdi wrote on June 9, 1873, saying that no thanks were necessary. It is by "an impulse, or better, a necessity, of the heart" that the composer is spurred to honor, as best he can, the departed poet. Here he adds: "When the musical work is well in hand, I shall not fail to notify you of what elements will be necessary so that the execution will be worthy of the city and of the Man whose loss we all deplore."

The word Verdi actually uses is *inoltrato*, which I have translated as "in hand," but it could more literally be rendered as "begun." Verdi was not a writer and did not choose his words with exceptional care. What he means is "When I get the work into the kind of shape in which I can tell what I need, I will let you know."

For, of course, a great deal of the Requiem was already written before Manzoni died. Professor Gatti, who should know, if anybody except Verdi ever knew, believes that the Mass was about two-thirds composed at this time. He also believes that, since Manzoni had been dying for the whole of the preceding year, the thought of Manzoni had dominated the writing during that period. Thus it is in a true sense "the Manzoni Requiem" even though the last piece in it (*"Libera me domine de morte aeterna"*) was composed in 1869 as Verdi's contribution to the combined requiem for Rossini.

A word should be said about that Rossini project, which caused so much excitement in its day, because it has since been thoroughly forgotten.

("Libera me" is all that remains of it.) Verdi himself proposed that the leading Italian composers should combine in a mass for Rossini's memory; the proposal was accepted and the work written; his assigned share was the "Libera me." After disputes and intrigues and hurt feelings almost without number, involving all the composers, conductors, cities, etc., etc., in a story as long and as complicated as the Trojan War, the project was abandoned and the separate pieces were returned to their composers. The composite mass would have been a curiosity, but scarcely more. When the project was abandoned, Verdi paid all the expenses incurred and retired again to Sant' Agata to nurse his wounds. His friendship with Angelo Mariani, dating back twenty years, never recovered from the dispute over this Rossini project—but, as we know too well, their relationship was already poisoned by Mariani's despairing jealousy over Teresa Stolz.

Aside from all this—and this but a hint of the complications!—I do not myself believe that Verdi's heart was inclined to mourn over the death of Rossini or that he could have written even the "Libera me" with his predecessor in mind. His feelings toward Rossini had always been mixed, so far as the man himself was concerned, and there was a clear resentment of the widow, whom he called "Madama Rossini." Furthermore, a great deal of the hubbub that went on at the time of Rossini's death left Verdi more than cold—a little disgusted. He thought the Italian government's decision to build a pompous monument to the composer at Santa Croce, in Florence, was "noble," but since it came from a government in such financial straits that it could not sufficiently assist the opera houses of the peninsula—could not support Rossini's work, the most valuable part of the man—the plan seemed "an affectation of sentiment, a [piece of] hypocrisy and worse."

Against these expressions can be set some others, of which that written immediately at Rossini's death is perhaps most exact. "It was the most extensive and most popular reputation of our time," he wrote, "and it was an Italian glory. When the other one, still living, is here no more, what do we have left?"

This is a tribute, if you will, but an external one: a tribute from the head and not from the heart. The reference to "the other one" is clear enough: the Requiem in Verdi's consciousness was already forming, not for Rossini, but for Manzoni—for Manzoni and out of the fear of death.

Perhaps the fear of death is the root impulse of all masses for the dead, at least when they are the work of composers not professionally liturgical. Palestrina might have written a dozen requiems in the course of him employment by the Pope, or Bach for the King of Saxony if such had been required; they were composers for the church, hired and paid for that work: but composers of "profane" music, for the concert hall or the opera house, are not compelled by any duty or likely to incur any reward when they turn to it. And yet an astonishing number of them have done just this: sometimes, as in the case of Cherubini's second requiem mass, with the frank intention of having the music performed at their own funerals. The same intention is attributed by legend to Mozart, who, of course, had no funeral and was buried in the grave of common paupers. In the period we are now considering, the two great requiems of the nineteenth century, those of Brahms and Verdi, appear to have arisen from that common, universal source, the contemplation of death, and to have entwined themselves in the natural process of creation with two specific deaths: in the case of Brahms, that of his mother, and in the case of Verdi, that of Manzoni (whom we might, in Freudian language, call a surrogate father). Most amateur Freudianism is dangerous, but it can do no harm to recall that in the year before he met Manzoni, Verdi had lost both of his "two fathers," old Verdi and Antonio Barezzi.

The fear of death may thus attach itself to a specific death but is in itself an absolute in human life, one of its determinants, not only for those who think they think, but also for primitives and savages, for the earliest as for the last of men. Anthropology and religion hardly need to be called to witness; every adult knows the feeling with its concomitant question, what then? What of the human soul? What is the destiny of being?

The experience is universal but it certainly does seem to have troubled Verdi far more than it does most active and practical men. His hypochondria was a symptom of it. At this late date one cannot really form an opinion about his countless illnesses, his frequent collapses and his appalling sojourns in the pit of melancholy. Perhaps some of his illnesses were "real" in the clinical sense. They were all real in the true sense, in that they caused him great suffering, but they can hardly be said to have shortened his life or interfered substantially with anything he wanted to do. His concern over his internal organs (stomach, liver, kidney, digestion) seems to have been unjustified by any disease, but no doubt the results are the same if one thinks they are. At all events, what we do know is that death itself daunted him in that it was not only inevitable and frequently expected, but that it seemed a cruel irony as life's culmination, a sort of impenetrable and unreasonable denial at the end of so many assertions.

In 1889 Italo Pizzi and his wife were on a visit to Sant' Agata when one of the company remarked to the composer, who was then seventy-six and had been complaining of a headache, that he ought to feel well in such lovely surroundings. Verdi said: "Eh, yes, to get out of the boredom of the city, and to feel only a little well, one must take refuge in this solitude or one must commit suicide!"

Pizzi further records—reverently, hesitantly—that his friend and erstwhile pupil, Dr. Domenico Battistini of Busseto, who was Verdi's physician in the late years, told him that the Maestro was inclined to emphasize his bad health (confirming an observation Pizzi had already made). The hypochondria, the consciousness of death and the frequent attacks of deep melancholy were shown in many ways to many persons, and we find them abundantly indicated in his letters to such friends as Countess Maffei and Count Arrivabene, with whom he had less reticence than with others. All of them agree with Pizzi, just the same, that between these fits of melancholy and premonitions of the grave he was bright and spirited or even downright lively, with a fund of observation and good sense, an acute perception and a gift for deliberate, clearly articulated expression.

We need only recall the fact, observed much earlier in this study, that the Maestro got a sore throat during the final stages of composition for every opera for years—a sore throat which the doctors could not treat, accompanied by a nervous disorder of the stomach which equally defeated them—to see that his maladies originated within his own being according to some laws which were not accessible to clinical analysis.

Such a creature, often or recurrently obsessed by the thought of death, could scarcely have grown into advanced age without finding the thought more frequent. In the case of an artist such thoughts take form; in the case of a musician he has ready-made forms to which he can turn. Once Verdi began to consider writing a mass for the dead—starting with the Rossini project in 1869—he never really gave it up in his own mind or on his writing board in the study at Sant' Agata. He kept on sketching and worrying at it. Some friends who had seen the music already written for the "Libera me" were insistent that he should go on from there (from the end!) and make his own requiem mass. Chief among these was Giulio Ricordi, who saw some of the pieces on which Verdi was actually working or sketching and evidently showed them to Albert Mazzucato. Mazzucato was chief conductor at the Scala from 1859 to 1869 and professor of composition at the Milan Conservatory from 1851; in 1872 he became its head. He was not only the composer of numerous unsuccessful operas, but had written books of theory and criticism as well: in sum, the exact kind of musician who could either impress or infuriate Verdi, depending on the circumstances. (Like all instinctive artists, Verdi either revered the intellectuals or despised them, sometimes in rapid succession.)

Mazzucato besieged Verdi in 1871 with a long, flattering letter, urging the composer of Aïda to get to his Requiem. This once Verdi seems to have been open to intellectual blandishments—undoubtedly because his own mind was already made up, underneath all its surface hesitations—and he replied to Professor Mazzucato in a letter which gives valuable indications of how far he had already gone in composing his Requiem. If he had done so much in February, 1871, he must have done a great deal more by September and October of 1872, when he mentioned the subject to Escudier with an idea of performances a year later in London and Paris. Part of the letter to Professor Mazzucato reads like this:

"If at my age one could still decently blush, I should blush for the praises you make of that piece of mine; praises which, I don't conceal it, coming from a Maestro and critic of your value, have great importance and caress my self-esteem not a little. And, see, a composer's ambition! Those words of yours might almost have engendered in me the desire to write, later on, the whole Mass; so much the more because with a little greater development I could find myself with the whole 'Requiem' and 'Dies Irae' already done, the latter having its restatement in the 'Libera me' already composed. Think then, and derive remorse, at the deplorable consequences those praises of yours might have! But be calm: it is a temptation which will pass like so many others. I do not like useless things. Masses for the dead there are already so many, many and many! It is useless to add another to them."

We do not know exactly what he means by "Dies Irae" and what he means by "Requiem" in this letter. If he means the entire "Dies Irae" as it appears in the printed score, and the entire "Requiem" which opens the work (along with the "Kyrie") this would be 97 pages to which the "Libera me" of 1869 (46 more) must be added: in all, 143 out of 229 pages. This is a high proportion—so high that my own guess on the probability would be that he did not mean either the whole "Dies Irae" or the whole "Requiem," but parts of them: i.e. (in the first case), the big opening chorus without any of the subsequent solos, duets, etc., and (in the second case) the opening quartet only. It would be strange indeed if Verdi had composed the greater part of this work by 1871, since he only—and very cautiously—hints at its existence, and at the possibility of performances, a year and a half later. It was his way to finish what he had begun, as a rule, particularly if it were so far advanced.

But there is not a doubt, from all these indications put together, that he worked at the Requiem off and on for about four years (1869–1873). How much was done at what point is another question, of interest more to musicology proper than to the study of the composer's character. My inquiry is simply, what did he mean by "Requiem Mass for Manzoni"? (*Messa da Requiem per Manzoni:* these words were used at the first performance and most subsequent ones, although they do not appear on the published score.) Did he mean that he had literally written this work as a homage to his hero? If so, how is one to explain that most of it was done before the hero died?

The answer lies in the nature of the artist, forever mingling the specific with the general and seldom able to distinguish them with any lucidity. Verdi as creator (not as farmer or businessman) was eminently intuitive, emotional, responsive and therefore sure of his course without being able to give reasons for it. The fear and contemplation of death were in him always, and he met the obviously dying poet-hero of Italy one year before he wrote the "Libera me." Consciously or unconsciously, he may have been thinking of Manzoni from the very first. (He never devoted that kind of thought to Rossini, as we have been at pains to show.) Is it not possible that the thought of death and the thought of the specific dying hero were intermingled from the beginning? I think it more than possible in a character like Verdi's. If so, this is "the Manzoni Requiem" indeed. The opposite extreme to which one can go—and to which some of his enemies did go—is to say that he had already written a mass for the dead, or nearly written it, and merely seized upon the great national figure as an excuse for its solemnization. This latter hypothesis does not meet the facts either of Verdi's own nature, of his passionate veneration for the old poet, or of the composition itself: for at least a third is supposed to have been written after Manzoni's death. His music drama on the death of the body and life of the soul was in him and would have been written, no doubt, sooner or later, but in my view it was elicited by his awe and piety before Manzoni, not wholly at the hour of death or afterward, but during the slow descent through the last few years of the poet's life.

4 Verdi and Peppina spent the summer of 1873 in Paris and its surroundings, returning to Sant' Agata on September 14th for the completion of the Requiem, and to Genoa (Palazzo Sauli—they had not yet moved to Palazzo Doria) for the winter. Evidently it must have been a painful winter for Peppina because the two German singers, Teresa Stolz and Maria Waldmann, were there a great deal of the time working with the Maestro, along with the Italians Capponi and Maini, tenor and basso. Verdi's time was taken, but not only his time: if there was a high point in his friendship with Madame Stolz it must have been between the rehearsals of Aïda at the Scala and the first performance of the Requiem Mass: the early months of 1874 must have seen the gifted soprano more certain of her fascination than ever. Mariani had died, poor fellow, that preceding summer, and all Verdi could think of, in Paris, when he was asked for a word on the subject, was, "What a misfortune for art!" While the conductor was dying Mme. Stolz was singing Aïda in a special season at Ancona. Peppina's depression in the early months of 1874 is shown by a letter to the Countess Maffei in which she says:

"True! Arrived at a certain age, one lives very much in memory. We all have gay ones, sad ones and dear, but oh! not everybody can be fortunate enough to keep unchanged the affections and friendships of the living, or anyhow the illusion of keeping these good things which make life dear. Blessed are you, who believe in, possess and deserve to possess the affections of your old and new friends! I, and I say it in deep discouragement, don't believe anything or anybody any more, or scarcely . . . I have suffered so many and such cruel disillusionments that I am disgusted with life. You may say that everybody treads the thorny path of disillusionment, but perhaps they, stronger than I, have kept some hope and some bit of faith in the future."

Such yielding to the dark forces of despair was not like Peppina—in spite of her somewhat rhetorical gloom in many letters—and she did not really surrender: before very long she had reacted characteristically by making of Madame Stolz, too, one of her dearest friends, a situation which, whatever its origins, attained and retained validity for all of them during the rest of their lives.

Of the numerous decisions involved for the first performance of the Requiem, only one, the choice of place, signifies much today. Verdi wanted the solemnity to take place in a church, of course—neither the concert hall nor the theatre could have given his sacred drama its proper frame. Not many churches are adapted to the performance of a work on such a scale, involving a full symphonic orchestra and a double chorus. The composer was urged to present it first in the Church of Santa Maria delle Grazie, famous throughout the world for Leonardo's fresco of the Last Supper. The church was in need of restoration and the excitement of such an event would draw attention to its appeal for funds. Verdi cut through this and other arguments by insisting on the Church of San Marco, obviously for reasons of musical acoustics. (San Marco, a Lombardo-ogival structure much restored, is off the Via Brera, north of the Brera Palace.) In this as in everything concerned with the project, all he had to do was insist: Count Belinzaghi and the rest of the city administration gave him anything he wanted. The choice of place presents the very same difficulties today, and always will, since this work is essentially double in nature: psychologically or spiritually it belongs in a cathedral, whereas musically it belongs in a very large theatre or concert hall.

The first performance took place at San Marco on May 22, 1874, with Verdi conducting. He had rehearsed every part of it himself, beginning with the quartet of soloists at his own apartment in Genoa months before. A voice-and-piano reduction, with Italian translations of the Latin text both in poetry and prose, was put on sale by Ricordi on the same day, and evidently Hans von Bülow, then in Milan, got a look at it ahead of time, for he writes: "A passing, contraband glance at this new emanation of *Il Trovatore* and *La Traviata* removed from me every desire to be present at this Festival."

Bülow was to make abject recantation two decades later, but at this time he was still in the throes of that venomous anti-Verdian disease which afflicted so many Wagnerians. (Bülow's wife, Cosima, had married Wagner four years before, but Bülow remained a Wagnerian.) His other remarks on this subject, written on the day before the Requiem was performed, are worth quoting as an example of the neurosis:

"*The second event of the season will be, tomorrow, the performance of Verdi's Requiem in the Church of San Marco, theatrically suitable, exceptionally conducted by the composer, Senator Verdi, with which the omnipotent corruptor of Italian artistic taste hopes to sweep away the last remains of Rossini's immortality, inconvenient to him. [This] his latest work, in churchly garb, will be exposed, after the first fictitious compliment to the memory of the poet, for three evenings to the world's* admiration, after which there will be undertaken, in company of the trained soloists, the journey to Paris, the aesthetic Rome of the Italians."

The word Bülow uses for "trained" is *dressiert*, which is used in German for circus animals and the like (not for the training of musicians).

Not content with sending these and other bilious remarks off to Germany, Bülow sent a note to the *Italian* press two days later, stating that "Hans von Bülow was not present at the stage performance which took place yesterday in the Church of San Marco. Hans von Bülow must not be listed among the foreigners who have come to Milan to hear Verdi's sacred music." The word I have translated as "stage performance" is, in Italian, *rappresentazione*, a word used only for the stage. (For a musical work not for the stage the word should have been *esecuzione*.)

These calculated insults probably had small effect on Verdi but they rankled in Bülow's own conscience and induced his public apology long afterwards; furthermore, they did him no good in Germany either, where judges of real eminence, such as Johannes Brahms, disagreed with him sharply. ("Only genius can write such work as this," Brahms said of the Requiem.) The triumphal progress of the Requiem in subsequent months throughout Europe was probably more impressive in Germany and Austria than anywhere else.

Verdi may well have resented many words or phrases in Bülow's published sarcasms, but none, we should think, more than the expression "fictitious compliment to the memory of the poet." The general implication that the Requiem was merely another stage work in disguise may have irked as well, but it was the obvious criticism of the superficial: Verdi must have known in advance, before he put pen to paper, that anything he wrote, if it were to have the characteristics of his inmost being as a composer, would be called "operatic" and would be, inevitably, through and through, a kind of drama. This was his genius and he could never have written otherwise.

However, the Latin mass itself is an opera: it is almost beyond question the origin of opera. What else? The mass for the dead, with its tremendous confrontations and assertions, is the most dramatic of all sacerdotal enactments, imposing an emotional intensity upon its audience which is deeper than the theatre could ever know. That which drew Verdi to it, that which he put into and got out of it, was both powerful and universal—felt by all men but by him expressed. Awe, pity and terror were evoked by this Requiem on that first day at the Church of San Marco and in all the time since then.

Verdi himself knew that in this work he had suddenly bounded far and away above anything that he had been able to write before. "It seems to me that I have become a serious person, and that I am no longer coming like a clown before the public, crying 'Come one, come all,' beating the tambourine and the big drum." These words are not bitter: they convey, to me, anyhow, a sense of discovery. In my own mind I contrast them with what he had written to Arrivabene about *Aïda* three years before: "Among my works it is one of the least bad." In the superb vocal polyphony and virile orchestra of the Requiem Mass we find a great master arrived at his mastery: and we find this aesthetic miracle fused with, indissoluble from, the august and terrible subject itself. A thing *inevitable*, and therefore true from beginning to end, has here come to pass. The fear of death, personal and general, the passion of grief for Manzoni, the tremendous question of destiny and its answer in prayer alone, came all together into the psychological unity of this work; but these momentous amalgamations were within the composer. To the external world the Requiem was given not because his soul had labored and brought forth, but because his mastery as a musician had just at this moment culminated and realized itself so as to express immensities which would have been (even if he had felt them then) impossible for him to get on to the paper only ten or fifteen years before. His erudition came to the aid of his experience, knowledge, feeling and natural resourcefulness: he thus had at his command a technical supremacy over harmony and counterpoint which equaled his skill with voices and instruments. For the first time in his life he governed his world, even if he did so only to offer it to God.

5   In calling the Requiem an "emanation of *Il Trovatore* and *La Traviata*" poor Bülow only made a fool of himself, as usual. He must have begun to suspect it almost immediately, because as a matter of fact the Mass gave musical Europe a rare experience, accompanied by the shock of surprise. The frame of mind which had been expressed by Jules Claretie in the *Journal des Débats* seven years before, after *Don Carlos*, began to be general in Europe: What does this man want? Claretie asked, in effect. Where is he going? Where will he stop? Nobody in his right mind could listen to the Requiem or read its score (and Bülow had done neither when he wrote his childish outburst) without knowing that here a genius was addressing mankind with the utmost seriousness. That the genius spoke through Verdi, in Verdi's voice, with all its echoes of lesser and different work, and that the mind of his listeners was haunted by the opera house—all this made the shock of the Requiem more bewildering. In June Verdi conducted the first Paris performances himself with the orchestra and chorus of the Opéra-Comique, not good, but the best at hand; he took his four soloists with him from Milan. He had previously conducted one performance, and Franco Faccio two, at the Scala in Milan for the benefit of the Manzoni monument. The Paris performances—seven of them, all in the afternoon—took place in the discomfort of great heat, but made a deep impression, after which it was arranged for the composer to conduct a series of them a year later in Paris, London, Berlin and Vienna. These engagements were fulfilled (at the new Opéra in Paris, rebuilt after the fire; at the Albert Hall in London with a chorus of—God help us!—twelve hundred voices; at the Court Opera in Vienna; the Berlin engagement alone could not be kept because the soloists could not get there on time). Verdi actually conducted the Requiem once more, in 1876, when he went to Paris for the first Aïda there (again with Stolz and Waldmann); his friend Escudier now had taken over the Théâtre Italien and wanted the Requiem as well.

There was a tumult in the musical press over the execution of a mass for the dead in the profane surroundings of a theatre. So far as I know Verdi never made a plain, sensible answer to the outcry, but if he had done so it would surely have consisted of the incontrovertible statement that the work sounds better in a theatre or concert hall. So does any other modern work composed for full chorus and orchestra (the *Deutsches Requiem* of Brahms, for example, after its first performance in the Bremen cathedral in 1868, has seldom been heard in a church). Churches with good acoustical properties are not common: most of them have the faculty of muddling up the voices or parts even in the most clearly defined contrapuntal music of an earlier age. Verdi's instinct told him with its usual authority, after the first rendition of the Requiem at San Marco and the second at the Scala, that it sounded better in the Scala. From that time on, imperturbably, he went on conducting the Requiem in opera houses or any other halls suitable for its sonority. He actually did conduct the Requiem more than any other work, either by himself or by anybody else, in his life: the fact gives some notion of the anxiety he had to make it properly heard, if it were to be heard at all.

But otherwise he was not on a high level of spirits. He had arrived at a destination in the Requiem, we know, but it seems that he himself suspected this destination was the end. Not death, perhaps, not instant death, and not death at ten o'clock next Tuesday morning, but the end of an artist's life and work. He had some valedictory feeling about Aïda, as we have remarked before, although not until after he had seen it on its way rejoicing; that is, he had some kind of hunch that this would be his last work for the theatre.

And, much as he may have detested the theatre, as he thought of a lifetime wasted in that abode of cardboard and grease paint, his melancholy would only have increased if it were never to be revisited. Surely, too, the experience of conducting the Requiem as often as he did in 1874 and 1875 could not have lightened his melancholy. His sixtieth birthday had oppressed him; he was now well past it, but the preoccupation with a mass for the dead made it seem a more final landmark than it might otherwise have been. Moreover, at any age, even long before, he was always unhappy when he was not composing something. To Countess Maffei he says (January 30, 1876): "You want to know about my doings, but I have nothing to say. My life is too stupid and monotonous. Every day the same thing, *nothing to do.*"

There were events in those years to add to his natural depression. His friend Camille du Locle, author of the French version of *Don Carlos* and prime mover, as well as second or semifirst author of *Aïda*, lost the directorship of the Opéra-Comique, on which he had set great store; Verdi regretted it deeply, no doubt feeling guilty that he had not been able to give Du Locle an opera in time to save him. The final catastrophe which cost poor Du Locle his job was, by the way, *Carmen*. The failure of that opera was the last straw for the French government authorities. Another misfortune, as it seemed to Verdi anyhow, was the death of Francesco Maria Piave in 1876 after years of illness. This amiable drunkard had Verdi's friendship and loyalty to the end and afterward—all through the years of his helpless imbecility; all through the subsequent vicissitudes of his family; Verdi's reward for a constant and considerable expenditure was to be accused of not having done enough. Piave had written the texts for ten of his operas, ten of the most popular, too: it constituted a claim, no doubt, although he had always been well and promptly paid. With the cruelty of another century we may be permitted to remark that no more spavined jade than Piave's ever climbed Parnassus; this "poet," so-called, achieved his immortality with less expenditure of talent than any other known to man. Verdi grieved, just the same, and it is highly probable that between friendship for the man and a certain obtuseness of taste for contemporary work he never really understood how bad Piave was.

In addition to worries and dissatisfactions of every sort, Peppina's increasing ill health, a sense of futility about composition, and other ailments of the time, Verdi had an acrimonious dispute with the House of Ricordi. It arose out of Aïda and the Requiem and is too involved to be recounted, but it empoisoned a lifelong relationship for at least two or more of these years.

The new artesian well at Sant' Agata, the breeding of cows, the irrigation schemes, the complicated affairs of the hospital at Villanova—all this, engrossing enough to Verdi, left one whole area of his being—and that the most important—without sustenance. Now he was reading scores and listening to the music of other composers; on his journeys to Paris, Vienna and elsewhere he took whatever opportunity offered for the hearing of new work of interest. He was paying far more attention to Wagner than ever before (Wagner, whom he had once thought "a madman"), not only through the scores themselves but in the theoretical prose work, which he obtained in French, and some books about Wagnerian theory and practice. He was delving into the Italian past more and more by means of reading, since performances of antique music were then rare; it was the period when he was preaching Palestrina to all the youth of music. He was ceaselessly, restlessly experimenting with polyphony and even with scales—his scala enigmatica, which has an effect rather like that of the whole-tone scale, was an adventure of the late part of this period. It was a period (the late seventies and early eighties) when he read a great deal of nonmusical literature as well, acquiring, for example, his marked predilection for Emile Zola, a writer one might have imagined to be far outside his field of sympathy, and becoming steadily more familiar with Dante and Shakespeare. His ventures away from home were rarer, but there was at least one worth mentioning because it laid a great ghost and consummated an aesthetic revenge. This was the first performance of Aïda at the Opéra in Paris on March 22, 1880.

Verdi had not been satisfied with Aïda at the Théâtre des Italiens in 1876 in spite of its resounding success. The stage in that theatre was too small, the chorus was bad and the orchestra mediocre; even though he had his own chosen soloists, including Mesdames Stolz and Waldmann, and was given full authority over rehearsals and production, he could not wring out of the material at hand the full effects he desired. (Peppina,

giving details, says that the harps in that orchestra "sounded like guitars,"
and that the timpani were very weak, "*debolissimi*"; the stringed instruments were feeble; the décor, "all gold, as Figaro says," cost a lot of
money but was unfaithful to the requirements and in bad taste; the chorus
had very little voice but by compensation a great deal of indiscipline!)
Obviously Aïda belonged at the Opéra—it is the supreme "grand" opera
of modern times, outgranding Meyerbeer—and to the new Opéra in all its
splendor it was accordingly transferred.

   Verdi supervised the entire production of Aïda at the Opéra, rehearsed
it and conducted the first five performances (not three, as he had intended
—the subscribers for the other two nights threatened a mutiny if he did
not). It was an arduous task for a man of sixty-seven, one might be
tempted to say, if Verdi had not himself greatly surpassed it later. On one
occasion he wrote to the Countess Maffei that he was spending "twenty-
six hours a day" in the opera house. Paris—which had already heard Aïda
a good many times at the Théâtre des Italiens—made this into a kind of
Verdi apotheosis only to be equaled (and surpassed) in the final Otello
and Falstaff fourteen years later. When the Maestro appeared on the conductor's stand at twenty minutes past eight on March 22, 1880, everybody
in the Opéra stood up, by some one of those spontaneous emotions which
do sweep audiences.

   This belated triumph with Aïda was an aesthetic revenge in that it constituted Verdi's final, conclusive proof that he could write a "grand"
opera, after a considerable number of trials.

   The President of the Republic (Jules Grévy) gave a dinner at the
Elysée for Verdi and Peppina, inviting all the snowy summits of art,
literature and politics to meet them. He bestowed upon the composer
the Grand Cross of the Légion d'Honneur, which at that time had never
been given to a French composer.

   These were highlights. So was the memorable concert at the Scala in
Milan, soon afterwards, when Verdi's Pater Noster and Ave Maria were
performed. (Both were "vulgarizations" by Dante of the familiar prayers:
the first is a five-part chorus, that is with two soprano lines, and the second
is for soprano over a string quintet: the Pater Noster from Purgatorio,
Canto XI, and the Ave Maria traditional or perhaps apocryphal.) The
two Verdi pieces came in the latter half of a program by Franco Faccio
devoted to Italian sacred music: Palestrina (motet Panis Angelicus for
unaccompanied quartet of voices), Cherubini, Lotti, Stradella and Rossini were the other composers. This gave Verdi keen satisfaction, because
his efforts in the direction of a religious return or revival, musically speak-

ing, were close to his heart, and because he welcomed any sign of appreciation for the older Italian composers.

None of this, just the same, took the place of composition—"real" composition, that is of some work on a big scale for voices and orchestra, something demanding passion and mastery: the only kind of composition for Verdi. His *Pater Noster*, an exercise in counterpoint, and his *Ave Maria*, a sort of study for a later and more famous work, cannot be called true Verdi in the full sense and cannot have given him the kind of satisfaction his restless creative instinct demanded. All of his friends—the invaluable, indispensable Countess most of all—were aware of this and never let an opportunity pass to remind him that his primary duty to himself and the world was to compose music. The Countess was never a nagger, but as we know, she knew when to strike and every time with effect. She had an exquisite sense of personal adjustment, combining her rare birds as if they were scents or flavors according to time and circumstance—just now was the moment, and here the place, for the blending of Verdi and Manzoni; now would be the time to weave and interweave the special essences of another springtime; let Boito come with cup in hand; she could choose the moment. She was aided by an ally of rare worth, Peppina, who in the whole delicate Boito-Verdi *rapprochement* showed a perception and indeed wisdom which surpassed even her own previous record. Much more blatantly, even flat-footedly, Giulio Ricordi was forever demanding of Verdi another major composition, but his wishes suffered the imputation of interest: he was, after all, head of the great publishing firm which had made a fortune out of Verdi and hoped to increase it. Tito Ricordi, with illness and age, and a quarrel with Verdi, dropped out of control of the business; he did not die until 1888, but during his last twenty years and more it is only his son Giulio with whom a Verdi student has to deal.

Giulio was certainly friend as well as publisher; he was an author and musician, under a pseudonym, and very well equipped to understand Verdi's work even in the composer's old age. He must have had, also, a salutary respect for any musician who could be such a good businessman as Verdi, as had been shown by the negotiations for *Aïda* in Cairo. Furthermore—a quaint detail—on one occasion (1867) when the House of Ricordi found itself temporarily short of cash for some heavy payments, Verdi actually made it a loan of a hundred thousand gold francs. This was equal to 40,000 gold dollars of that time, or about 100,000 in today's money. Verdi said: "It's quite a lot for a music master." One might think it quite a lot for anybody, and it is impossible not to wonder if any other such reversal of roles has occurred in the history of music.

None of them, the Countess or Giulio or Peppina, could do much against the prevailing melancholy and discouragement of Verdi's mood in the late 1870's. He had, of course, often thought of a lyric comedy to be written sometime in utter freedom from engagements or obligations: *Don Quixote* was the subject he had dreamed about in his youth. He was also drawn more and more to Shakespeare, and had never wholly surrendered the notion, also decades old, that he might some day be able to write about *King Lear*. He was even gravitating closer and closer to the actual subjects which were eventually to fulfill his genius as a composer, *Otello* and *Falstaff*: we can find both discussed in his celebrated letter of September 20, 1876, to the Countess, so often reprinted, in which he reiterates his maxim, "Invent the truth," and says there is no contradiction in it. If you doubt me, he tells the Countess, you must inquire of "Papà" (Shakespeare). Since he mentions both Falstaff and Iago as examples of the invented truth, we are entitled to believe that the Countess bore this in mind, also. (The letter will be given in full where it is most appropriate, later on.)

In 1878 both Victor Emmanuel II and Pope Pius IX died, landmarks of the past, mementos of a heroic struggle now dim in memory and clouded by the preoccupations of a more sordid time. ("The stock market and the labor union," Verdi called the thoughts of the hour.) He felt these and many other deaths; his first librettist, the fantastic Temistocle Solera, who had gained a fortune and lost it, once a favorite of Queen Isabel II and now a beggar in a garret, died on Easter Sunday of 1878; soon afterward the Countess della Somaglia, one of the loves of his youth, went her way. "Everybody is dying, everybody!" he said. In his old age, at least after sixty, he had the not uncommon tendency to regard every death on the part of an old friend or acquaintance as a form of desertion or treachery, and, of course, such desertions became more frequent with every year.

He was, in spite of his triumphs and his devoted friends, in some curious way solitary (he uses the words "solitary" and "solitude" often). He always slept in his workroom or study, even in early days, and the splendid apartment in Palazzo Doria in Genoa, to which the couple now had moved, was furnished to provide for this idiosyncrasy. It was a very beautiful and even princely apartment with the mountains on one side and the sea on the other; there was room for all the numerous retinue and the books and the grand pianos. ("Life grows easier, more comfortable," says Verdi, "and more boring.") In Genoa, as at Sant' Agata, there were scores open on the music stand in the middle of the room and he sometimes got up at night to read them. He actually worked at the writing board also a good deal of the time, sometimes in the middle of the night, although much of what he did—contrapuntal and polyphonic exercises— was by himself destroyed. They were not cheerful years, as we can see, but somehow his gigantic creative gift was taking into itself new powers, enlarging its frame, giving itself a longer and solider and smoother and stronger airfield for the take-off of a bigger aircraft than it had ever launched before.

We know now, of course, what he was waiting for. He was waiting for Boito.

6 Arrigo Boito, born in Padua on February 24, 1842, was almost twenty-nine years younger than Verdi; he came not only from a different generation but from a different world, formed by quite other ideas than those which shaped the development of the peasant from Le Roncole. Boito's father was Italian, his mother Polish, his education polyglot, his tastes European; he was full of talent, charm and temperament; he was bourgeois or upper-class to his finger tips, and could hardly have discerned one end of a cow from the other except by direction; witty, elegant, precocious and distinguished, he had no difficulty in anything he undertook up to the advanced age of twenty-six. He entered the Milan Conservatory when he was twelve (violin, pianoforte and composition) and got out of it seven years later with success, although it was observed by his teachers that he was deficient in the sense of rhythm. He had formed some friendships, notably that with Franco Faccio, which were to influence not only his own youth but the development of the younger school of music in Italy. In these very early years he was already welcome to the salons of musical ladies who patronized talented young men; there was no straw in his hair. His mother, Countess Josephine Radolinska, had given him the fluent grace, volubility and responsiveness of the Polish aristocracy, along with their exquisite manners and eagerness to please·

before he was twenty Boito had already made more conquests than were good for him. Among these may be counted the Contessa Maffei, who saw both in him and in his friend Faccio talent which flashed forth all sorts of promises for the future of Italian music. Boito, who was not reticent, did not discourage her: indeed he was lavish with "new" ideas, "new" principles and "new" theoretical objectives for music. He and Faccio between them were capable of a manifesto any evening between dinner and supper; they both talked and wrote indefatigably and burgeoned with plans for new musical organizations, critical reviews and the like.

Boito and Faccio had shared their successes at the Conservatory, which were not negligible for such very young men. Aside from a symphony by Boito which was played when he was sixteen and has since vanished, the works by which they came to be known in Milan were done in collaboration: a cantata called *Il Quattro Giugno* (The Fourth of June), performed at the final exercises of 1860 (September), and a "mystery" called *Le Sorelle d'Italia* (Italy's Sisters) performed one year later when both the youths received their own diplomas. Boito wrote all the verses of both works; Faccio composed the music for some of the separate pieces and Boito for the others. They are patriotic efforts, the first in commemoration of the Battle of Magenta and the second in honor of Italy's fellow strugglers for freedom—Poland and Greece; too much could not, perhaps, be expected under the circumstances, but it is quite astonishing what a stir they made in the Milan of that time. Faccio's music, in spite of the great importance it gave to the orchestra, was judged to be more "Italian" in spirit than Boito's, which was tinged with "Germanism." Not much was said of the verses but to subsequent minds they have seemed to exhibit, at least in some passages, foreshadowings of the peculiarities of Boito's style as it was to develop within a few years. The combination of talents aroused a good deal of interest and the two young men were welcomed to the houses of Milan society in which music, poetry and art in general were most esteemed.

Social favor and critical success could not, however, take the place of money or work. Boito's mother had died in 1859 with her once comfortable fortune reduced to almost nothing (his father, Cavaliere Silvestro, a decidedly rakish painter of miniatures, had helped in the reduction). Now the question was what two young men of such gifts could do to obtain funds, and, with strong recommendations, they applied to the Ministry of Public Instruction at Turin—Turin was still the capital—for a subsidy. It was granted. They were to have two thousand gold francs each for one year so as to "perfect themselves in the musical art." The Ministry's grant declares that both boys, "by examples given and upon information received," give hope of excelling in their art, and without government aid may be compelled to have recourse to private teaching, which might cause their "happy auspices for the future" to evaporate. It is an oddly generous and intelligent provision for a new government to make, but we can suppose that Boito and Faccio had powerful backing. They left Milan for Turin in November to make sure of their first payments and from there went on to Paris by the end of the month. Countess Maffei's letter of introduction to Verdi reached them there.

Verdi had not yet arrived from Russia at this moment: he and Peppina were sightseeing in the snows, having little hope of an immediate production of *La Forza del Destino* in the absence of a competent soprano. They were to arrive in Paris soon, as Countess Maffei no doubt realized, on their way home, and would go back to Russia in the following season. December and January passed before Boito met Verdi; during this period he and Faccio were busy seeing and hearing everything they could in Paris. Among the sights of Paris old Rossini was certainly one, and they had a letter of introduction to him from Tito Ricordi.

Rossini welcomed them to his hospitable table once a week for dinner and talk, and seems to have taken a liking to them in spite of the half-century that gaped between his age and theirs. He played all sorts of jokes on them, of course, as was his habit with everybody. One evening he had indulged in a good deal of anti-Wagnerian witticism, with the help of some of his guests, while the two "modern" youths sat in tight-lipped, embarrassed silence. The next time they came the old man made the boys eat their meal very fast, pretending some unexplained haste; and when they had wolfed the food he said: "I see you have futurist ears, so of course you have futurist stomachs as well!" Boito and Faccio left cards at the Casa Rossini after each such dinner, as was the custom of the time; Madame Rossini would have thought them boors if they had not done so. The old composer saved all their cards for many weeks and when they were ready to leave Paris, after their last dinner in his house, he sent a footman after them down the stairs to give each one a neat packet. In these packets were all the cards, with Rossini's note: "To youth everything is useful."

Verdi's arrival gave both the boys a chance to see how very different a composer nearer to themselves could be. Verdi was in the full flood of active life and probably had not much time to give them, but he found in Boito a ready volunteer for the text he was seeking for the London

Exhibition. It was due in March and the young poet had to turn it out in a hurry: the *Inno delle Nazioni*, and here again, although the verses are not inspired, they give some suggestion of the verbal richness and originality of phrase which were so soon to be at Boito's command. And with Verdi they could never have found that constant snicker at other men's work which was Rossini's idea of conversation—or those incessant jokes, some of them slightly "practical"—which cannot always be funny.

Verdi and Peppina went on back to Sant' Agata, where they stayed until April, and Boito's acquaintance with them was necessarily limited to a few talks. It is possible to guess—I am inclined to do so—that perhaps the boy talked a little too much in his few meetings with Verdi, or expressed himself with some extravagance at the expense of various brass tacks. At all events Verdi's present to him at the conclusion of the episode was a handsome gold watch with the words: "Remember my name and the value of time." When we consider that their conjunction was to become, in the third decade afterwards, an event of incomparable interest to Italian art and indeed to all music, these brief, sober words have the air of prophecy. Verdi probably only meant: "Thanks for the verses but don't waste so much time talking."

We have no record of what the twenty-year-old Boito thought of Verdi after these first brief meetings. Whatever his aesthetic development was afterwards he never once referred to Verdi in disrespectful terms: the "bad words," as Verdi considered them, were all by implication. He and Faccio parted company then: Faccio was for London, Boito for Germany and Poland. He had a rather extraordinary spring and summer in Poland with his mother's family, country gentlemen who took him into the woods to shoot; Boito would not use a gun but used to sit in a remote dell all day and hope that the birds escaped his cousins' bullets. His pocket edition of the *Divina Commedia* accompanied him in Poland as it did through almost all his life.

He had already, at this period, sketched out his idea for the opera *Mefistofele*, and his older brother Camillo was urging him to come back to Milan and write it. He had also agreed to write the *Hamlet* libretto for Faccio, and had in fact started it in Paris—Faccio had composed some of the music and was anxiously awaiting more of the text. Thus we see him at the very beginning of his adult existence hypnotized, or, in a more permanent and pervasive meaning, obsessed, by greatness: only Dante, Shakespeare, Goethe, Beethoven, Wagner, Verdi—only the great commanded him. The love of his life was to come twenty-two years later, but we cannot refrain from observing that when it came, it was and had to be in the form of a woman of genius, the greatest "soul," among all the women of modern Italy, Eleonora Duse. It was Boito's fate to be like this: his fate because it was his character, and his character because it was his fate.

7 Boito's return to Milan was followed by the brief but remarkable period of rebellious youth which culminated when he was twenty-six in the production of his *Mefistofele* at the Scala. During these five years he wrote criticism, essays and journalism of one sort or another; he composed music, including *Mefistofele*; he produced verses of a nature distinct from anything known to Italy before, both technically and in their imaginative range; he provided Faccio with the *Hamlet* libretto at last, and its success, although ephemeral, seemed a landmark in the culture of the time (Genoa, 1865). At twenty-one he had even invaded the prose theatre with a comedy called *Le Madri Galanti* (1863) in collaboration with his friend, the poet and painter Emilio Praga; they obtained an extremely sensational and noisy failure with it in Turin, after which Boito never again tried to write for the stage without music. The apex of his rebellious period, before *Mefistofele*, came in 1866, when he was twenty-four; he and Faccio left Milan to join Garibaldi in the campaign against the Austrians. It ended, as all know, in the ignominious armistice which disappointed Garibaldi as much as anything ever did in his whole career—and produced in Verdi one of the worst periods of gloom of all his life (the "accursed year" of 1867). The boys did not see much action. We know some of the privileges given them. Although Boito was tall (he had long, Polish legs) and Faccio short, and companies in Garibaldi's force were formed by stature, by special dispensation these two were allowed to be in the same company (Boito's, the taller one). Furthermore, they were allowed to go on sentry duty together and both were kept at Como, the General's headquarters, without experiencing any sharp peril.

It was not the first or the last time that young men of good connections or special qualities got through a war without danger. Even so, the very nature of the experience and all the surrounding circumstances, the character of Garibaldi, the terrible disappointment of the armistice imposed by the French before there was a chance of an Italian victory—all this had a powerfully sobering effect upon both Boito and Faccio. It was a long way from Countess Maffei's salon to sentry duty in the mountains. (Faccio's diary tells us how he had to "medicate" and bind up Boito's feet.) They returned to Milan somewhat less *scapigliati* than before. They were rapidly to lose their *scapigliatura* altogether.

The word "*scapigliato*," meaning disheveled—uncut, uncombed—was used to describe a whole set of young men who were supposed to live in a manner which gave free rein to their talents without subjecting them to middle-class standards of morals or manners. They were the bohemians of the time; they were in a general state of rebellion against their predecessors, tended to give fancy its freest rein, and did not mind shocking the good citizens. But Boito as a drunken bohemian, waking up worthy citizens by singing and dancing in the streets after midnight—the sort of picture one might obtain of him by reading his own autobiographical sketch called "*La Musica in Piazza*" of 1870—rapidly ceased to exist, if indeed it was ever a true picture for more than a few special occasions. For the greater part of his life, after 1868–1870, he was dignity itself so far as the public could ever know; having become "important," and even successful, he remained "important" for fifty years, constantly going on committees and commissions for the improvement of Italian art but otherwise avoiding attention. His youth, so intense, various and astonishing, seems to have ended in 1868 with the first night of *Mefistofele* at the Scala.

It was a riotous night, because a failure at the Scala in those days was not only a misfortune but a brawl. Boito, at twenty-six, had not only written the poetic drama and set it to music but himself conducted it. This last supererogatory flourish was due to the enthusiasm of his friends. (They were called the "claque" and the "modernists" and the "Germanists" and the "ultramontanes" as well as other things.) They decided that the young man of genius—the "hope of the future"—should present himself not only as poet and composer, but as conductor of his own work. Since he was also responsible for the stage direction and the production in general, it gave him a concentration of authority, and responsibility, which had never yet been known in an Italian theatre.

He was not a conductor, of course, and never conducted again; but it should be observed that our concept of "conducting an orchestra" had hardly been born in those days. Up until only a short time before, the first violin did whatever conducting was necessary: the innovation of a full-fledged conductor who did nothing whatever except conduct was still new. Wagner was only now, at this time, forcing the authoritative concept upon the musical world (*Tristan und Isolde*, 1865, *Die Meistersinger von Nürnberg*, 1868, both conducted by Hans von Bülow). Therefore, in the very infancy of orchestral conducting as we understand it, there seemed nothing particularly outrageous about putting a young man of twenty-six, without sufficient orchestral rehearsals, into the conductor's place for a work as complex as *Mefistofele*. After all, had he not written it, words and music both? Therefore, he must be able to conduct it. That was the reasoning. We know now that it is like saying that a playwright ought to be able to play every part in his own composition as well as any actor. It is nonsense to our minds; but the year was 1868.

The result was an appalling fiasco, one of the worst in the annals of the Scala. At times the music was completely inaudible, and frequently the singers on the stage could not hear the orchestra well enough to keep in tune with it. The performance was halted again and again by the noise of the protesting audience. Boito went through that evening with an impassive courage which earned him the respect of many who had hitherto thought of him as a merely fashionable innovator, a "faddist" and a false intellectual. He stood quiet when he was obliged to do so and resumed conducting whenever it was possible. The work, which was tremendously long to start with, was so stretched out by interruptions that it lasted about six hours. The administration of the Scala then decided to try it in a bifurcated version for two evenings: the first would contain the Prologue in Heaven, Acts I, II, and III; the second evening would consist of Prologue, Act IV, Symphonic Intermezzo and Act V. The administration kindly explained that this was in accordance with the poetic concept of Goethe in the two parts of *Faust*.

The bifurcated version had worse luck than the original mastodon. The third night produced a real riot, with fisticuffs; all pretense at a musical or aesthetic exercise had to be abandoned for a good deal of the time, and thereafter the work was withdrawn from the list at the Scala. It was to return there—and to most other opera theatres—after its author-composer had cut it and trimmed it and put it into the shape it has since retained; but that revenge did not take place until after 1875, seven years later, when the reduced version of *Mefistofele* triumphed at Bologna.

The merits of *Mefistofele* as a poetic drama and as an opera are great but do not concern us; what does concern us is that Boito never went through the ordeal again and evidently did not want to do so. He had already, by this time, begun to compose his *Nerone*, the work which was to occupy all the rest of his life: it was his only other work and by dint of inconceivable effort for over fifty years he made it almost impossible for any theatre to perform and, furthermore, left it unfinished. Arturo Toscanini produced it at the Scala in 1924 as an act of piety; in spite of lavish effort, if failed; it is not likely to be heard again. *Mefistofele* remains Boito's one opera, his only integrated effort as poet and composer. Its extraordinary individuality and beauty form a sort of swan song—and at the age of twenty-six.

His literary and journalistic work kept to a very high level, just the same, and he versified constantly, skillfully, imaginatively and with a degree of originality which has been more appreciated in recent decades than it was when his poetry appeared. He provided a number of composers with texts and was thus a "librettist" of experience before he worked with Verdi. These dramas for music could only have been written by a composer—that is, he knew or felt the musical effects in advance, and more or less dictated them to the composer of the music—and are unique of their kind. *La Gioconda* (Scala, 1876) is the one of these which has remained on the stage almost constantly ever since: the music, by Amilcare Ponchielli, is not equal to the language it clothes, but appeals to successive generations with considerable authority. *Ero e Leandro* was a classic effort (some passages are almost literal translations from the Greek) and he wrote a good deal of the score himself before he decided that it was not good enough; he then gave it to Bottesini, who failed with it in 1880, and afterwards to Luigi Mancinelli, who obtained some success with it in Madrid in 1897. There were others, to a total of seven, exclusive of the two he wrote for Verdi, but it is vital to observe that they were all signed by the anagram "Tobia Gorrio."

Boito's juggling with his own name is in itself an exemplar of the behavior which psychoanalysts have since made too familiar for imitation. He was baptized Enrico, but his second composition with Faccio, performed when they received their diplomas at the Conservatory, bears the name of Arrigo Boito. Linguistically, Enrico is the same as the English Henry, while Arrigo is the English Harry; but psychologically there is no such equality between them. Enrico is one of the commonest of all names in Italian and Arrigo one of the most uncommon; moreover, Arrigo is a "romantic" name, associated with the days of chivalry and, at the latest, with the Renaissance. (Harry, in English, is colloquial: you meet with it every day: but you could scour Italy without finding anyone called Arrigo in modern times.) Boito assumed a costume, a plume or, if the psychoanalysts prefer, a mask, when he changed his name from Enrico to

Arrigo. This, however, was permanent—he was Arrigo from the age of nineteen onward and expected his friends to use that name: even Eleonora Duse used it.

When it came to his work, literary and musical, he made another transformation. That which was deeply his own and belonged to the lifelong aspiration was signed Arrigo Boito; everything else was signed by the anagram Tobia Gorrio. This means that the two operas, *Mefistofele* and *Nerone*, are by Arrigo Boito, as are the dramatic poems for Verdi's *Otello* and *Falstaff*, as well as the books of verse (the early and extraordinary *Rè Orso*, which makes one think of Edgar Allan Poe, and the *Libro dei Versi*, a comprehensive collection in 1875). All the critical articles, short stories, incidental sketches and journalism, all the dramatic poems for other composers, and indeed all the work aside from that handful we have named, was signed Tobia Gorrio. The anagram never fooled anybody, and since Boito was always celebrated—he had the misfortune to achieve celebrity before he was twenty and never shed it afterward—there was something akin to pathos in the obstinacy with which he went on, decade after decade for half a century, using two names for two kinds of work when the entire public knew they were really one. Curiously enough, we cannot say or believe that the work signed Tobia Gorrio was in any way shameful to him; he valued it and it was his own; he was adamant with any musician who, after receiving a libretto by Tobia Gorrio, tried to obtain changes in it; in fact, poor Ponchielli, who was somewhat terrorized by the poet, complained that Boito wrote the libretto of *La Gioconda* not for the composer but "for himself." Still, one kind of work, obviously on a lower shelf than that reserved for himself and Verdi, had to be signed Tobia Gorrio and he maintained the distinction to the end. With all his philological erudition he had not heard the word schizophrenia because it was not yet invented, but we have an idea that it would not have bothered him if he had. His nature exacted this division and he perpetuated it.

But—the most important thing of all—he was never really Tobia Gorrio. Tobia Gorrio was that part of him which could not rise to the level demanded by the taste, learning, talent and critical perspicacity of Arrigo Boito. Tobia wrote for the papers but Arrigo wrote for God, and of the two scriveners there can be no doubt whatsoever that Arrigo was the true being. It was, however, a being which could not always fulfill or realize itself: it could not always be. In that fact alone we find reason enough for the increasing reserve, the shell of dignity in which this essentially tragic personality took refuge against the arrows of the world after his youth was over. By the time he was forty—which is to say, before *Otello* and before Eleonora Duse—Boito had already taken on an air of age. The best of his work failed to please him and his individual life seemed to be at an end. According to Benedetto Croce, this poet was "the only romantic of Italy" —the only true romantic in the land of Leopardi and Manzoni—and perhaps romantics should always die young. Surviving his youth, but without faith or hope in the one great work that remained to him—the colossal, impossible *Nerone*—he needed some more august command than any he had yet received, some reason for living in a world he had found cold and alien. He was solitary, with the ideal "impassibility" of the Chinese sage in his short novel, *Il Trapezio*; aside from his older brother Camillo and the unwavering friend Faccio, he had no family; the emotions existed (he thought and wrote) only to be conquered. His biographer Professor Vajro believes that at this period a profound psychological necessity, more than a necessity in poetry or music, drove him to Verdi. "The exigence of a finality, of an *idol*,"says Vajro (and the italics are his), "around which he could make his own life gravitate, conducted Boito unconsciously to Sant' Agata."

8 Verdi's coolness toward young Boito in the 1860's and 1870's arose from two distinct categories of thought, and neither one was purely "personal." In fact I think, on all the evidence, that Verdi hardly knew the young man who had come to him so providentially in Paris that winter when he was looking for some verses. Their occasions for any kind of meeting afterwards were rare, if they existed, and when Peppina says that she knows Boito "pochissimo," very little indeed (as she tells Ricordi in 1879), she is undoubtedly speaking also for the Maestro.

But Boito had filled Italy with his celebrity during the 1860's, and all his hermitlike reticence and severe retirement afterwards did not enable him to live it down. It was impossible to read the newspapers, the musical reviews or even the letters of one's friends without hearing about Boito. He and his friends were always delivering themselves of large statements

about art, music, the past, the future, and other portmanteau subjects
which can be so easily handled by thinkers under twenty-five. He and
Faccio had founded the Quartet Society in Milan and provided it with
a gazette in which Boito in particular found an outlet for many pronouncements. Faccio was becoming more and more concentrated on the
orchestra, and after the failure of his two operas (*I Profughi Fiamminghi,
The Flemish Refugees*, 1863, and *Amleto* in 1865 to Boito's text) he
ceased to compose except occasionally; in compensation he became the
finest Italian conductor of his time, an immediate precursor of Toscanini.
I have called his operas "failures," which they were, but each of them
had the excitement and réclame of first productions which interested all
Italy, so that it was impossible to tell for some time that they had in fact
fallen dead. Anything by Faccio (or by Boito) in those days aroused such
an agitation among the musical and the general public that judgment had
to be suspended, remitted to the hands of time.

The root reason for this was obviously the revolutionary ferment which
had been set up all over Europe by the theories and practice of Richard
Wagner. *Lohengrin*, which seems a very tame cat nowadays, and was already left far behind in Wagner's development, came to Italy in 1871;
it stirred up a Wagner-Verdi storm in which neither of the composers
took any direct part, although partisans of each went to absurd extremes.
The opera was twenty-one years old by then. In the meanwhile Wagner
had gone far beyond it, had composed (although not produced) half of
the *Ring*; the immense, mature works of high genius, *Tristan* (1865) and
Die Meistersinger (1868), had already received their first performances
in Munich with Hans von Bülow conducting.

So it was in the 1870's that the Verdi-Wagner dispute, such as it was,
had its heyday. By the next decade, and especially after Wagner's death
in 1883, Verdi himself had no disposition to encourage it. His view of
Wagner changed a great deal during the decades 1871–1891, and although he was always ready to poke a little gentle fun at the length of
these German works or their ponderosity—and found the world of Wagnerian gods and heroes, as distinct from the music, downright repulsive—
he had not the slightest desire to lead a charge against them. For the last
twenty years of his life, and more, his point of view was more or less to be
put evangelically: "In my Father's house there are many mansions."

Such was not the case during the period when young Boito incurred
his displeasure. During the 1860's and 1870's Verdi sincerely dreaded
German influences on Italian youth and deplored the deviations which
he foresaw as a result. Moreover, we observe in his letters during the silent

years many remarks which indicate a feeling that the world had passed him by, and even though he was glad to get rid of it, the feeling cannot have been pleasant. After Madame Stolz had taken an apartment in the Palazzo Loria (that which is now the Hotel Continental) and started living a highly social existence, Verdi complains that she no longer has time to write to "an old music master." To another correspondent, commenting upon new work which did not please him, he says: "You see what it is not to be *dans le mouvement.*" Such points, from the years of retirement, suggest an oddly uncharacteristic pathos, something which might almost be called wistful if the word could ever be used about the old bear of Busseto.

Before he retired, however—that is, before Aïda and the Requiem and during the period of their first performances—he was as combative and vigorous as ever. During this time he expressed his views both privately and in public on numerous occasions. We venture to sum them up as follows:

Italian music is primarily and fundamentally vocal, and can only incidentally be instrumental; German music is primarily and fundamentally instrumental. (The unaccompanied vocal polyphony of Palestrina is Italian genius, just as the B Minor Mass or the Ninth Symphony is German.) In the German influences now flooding into Italy—that is, in the '70's—a great emphasis on chamber and orchestral music or on opera composed over a symphony orchestra is bewitching the Italian youth and leading it astray from its own sources of strength. Italian music must remain Italian, that is, primarily vocal, and if it deserts its own native genius it will fade into imitation and sterility.

Verdi's fears were groundless, but they did not seem so in 1870 when "the music of the future" was invading Italian youth. For one thing, Wagner—however little known—was intensely fashionable at that time and for years afterward. The young could speak and write with gathering excitement about "the music of the future" and not run much risk of correction since nobody was quite sure what it was. The temptation to denigrate the familiar while yielding to the fascination of the new and strange—well, that, too, was rampant, as it so often is in the history of any art.

The formation of the Quartet Society in Milan (Boito and Faccio) and the development of the Scala orchestra for symphonic purposes (Faccio) were events in musical life, as distinct from musical journalism, and both ran into Verdi's disapproval. The tremendous success of Hans von Bülow as piano virtuoso and orchestral conductor was another part of the process which Verdi fiercely resented. Bülow was a very foolish man, of course, and never stopped denigrating Italian music, especially Verdi's, during his years in Italy (his recantation was late). For the Beethoven centenary, which made him an idol in Milan, he played the "Emperor" concerto and conducted an all-Beethoven program, which included the overture Zur Weihe des Hauses (*Consecration of the House*); the Eighth Symphony, two movements of the Ninth, and the Egmont Overture for good measure (December 4 and 8, 1870). Such programs had never been heard in Italy and the time was ripe: Bülow's success, like Wagner's, or Anton Rubinstein's—for that virtuoso also came along at about the same time—helped to instigate a general enthusiasm for German work.

And Boito was responsible for a good deal of this, too, not only by his journalism which whipped up interest, but by direct arrangement: his Quartet Society brought Bülow to Milan.

We can readily see, therefore, that in one category of thought, in the general defense of Italian music against German influences, Verdi could hardly regard young Boito as a friend. There was, however, another and more specific cause for offense: Boito had written some verses which Verdi chose to regard as personally insulting. In the first category (the general) there were many besides Boito to be considered, chief of them being Faccio, of course, who also had to be forgiven and received as a prodigal son before long. In the second category, and more emphatically because of their association in *The Hymn of the Nations*, there was only Boito.

The specific offenses of Boito were several; the insulting verses were only the worst of them. One, for example, was the fact that Boito had written a polka for pianoforte on the tune of "*La donna è mobile.*" When you consider that this polka was a composition of Boito's childhood in Venice, and that his mother the Countess seems to have been proud of it—the boy was only ten—and furthermore that it never reached publication, you wonder why Verdi was offended. Verdi, however, was always a bit sensitive about that tune, partly because he had written it at the very last minute to suit the whims of a tenor who felt he did not have enough to do in the opera, and partly because it had become, instantaneously and forever, the kind of popular favorite which can be heard in scraps, whistled or hummed out of tune or otherwise maltreated in almost any street of any country at any time. It governed the hand organs of the whole world for fifty years or so, and much as Verdi may have been inured to the hurdy-gurdy, we cannot doubt that he had to wince over it many, many times.

So, when it was reported to him that Boito had written a polka on this tune, he concluded at once that it was a gesture of ridicule.

The verses, however, were the worst thing to Boito's personal debit. They were in the form of an ode to Italian art, composed in a hurry for a banquet of the *scapigliati*—the long-haired gang, we might call them— in 1863, when Boito was twenty-one. The boys had not been doing very well with the great public: Boito's comedy in collaboration with Praga, *Le Madri Galanti*, had recently failed in Turin, and this drinking party had been organized as a form of consolation to Faccio, whose opera *I Profughi Fiamminghi* (to a text by Praga) had just failed at the Scala. Boito's "poem," a slapdash affair of no quality, which was not included in his collected verse, is actually called "Sapphic Ode with Glass in Hand," so we do not think he meant it to be taken too seriously. The first line declaims "*Alla salute dell' arte italiana!*" and by art we are evidently supposed to understand opera, or at least music. The bard then tells us that this sadly degenerated art is about to be put on its feet again by some young genius, some mysterious young genius seated on the other side of the table, and for three stanzas the promise is reiterated, along with the statement that the first sound emitted by this genius had been that of a lion. The effort to console Faccio for the bad taste of the public is not too subtle. We then come, however, to the famous fourth stanza which, much repeated and reprinted far and wide, caused so much trouble. In Italian it goes:

> *Forse già nacque chi sovra l'altare*
> *Rizzerà l'arte, verecondo e puro,*
> *Su quell' altar bruttato come un muro*
> *Di lupanare.*

In literal English prose this means: "Perhaps the one is already born who will once more raise up art, truthful and pure, upon the altar, that altar defiled like the wall of a whore house."

Later on there is another stanza which laments "Italian art" which once was teacher to a "Nordic country" (three guesses!) with the "holy harmonies" of Pergolesi and Marcello.

Nobody in his right mind can acquit Boito of insolence toward his elders and betters. At this moment (1863) Verdi had already written all of his most popular operas and there were incessant performances of them throughout Europe. Who, then, is supposed to have "defiled the altar"? Certainly not the lesser Italian composers of the day, who were so thoroughly overwhelmed by the flood of Verdi's work that they hardly dared produce.

No: he meant Verdi, all right, and could have meant no other. But Boito was only twenty-one and the occasion was ribald. Perhaps, after having given Verdi the verses for London, the year before, he had expected some continued favor from the composer; perhaps he had been offended in his youthful amour-propre; we do not know. The "Sapphic Ode with Glass in Hand" traveled all over Italy and came to Verdi's knowledge in no time at all, as such morsels generally do; he was deeply offended and the offense rankled for many long years. Fifteen years later he was still quoting it in a letter to Faccio, although by that time Faccio himself, like Boito, had become a passionate and devoted Verdian.

Against these and lesser offenses given by the young Boito there can be set a number of passages from his journalistic work during the 1860's which declare his respect and reverence for Verdi. In fact, every time he mentions Verdi by name it is an acceptable reference, although—as in his very first piece for the weekly Figaro, shortly after the famous "Sapphic Ode"—not uncritical. In that first effort for their short-lived paper in which he and Praga, under various names, wrote the entire text, he dealt with a revival of I Lombardi at the Scala and judged it aged and faded, as indeed it must have been. "Time has laid upon it the first dusty hand," says Boito, but there is no disrespect to Verdi: the critic points out that Verdi's own later work is largely responsible for the eclipse of his first efforts. The time for Verdi's advice, "keep one eye on the public and one on art," has now passed, says Boito: that was good advice in a period when most composers had both eyes firmly fixed on the public; what the artist now must do is keep both eyes serenely and securely on his art alone.

In short, whenever Boito spoke of Verdi by name there was no nose-thumbing, no outright flouting of Italy's principal living composer, although there was no adulation either. It was by indirection, in articles on other subjects or by implied meanings, that Boito's critical judgment on the existing state of Italian music (which meant Verdi) could be understood. His outburst in praise of Beethoven, January 28, 1864, was in terms so ardent that they could hardly be reconciled with an acceptance of Italian opera at all. It was safe enough to praise Beethoven, and Verdi himself was as much an admirer and knower as Boito in that respect. But to proclaim the necessity of "educating the public" to the realization that all the marvels of the art, past, present and future, were "miraculously contained within that sublime intellect"—well, is this not equivalent to saying that other composers might as well cease work? What Boito says is so extreme that it would sweep away not only Verdi but everything that had ever been written in Italian music. Fervently the young man perorates: "Those nine symphonies of his are the Bible, Gospel, Koran of everybody who cultivates the art." One is not far from agreeing, but the excess of zeal turns the pronouncement sour. Beethoven may be, as Boito says, a god—and of course he was—but the pantheon also includes Mozart and a great many others. It is easy to imagine what an effect such fiery proclamations had upon Verdi in his early fifties after a lifetime of hard work: they said to him, in effect, that he might as well never have put pen to paper, that everything good had already been written, somewhere beyond the Alps.

Offense by indirection is a subtle thing. We do not know how many of Boito's pronouncements injured Verdi in the recesses of his being, but it is my own belief that for some years almost everything the young man published had this effect. Its general line was ultramontane, its temperature and tone were feverish and it always seemed to be militant in purpose, as if the author were leading a crusade. If you read Boito—in the *Quartetto*, the organ of his Quartet Society, he continued as he had begun in *Figaro*—you might feel quite certain that you were being "up-to-date" and "modern" or even fashionable, but you could hardly avoid suspecting that to attain these results you would have to abandon Italian music altogether. That is, of course, always excepting the fathers: from Palestrina to Marcello all was permitted, sanctified as antique. In short, the only good Italians were the dead Italians.

But by the middle of the 1870's it was imperative for Boito, as for everybody else in musical Europe, to reconsider previous opinions about Verdi. Two startling events had upset the judgments of other years. First came *Aïda* and the Requiem. And after that, nothing: for one of the most dramatic developments of all, ranking really as another event, was Verdi's prolonged retirement. We know now that he was working and studying as never before, but his contemporaries were merely puzzled and his friends distressed.

It was in this period that Boito "came home," so to speak, as a prodigal son, and made his humble submission. He was now free of financial worries. *Mefistofele*, in the revised and severely cut version of 1875, was conspicuously successful everywhere. Aside from his loneliness, his uncertainty, his corroding self-criticism, his search for a god or an idol or a hero, there was that additional detail that *Mefistofele* set Boito free to do as he wished. Fully conscious of what he was doing, this poet and musician of high attainment made up his mind, after the Verdi Requiem, that what he wished to do was to dedicate himself to Verdi.

Easier said than done.

9   Countess Maffei had never given up either Faccio or Boito: both frequented her house and engaged her interest and support during years when the "Mago" would have none of them. She was in Verdi's confidence, we think, more than anybody else in some respects—more, certainly, than Giulio Ricordi, whose constant efforts to get new work out of the old man may have become an annoyance. Peppina was too close to her Mago to receive that kind of explicit revelation which he so often made to the Countess in letters. Very likely Peppina had to judge his frame of mind more by half-statements and mutters than by direct communication, but by this time she had learned to interpret all his moods, even without a word. She must have known, more than anybody else, that he was boiling with the desire to compose music—not merely contrapuntal exercises, but something of his own on a big scale, something for voices and full orchestra, an expression.

Verdi's letter of September 20, 1876, to the Countess, in which the famous words "invent the truth" occur, has already been quoted, and should now be given in full. Written from Sant' Agata, it reads as follows:

"I saw Color del Tempo *in Genoa.*[3] *There are great qualities in it, above all a swiftness of touch which is a French particularity; but there is little in it at bottom. To copy the truth may be a good thing, but to invent the truth is better, much better.*

"There seems to be a contradiction in these three words, invent the truth, but just ask Papà. It may be that he, Papà, might have found himself with some Falstaff, but he would have had difficulty finding any scoundrel

---

[3] Color del Tempo was a "veristic" comedy by Achille Torelli, a young protégé of Verdi, son of an old friend.

as scoundrelly as Iago, and never and never such angels as Cordelia, Imogene, Desdemona, etc., etc., and yet they are true!
"To copy the truth is a fine thing, but it is photography, not painting.
"What useless chatter! We are leaving today. A good journey, you'll say! I hope so. Love us, and good-bye."

Remembering that Papà means Shakespeare, as it did in Verdi's letters and conversation for a long time, and that these years of retirement were in part consumed by the reading of Dante and Shakespeare, we can easily enough amplify the meaning of this brief but momentous letter. He did not mean that Iago and Falstaff were "abstractions," but that they were truer than mere copies of the truth: that they embodied truth. Hatred, as we find it in Iago, cannot be found every day if at all, but when it is expressed as Shakespeare expressed it, there is a truth above facts, a true element of human existence.

There is not the faintest doubt in my own mind that the Countess made good use of this letter. It gave her two broad hints, one for *Otello* and one for *Falstaff*. Everybody in Verdi's circle knew that he had been thinking about Falstaff as a character for a lyrical comedy for over thirty years; they all knew he had repeatedly dreamed of a tragic opera on King Lear; they were aware of his preoccupation with Shakespeare in just this period; and now they were given the additional information that he was fascinated by the character of Iago. Intimate as she was with Boito and Faccio, as well as with Giulio Ricordi, could anybody doubt that the Countess either showed this letter to them or quoted it?

In early July, 1879, Don Giulio, as they called him, persuaded Verdi to come to Milan and conduct a performance of the Requiem at the Scala for the benefit of flood victims. Teresa Stolz made her farewell to the public in this performance. The orchestra played a serenade to Verdi under the balcony of the Grand Hotel afterward and voices were heard from the crowd: "When will you write another opera?" Verdi answered, from the balcony, that he was too old now and was leaving the field to the young; but he added that for such a wonderful orchestra he might be tempted to compose a symphony, that is, a regular symphony in four movements (not a *sinfonia*). The words, or a paraphrase of them, were reported in print; they may have corresponded to some vague idea of his; they certainly encouraged his friends to hope for something.

One evening soon afterward, perhaps the very next, Verdi and Peppina had Don Giulio and Faccio to dinner with them at the hotel. The atmosphere of conspiracy grows very thick just here: Don Giulio, Faccio, Peppina and Boito (who was absent) were undoubtedly all in it, we think, and the Countess was behind the scenes. Ricordi kept on talking about Shakespeare and Boito, claiming for the latter a special comprehension of the former. Verdi did not grant this but could not conceal the eagerness with which he welcomed the discussion or the fascination which the characters of Iago and Othello exercised over him. He was only cold toward the idea of Boito.

On the following morning Franco Faccio brought Boito to the Grand Hotel to see Verdi. It must have been a very serious meeting for all three of them. We have no record of what was said beyond the fact that Boito set forth—no doubt with eloquence—the merits of Shakespeare's *Othello* as a subject for Verdi's music. Verdi did not reject the idea but he was careful not to encourage it. Boito must have made it plain, probably by indirection and allusion, that he was humbly offering Verdi his talent and his life. Verdi must have pulled his beard and scratched his ear and frowned mightily, as was his wont, and interposed many a "but" and "nevertheless," meanwhile feeling in his own heart a glow of warmth at the thought that the youth of Italy had not, after all, wholly deserted or forgotten him. Some spark there must have been; and we know that the anxious Faccio must have fostered that nascent flame by any means in his power, with any words he could find.

Three days passed, and no more: Boito was back again at the Grand Hotel with a complete scenario or outline of the opera.

Had he really done it in three days? It is possible. Had they all been conspiring about it for weeks or months? That is also possible. Three whole years had passed since the celebrated letter about *inventare il vero*, and the conspirators had had plenty of time to talk it over.

Verdi did not accept it outright but told Boito to go ahead and write the poem, which, as he said in a letter, would be good anyhow, whether for himself, for Boito or for another. He was still testing the younger man, considering, wondering, weighing all the elements including his own powers. He was sixty-six; Boito was now thirty-seven and had left his rash youth far behind. For Verdi there were many things to be considered aside from old resentments and misgivings, aside from any thought either of his own powers or those of Boito. He must (for he was a man of deep humility) have been awed and perhaps a little frightened at the magnitude of the offering: for Boito was the best young Italy had to offer, the most talented poet, the most gifted composer, the one whose future seemed most sure. He never learned to take it lightly; to the very end he worried over Boito's own work (the completion of *Nerone*) and felt his own full responsibility for its frustration. In his fulfillment there was ever and always one aching nerve, the sense that to attain this end Boito had been sacrificed.

With passionate enthusiasm Boito hurled himself into the composition of the poem. There now began for this troubled spirit the only period of happiness it was to know: the two decades of dedication to Verdi, upon which there was soon to be superimposed, like sunlight on the Alps, the love of Eleonora Duse. He wrote the entire poem of *Otello* between July and November of 1879, and although there were numerous adjustments and accommodations afterward, both for Verdi's needs and for his own, the work as performed at the Scala on February 5, 1887 was substantially as his genius had conceived it after that first reconciliation with Verdi.

It has no parallel in either literature or music because, without being an original poem, it has the aspect and imprint of originality. *Otello* is not a translation, although it is for pages upon pages very close to the original English; it is not paraphrase, though it often adheres to the significance by departing from the text; and it is not an adaptation, because it does not adapt, but fully accepts, every premise and postulate, every enactment. It is rather a kind of re-creation. By suppressing the first act but transferring some of its most potent concepts to his own (Shakespeare's second, his first); by gently, powerfully accentuating the part of Desdemona so as to make it musically valid, as a minimally written part cannot be in the lyric theatre; by few, slight, but unutterably brilliant eliminations and additions, Boito transferred into Verdi's hands an incomparable jewel of dramatic poetry for musical composition. It is by common consent the best "libretto"; but what strange, what incomprehensible sorcery ensues? That old man, that bear of Busseto, rises to the challenge; he understands it; he composes it. There are no reticences or artificial refinements in the way: this is the full flood of impetuosity, just as lavish as it ever was, but there is a whole new world of harmony, counterpoint and instrumentation to support it. The whole thing, poem and music, from whatever point of view you may consider it, is a Vesuvian event.

All this Boito may quite possibly have foreseen, although we doubt it. We think he was simply obeying the law of his own nature, submitting himself to a god without thought for the result. It certainly took the god a long stretch of time to fall in with the foreordained design. Verdi perhaps felt that they were all attempting to rush him into obligations, specific promises, without due reflection. He liked what he had seen of Boito's poem by midsummer, but he did not want the young man to come to Sant' Agata. Giulio Ricordi wanted to come there and bring Boito; Verdi said no, because any expression he made under his own roof, affirmative or negative, would have too much weight, would become a sort of pledge. He wanted time.

Peppina's views in the matter show her essential wisdom more than almost any that have come down to us. Her letter of early November, 1879 (when the poem of *Otello* was in fact completed) implores Ricordi to be patient and says:

"I know Boito very little, but I believe I have divined him. A nervous nature, most excitable! When invaded by admiration, capable of unconfined enthusiasms and perhaps also of brief paroxysms . . . Firm in friendship and at the same time pliable as a boy, when his own fiber is not, so to say, plucked. I say all this to make you understand that it seems to me I have understood the man; and for this I am not surprised at his feverish state in the present moment. In the hope of giving him a little calm, I will whisper into Giulio's ear a small confidence on the condition that it does not become Punchinello's secret. Toward the 20th of this November we are coming to Milan to pass several days, and I am of the opinion that one should await that moment, which seems to me most opportune, so that without being seen or attracting the attention of the curious Boito can speak quietly and at length with Verdi. Inter nos: what he has already written of the African seems to be to his taste and very well done. . . . Let him finish the poem calmly, abandoning himself (without torturing it) to his own imagination; as soon as it is done let him send it without delay or hesitation to Verdi, before we come to Milan, so that he can read it tranquilly and, if it so happens, make his observations on it in advance."

She urges Ricordi not to write to Verdi, not to importune him, not to say that she herself had written, and above all not to let Verdi for one moment suspect that any pressure is being brought to bear upon him. Let the stream flow to the sea, she advises, in its own way and time. And then she adds some words which, even for so wise a woman as she had become, are unusually weighted with meaning. "It is in the ample spaces that certain men are destined to meet and understand each other," she says. "If my advice seems good, follow it." Beyond a doubt she already knew that Boito and Verdi formed such a conjunction in "the ample spaces," and that nothing more was needed but patience.

From Boito's first sketch of the text of the opera to the night of its first performance at the Scala was a long time, just the same—seven and a half years or more (July, 1879 to February, 1887). There were many times during that period when the outcome seemed in doubt, not only because of Verdi's slowness in accepting the poem and going to work on it, but also at later stages. Everything depended not only upon the health and spirits of the old composer but upon his will to carry out so large and difficult a scheme, his confidence in the poet and in himself. He was easily annoyed, and as he grew older he found it more and more difficult to bear the constant mention of his supposed doings in the newspapers. There was no possibility of keeping the *Otello* project secret; as soon as Verdi had accepted even the idea of doing it, before he put pen to paper, it was bruited about the Western world. In the vain hope of keeping his own counsel for at least a while, Verdi adopted all sorts of absurd mystifications: he called the Boito poem "the chocolate," for example, for a long time—"I have received the chocolate," for instance, or "the chocolate is good."

Thus an entire year went by without any promise on Verdi's part that he would undertake the work. He was studying it (November, 1879, to November, 1880) and undoubtedly found it good as a poem in Italian, as a work for the theatre, and as a libretto for somebody's opera: the question was whether he was the right person to compose this opera. Musical taste everywhere, including the Italian opera houses, had changed almost out of recognition in the last decade or two. If Verdi returned to the theatre much would be expected of him: the fall would be great indeed, if there were a fall. These were his considerations, in some part, but most of all his task was to convince *himself* that this was his work, that he was the composer most suited to a text so rare and wonderful.

10　During the *Otello* years (1879–1887) the old bear of Busseto became a fox. Nobody knew what he was up to; nobody could be sure what might result. Aside from the documentary proof that he was working on the score of this opera from the autumn of 1884 to the autumn of 1885, and on its orchestration until the autumn of 1886—that is, about two years in all—we cannot nail down that sort of incontrovertible proof which is the delight of historians. For 1884–1886 the documents exist, both in the archives of Sant' Agata (the sketches of earlier composition) and in those of the Casa Ricordi, and in the composer's own hand so that there can be no doubt. But during the five years which lead up to these papers . . . ?

I have already made one guess which is without basis in recorded evidence but must seem probable to anybody familiar with the characters involved: that is, that Verdi's great year of hesitation was between the November of 1879 and the November of 1880. In this year he studied and restudied the poem which had been submitted to him; he read other versions of Shakespeare's play; he tried to fix in his own imagination the shape, content and innermost meaning of the characters, of whom—to begin with—it was Iago who fascinated him. He asked his painter friend in Naples to paint Iago for him (which the friend, Domenico Morelli, never did). Quite possibly, as a confirmed hypochondriac, he was also testing his own physical powers. He went to Paris, for instance, to conduct those triumphant first performances of Aïda at the Opéra, of which he said, in a letter to the Countess dated March 15, 1880, that they were "a success." Such words were seldom on Verdi's lips or pen, and if he said Aïda was "a success" he must have been feeling inspirited, even though he immediately added that "we must wait to see if it lasts."

The year obviously shook him to the depths in one way, which was literary rather than musical: the more he read it, the more he realized that one of the most remarkable poets of modern Italy had given him a text. This realization comes out in letters written even some years later: he rejects outright any suggestion that this text should be heard in another language first, and his reason given is that Boito's poetry is not only Italian, but good Italian. It was the first time in his entire life that he had been afforded the opportunity to compose music to anything written in good Italian, and the entire Rothschild Bank could not have persuaded him to see it put forward in French or any other foreign language.

The crucial year at which I guess (1879–1880) culminates with Verdi's acceptance of Boito as collaborator on a new version of Simon Boccanegra. This grandiose work, written twenty-three years before to an almost unimaginably bad text by Piave, was close to Verdi's heart for a number of reasons. "Figlia" is one: the father-daughter relationship always aroused deep feeling in him; furthermore, it was his only treatment of a Genoese subject and he loved Genoa; but most of all, no doubt, was the fact that it contained notable musical advances, maturities and depths, which had not been appreciated at the time it was written. It had been defeated by its libretto, like La Forza del Destino, but Verdi certainly knew that it contained some of his finest music of that middle period, and perhaps even of any period. Ageing and regretting, he may have been willing to throw away a dozen or so of his juvenile works, but *Boccanegra* did not deserve to perish.

Giulio Ricordi—ah, what a publisher!—divined all this, and when he found at the end of a whole year that he could not get a new opera out of the old man, he suggested a thorough revision of *Boccanegra* with Boito to work on the text. This was extremely wily and fruitful, because all concerned (which includes Peppina and the Countess) immediately understood that if the *Boccanegra* project came to a good conclusion there was every chance that Verdi would compose *Otello*. Boito himself, by no means the kind of poet who could be hired to patch up the work of others, consented under the same understanding. He only made one condition: that his name should not be used. Even today his name does not appear on the *Boccanegra* text, although the changes he made in Piave's wretched libretto were radical.

Verdi's changes were equally radical. He threw himself into this work with enthusiasm and even with a sort of joy—it was good to be composing again for voices and orchestra, on the large scale native to him; it was good to find that the orchestra had somehow or other grown immensely bigger under his very fingers. Perhaps he did not even himself realize, until these weeks, how much the silent years had enlarged and deepened his resources. At first he made the usual excuses, which met with some of the usual arguments (the Scala was in peril, had had too many failures, needed a new work by the Maestro, etc., etc.). But once he and Boito had agreed about what should be done he caught fire rapidly. Both of them thought there was little work involved, a bit of cutting, a new end for the first act, an additional scene or two: Petrarch's wonderful letter to the Doge of Genoa and to the Doge of Venice, adjuring them to avoid fratricidal strife —these were the main points. Before they had done with it, *Boccanegra* had experienced so many changes that it counts in the minds of many good judges as a "new opera."

It went on at the Scala in its rewritten version March 24, 1881, and for ten evenings drew applause from large audiences. Critical opinion in general was surprised at the degree to which Verdi had enriched the score. Boito had done an astonishing amount of sheer cobbling—a line here and a line there—as well as big changes like the new end of Act I (including part of the old Act II). The work is cursed by a libretto which even Boito could not redeem in full. Like so many of those dramas in which essential parts take place off stage, or have taken place years before the curtain rises, *Boccanegra* gives its public very little chance at intelligent participation: even persons who have heard it fairly often must constantly be consulting programs, or the libretto itself, to find out where and what is the action at any given point. Boito called Piave's drama a "crooked table," or perhaps we should say a "crippled table," and since this was the fundamental structure, the most gifted poet could not do much to it. The enduring merit of the opera arises from some noble music in a few great scenes. There were moments during the rehearsals when even Verdi was carried away by the dramatic power of his own music. The men in the cast were among the greatest performers of operatic history, including Tamagno, Victor Maurel and Édouard de Reszke. Verdi had already worked with Maurel the year before, in Paris (in that famous first Aïda at the Opéra), but this Boccanegra seemed even more remarkable. At the end of one scene during the Scala rehearsals Verdi cried out to him; "Maurel, if God gives me health I'll write Iago for you."

He was to regret these words bitterly for some years, since Maurel had about as much discretion as a parrot. The words were rash anyhow. Verdi never really wrote an opera or a part in an opera for any performer; it was a cry of admiration for Maurel's power in one scene; but Maurel (and his "intelligent" wife, Madame Maurel!) never allowed Verdi to forget it. The newspapers of Europe from then on periodically mentioned "Verdi's Iago," although nothing of the kind yet existed.

However, it is in this outburst, as well as by indirection from a few letters, that I find justification for my guess that the great year of hesitation over Otello was 1879–1880. By my reading, as soon as Verdi accepted Boito as a collaborator for Boccanegra he had already, in his heart, accepted Otello as well. His unconsidered words to Maurel, although only a cry in a darkened theatre, came from his own inner depth. His doubts about his own health, of course, were real—they had been real for seventy years—but nothing was more curative to his numerous diseases than the practice of putting black pothooks, as he called them, on white paper. He loved to quote the story of a peasant girl who worked in his house at Sant' Agata and was once shown a sheet of paper with notes of music on it (perhaps when she was helping to clean the study). "What?" said the girl, aghast. "He's made all this money just from those pothooks?" The pothooks had conquered Verdi's bad health before and could do so again.

He resumed his discourse with the painter Morelli, in Naples, about the character of Iago, and their letters on the subject are in print. Morelli, who had already made some gory "historical" canvases on the Othello subject (rather like some of the Victorians in England, or like Repin in Russia), was curiously reluctant to attempt Iago and did not see him in the same way as Verdi. The small, sly, dirty conspirator he had in mind would not have deceived a gnat. He was puzzled over certain details (the "inside" or the "outside" of the castle, for instance, which as Verdi said made not the slightest difference, since in Shakespeare's time it was merely indicated on a placard). Verdi's view of Iago, as shown in this correspondence, is already well established. At this period (September 24, 1881, is the date of the letter) he was undecided about how Othello should be dressed, and was inclined to think he might be presented as an Ethiopian, but without a turban. He points out that the so-called Moor was not in reality a Moor at all, but a Venetian by the name of Moro: since the "Signor Guglielmo" (i.e., Shakespeare) wished to commit the error of making him a Moor, let Signor Guglielmo take the responsibilty. But so far as Iago is concerned there is no such uncertainty in his mind. He says: "If I were an actor and had to represent Iago, I would want to have rather a thin, long face, thin lips, small eyes close to the nose like the monkeys, a high forehead slipping off to the back, and the head developed in the back; manners distracted, *nonchalant*, indifferent to everything, flippant, uttering good or evil almost with levity, and having the air of not even thinking of what he says. . . ."

Christmas of that year (1881) brought a curious present to the composer from his publisher. The Verdi establishment in Genoa was princely indeed—a whole floor of the Palazzo Doria; it had been sufficient for Napoleon Bonaparte and other sovereigns in the past—and there was room for many guests. ("Some Russian prince," Peppina used to say, "must have come into Busseto with the allied armies; this man didn't get his taste from peasants." She was off by a year, since Verdi was born before Napoleon fell, but the Palazzo Doria gave her little joke its point.) That Christmas of 1881 brought Teresa Stolz and Emanuele Muzio, among others, and with them an official ambassador from Giulio Ricordi bringing the traditional *panettone*. The *panettone*, a cross between bread and cake (something like French *brioche*, only baked into a big cake), is inseparable from Christmas week in Italy. This time, however, a novelty had been introduced: in the midst of the sugary designs on top of the cake there was a small, very small boy made of chocolate. The hint was appreciated, but it had to be repeated for several more Christmases before *Otello* reached the stage of the Scala. At that same holiday season—for the New Year of 1882—Domenico Morelli sent Verdi a drawing of Othello, which was his way of answering the repeated requests of the past two years for one of Iago.

And so it went on—hints, gossip, chatter, newspaper articles, reminders from Maurel. Madame Blaze de Bury, wife of the music critic of the

Revue des Deux Mondes, wrote to Boito to ask if her husband could translate the work for Paris: *"Un jour ou l'autre,"* says she, *"le* Iago *ex-istera."* Verdi wrote from Sant' Agata that summer: "I am surprised at this certainty, . . . I in person don't know whether it *existera* or not." The year passed without a real decision, and another *Moretto,* as they called him, another Negro baby, appeared on Ricordi's Christmas cake. In 1883 Verdi, who still could not take the plunge for new work on the scale demanded, decided to see what he could do with *Don Carlos,* the somber and beautiful *Don Carlos* which in its sixteen years of existence had never quite satisfied his own taste.

The results of this enterprise are debatable: to many judges it has seemed that some of Verdi's cuts (especially in the first act, the scene between Elizabeth de Valois and Don Carlos) were injurious to the opera. This, however, was his last attempt to retouch or improve any of his older work, and we may be glad of that for two reasons: first, because such retouching is always perilous, superimposing the values of one stage in life upon the inspiration of another; and, second, because the uncertain results of the Don Carlos experiment may well have been his incentive, the final, necessary goad, which got him started on *Otello.* He had to compose; all the agriculture and philanthropy in the world could not absolve him from the most imperious law of his own being; and since he could not compose by retouching or rewriting, he was forced to turn to new work. Boito probably guessed as much; at all events, he had nothing to do with the revision of *Don Carlos.* With patience, deference, tact, skill, perseverance and something else which deserves the name of love, he was still working on his *Otello,* changing a line or rewriting a whole scene after every long talk with the "Mago." (This, Peppina's favorite word for her husband, was adopted also by Boito, and as we shall see, through him by Eleonora Duse.) To take one single example of the kind of work Boito did even after the poem was complete: Verdi had thought of the Othello subject, when he first began to reflect upon it seriously, as one which should be set to music for the characters of the drama only: that is, without chorus or ballet. The requirement of a ballet, or *ballabile* music as Verdi called it (*"danceable"* is the exact English), was always irksome to him. Certain opera houses in France and Russia made it a fundamental requirement, whereas others in Italy and the two Americas valued it without so insisting. Undoubtedly one of Wagner's innovations with which Verdi sympathized was the omission of this kind of music. The chorus, on the other hand, was an almost ideal form for Verdi's highly personal gift, and even many of his early choruses are immortal.

Was he to write *Otello*—provided he did write it—without a chorus as well as without a ballet?

Boito undoubtedly knew every chorus Verdi had ever written, including those in operas which nowadays are forgotten by everybody. There is the documentary proof that he disagreed with the composer in this matter of choruses, and they not only discussed it in talk, but continued the discussion in their letters. His problem, then, was to write choruses which had such excellent musical possibilities—words with such suggestive power to the old composer—that they were, in effect, irresistible. He had to persuade the old man by the text *itself* (since argument made little headway) that choruses were necessary in some scenes of the drama. His success in this matter alone is something very notable, because as it turned out the choral writing in *Otello* is beyond comparison. The great chorus called "*Fuochi di gioia*," in Act I, has so much dramatic brilliance and musical originality that in all the early years of *Otello*, when even the greatest theatres permitted the repetition of separable pieces on public demand, this chorus had to be repeated. It was so at the Scala, at the Opéra, and at the imperial houses in Vienna and Berlin. Although the encore—or the *bis*—was common enough at that period, it was very rare to have it demanded for a chorus.

As late as 1884 (late January or early February) this kind of rewriting was still going on, and at Verdi's request. Boito went to see him in Genoa at that time and the old man—disgruntled over *Don Carlos*, as we have just said—asked him to make some new modifications in his poem. Boito cheerfully consented. He had made up his mind to anything by now.

But he was on his way to Naples, for the first production of his *Mefistofele* at the San Carlo, which brought about the final spasm of Verdi's curious fears and uncertainties over *Otello*.

We know that *Mefistofele* in its new version, cut, trimmed and even manicured, had been a success after 1875. Now the San Carlo yielded and the production there (March, 1884) was also triumphant. Boito was much courted and flattered in Naples, where the press and the opera administration had more than one gathering in his honor. At one of these dinners (the one given by the Naples Conservatory) he made some remarks, in answer to questions, which got into print in a distorted form. The newspaper was the *Piccolo* and the exact words were: "With regard to *Iago*, Boito said that he had taken up this theme against his own will, but that, once the libretto was finished, he had regretted not being able to set it to music himself."

Obviously these words reached Verdi almost at once. After all the pressures and hints to which he had been subjected for five years by his own wife, by Ricordi, Faccio, Countess Maffei and Boito himself, it was really a little too much.

He may have already begun composing, or at least sketching, the music. We know the subject had dwelt in his mind for these same five years, and he would not have been Verdi if he had not tried over some of the verses in music (even if only in his own mind).

He wrote to Franco Faccio (March 27, 1884):

"That I forced his hand to treating this subject!—and you know how things really were.

"The worst is that Boito, regretting that he is not able to set it to music himself, naturally allows it to be supposed that he cannot hope to see it set by me as he would wish. I admit this perfectly, I admit it completely, and for this reason I turn to you, the oldest and firmest friend of Boito, so that when he returns to Milan you can say to him in speech, and not in writing, that I, without the shadow of resentment, without rancor of any sort, give him back his manuscript intact. More, since this libretto is my property, I offer it to him as a gift whenever he wants to set it to music. If he accepts, I shall be happy in the hope of having thus contributed to and enhanced the art which we all love."

Boito, knowing nothing of this, stopped in Genoa on his way back from Naples and saw the old man for a few minutes—just long enough to give him a photograph of his friend Morelli's last big picture. Evidently Verdi said nothing; the poet did not know what had happened until he got to Milan and was informed by Faccio. The long letter he wrote then to the Maestro reveals not only the deep strength of his faith in Verdi as composer, but also the sad and subtle structure of his own character, his tragic flaw.

The Boito letter, after its salutation, reads as follows:

"This is the origin of the misunderstanding. (Blessed are you who have so much fame and authority that you can refuse dinners; I cannot permit myself that luxury, because I should be accounted presumptuous and nothing else.) At the dinner offered me by some colleagues after Mefisto-fele in Naples, a polite journalist, a courteous and cultivated man, Signor Martino Caffiero, made this observation to me point-blank: 'Otello would have been also a subject for you.' (This proves how even a nice man can say words which embarrass his listener.) I answered, denying it, added that I had never thought of Otello on my own account, but then, perceiving that to persist in this negative without explaining it might be interpreted as if I had little love for the theme which Verdi was to set to music, I

explained my answer. I said I had never thought of it because I felt too passionately Shakespeare's masterpiece in its tragic form to be able to abstract it into a lyric manifestation. (And this is true in part.) I added that I should never have believed it possible to transmute the tragedy of Shakespeare into a good libretto before I did this work for you, Master, and with you (which is true), and that only now, after many retouches, I saw with satisfaction that my work, begun in great trepidation, came out gifted with eminently lyrical qualities, in forms perfectly suited to musical setting and adapted in every way to the needs of music drama.

"I said these words with the accent of profound conviction and Signor Caffiero who heard them correctly did not publish them, because he is not one of those who publish table conversations. Another, to whom obviously I was not speaking and who heard [my words] all wrong, published them in the Roma after his own fashion, perhaps without malignant intention, but turning the meaning upside down and attributing to me a desire of which the motive offends me and which is precisely the opposite of my great desire: this is to hear, set to music by you, a libretto which I wrote only for the joy of seeing you take up your pen again on my account, for the glory of being your working companion, for the ambition to see my name coupled with yours and ours with that of Shakespeare, and because this theme and my libretto devolve upon you by a sacrosanct right of conquest. You alone can set Otello to music, all the work you have given us in the theatre affirms this truth; if I have been able to perceive the powerful musicability of the Shakespearean tragedy, which at first I did not feel, and if I have been able to demonstrate it by fact in my libretto, it is because I placed myself at the point of view of the Verdian art; it is because I have felt, in writing those verses, that which you might feel illustrating them in that other language, a thousand times more intimate and commanding, the language of sound.

"And if I did this it was because I wanted to seize an opportunity, in the maturity of my life, at an age which no longer changes its faith—an opportunity to demonstrate, better than with all the praises one could give face to face, how much I loved and how much I felt the art that you have given us.

"Now you can tell me whether you believed the item of the Roma's reporter, reprinted in the Piccolo and the Pungolo. I hope not. Even so, the printed item existed, and because you read it, you felt the same need I felt, to cut the tangled knot—a delicate task—and you cut it in the most exquisitely suitable manner possible. You turned confidentially to the most faithful of my friends so that he, talking to me, could question my soul, and see if he could recognize a far-off germ of truth in the note published by the journalist. You were ready to give me Otello so that I should set it to music.

"You had for a moment, on my account, the doubts of the wise man, who observes in mankind the weakness of Adam, but this doubt resolved itself in you by a benign and generous offer. Maestro, what you cannot suspect is the irony that seemed to me to be contained in that offer, without any fault of yours. Look: now for seven or eight years, perhaps, I have been working on Nerone (and you can put the perhaps wherever you like, attached to the word years or to the word working). I live under that nightmare; on days when I don't work I pass the hours calling myself lazy, and on days when I work I call myself a donkey, and so runs my life away while I continue to exist, slowly asphyxiated by an ideal too high for me. For my misfortune I have studied my period too much, that is, the period of my subject; and I am terribly enamored of it and no other subject on earth, not even Shakespeare's Othello, could detach me from my theme; it corresponds in every way to my nature as an artist and to my concept of the theatre: I shall finish Nerone or not finish it, but certainly I shall never abandon it for another work, and if I do not have the strength to finish it I shall not complain, but shall pass my life, neither sadly nor gaily, with that dream in mind.

"Judge now if I—with such an obstinacy!—could accept your offer. But for Heaven's sake do not abandon Otello, do not abandon it. It is predestined for you, do it; you had already begun to work on it and I was already comforted and already hoped that one day, not too far off, I should see it finished.

"You are healthier than I, stronger than I, we have measured arms and mine bent beneath yours, your life is tranquil and serene, so take up your pen and write to me soon: Dear Boito, do me the favor to change these verses, etc., etc., and I shall change them immediately with joy and shall know how to work for you—I who do not know how to work for myself—because you live in the true and real world of Art, I in the world of hallucinations."

11 From Boito's letter, aside from its revelations of character, we learn one fact of which no proof otherwise has appeared: that Verdi had already (April, 1884) been working on the score of *Otello*. Perhaps these were preliminary sketches for this, that or the other scene, some of those furious squiggles and squaggles in which he made his early notes; they probably antedate any of those which have been preserved. But Boito, who was by now on an intimate working relationship with the composer, must have known the truth. If Verdi wanted certain changes in certain verses here or there, and in a hurry, it usually meant that he was trying to compose the scene in which they occurred. His impatience at times—as when they had been working on *Boccanegra* three years before— was so irresistible that he could not wait for letters, but sent telegrams. Verdi might even have shown Boito some of these early *Otello* sketches, or at least described them to him. That they existed we could have guessed, and from Boito's letter we may be sure. Verdi's reply, accepting Boito's statements, acknowledges that too much talk about *Otello* (as he now calls it—not *Iago*) had thrown a chill over it, "stiffened the hand that had begun to trace a few lines." This, too, makes it plain that some work had already been done on the score.

Boito's reply was characteristic: he sent the Maestro an entirely new set of verses, with no corresponding original in Shakespeare's play but thoroughly in the character of Iago. They were the dramatic verses beginning "*Credo in un Dio crudel,*" which subsequently became one of the notable passages in the score and is known even to many who have never heard the whole opera as the "Credo." Verdi thought these verses "most powerful and Shakespearean," but advises Boito to "leave that poor *Otello* alone for a while, he's getting nervous and so are we: you perhaps more than I."

For the spring and summer, therefore, *Otello* remained on the shelf while the old composer, now in his seventy-first year, made some new experiments with diet, massage, "the waters" and health in general. In June he and Peppina went to the Turin Exposition and heard Faccio conduct a concert, after which—rare for him—he asked to have the full score of Liszt's symphonic poem *Mazeppa* sent to his hotel so that he could study it. He even went to Faccio's orchestral rehearsal for the next concert: his esteem for Boito's friend, founded on the experience of *Aïda* and *Boc-*

canegra, was higher than ever: this was his conductor for Otello. He then proceeded to Montecatini, in the hills above Florence, which old friends had recommended to him: and from that time onward Montecatini was his annual refuge to "take the cure" and stay cool.

"Cure," one may well inquire, for what? We have no evidence of any real disease in Verdi aside from melancholy and the fear of death; but he was convinced that his heart was weak (on the ground that his father had died of heart trouble) and that there was something wrong with his digestion. The medical chief at the baths of Montecatini, who had the reassuring name of Fedeli, gave him a thorough examination, told him his heart was sound and his general condition good, and that there was no reason why he should not compose a new opera if he did not overwork at any one time. In fact, Dr. Fedeli's advice was better than medical—it was almost aesthetic—for he said something that would have been useful to Verdi at any period: "Do not bind yourself to deliver the work at any precise date, since this might force you to excessive effort and fatigue, but go ahead and write as it comes." The words are my paraphrase, but we know from Verdi himself that this was the gist of the doctor's counsel.

He had a visit from Boito in September at Sant' Agata and had apparently already begun to compose at that time. Boito's visits were becoming a high point in Verdi's life; this time he was accompanied by the playwright Giuseppe Giacosa, one of his great friends, and there was much to discuss in the evenings. When Boito and Giacosa had departed, Verdi set to work in earnest, and we have thus (October, 1884) a sort of "official" date, so to speak, for the beginning of the Otello score. It evidently went well right away (some of the existing sketches show this) because Verdi was vexed and annoyed when he had to stop work a month later and go through his annual accounts with the farmers and shepherds. Even to him, archpeasant as he claimed to be, there was something absurd about interrupting the composition of Otello to haggle over crops, flocks and pastures. He made up his mind then and there to rent all his farms and pastures henceforth so as not to be directly responsible for them. The decision evidently set his mind free, for on December 9 (after he and Peppina had gone back to Genoa for the winter) we find him informing Boito: "It seems impossible, but nevertheless it's true! I am busy and I am writing! I am writing—because I am writing; without aim, without preoccupations, without thinking of what comes after—indeed with a decided aversion toward what comes after."

In short, he was now in full flight and there was no turning back. From then on until the October of the next year (1885) he was composing, and from that October to the following one he was orchestrating the whole work, which in his case meant also constant changes. The original full score of *Otello* is preserved at the Casa Ricordi in Milan, an immense pile of manuscript, and no other work of Verdi's pen exhibits such intense application to every detail, such endless emendation, such an unremitting search for perfection. We have it on the authority of Professor Gatti, who no doubt examined every scrap of Verdi's writing in existence before he said so, that this score contains more changes than any other, and from looking at only a sheet or two of it one can well believe that this is so. The old man, after a decade and a half of silence, was determined that nothing but the best he could offer should go into this phoenix, this towering monument of his immortality.

Boito came to Sant' Agata on October 16, 1885, hoping to hear as much as he could of the last act: he thought he had heard everything else up to then, "heard" it, that is, partly by reading the score and partly by illustrations or suggestions at the piano. In proposing the visit he says that if Verdi has "captured all the terribility of the truth" in this last act, as he has done "with such power and simplicity" in the preceding ones, he experiences actual fear at the thought of hearing the music. Verdi told him to come ahead, just the same, and evidently gratified at least part of his wish for the last act.

The news that Verdi had practically finished his opera was spread all over Europe by this time and various offers or requests reached Sant' Agata. Maurel was a nuisance, as usual: he had been offering his services to "create the title role," as opera jargon has it, for the past four years, and he now generously proposed to do so at the Opéra-Comique in Paris! A work of the dimensions of *Otello* woud probably take the roof off that theatre—and besides, of course, Maurel constantly referred to the work as *Iago*, which by this time irritated Verdi very much.

To Maurel, to the Opéra (now directed by Gailhard) and to the Comique (now directed by Carvalho) the composer made the same replies: the opera was not finished, and when it was finished it must be done in Italian, in Italy, because its text was "most powerful" and would lose quality in any other language.

And to all concerned he served notice that the score was to be called *Otello*, not *Iago*. He had already said so and it was offensive to him to have these people (he was thinking of Maurel) go on calling it by the wrong name. The correct title, Verdi felt and said, was that of the prime doer in the drama, not of the prime mover: it is Othello who acts and suffers, Iago who pulls the strings. That Rossini had written an *Otello* and thus preëmpted the title seemed to Verdi a foolish argument, as it seems to us: rather "struggle against a giant and fail," Verdi thought, than to misname the tragedy out of a cowardly effort to avoid comparisons.

So we come to 1886, the year in which Verdi could no longer deny that the composition was finished ("or nearly finished"), but which was nevertheless a year of incessant work on it. He had probably completed the score, without full orchestration and not in final form, but anyhow the whole opera, by October 16th, the date of Boito's one-night stay at Sant' Agata. The amount of work the old man—now past his seventy-second birthday—lavished upon this opera is awe-inspiring. He must have spent many, many hours out of every twenty-four at his writing board. For one thing, he wrote out all of Boito's poem, over and over; that is, once in its entirety and then separate scenes at separate times, so that each word was engraved in his mind as he composed: if it were not so engraved, there was something wrong, and he called for more changes. After he had composed the work as a whole he was dissatisfied with great sections of it. Thus we find him (January, 1886) telling Boito that he intends to rewrite a large part of the first act.

Boito had never heard the final duet of Act I, which seems strange, but Verdi's secretiveness and sensitivity about this opera really knew no bounds. That wonderful duet ("*Già nella notte densa*") which brings Boito's first act to a magical conclusion—and we say Boito's because his first is largely Shakespeare's second—is such a very high point of achievement for the composer's genius that he may have dreaded showing it to anybody; he may have rewritten it many times more than the existing copies show; he may have put off composing it on paper until the last possible minute. Both Boito and Verdi are at their best in this scene; Boito by salvaging Othello's magnificent speech from Act I and putting it in the middle of the love duet; Verdi by an ecstatic intensity of creation which is seldom reached in any music.

And yet the poet of the piece, who knew all too well what a tremendous demand the scene made upon its composer, still knew nothing of its results.

He asked if he could come to Genoa in mid-February so as to see and hear—a complicated procedure, involving all sorts of indications as well as reading and playing the piano—the finished opera. He was careful not to mention the love duet, but in such a matter it would not be possible to deceive the old man. Oh, no, says Verdi: "You certainly can't hear the whole of *Otello* a month from now!" No, indeed: too much still to be done. Instead, the Maestro asks him if he can go very quietly to the Scala and hear two young sopranos who were appearing there at the moment, and report ("in all secrecy") on their respective qualifications for the part of Desdemona. Both were said to be young and beautiful; one of them was Gemma Bellincioni, afterward renowned throughout Europe. Verdi preferred young people because "one can do what one wants with them," but in this case he wanted something a little rarer than youth. He tells Boito to pay careful attention to the quality of the voice and its intonation (a Desdemona who sang off pitch would be a torture), but, "first above everything," there must be "intelligence and feeling." (Italics Verdi's.) He then makes a fine, sweeping statement: "Even if they sing badly," says he, "it doesn't matter! In that case they'll sing more easily in my style. . . ."

Verdi, of course, as we have often noticed, made essentially dramatic demands upon the voices and was consequently accused of "ruining" Italian singing. He certainly changed it from the limpid, instrumental style of *bel canto*, which made hardly any demands upon "intelligence and feeling," but whether this was "ruin" or not depends upon taste. With his profoundly and even exclusively dramatic genius there was no other possibility: he *had* to have singers who could convey the passions he wrote into his music. An artist who sang like a violin—Melba, for instance—was not really suited to his music, although she often sang Desdemona with success. Some singers who were vocally imperfect (as seems to have been the case with La Frezzolini in Verdi's early years) were able to express the emotions which were the very material of his compositions from the start. An artist like Adelina Patti, who could do everything, seems to have been Verdi's ideal: she had a highly developed dramatic sensibility and could color her voice to express almost any emotion, reducing her audiences to tears very often, even in such a period piece as *La Sonnambula*; we have Verdi's word for it. But she also commanded a birdlike lyricism at will, and all her early triumphs were based upon it. An Italian born in Madrid, she made her first appearance on any stage as Lucia when she was sixteen, in New York; Verdi heard her for the first time in London three years later and was profoundly impressed. We have a number of letters of his, notably one to Ricordi, in which he describes and even tries to analyze her unique quality. He was expounding her virtues to his friends in Milan years before she sang at the Scala, and he was saying "I told you so" for years afterwards. I think it probable that the Verdi soprano, that passionate but lyrical heroine of everything he wrote in maturity, owes something to Patti: at least, after he had heard Patti, he realized that the kind of artist he had in mind really did exist, and there was therefore no need to hold himself down, to curb his natural demand for emotional expression.

Verdi's problem in finding the right singers for *Otello* was, obviously, more acute than usual. In this work the drama is equal to the music, and the kind of singer whose idea of dramatic expression is three-steps-left and two-steps-right, accompanied by a sawing motion of the right arm, would not do for any of the characters. There was no lack of volunteers: to "create" the characters in a Verdi opera—and how Verdi hated that use of the word "create"!—was by this time a tremendous honor. Among these volunteers was the persistent Maurel, and to them was now added (winter of 1886) Tamagno, both of whom eventually achieved their ambition. A young, beautiful, ingenuous Desdemona with voice enough and feeling enough to express Verdi's music was difficult to find. The character has more substance and color in the opera than in the play, partly because of the wonderful music she has to sing, and partly because Boito's compression of other parts has thrown Desdemona into greater prominence, even without the extra lines he wrote for her. In the Boito terms, the old dichotomy, she is Good and Iago is Evil and Othello is the tragic hero suffering between them. Her significance to the opera is thus greater, aesthetically speaking, just as her actual scenes are bigger, than in the play.

Verdi in the midst of his rewriting and orchestrating was conscious of all these practical problems—those which a year before he had scornfully called "what comes after"—and it is significant of the growing solidity of his substitute father-son relationship with Boito that he tended to throw a good many of the odd jobs onto the younger man. It was not only singers but costumes, stage settings, stage action which required much thought, and Verdi was constantly asking Boito's opinion or assistance. He still would not admit, to the world at large, that *Otello* was finished: as late as March, 1886, he wrote to Arrivabene and said: "Will I finish it? Perhaps yes. Will I produce it? The answer is difficult even for me!"

But on March 17th he suddenly made up his mind to go to Paris again— "partly to see if they are as crazy as ever" but principally to hear Maurel and decide in his own mind whether he really wanted this extremely "starry" baritone as Iago. Meanwhile he had told Tamagno, who was then singing in Madrid, that he could come to Genoa afterwards and talk things over; there was no doubt that Tamagno had the trumpet voice for the Othello part, but Verdi doubted (with good reason) how much he could understand and learn of an almost new art in a relatively short time.

These preoccupations, along with his work at the writing board, filled his mind and his life through the greater part of 1886, but there was one interruption of overwhelming sorrow to the composer. Clarina Maffei was stricken with meningitis, and during the summer the Verdi pair at Montecatini ("taking the cure") learned that there was not much hope for her life. Verdi kept himself informed, and when he thought he had no more time to waste he went to Milan to see his wonderful friend once more. The Countess did not even recognize him; she died on July 13. No friend Verdi ever had had done more for him, often in ways he did not notice or remember.

From Montecatini the Verdi ménage returned to Sant' Agata and work: on October 29th Verdi was able to write to Boito, "tomorrow or soon after, I hope, the last note of the instrumentation will be written." It was written on November 1, 1886, and the composer gave his poet the news in these words: "It is finished! Salute to us . . . (and also to *Him!*) Farewell."

He then sent three-fifths of the manuscript of the full score—by his own calculation—to Ricordi to have the instrumental and vocal parts copied out, retaining, for some reason of his own, the whole second act and the ending of the third. At the end of that month he made the annual move from Sant' Agata to Genoa, where the head of the music-copying service of the Casa Ricordi came to receive the rest. In early December this enormous mass of manuscript was in the hands of the copying artists.

Verdi had a feeling almost of grief—a "*stretto di cuore,*" a squeezing of the heart—when he let the work go at last. He had dwelt with it a long time and had often doubted that he could ever finish it. "Poor *Otello!*" he says. "He never will come back here again!" Into this he had put everything he had to give, the whole of his genius and his life, without any reserve except that imposed upon him by new severities of taste and judgment. As his first opera in sixteen years, it had seemed to him, all along, very nearly an impossibility; and except for Boito's unremitting ministrations to the text as to the composer, it would never have produced this result.

From now on everything went with lightning speed. The Scala was avid to produce the work; Europe and the two Americas were waiting and had sent special correspondents to report upon it long before the rehearsals were over; the singers, chorus and orchestra were, although a little frightened, anxious to do their best. Verdi, entering his seventy-fourth year, was determined to work as many hours a day as might be necessary to bring about the result he had in mind.

Maurel was Iago and Tamagno was Othello; these had been more or less inevitable all along, in spite of Verdi's reservations about both of them. They were the best dramatic baritone and tenor of the age, by common consent, and it would have been hard to refuse their services. The Desdemona problem was solved when Verdi accepted Romilda Pantaleoni, a soprano whose temperament and artistic aspirations, along with her personal beauty, had brought her into an intimate relationship with Franco Faccio. Faccio was, of course, inevitably, the conductor—there was evidently nobody else in Europe at the time who could compare with him: he was a sort of pre-Toscanini. Verdi was not truly satisfied with any of the three singers, and the fact should be emphasized because all of them endure in history chiefly because they sang this opera in its first production. Indeed Tamagno became so renowned as Othello that he sang scarcely anything else, and Madame Pantaleoni's lines in the reference books mention nothing but Desdemona. Maurel, of course, had Falstaff still to come, but even he, so notable in many parts including that of Don Giovanni, is remembered as the first Iago. (He even wrote a whole book about it a year later, entitled A Propos de la Mise en Scène du Drame Lyrique Otello.) The three of them, but especially the two men, were announced throughout Europe, even in such musically respectable places as Vienna, as the "creators" of Otello.

From the time the whole score went to the copyists until its first performance at the Scala on February 7, 1887, only two months passed. They were months of intense work for all concerned. Verdi, with what mixed emotions we can only guess, was back in the theatre again, discussing costumes and settings, following orchestral rehearsals, rehearsing the principal singers himself, as indefatigable as a healthy man of half his age. By now almost everything at the Scala was electrically operated, the reign of the orchestral conductor as supreme dictator had been thoroughly established, and dozens of other details had changed since the time when he first entered that house, but it was observed that he was as thoroughly and unreflectingly a man of the theatre as he had ever been. The story goes that in one rehearsal, exasperated at the stupidity and woodenness of Tamagno, the composer himself took the tenor's place beside Desdemona's bed and fell as he wanted Othello to fall, half down the steps. If this ever did occur it was the natural action of a man to whom the theatre was home, and who had a very definite idea of what he wanted at that point; he would not even have noticed the consternation of the beholders at this violence on the part of a (supposedly) fragile old man. The big bull Tamagno was, by all accounts, a far less gifted actor than Verdi would have liked, but at least he sang the notes as written, which can scarcely be said of his successors; and by dint of long, hard work Verdi succeeded in making him understand the character and convey some of its meaning.

Maurel was much less difficult. Indeed, however vain and foolish he may have seemed in ordinary life, this singing actor evidently possessed the quality of being transformed on the stage. His gift for characterization never caused him to lose the musical line, and that rare, peculiar, unteachable art of *musical* acting—so different from acting without music—was his by nature. His Iago and Tamagno's Othello established an operatic tradition from the very first performance, and everybody who sings those parts even today is carrying out, by and large, the Tamagno-Maurel stage action as fixed by Verdi.

Perhaps I should be very specific, since the point has its importance, about Verdi and tradition. He respected the traditions of the theatre and of the separate operas; he thought of himself as a conservative in such matters; and in Italy, where opera traditions are quickly established, he accepted them without rebellion. But he never did believe in *blind* tradition, that is, in doing things for no reason at all: he always wanted the performers to understand what they were doing, and indeed his prolonged, exhausting rehearsals with them individually were intended to bring about this result if possible. If the public set up a tradition of its own, particularly in such matters as applause, Verdi shrugged his shoulders and accepted it. His fierce disciple Toscanini never tolerated a fraction of the freedom which Verdi conceded to his audiences. There are many examples which everybody can think of: in *Boccanegra*, for example, the long cry of *"Figlia!"* which the baritone emits when he recognizes his daughter. This is only two notes, but they are beautifully placed for a baritone voice and ring out with the most powerful effect; consequently they are always applauded in Italy, even at the Scala, thus drowning out Verdi's music for two or three minutes. The old man never complained, although we may suppose he did not like it. A rather similar case occurred during the first *Aïda* at Parma (Parma, which claims Verdi as its own, as well as Boito and Toscanini). The audience was wildly excited and many sections of the work had to be repeated, as was common at the time. When, in the Nile scene, the great, sweeping melody of the Aïda-Amonasro duet first came out (*"Rivedrai le foreste imbalsamate"*), the enraptured audience could not even wait to hear the rest of the scene, but stopped the performance then and there, demanding the repetition of that single phrase. Professor Pizzi, who was present that night, says the audience emitted "almost savage cries," and long years afterward he recalled the circumstance to Verdi, who merely smiled tolerantly.

In all these respects Verdi was neither rebel nor tyrant; he thought Italian audiences exaggerated their enthusiasms, but he preferred this excess to the German custom of sitting "like dead fish" until the entire act of a work was ended. He believed (or professed to believe) that German audiences were asleep most of the time, owing to the silence and darkness of their theatres and their tradition of restricted applause.

And in only a few years Toscanini had imposed the no-encore rule at the Scala! Indeed, as all know, the refusal of the public to obey his rules caused him to leave that theatre once, and he was never disobeyed again. Today the Scala audience has a new tradition—traditions are easy enough to create—and would never dream of demanding that any piece be repeated, even in old operas written at a time when repetitions were customary and expected.

12 The dress rehearsal of *Otello* took place Thursday, February 3, and the first performance Saturday, February 5, 1887. No person not immediately concerned in the production was allowed inside the theatre at the dress rehearsal; this was in accordance with Verdi's edict but caused a rebellion among the musical journalists, especially the foreigners who had come to Milan for *Otello*. They were obliged to write their accounts after the first performance—and on a Saturday night, too—so that haste and unfamiliarity conspired to increase their astonishment.

Otello was a towering success, of course, even from that first night, but among the critical fraternity the predominant response was certainly astonishment. Nobody had expected such an eruption of genius from a man of seventy-four; nobody was prepared to hear such "advanced" harmony and instrumentation; nobody knew what had been going on inside Verdi's head for the past sixteen years. We who are used to *Otello* can relate it organically and simply enough to all of its predecessors. We can see it as the coming of age of a creative talent, the culmination of a long growth, every element of which had been there from the very beginning. To the stunned and somewhat bewildered critics of 1887 it seemed "a new Verdi," and they used that expression with nauseating frequency; they thought he had abandoned his past, whereas, of course, he was only fulfilling it. They noted the complexity of his orchestra, the variety and power of the different kinds of recitative or declamation, the continuous symphonic flow of the whole, and when they remembered *Rigoletto* they could hardly believe the evidence of their own senses. Some isolated cries of "Wagner!" were heard here and there, soon to be drowned out and forgotten. To a superficial listener the recurrence of the "kiss" theme from the first act duet in the finale seems Wagnerian; and the theme itself, wondrously beautiful though it is, does suggest *Tristan* in the orchestra; the whole love duet has some remote natural cousinage with *Tristan*; but everything from the first note to the last is so inspissatedly Italian that to speak of Wagner at all is foolish. It is quite easy to prove that the recurrence of a characterized theme (as a reminiscence) is a musical device far antedating Wagner; Verdi himself had used it before he had ever heard Wagner's name; and anyhow this kind of recurrence is not in the very least like the web of leading motives, *Leitmotive* as they are now called, which constituted Wagner's fundamental system of composition in the *Ring*. Incidentally—not that it mattered to Verdi—the word *Leitmotiv* was coined by Hans von Wolzogen in this very year, the year of *Otello*, to describe the elements of the Wagnerian web; Wagner himself, now three years dead, had never heard the word and had been content to call these elements the "fundamental themes."

Verdi's orchestra in *Otello*, although not Wagnerian in anything but size and arrangement, and not used in a Wagnerian manner, was nevertheless novel in many respects to those who heard it first. Aside from harmonic complexities, the actual instruments themselves were adapted to dramatic purposes in a way Verdi had never so fully developed before. Thus Othello himself has a trombone color (we can hear it in his voice, too, when the part is sung as written), and Iago is very often harmonized with bassoons. The parts call for four trombones and four bassoons. The bass trombone was a real trombone (not, as hitherto, a tuba) especially made for the occasion, and the instrument is hence known as a "Verdi trombone." Woodwinds and brasses are very fully exploited without sacrificing the wonderful string writing which—when required—gives such beauty to the work. All this wealth and power in the orchestra was the source of much of the general astonishment; nobody at the time seems to have remembered that in 1871 at Cairo the writers sent from Europe (some of them the same men) were expressing the same astonishment about Aïda. The "new Verdi" of 1887 represented an enormous augmentation of technical resource over the "new Verdi" of 1871: there was a new refinement and variety of singing declamation—a refinement amounting to subtlety, not instantly discernible by those who were hearing it for the first time—and there were depths upon depths of expressive richness in the wedding of voice to orchestra, a wedding here consummated as never before in music. All this was new but *the thing itself*, the essential Verdi, that which is expressed by this new wealth of means, remains itself and forever true. *Otello* is not only the greatest of Italian operas—that is, removing *Falstaff* from that classification altogether, as I think one must—but it contains the best of all Verdi's preceding work just as the greater contains the lesser. If you have that kind of mind you can hear *La Traviata*, *Boccanegra*, *Il Trovatore* and any number of other Verdian works through the music of *Otello*, right on back to *Ernani* and *Nabucco*. Verdi himself was fond of pointing out the resemblances between his early and late work, perhaps because all the "new Verdi" talk annoyed him, and the resemblances are there. It is the relationship of the bud to the flower, but it exists far more naturally and inevitably than anybody was able to perceive in 1887.

The singing declamation in *Otello*, I have said, has a subtlety and range which its first audience could scarcely perceive. This is because nothing like it had been heard before all at once. Verdi employs, with consummate art, every kind of recitative known to Italian music since the seventeenth century—"since Peri and Caccini . . . built the foundations of the recitative style," says Professor Gatti. It can touch *Sprechgesang* at one extreme and melodic lyricism at the other, moving with such smoothness, eloquence and apparent ease through the dramatic poem that every expression (however erudite in origin) seems precisely suited to the words and to the situation on the stage. Some of it is free of tempo, that is, "a *piacere*," and most singers of Iago deliver these passages almost like speech; some of it is extremely heroic declamation, as when Othello addresses the people:

> *Esultate!*
> *L'orgoglioso musulmano sepolto è in mar,*
> *Nostra e del ciel è gloria!*

Some of it is melodious, in strict time, and can pass into the "lyric effusion" as Gatti calls it (pure song) with an effect of such naturalness and inevitability that the listener has no sense of being nudged or prodded into special attention, as one does with the old-fashioned aria or set piece.

Those who heard *Otello* on its first night may have had the voice-and-piano reduction of the score, for Ricordi put it on sale in his big shop the morning of the performance. It would not have helped much in judging a work of such complexity and technical invention, partly because the piano reduction can give no remote idea of this orchestra, and partly because the declamation itself—or, if you prefer, the entire vocal composition—shows its style to the ear far more readily than to the eye. For it must be said, loud and long, that *Otello* is an opera, and in Verdi's concept this means that the stage (and those upon it) must predominate. To the very end he maintained that his music was all written for the stage. The great and wonderful ocean of sound which sustains *Otello* is not to be considered as orchestral composition alone: it is there to carry the drama onward, to sustain the wings of song, but *never to take their place*. Wagner put his drama primarily in the orchestra and used singers to illustrate the dramatic idea, but he was not much interested in action on the stage, and hours upon hours of his *Ring*, for example, are consumed by an orchestral drama, while various singers stand motionless on the stage and declaim the poem if they can. (Very few can.) Wagner did not write opera at all; he spent his life saying so; and Verdi agreed with him heartily. His orchestral dramas, supreme in their own beauty, contain practically no action and very little pure singing; the stage is merely there to illustrate, in a static way (as if by post cards), the tremendous conflicts and resolutions of a magnificent orchestra. The procedures of the two giants were thus exactly opposite, as they started from opposing concepts; and if, in the result, there sometimes may seem to be distant relationship in the effect given—as one may feel at times between *Otello* and *Tristan* —it is accidental.

Bewildered though they were, the critics, writers and general public of 1887 realized that this was an event verging on the miraculous. The ordinary public—perhaps out of simple curiosity—besieged the theatre, and every opera house in the world clamored to produce the work. At every performance the public of the Scala demanded certain repetitions (the "Credo," which Faccio refused to repeat, and the "*Fuochi di gioia*" chorus, the "Ave Maria," the tenor-baritone oath, the contra-bassoon interlude in the fourth act, and other passages which are heard nowadays in an almost religious silence throughout the world).

Perhaps there was some vitality or at least vulgarity in the public of those days which was healthy, good for the system; perhaps we have grown too refined in such matters. At all events I confess that as a child of the twentieth century I find the notion of "encores" for *anything* in *Otello* downright repulsive; the thought of asking Desdemona to repeat her "Ave Maria" actually shocks me, as very few things can. Verdi did not mind; he was born, remember, in 1813. But he wrote a work of such homogeneity and incandescent unity that to our taste, seventy years later, it is sacrilege to interrupt it. "Bows" and even "encores" may be suitable to the Mozart operas, at least as they are done in Vienna nowadays, but they are no more permissible in *Otello* than in *Tristan* or the B Minor Mass. One thinks of Toscanini and his frequently repeated words, "Poor Verdi!" by which he meant to express his pity for the great old man who never dared, or even cared, to enforce his true will. We think of many things in the score which indicate an aspiration crossed with unbelief —a form of despair peculiar to the theatre—because the composer knew that he could never get what he wanted in an opera house. We may mention the dynamic ranges in particular as a proof of this despair. When the composer puts down so many *p*'s and *f*'s he is not really hoping for an exact rendition of the marking: he is only giving the singer or instrumentalist a target. You will find in the late scores of Verdi a dynamic range of *pppppp* to *ffff* for the soprano soloist, for example, and one may safely assume that no singer in real life has the technical skill to sing either so soft or so loud as this. (We are doing well if we can get anything but a monotonous *mezzoforte* out of most of them.) By this ferocious emphasis the composer means simply: "Do the best you can to approximate this marking because this is the way I hear it in my head." Actually in the opera house he accepted all sorts of things which were not at all what he had heard in his head while composing.

Toscanini used to tell a story in this very connection which shows Verdi's sad compliance with necessity. Arturo Toscanini, born at Parma on March 25, 1867, was approaching his twentieth birthday when *Otello* was first produced at the Scala. He was a violoncellist and in that capacity had gone with a traveling opera company to South America, where, in a sudden emergency, he was called upon to conduct an opera—no less than *Aïda!*—by memory and without rehearsal. His phenomenal success in Rio de Janeiro was quickly known in Italy and he was already engaged to conduct in Turin, but he asked, as a special favor, to be allowed to play a second-row cello in the Scala orchestra when *Otello* was produced. He went through all those rehearsals with Faccio, then at his very peak as a conductor, and with the composer. There is one place in the cello part which is marked *pppp*. Toscanini played it *pppp*. Verdi said to Faccio: "I cannot hear that cello. Do it again." They tried it over and Faccio said to Toscanini: "You must play louder, no matter how it is marked. Verdi must hear the notes." Toscanini ground his teeth and relaxed his pianissimo.

Later on when he knew Verdi (I think it was at the time when he went to Genoa to go over the *Te Deum* and the other sacred pieces with the old man) he told the story to the composer. One can imagine the young man's desire to justify himself, or at least his musicianship, to the artist he worshipped. He explained that he had played the notes in question louder because Faccio insisted, but that actually they were marked *pppp* and he had played them *pppp*. Verdi sighed and said: "Who can tell the difference in an opera house?" It is for this and kindred reasons that Toscanini used to say, in such a heartfelt manner, "*Povero Verdi!*" One part of his own fanatical and exhausting struggle for perfection may even have been a desire to avenge this composer, the greatest he ever knew and the closest to his own innermost being, for all the sad necessities of a long life in opera. Toscanini did the same for Wagner, of course, as for Mozart and Beethoven, but they were not blood of his blood and bone of his bone as Verdi was. Anybody who ever attended a Toscanini rehearsal knows that this conductor very adequately avenged them all.

13 The resounding first night of *Otello* brought new honors to Verdi, of course, although he had long outgrown any appetite for honors. There was a new decoration from the King, there were demonstrations in the streets, official ceremonies; the city of Milan (rather late in the day, one might think) made him an honorary citizen. The Mayor of Milan, on this civic occasion, said that all were looking forward to Verdi's next opera, which he (Don Gaetano Negri was his name) hoped would be an *opera buffa*; he even went so far as to suggest a subject, Don Quixote, knowing full well that Verdi had dreamed for years of a lyric comedy on that character. The Maestro did not specifically deny this possibility, but in his brief reply he said: "My long career is now over."

The call for a new opera rose also from the crowds in the street before the Grand Hotel, after the first performance. Verdi and Boito came out onto the balcony with the conductor and chief singers: Tamagno, beside him, suddenly opened his cavernous throat and sang Othello's *"Esultate!"* which seems to have been enough to put any crowd into a frenzy. Verdi went through all this calmly enough, but as soon as the third performance was over he went home. "Up to midnight I am still Maestro Verdi," he said in the farewell reception at the Scala, "but then I go back to being the peasant of Sant' Agata."

There were numerous incidental or concomitant results of the *Otello* triumph, most of which Verdi either did not know or did not notice. The impressions made on the genius of the young Toscanini were indelible and helped to create the greatest Verdian of all, the incomparable Verdi conductor; the impressions on the strange, hypersensitive mind of Arrigo Boito were such as to make him Verdi's slave thereafter. Verdi quite rightly insisted that Boito's part in the achievement was equal to his; he forced Boito to share his bows, his public appearances, his honors as much as possible. He had to pull Boito along by the hand on some occasions, but he did it. Beyond any doubt Boito was overwhelmed by the grandeur of the creation, because *Otello* in the opera house, where it belongs, is a thing one could not fully realize from the printed page, from the piano or even from a rehearsal. Boito knew the score as well as anybody did except Verdi and Faccio, but even he could not tell in advance what a volcano this was going to be in the theatre, with a dense, excited and attentive audience, in all the magic and mystery of a great night in the greatest of opera houses. The electricity engendered seems to have pervaded everything and everybody except, perhaps, Verdi. It played its part in igniting a great flame, one of which Verdi may not even have been too conscious: the loves of Boito and Eleonora Duse.

Duse had met Boito at a supper party in the Cova Restaurant in Milan three years before. She had been playing a brief season at the Carcano Theatre—*La Dame aux Camélias* and *Cavalleria Rusticana*—in which her unique gifts, then on the very brink of their world-wide fame, were for the first time appreciated by the Milanese intellectuals at something like their true worth. The supper party in her honor, in that celebrated and luxurious old restaurant which has now disappeared, was so memorable that it has been described at length by several participants. The guests were men only, since the Milanese countesses still could not have supper in restaurants or meet "theatre women"; but the men were the most notable specimens obtainable, including some of the best writers in Italy. La Duse sat at supper between the Mayor of Milan (Count Belinzaghi) and Boito. After supper she circulated among the groups in the private sitting rooms, talking to everybody with, we are told, the grace and simplicity of a great lady. Boito was very smitten; he asked for her photograph and sent her some verses after she went away.

But Duse was already beginning her forty years of wandering over the earth, and her first tour of South America came soon afterward. Boito did not see her again for three years; they met in all the thunder and lightning of the *Otello* first night at the Scala.

Duse was now twenty-seven and he was forty-four. She had been on the stage since her fifth year, when her father led her on as Cosette in *Les Misérables.* The child of vagabond actors from Venice, often with nothing to eat except the greenery her mother gathered in the fields near their tents, she had received practically no schooling. When her mother could occasionally get her admitted to a class in some town where the troupe played, she was obliged to sit apart from all the others because she was the "child of the comedians." At fourteen she played Juliet in the Arena at Verona and seems to have undergone a mystical experience: she "became" Juliet. She had already been acting constantly for ten years without understanding the words she recited—and perhaps, in one sense, she never did understand them—but on that night in May, 1872, she "became" Juliet and the words took care of themselves. Poetry poured through her; the character lived; some strange species of trance, almost like an illness, was upon her. It seems to foreshadow her whole life, which, with gathering intensity, turned into a series of such "becomings" upon the stage. Before long she had discarded most of the trappings of the theatre, including make-up: she was working toward that bare, essential creation or re-creation which was so soon to subdue the audiences of all Europe and the Americas. We have ample accounts by Chekhov, Bernard Shaw, Hermann Bahr and others of how utterly unlike ordinary "acting" this was. Through Chekhov and Stanislavski it founded a superb school of the theatre—almost precisely the opposite of that represented by Sarah Bernhardt and the Comédie Française—but nothing that followed her seemed to "be" or to "become" in quite the same way.

This, then, was the woman of genius who tapped on Boito's window at three o'clock in the morning a few nights after the first performance of *Otello.* She was in love and could wait no longer. From their letters— only made public in recent years—we know now that it was a fully sexual and highly romantic relationship; at the time, owing to Boito's fanatical secretiveness, it was generally considered a "platonic friendship." He made his translation of Shakespeare's *Antony and Cleopatra* for her, subtly adapting it here and there for her talent; they had a few intervals of happiness for two years; the first of these two years—the one after *Otello*— was always referred to thereafter by the Duse as "the year of the dream."

Boito was by this time elderly, sedentary, habitual in his ways, far more so than his age required. What he liked to do of an evening was to play Bach to himself and look at the Velasquez drawings he had brought back from Madrid. All the fire and flame of the Duse may have frightened him a little; he very soon took to calling her "my child" and otherwise emphasizing the difference in their ages; in the letters we find him constantly urging her to more and more hard work, which, he felt, was the only salvation for both of them. Permanent union was out of the question. She was constantly on tour, as Italian actors must always be (they get, even today, only a brief season in each city), and he could not go with her. He tried it in the first year—a tour of Sicily and the south—and could not endure it. Their happiness was restricted to some few months up in the mountains above Bergamo. He could not take the journey even from Milan to Turin to see her, after a while.

In the slow decline and fall we are most concerned, of course, with Verdi, and we see that he played his part. "Lenor," as Boito always called her, never complained when Boito was called to Sant' Agata, but she could not help noticing it. Aside from her own long absences on tour, not only in Italy but abroad, and Boito's utter inability to live in (so to speak) a circus tent, it was Verdi himself, the Mago, who presented one of the principal impediments to their continued happiness. Boito's worship of the old master had now reached such a point (with the beginning of *Falstaff*) that it dominated every other element in his life: even Lenor could not stand against it. If Verdi wanted him to come to Sant' Agata, he went to Sant' Agata. Lenor observed, with a woeful sadness but not bitterly, that if she wanted Arrigo to come to Turin or Venice or somewhere else, while she was engaged there, he was unable to do so: he was busy composing his *Nerone*. If Verdi, on the other hand, expressed the slightest wish, Boito would drop *Nerone* immediately and take the first train. As an artist Duse understood this; as a woman Lenor was sad. And we can discern in her, even as an artist, a wish that he would put his own work first—that his *Nerone* could really be done, Verdi or no Verdi.

The flame flickered and finally died. There came a time when she met "a young Mago" (Gabriele d'Annunzio) to whom she devoted the next seven years of her life. In her use of those words "a young Mago" is the only suggestion that she resented Boito's "old Mago." Her attitude toward Verdi was serene enough: she called him a *galantuomo*, an honest, brave and true man (perhaps "gentleman" would translate it), "who understands everything, and does not judge, for good or for evil, the affairs of other people."

We have proof of only one meeting between Verdi and Madame Duse. This must have been soon after the *Otello* first night, because the Verdi pair did not remain long in Milan. Duse was playing Goldoni's *Pamela Nubile* at the Manzoni Theatre. Boito took the Verdi couple to the performance and to Duse's dressing room afterward, as she recalls in a letter some years later. We cannot be sure that Verdi knew of the relationship between his poet and the great actress, but his instinct was profound; he probably did. What he would never have guessed, because it was not in his nature to do so, was that Boito sacrificed this rare creature to him.

And yet, to a considerable extent, that is just what Boito did.

14 There was another sacrifice Boito made which Verdi bore in mind at all times: that of his own work, the *Nerone*. Actually Boito was incapable of finishing the work, by now—he had compiled too many notes; he had worked too hard—and it was not Verdi's fault. Boito lived on for seventeen years after Verdi's death and never could finish *Nerone*. But Verdi, in all his highly justified gratitude to Boito, could never get rid of the feeling that this gifted young fellow ought to be doing his own work, finishing his own opera, instead of supplying texts, ideas, time and devotion to an old man. Again and again Verdi returns to this subject; he loses no chance to urge Boito to work at *Nerone*, to finish it, to give it everything he has to give. Boito had mountains of notes by this time on every subject it is possible to imagine from the period of Nero: every garment the people of the time wore, every dish they ate, their weapons and furniture, their music and poetry, their measurements, income and expenditure, their habits and schedules. There was practically nothing he had not been able to dig out of some Latin or Greek text. In

his drama—the libretto—he names in one place over thirty different kinds of armed men who come onto the stage, in accordance with their Roman nomenclature, and evidently expecting an ordinary theatre to go to the trouble to get all the different weapons, headdress, etc., etc., which made each distinct. It is a male chorus, as a matter of fact, and Verdi's earliest librettists (up to and including the ineffable Piave) would have called them all, succinctly, "warriors," and been content with a helmet and spear for each. Boito's immense erudition and his sheer delight in it for its own sake, aside from any ultimate stage production of the work, made him dawdle over details and postpone, in his usual dreamy way, any serious consideration of an end to it all. When it came to working for Verdi he was brisk and precise and could finish any given task with remarkable speed.

It never seems to have occurred to any of them (Verdi, Ricordi, Duse or even Boito himself) that in writing *Otello* and *Falstaff* for Verdi he was perhaps doing his "own" work, doing a work of more permanent value than any other within his range. With all his talent he never had been within planetary distance of Verdi as a composer, and his stories and verses—although they echo Hoffmann and Poe and foreshadow D'Annunzio—are not, independently, of the most exalted species. His most peculiar, indeed his unique, gift as a poet or dramatist was that of supplying dramatic form and versified content to work which could be set to music. He was a bridge between Shakespeare and Verdi: this was the strange, rare fruition to which he comes when all is said. There is nothing quite like it in literature or music, and although it was not what is called "original" work, in that it arises from one master and is destined for the purposes of another, it has more merit and will survive far longer than most "original" work of its time and country.

Verdi himself, aside from worrying over Boito's *Nerone*, had a quantity of preoccupation in the year or two after *Otello*. First of all came his own Golden Jubilee, a national festival to commemorate the fiftieth anniversary of his first opera (*Oberto, Conte di Bonifacio*, at the Scala in Milan in 1839). Ricordi was responsible for the idea in the first place, although not under his own name, and the indignant Verdi forced him to recant by a public letter calling the whole thing off, but of course it was too late. After *Otello* and the stir it made throughout the musical world of the West, some kind of observation of Verdi's fiftieth year on the stage could not be avoided. In the end, after a struggle lasting many months, Verdi was obliged to submit and did so with good grace. The King, the Prime Minister (Crispi), the poet Carducci, and everything or everybody else of eminence in Italy united to do him honor: he acknowledged it all as best he could, even though he maintained throughout this time that of all useless things, a "jubilee" was the most useless.

But graver sorrows were upon him: his friends, his best and oldest and dearest, were now dying in an ineluctable sequence, close together, in accordance with age and human weakness. The Countess Maffei, as we have seen, departed without recognizing him; Count Arrivabene, that lifelong strength to Verdi, died on New Year's Day, 1887; neither of them lived to see *Otello*. He had to go into the *Otello* rehearsals in mid-January with the certainty that these two, the stalwarts, would never be his to claim again, and that whatever he did, they could neither see nor hear it. In some ways the next death in the series, that of his devoted pupil Emanuele Muzio, was even worse: Muzio had been so wholly Verdi's all through life, so selfless and pure in his childlike adoration, that something rare or unique was taken away with him. Muzio had met and married an American girl, much younger than himself, on a tour of the United States; there had been a child; the child died and the girl took herself off elsewhere; it was the only private or personal life he ever had, and it left him solitary in Paris, in his old age, as a teacher of music or of repertoire to singers. His operas were unproduced or, if produced, were unsuccessful; his career as an orchestral and operatic conductor had been good but in no way remarkable. The whole point and center of his life from beginning to end was his connection with Verdi—that he was "Verdi's pupil," in fact Verdi's only pupil, was his title to consideration. And for him Verdi mourned, it would appear on the evidence, more than for all the others, because in Muzio there was something downright unique. This may be illustrated by one fact alone: of all Verdi's friends, without exception, he was the only one who obeyed the composer's wishes about letters. Muzio had probably received more letters from Verdi than anybody else in that circle, and over a larger number of years. He kept them all, of course, and could not be blamed for doing so; but in his last will and testament he gave explicit directions about destroying them, and it was done. All the letters of half a century had been made into neat packets with the exact dates on the outside; all went to the furnace.

Muzio died November 27, 1890, in Paris, only a few days after writing to Verdi a farewell letter which is kept at Sant' Agata. "Remember me sometimes," he says, "and let us meet as late as possible in the other world."

By this time *Falstaff* was, so to speak, in existence already: it had taken form in the minds of its two creators a year before.

Verdi was on his way to Montecatini in the summer of 1889 when

Boito sent him the first sketch, or scenario, for *Falstaff*. Obviously the idea set the old Master on fire at once. There is not a trace of the long hesitations and fears which beset the composition of *Otello*. Verdi has only one real doubt, which is of his own health and powers. In his first letter to Boito after receiving the sketch (July 6th) we can see how he felt. He got out his Shakespeare (which he read in Italian and in French) and went through *The Merry Wives of Windsor* and *Henry IV* once again. He knew them well, because an opera on this subject had been in his mind for many years. He makes a few very tentative (and for him even timid) suggestions, but tells Boito to pay no attention to them. On the following day (July 7th) he writes to Boito again at great length. "I want it but I can't believe it," is the gist of this letter. Again Boito had to convince him, but with nothing like the difficulties and delays which attended the composition of *Otello*.

Verdi composed *Falstaff* in a manner unlike his working habit of so many long years. Sometimes the work came pouring out so fast that his pen could hardly keep up with it, and at other times months would pass without his being able to do more than an occasional desultory correction or improvement in the score. We have seen how the *Pancione*, the "Big-Belly," took possession of everything at Sant' Agata sometimes—to Boito's delight—and there was an obsessive concentration upon it even when the actual pen was idle. After he had decided to write it and was waiting for a text (1889–1890) he "amused himself" (his own words) with contrapuntal exercises, and in particular with fugues, and he tells Boito he has composed a "comic fugue" which might very well go into *Falstaff*. There is, of course, a great comic fugue at the end of *Falstaff*, but from all indications it is a different one; what is curious, just the same, is that Verdi's mind should have turned to polyphony just at this time, and that the "canons and fugues in all the sauces" which had consumed so much of his youth were coming back to him again.

In this precise period, when the creative effort was at last turned upon lyric comedy—the dream of a lifetime—Verdi had more than the usual anxieties. Aside from the great and recurrent grief of so many deaths among his oldest friends, he was greatly worried over Franco Faccio, now the chief of his disciples aside from Boito. Faccio was showing signs of mental and physical collapse, not much helped by a passion of overwork on the first production of *Die Meistersinger von Nürnberg* at the Scala. The Scala itself was having one of its periodic crises, too; the Conservatory at Parma was without a director; Verdi felt to some degree responsible for all these troubles. He took Faccio out of the Scala and made him director of the Parma Conservatory—that is, he said the words which caused others to do these things—and put in Leopoldo Mugnone as temporary director at the Scala. Eventually he employed his influence, which was more or less the same as absolute power, to give the directorship of the Scala, and with it the first *Falstaff*, to the conductor Mascheroni.

But Faccio never took up his duties in Parma; he degenerated so rapidly that soon he had to be put into a private asylum for the insane. Boito, in an act of characteristic generosity, volunteered to carry out Faccio's duties in Parma if the administration there would pay the salary to his poor friend in the asylum. This unprecedented arrangement went on for a year and more, until Faccio died (July 21, 1891) and the Parma Conservatory (which now bears Boito's name) tried in vain to keep the illustrious substitute.

With all these preoccupations, with Peppina's health and his own to worry about and with the business of creating his House of Rest for Musicians, which was coming into legal existence just then, Verdi had enough to do, but none of it counted against the imperious necessities of *Falstaff* when the fit was upon him. Indeed, we can tell by the ear alone that much of this score must have been written in a continuous flood of inspiration, melody, harmony, counterpoint and instrumentation all at once: it has an organic simultaneity of life unlike almost anything else ever written for the stage. And indeed we have proof, from the letters, that Verdi wrote out more of the orchestration than ever as he went along: his excuse was that he was "afraid he might forget" some of the things he had intended to do with the instruments and could not depend on his own notes. This, however, must be only part of the truth, although, at his age, a valid part: more vital to the masterpiece is the fact that it compelled this simultaneity of composition, roughly speaking, of all parts at once.

By 1892 we find the Maestro already discussing interpreters, stage settings and the like, although he still had not finished the work. He was even specifying instruments of a certain character for certain passages— flute in D Flat for the Honor soliloquy; A Major clarinet in one place; and a true hunting horn, "genuine antique," for the last scene in Windsor Great Park. Where his requirements run counter to custom (as in the case of the low oboe in the orchestration which goes with Dame Quickly in Act II) he says sourly: "They'll say I don't know the *tessitura* of the instruments," although any such criticism was by this time unlikely or impossible: somebody had probably said something of the kind years before and he never forgot it.

At this very moment there came the much advertised "recantation" of Hans von Bülow, once the most vehement and sarcastic of anti-Verdians. Why Bülow felt it necessary to make this public apology and confession of error is a matter of his own conscience; it was not necessary, and Verdi, although he acknowledged it with courtesy, did not so consider it. If it had come two decades earlier it might have had a calming influence on the polemics of the 1870's, but now it had not much weight.

"Deign to hear the confession of a contrite sinner!" Bülow begins his letter. There follows a tremendous rigmarole about art, music, justice, history, fanaticism, enthusiasm, ultra-Wagnerism, journalistic stupidity, and other large subjects, culminating in an outburst of homage to Verdi. He (Bülow) had been studying Aïda, the Requiem and Otello, the works —so far—of Verdi's last phase, and saw how wrong he had been before; an indifferent performance of the Requiem lately heard had moved him to tears; and he perorates: "Illustrious Master, I admire and love you!" This might have been all right, more or less, if he had not added a final bit of nonsense: "Evviva Verdi, the Wagner of our dear allies!"

Verdi answered kindly, sensibly, that there could be no question of sin and repentance; that Bülow's opinions at one time or another were his own, and that he was entitled to express them; and that, after all, he might have been right the first time. He adds what had now become his creed in such discourse: "If the artists of the North and of the South have different tendencies, then let them be different! Everybody should maintain the natural characteristics of his own nation, as Wagner so rightly said." The Germans are the children of Bach, the Italians the children of Palestrina.

Wise Verdi, knowing the inclination of Bülow (and the other Wagnerians) toward newsprint, sent the two letters to Ricordi so that if a "leak" occurred in Germany the publisher would be ready in Milan with the Italian originals: and thus, quite promptly, it happened.

We have already seen, at the very beginning of this meditation upon a life, that Verdi at eighty needed no apologies as he needed no defense. He had struggled through every obstacle toward a final fulfillment such as few artists ever attain. Other Italians—Michelangelo, Titian—did great work at an advanced age, but they did not have so far to travel. The distance between Michelangelo's early and his late work is not too difficult to perceive: there is a great distance, of course, between the David and the unfinished works in the Accademia in Florence, but it is measurable and recognizable. In the case of Verdi the distance traversed between Nabucco and *Falstaff* very nearly defeats the imagination, even though a relationship between early and late does exist. The relationship is mainly in a sort of vocal magic, a way of singing in pen-and-ink, which was Verdi's peculiar genius: but in every other respect the whole world of this creative artist is different at eighty from what it was at thirty. In every dimension, breadth, depth, height, his work has assumed a greatness which has no superior and hardly any equal in the music of the world. *Otello* was the greatest of Italian operas but *Falstaff*, in all its joy and sadness, is no longer exclusively Italian: it is universal. We hear Italian melody all through it, but we hear everything else too; we hear Shakespeare; we hear Greece and England and a great many things that never grew in the soil of the Piazza della Scala at Milan. In the wonderful swing and dance and lilt of the music, as well as in its musical erudition—a combination rare since Bach— there is a touch of eternal youth, of something age cannot wither; there is sorrow, too: "How sad is your comedy!" Eleonora Duse wrote to Boito. She had gone to it and wept, and rightly, for every regret is in it along with the gaiety and wit.

We have returned to our point of departure, and need follow the fortunes of *Falstaff* no further: we have already pursued them from Milan to Rome and to Paris, and with them all the years that went into them. Any survey of Verdi's life as a whole, particularly from the point of view of his last work, must take in so many glimpses of other lives and perceptions of past time that it begins to look like a view of the whole nineteenth century in Italy. Thus it must have seemed to Verdi himself when he thought things over, down at Sant' Agata or even in his room at the Grand Hotel in Milan, on the night of his last farewell to the theatre, on the third night of *Falstaff*.

A Brief Chronology of Verdi's Life

1813. Birth at Le Roncole, near Busseto (October 10).

1823. Admitted to school (gymnasium) at Busscto (November).

1832. Goes to Milan on funds from Busseto charity (May).

1832. Refused admission to the Conservatory (June); becomes pupil of Vincenzo Lavigna.

1835. Appointed choirmaster, organist and music teacher at Busseto (March 5).

1836. Married (May 5) to Margherita Barezzi, daughter of his bene-factor.

1837. Daughter Virginia born (March 26).

1838. Son Romano born (July 11).

1838. Death of Virginia (August 12).

1838. Verdi to Milan (September 8) with Margherita.

1838. Resignation as choirmaster, organist and music teacher at Busseto (October 28).

1839. First opera: Oberto, Conte di Bonifacio, produced at the Scala on November 17.

1839. Death of Romano (October 22).

1840. Death of Margherita (June 18).

1840. First and most crashing failure, the "jocose melodrama" Un Giorno di Regno (Scala, September 5), which lasted one night.

1842. First success: Nabucco (Scala, March 9).

1842–1852. The "galley-slave years," as Verdi called them: fifteen operas in ten years, ending with Rigoletto.

1847. Open union with Giuseppina Strepponi ("Peppina") in Paris.

1853. Il Trovatore (Rome, January 19) and La Traviata (Venice, March 6) bring Verdi's youth and his early or first creative period to an end.

1859. Marriage to Giuseppina Strepponi, at Collange, Haute-Savoie (then still part of the Savoy dominions) on August 29, with church ceremony carrying civil validity.

1853–1867. The middle period, a time of struggle and experiment, ending with Don Carlos (Paris, March 11, 1867).

1859. First meeting with Cavour (September 17).

1860. Garibaldi's expedition with "The Thousand" to Sicily and Naples (beginning May 5).
1860. First all-Italian parliament summoned to Turin to proclaim the Kingdom of Italy.
1861. Verdi elected deputy to first parliament of Italy (January 27) at Cavour's wish and with his public support.
1861. First parliament meets (February 19) and proclaims the united kingdom under Victor Emmanuel II.
1861. Death of Cavour (June 7).
1867. Death of the composer's father, Carlo Verdi (January), and of his "other father," Antonio Barezzi (July).
1868. Meeting with Manzoni (June 30) in the house of the Countess Maffei.
1871. Aïda (Christmas Eve at the Khedivial Theatre in Cairo—the following February 8, 1872, in Milan) opens the final period of Verdi's creative work.
1873. Death of Manzoni (May 23).
1886. Otello (February 5).
1893. Falstaff (February 9) and farewell.
1897. Death of Peppina, at Sant' Agata, November 14.
1901. Death of Verdi, January 27, at the Grand Hotel in Milan.

List of Verdi's Works

I. Operas

(This is, of course, a complete list, which means that some works have been counted twice. Macbeth, La Forza del Destino, Simon Boccanegra and Don Carlos were drastically revised years after their first presentations; Stiffelio was reborn under another and equally unlucky star; I Lombardi was considerably touched up for its French version as Jérusalem. Thus, although we are obliged to list thirty-one separate titles, the captious might contend, with reason, that these in fact stand for only twenty-five original compositions.)

Oberto, Conte di Bonifacio, two acts, text by Antonio Piazza, retouched by Temistocle Solera. Scala, Milan, November 17, 1839.

Un Giorno di Regno, or Il Finto Stanislao, comic opera ("*jocose melodrama*") in two acts. Scala, Milan, September 5, 1840.

Nabucodonosor (Nabucco), four acts, text by Temistocle Solera. Scala, Milan, March 9, 1842.

I Lombardi alla Prima Crociata, four acts, text by Temistocle Solera. Scala, Milan, February 11, 1843.

Ernani, four acts, text by Francesco Maria Piave. La Fenice, Venice, March 9, 1844.

I Due Foscari, three acts, text by Francesco Maria Piave. Teatro Argentina, Rome, November 3, 1844.

Giovanna d'Arco, three acts, text by Temistocle Solera (from Die Jungfrau von Orléans, by Schiller). Scala, Milan, February 15, 1845.

Alzira, a prologue and two acts, text by Salvatore Cammarano. San Carlo, Naples, August 12, 1845.

Macbeth, four acts, text by Francesco Maria Piave. La Pergola, Florence, March 14, 1847.

I Masnadieri, four acts, text by Andrea Maffei (from Die Räuber, by Schiller). Her Majesty's Theatre, London, July 22, 1847.

Jérusalem, four acts, text by Alphonse Royer and Gustave Vaëz from the original I Lombardi. Opéra, Paris, November 26, 1847.

Il Corsaro, three acts, text by Francesco Maria Piave. Teatro Grande, Trieste, October 25, 1848.

La Battaglia di Legnano, four acts, text by Salvatore Cammarano. Teatro Argentina, Rome, January 27, 1849.

Luisa Miller, three acts, text by Salvatore Cammarano (from Kabale und Liebe, by Schiller). San Carlo, Naples, December 8, 1849.

Stiffelio, three acts, text by Francesco Maria Piave. Teatro Grande, Trieste, November 16, 1850.

Rigoletto, three acts, text by Francesco Maria Piave. La Fenice, Venice, March 11, 1851.

Il Trovatore, four acts, text by Salvatore Cammarano. Teatro Apollo, Rome, January 19, 1853.

La Traviata, three acts, text by Francesco Maria Piave. La Fenice, Venice, March 6, 1853.

Les Vêpres Siciliennes (*I Vespi Siciliani*) five acts, text by Eugène Scribe and C. Duveyrier. Opéra, Paris, June 13, 1855.

Simon Boccanegra, prologue and three acts, text by Francesco Maria Piave. La Fenice, Venice, March 12, 1857.

Aroldo, rewritten version of *Stiffelio*, four acts, text by Francesco Maria Piave. Teatro Nuovo, Rimini, August 16, 1857.

Un Ballo in Maschera, three acts, text anonymous (but written by Antonio Somma). Teatro Apollo, Rome, February 17, 1859.

La Forza del Destino, four acts, text by Francesco Maria Piave. Imperial Theatre, St. Petersburg, November 10, 1862.

Macbeth, revised to a French text by Nuitter and Beaumont (from the original version of Florence in 1847). Théâtre Lyrique, Paris, April 21, 1865.

Don Carlos, five acts, text by Camille du Locle and J. Méry. Opéra, Paris, March 11, 1867.

La Forza del Destino, revised version. Scala, Milan, February 20, 1869.

Aïda, four acts, text by Antonio Ghislanzoni. Khedivial Theatre, Cairo, December 24, 1871.

Simon Boccanegra, revised version with text partly written (although not signed) by Arrigo Boito. Scala, Milan, March 24, 1881.

Don Carlos, revised version of the French *Don Carlos*, reduced to four acts. Scala, Milan, January 10, 1884.

Otello, four acts, text by Arrigo Boito. Scala, Milan, February 5, 1886.

Falstaff, three acts, text by Arrigo Boito. Scala, Milan, February 9, 1893.

II. *Principal Other Works*

Messa da Requiem for four voices, chorus and orchestra. Church of San Marco, Milan, May 22, 1874.

String Quartet in E Minor. Naples, April 1, 1873.

Inno delle Nazioni, cantata composed for the London Exposition of 1862, for tenor (or soprano) with chorus and orchestra, to a text by Arrigo Boito. Her Majesty's Theatre, London, May 24, 1862.

Quattro Pezzi Sacri (comprising the Ava Maria on a scala enigmatica, approaching the whole-tone scale; a Stabat Mater to the text of Jacopone da Todi; Laudi alla Vergine, for four female soloists and orchestra, on the text from the ending of Dante's Paradiso; and the Te Deum for double four-part chorus and orchestra, to the traditional Latin text). Opéra, Paris, Société des Concerts, April 7, 1898.

This list omits all the juvenile works, which are in any case either out of print or unpublished. The exception is the "romanze," early compositions for voice and pianoforte, more or less what we could call "songs," although generally more elaborately written than our word suggests. Ricordi published a collection of these (sixteen, comprising all except a vocal trio) in 1935 under the title of *Composizioni di musica da camera per canto e pianoforte, da Giuseppe Verdi.*

Bibliographical Note

The preëminent authority on Verdi's life is Carlo Gatti, now over eighty, who became Professor of Harmony and Counterpoint at the Milan Conservatory in 1898, and had ample opportunity to know Verdi's friends and family in the early part of this century. His researches in the Milan archives (those of the Conservatory, of the city and of the Austrian viceregal government) have cleared up many shadowy episodes, such as that of Verdi's failure to obtain admission to the Conservatory in 1831. Professor Gatti's *Verdi* (Milan, 1930) was originally in two volumes but in 1951 was combined into one, which, however, lacks an index. It is an invaluable work of reference and has been translated into the principal languages, but was not intended for the general reader.

Alessandro Luzio, originally a journalist and afterward an archivist and essayist of attainment, especially on the Risorgimento, worked with Gaetano Cesàri, librarian of the Milan Conservatory, on the original *Copialettere* of 1913. This collection of Verdi letters in one volume was the first attempt at a comprehensive edition. Since then Luzio has edited the *Carteggi* (Milan, 1945) in four volumes, but new Verdi letters are constantly being discovered and brought out in one way or another. There are also many special selections in print, such as the letters to Countess Maffei, those to Maria Waldmann, etc. *Verdi Intimo*, edited by Annibale Alberti, consists of the correspondence with Arrivabene, arranged chronologically and whenever possible in collocation so that we have both sides of the discourse, with notes and useful excerpts from the press of the time. Aldo Oberdorfer's *Autobiografia dalle Lettere* (Milan, 1946) is a selection of letters arranged by subjects and linked by biographical essays. All these and others (and there will be more) constitute a source of high importance, mostly in Verdi's own words, for our concept of his personality.

It has not been necessary, in this essay, to consult works in French, German or English, since these are all based on the original Italian work anyhow.

For Boito's life the chief authority is Piero Nardi, who brought out his *Vita di Arrigo Boito* in 1942, the centenary of the poet-composer's birth. In that year Nardi also edited his collected writings, complete (*Tutti i*

Scritti). Both are published by Mondadori in Milan. Nardi's work was based upon the immense collection of papers Boito left, and among other surprises it contained much of the correspondence with Eleonora Duse. For Duse's own life it is safe to recommend Olga Signorelli's *Eleonora Duse* (Rome, 1955), which combines personal knowledge of the subject with competent use of all the material published in the thirty years after Duse's death.

The Museum of the Teatro alla Scala contains portraits, sketches, busts or photographs of a great many persons mentioned in these pages besides Verdi himself and his Peppina. Some of the portraits are conventional, but many (such as the commanding and beautiful head of Teresa Stolz) give a vivid notion of character.

There are two Boldini portraits mentioned in the text of this book. The more celebrated is the one made in Paris in 1886, in which Verdi wears a top hat and a blue scarf. It hangs in the Museum of Modern Art in Rome. Boldini himself made copies or studies of this same subject. The pen-and-ink drawing in the Scala Museum, Milan, is one, and so is the very dark version which hangs in the Grand Hotel, Milan, where Verdi died. The other portrait (the "dandified" one, as I have called it), which has no top hat but some carefully curled hair, belongs to the family. Of the almost innumerable representations of Verdi in painting and sculpture the Boldini pair, in whatever versions one may see them, are clearly the best.

A brief list of Italian books I have kept at hand during the writing of this study will follow. It includes nothing from the large literature printed in periodicals such as *Il Pianoforte* or *Musica d'Oggi*, which may be consulted in libraries; nothing in foreign languages or by foreign writers; nothing of a strictly musicological nature. For students who wish to pursue the subject further, Verdi's own scores will be the best guide to his work, while his letters must always be the final authority on his life and character, subject to an occasional emendation of a critical or historical nature by Professor Gatti.

The list:

Carlo Gatti: *Verdi* (Milan, 1930—latest revised edition, 1953).

A. Luzio and G. Cesàri: *I Copialettere* (Milan, 1913).

A. Luzio: *Carteggi Verdiani* (Milan, 1945—four volumes).

A. Luzio: *Garibaldi, Verdi e Cavour* (Milan, 1924).

A. Alberti: *Verdi Intimo* (Milan, 1931).

Aldo Oberdorfer: *Giuseppe Verdi: Autobiografia dalle Lettere* (Milan, 1941—published pseudonymously because the author, as a Triestine Jew and a Socialist, was in a concentration camp; Rizzoli has since brought it out in the cheap, convenient form of his Universal Library).

Italo Pizzi: *Ricordi Inediti Verdiani* (Milan, 1901).

G. Monaldi: *Verdi* (Milan, 1899).

P. Nardi: *Vita di Arrigo Boito* (Milan, 1901).

M. Vajro: *Arrigo Boito* (Brescia, 1955, in the series called "Men and Civilization," published by La Scuola).

Olga Signorelli: *Eleonora Duse* (Rome, 1955).

Other works ranging over the nineteenth century (history, biography, musicology, musical dictionaries and the like) were occasionally consulted, of course, but are too numerous to be listed. Almost every character who moves across the scene has given rise to a large literature—Cavour, for instance, whose more intimate letters are only now coming to light; Mazzini, upon whom a library has been written; or, for that matter, Richard Wagner, the character who never appears on our scene but often seems more present than those who do. Ernest Newman's four-volume *Life of Wagner* is definitive. Some readers might like to read William de la Rive's *Vie du Comte de Cavour*, a hero-worshipping volume, full of charm and character; others might enjoy Barbiera's book, *Il Salotto della Contessa Maffei* (Milan, 1900), or the Verdi biographies by Barrili, Resasco, Bragagnolo and Rettazzi, Bonaventura, Della Corte, Rinaldi, Radius and Roncaglia, which do not appear on my own bedside list.

Index

Index

A B O U T   T H E   A U T H O R

During his three years' work on *Orpheus at Eighty*, VIN-
CENT SHEEAN lived in Italy, close to his sources, the
opera houses of Rome and Milan, and the great libraries in
those cities and in Florence. His complete familiarity with
the Italian language enabled him to read the vast literature
and discuss Verdi freely with the scholars. Not only that, as
a lifelong follower of the opera, he has for many years stored
up knowledge and understanding of Verdi's and his contemporaries' music. Certainly, this book was done *con amore*.

Prior to this work, Sheean wrote *First and Last Love*, an
autobiography of his life in music. Although he is perhaps
best known as a foreign correspondent, the author of *Personal History* and other books about world crises since the
nineteen-twenties, his second interest has always been music,
especially opera.

Born in Pana, Illinois, and graduated from the University
of Chicago, he worked as a reporter in New York and later on
the Paris *Herald*. Thereafter he showed an uncanny ability
for being on the spot for most of the world-shaking news
events. He was in Vienna when Hitler moved into Austria,
in Prague when the Nazis took Czechoslovakia, in France
during its fall, getting off to England just in time to avoid
capture by the Germans. He was in London from Dunkirk
through all phases of the blitz, and left Wake Island one
plane ahead of the attack on Pearl Harbor, and then served
in the Air Force during World War II. In 1946, he was in
the garden at Birla House in Delhi when Gandhi was assassinated.

During all his journalistic wandering, Vincent Sheean has
maintained his interest in the opera and has attended,
through the years, some of the most notable performances in
the European music centers.